D1477053

UNIVERSITY OF WINCHESTER
LIBRARY

TWENTIETH-CENTURY
PHILOSOPHY OF RELIGION

KA 0382671 6

THE HISTORY OF
WESTERN PHILOSOPHY OF RELIGION

TWENTIETH-CENTURY PHILOSOPHY OF RELIGION

Edited by Graham Oppy and N. N. Trakakis

VOLUME 5

THE HISTORY OF WESTERN PHILOSOPHY OF RELIGION

ACUMEN

UNIVERSITY OF WINCHESTER
LIBRARY

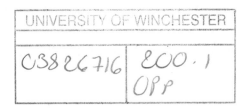

UNIVERSITY OF WINCHESTER

03826716 | 200.1
OPP

© Editorial matter and selection, 2009 Graham Oppy and N. N. Trakakis.
Individual contributions, the contributors.

This book is copyright under the Berne Convention.
No reproduction without permission.
All rights reserved.

First published in 2009 by Acumen
First published in paperback by Acumen in 2013

Acumen Publishing Limited

4 Saddler Street
Durham
DH1 3NP

ISD, 70 Enterprise Drive
Bristol, CT 06010, USA

www.acumenpublishing.com

ISBN: 978-1-84465-685-1 (paperback Volume 5)
ISBN: 978-1-84465-679-0 (paperback 5 volume set)
ISBN: 978-1-84465-224-2 (hardcover Volume 5)
ISBN: 978-1-84465-181-8 (hardcover 5 volume set)

British Library Cataloguing-in-Publication Data
A catalogue record for this book is available from the British Library.

Typeset in Minion Pro.
Printed and bound in the UK by CPI Group (UK) Ltd, Croydon, CR0 4YY.

CONTENTS

EDITORIAL INTRODUCTION

Bertrand Russell's *History of Western Philosophy* (1946; hereafter *History*) provides a model for *some* of the significant features of the present work. Like Russell's more general history, our history of Western philosophy of religion consists principally of chapters devoted to the works of individual thinkers, selected because of their "considerable importance". Of course, we do not claim to have provided coverage of all of those who have made important contributions to Western philosophy of religion. However, we think that anyone who has made a significant contribution to Western philosophy of religion has either seriously engaged with the works of philosophers who are featured in this work, or has produced work that has been a focus of serious engagement for philosophers who are featured in this work.

Like Russell, we have aimed for contributions that show how the philosophy of religion developed by a given thinker is related to that thinker's life, and that trace out connections between the views developed by a given philosopher and the views of their predecessors, contemporaries and successors. While our primary aim is to provide an account of the ideas, concepts, claims and arguments developed by each of the philosophers under consideration, we think – with Russell – that this aim is unlikely to be achieved in a work in which "each philosopher appears as in a vacuum".

Again like Russell, we have only selected philosophers or religious writers who belong to, or have exerted a significant impact on, the intellectual tradition of the West (i.e. western Europe and the Anglo-American world). We realize that this selection criterion alone excludes from our work a number of important thinkers and religious groups or traditions, such as: Asian philosophers of religion, particularly those representing such religions as Hinduism, Buddhism, Confucianism and Taoism; African philosophers of religion; and individuals, texts and traditions emanating from indigenous religions, such as those found in the native populations of Australia and the Pacific Islands. Clearly, the non-Western world has produced thinkers who have made important, and often overlooked, contributions to the philosophy of religion. We have decided, however, not to include any entries on these thinkers, and our decision is based primarily on the (admittedly not incontestable) view that the Asian, African and indigenous philosophical and religious traditions have not had a great impact on the main historical narrative of the West. It would therefore have been difficult to integrate the various non-Western thinkers into the five-volume structure of the present work. The best way to redress this omission, in our view, is to produce a separate multi-volume work that would be dedicated to the history of non-Western philosophy of religion, a project that we invite others to take up.

Where we have departed most significantly from Russell is that our work has been written by a multitude of contributors, whereas Russell's work was the product of just one person. In the preface to his *History*, Russell claimed that:

> There is … something lost when many authors co-operate. If there is any unity in the movement of history, if there is any intimate relation between what goes before and what comes later, it is necessary, for setting this forth, that earlier and later periods should be synthesized in a single mind. (1946: 5)

We think that Russell exaggerates the difficulties in, and underestimates the benefits of, having a multitude of expert contributors. On the one hand, someone who is an expert on the work of a given philosopher is bound to have expert knowledge of the relation between the work of that philosopher, what goes before and what comes after. On the other hand, and as Russell himself acknowledged, it is impossible for one person to have the expertise of a specialist across such a wide field. (Indeed, while Russell's *History* is admirable for its conception and scope, there is no doubt that it is far from a model for good historical scholarship.)

Of course, Russell's worry about a multiplicity of authors does recur at the editorial level: the editors of this work have no particular claim to expertise concerning any of the philosophers who are featured in the work. In order to alleviate this problem, we invited all of the contributors to read drafts of neighbouring contributions, acting on the assumption that someone who is an expert on a particular philosopher is likely to have reasonably good knowledge of contemporaries and near contemporaries of that philosopher. Moreover, each of the five volumes comes with an expert introduction, written by someone who is much better placed than we are to survey the time period covered in the given volume.

Obviously enough, it is also the case that the present work does not have the kind of narrative unity that is possessed by Russell's work. Our work juxtaposes contributions from experts who make very different theoretical assumptions, and who belong to diverse philosophical schools and traditions. Again, it seems to us that this represents an advantage: there are many different contemporary approaches to philosophy of religion, and each of these approaches suggests a different view about the preceding history. Even if there is "unity in the movement of history", it is clear that there is considerable disagreement about the precise nature of that unity.

Although our work is divided into five volumes – and despite the fact that we have given labels to each of these volumes – we attach no particular significance to the way in which philosophers are collected together by these volumes. The order of the chapters is determined by the dates of birth of the philosophers who are the principal subjects of those chapters. While it would not be a task for a single evening, we do think that it should be possible to read the five volumes as a single, continuous work.

* * *

Collectively, our primary debt is to the 109 people who agreed to join with us in writing the material that appears in this work. We are indebted also to Tristan Palmer, who oversaw the project on behalf of Acumen. Tristan initially searched for someone prepared to take on the task of editing a single-volume history of Western philosophy of religion, and was actively involved in the shaping of the final project. He also provided invaluable advice on the full range of editorial questions that arise in a project on this scale. Thanks, too, to the copy-editors and others at Acumen, especially Kate Williams, who played a role in the completion of this project, and to the anonymous reviewers who provided many helpful comments. We are grateful to Karen Gillen for proofreading and indexing all five volumes, and to the Helen McPherson Smith Trust, which provided financial support for this project. We also acknowledge our debt to Monash University, and to our colleagues in the School of Philosophy and Bioethics. Special thanks to Dirk Baltzly for his suggestions about potential contributors to the volume on ancient Western philosophy of religion and for his editorial help with the chapter on Pythagoras.

Apart from these collective debts, Graham Oppy acknowledges personal debts to friends and family, especially to Camille, Gilbert, Calvin and Alfie. N. N. Trakakis is also grateful for the support of family and friends while working on this project, which he dedicates to his nephew and niece, Nicholas and Adrianna Trakakis: my prayer is that you will come to share the love of wisdom cultivated by the great figures in these volumes.

Graham Oppy
N. N. Trakakis

CONTRIBUTORS

Paul Badham is Professor of Theology and Religious Studies at the University of Wales Lampeter and editor of *Modern Believing*. His publications include *Christian Beliefs about Life after Death* (1976), *Immortality or Extinction?* (1982) and *The Contemporary Challenge of Modernist Theology* (1998). He was a research student of John Hick's at the University of Birmingham, has edited *A John Hick Reader* (1990), and contributed the article "The Life and Work of John Hick" in *God, Truth and Reality* (ed. Sharma, 1993). His pamphlet, *John Hick's Global Theology* (1994) has been published in English, Japanese and Chinese.

Lewis S. Ford is Professor of Philosophy Emeritus, Old Dominion University, Norfolk, Virginia. He taught a year-long seminar at the Catholic University of Louvain, Belgium, exploring the development of Whitehead's *Process and Reality* and showing ways in which his thought could be modified. He has written *The Lure of God* (1978), *The Emergence of Whitehead's Metaphysics* (1986) and *Transforming Process Theism* (2000), and has co-edited *Exploring Whitehead's Philosophy* (with George L. Kline, 1964). He has also written some 135 articles for learned journals, mostly about Whitehead, and was the editor of *Process Studies* from 1971 to 1995.

Richard M. Gale is Professor Emeritus at the University of Pittsburgh, where he held a full position from 1964 until 2003. He is the author of two books on William James – *The Divided Self of William James* (1999) and *The Philosophy of William James* (2004) – as well as a range of books on other philosophical topics, including *The Language of Time* (1967), *On the Nature and Existence of God* (1991), *God and Metaphysics* (2007) and *On the Philosophy of Religion* (2007). He is also the editor of the *Blackwell Companion to Metaphysics* (2002), and co-editor of *The Existence of God* (with Alex Pruss, 2003).

A. C. Grayling is Professor of Philosophy at Birkbeck College, University of London. He is the author of nearly thirty books, including *The Refutation of Scepticism* (1985), *Russell* (1995), *An Introduction to Philosophical Logic* (3rd edn, 1997), *The Quarrel of the Age* (2000), *The Mystery of Things* (2004), *Descartes* (2005), *Against All Gods* (2007), *Towards the Light* (2007) and *Truth, Meaning and Realism* (2007).

Kevin Hart is Edwin B. Kyle Professor of Christian Studies at the University of Virginia, and the Eric D'Arcy Professor of Philosophy at Australian Catholic University. Among his publications are *The Trespass of the Sign* (1989), *Post-modernism* (2004) and *The Dark Gaze* (2004). He has co-edited *Derrida and Religion* (with Yvonne Sherwood, 2005).

Laurence Paul Hemming is Senior Research Fellow in the Institute for Advanced Studies of the Faculty of Arts and Social Sciences at Lancaster University. His books include *Heidegger's Atheism* (2002) and *Postmodernity's Transcending* (2005). He has also written many articles concerned with Heidegger's thought, the philosophy of religion and theology, and the liturgy of the Catholic Church.

Daniel Howard-Snyder is Professor of Philosophy at Western Washington University. He studied with William P. Alston for seven years at Syracuse University, and Alston was also his dissertation advisor. He has published numerous articles in the philosophy of religion and epistemology, many of which focus on themes also found in Alston's work, especially epistemological foundationalism and the problem of evil. He has also edited *The Evidential Argument from Evil* (1996) and co-edited *Faith, Freedom and Rationality* (with Jeff Jordan, 1996) and *Divine Hiddenness* (with Paul K. Moser, 2002).

Paul Dafydd Jones is Assistant Professor of Western Religious Thought at the University of Virginia. He is the author of *The Humanity of Christ* (2008) and various scholarly essays on modern Christian thought.

Anne-Marie Korte is Associate Professor of Systematic Theology at the University of Tilburg and Honorary Professor of Women's Studies in Theology at Utrecht University, The Netherlands. She has written a dissertation on the concept of faith in the oeuvre of Mary Daly, *Een passie voor transcendentie* (A passion for transcendence; 1992), and has published several interpretations of Mary Daly's work, including two essays in *Feminist Interpretations of Mary Daly* (eds Hoagland & Frye, 2000).

Jeffrey L. Kosky is Associate Professor in the Department of Religion at Washington & Lee University. He is the author of *Levinas and the Philosophy of Religion* (2001) and serves on the editorial board of *Levinas Studies: An Annual*

Review, the first volume of which he co-edited. He is also the translator of several books in phenomenology and religious thought, including *Being Given* and *On Descartes' Metaphysical Prism*, both by Jean-Luc Marion, as well as co-translator of *Phenomenology and the "Theological Turn"*.

Bruce Langtry is Senior Fellow in Philosophy at the University of Melbourne. He is the author of *God, the Best, and Evil* (2008) and numerous journal articles on divine providence, the problem of evil and miracles (and on topics outside the philosophy of religion). He is a member of the International Editorial Advisory Board of *Sophia*.

Graham Macdonald is Professor of Philosophy at the University of Canterbury, Christchurch, and Distinguished International Fellow of the Institute of Cognition and Culture at Queen's University Belfast. He undertook postgraduate study at the University of Oxford, where one of his tutors was A. J. Ayer. He edited *Perception and Identity* (1979) and co-edited *Fact, Science, and Morality* (with Crispin Wright, 1986), a volume celebrating the fiftieth anniversary of Ayer's *Language, Truth and Logic*. Recent work includes two co-edited volumes: *McDowell and His Critics* (with Cynthia Macdonald, 2006) and *Teleosemantics: New Philosophical Essays* (with David Papineau, 2006).

John Mullarkey is Lecturer in Philosophy at the University of Dundee. He is the author of *Bergson and Philosophy* (1999) and editor of *The New Bergson* (1999) and Bergson's *Introduction to Metaphysics* (2007), as well as having published numerous articles on Bergson. He is also the author of *Post-Continual Philosophy* (2006) and *Refractions of Reality* (2008).

Graham Oppy is Professor of Philosophy in the School of Philosophical, Historical and International Studies at Monash University. He is the author of *Ontological Arguments and Belief in God* (1996), *Philosophical Perspectives on Infinity* (2006), *Arguing about Gods* (2006) and *Reading Philosophy of Religion* (with Michael Scott, 2009), and has also written many articles on topics in philosophy of religion. He is on the editorial boards of *European Journal for Philosophy of Religion*, *International Journal for Philosophy of Religion*, *Oxford Studies in Philosophy of Religion*, *Philo*, *Philosophy Compass-Philosophy of Religion*, *Religious Studies* and *Sophia*.

Stephen Plant is Lecturer in Theology at the University of Durham. He was Senior Tutor at Wesley House, Cambridge, from 2001 to 2008, and an affiliated lecturer in the Faculty of Divinity, University of Cambridge. He is editor of the journal *Theology*, and has edited or written several books, including *The SPCK Introduction to Simone Weil* (2007), also published as *Simone Weil* (2007).

Peter A. Redpath is Professor of Philosophy at St John's University, Staten Island, New York, and former vice-president of the American Maritain Association. He has written and lectured extensively on, and organized many national and international conferences devoted to, Jacques Maritain's thought. Two of his most well-known works on Maritain are his collected volume *From Twilight to Dawn* (1990) and his article "Romance of Wisdom: The Friendship between Jacques Maritain and Saint Thomas Aquinas", in *Understanding Maritain* (eds Hudson & Mancini, 1987).

Steven C. Rockefeller is Professor Emeritus of Religion at Middlebury College, Vermont, where he taught for thirty years and served as Dean of the College and Chair of the Religion Department. He is the author of *John Dewey* (1991), an intellectual biography of John Dewey that gives special attention to the evolution of his religious and ethical thought. He has also published essays on Dewey's philosophy in a variety of books and journals.

William L. Rowe is Professor Emeritus of Philosophy at Purdue University. He has made many significant contributions to the philosophy of religion, particularly in the areas of the problem of evil, the cosmological argument and divine freedom. In addition to over seventy journal papers, he has written five books, including: *Can God Be Free?* (2004); a widely used textbook, *Philosophy of Religion* ([1978] 2006), now in its fourth edition; and a philosophical study of Tillich's theology, *Religious Symbols and God* (1968). A selection of his work was published in 2007 as *William L. Rowe on Philosophy of Religion*.

Kurt Salamun is Professor of Philosophy in the Department of Philosophy, Karl-Franzens-University of Graz, Austria. He is author of *Karl Jaspers* (2nd edn, 2006), co-editor of *Karl Jaspers' Philosophy* (with Gregory J. Walters, 2008) and author of articles in German on Jaspers' conception of 'philosophical faith'. He is the founder and president of the Austrian Karl Jaspers Society, co-editor of the yearbook of the Austrian Karl Jaspers Society, member of the Stiftungsrat of the Karl Jaspers Foundation Basle, and a member of the advisory board of the online periodical *Existenz*, a journal in the tradition of Jaspers' thought.

Genia Schoenbaumsfeld is Senior Lecturer in Philosophy at the University of Southampton. Her publications include *A Confusion of the Spheres* (2007), "Words or Worlds Apart? Wittgenstein on Understanding Religious Language" (*Ratio*, 2007) and "Wittgenstein über religiösen Glauben", in *Der Denker als Seiltänzer* (eds Arnswald & Weiberg, 2001).

James F. Sennett is Associate Professor of Philosophy at Brenau University in Gainesville, Georgia. He is the author of *Modality, Probability, and Rationality* (1992) and articles on Plantinga in the *Cambridge Dictionary of Philosophy* and

The Dictionary of Modern American Philosophers. He has published numerous journal articles dealing with Plantinga's work and is the editor of *The Analytic Theist* (1998). Plantinga once quipped, "I have learned much about my work from reading Sennett".

Quentin Smith is Professor of Philosophy and University Distinguished Faculty Scholar at Western Michigan University. He has published over a dozen books and over a hundred articles, with the philosophy of religion being one of his areas of specialization. He has also worked extensively in the area of phenomenology, beginning with his 1976 dissertation "The Phenomenology of Feeling", which focused largely on the work of Max Scheler. Since then he has published several articles on Scheler, including "Scheler's Stratification of the Emotional Life" (*Philosophical Studies*, 1977). His own phenomenological theory of feelings, partly influenced by Scheler's, was published in *The Felt Meanings of the World* (1986).

Charles Taliaferro is Professor of Philosophy at St Olaf College, Minnesota. He has published extensively in philosophy of religion, with authorship or editorship of thirteen books, including *Consciousness and the Mind of God* (1994), *Contemporary Philosophy of Religion* (1998) and *Evidence and Faith* (2005). Taliaferro is also a co-editor of the *Blackwell Companion to Philosophy of Religion*. He serves on the editorial boards of *American Philosophical Quarterly*, *Religious Studies*, *Philosophy Compass*, *Sophia*, *Religious Studies Review*, *Ars Disputandi* and *Continuum Studies*, and currently serves on the American Philosophical Association committee on lectures and publications.

N. N. Trakakis is Research Fellow and Senior Lecturer in Philosophy at the Australian Catholic University. He works primarily in the philosophy of religion, and his publications in this area include *The God Beyond Belief* (2007) and *The End of Philosophy of Religion* (2008). He has also edited, with Graham Oppy, *A Companion to Philosophy in Australia and New Zealand* (2010) and *The Antipodean Philosopher*, vols 1 and 2 (2011).

Tamra Wright is Director of Academic Studies at the London School of Jewish Studies and a visiting lecturer in the Department of Theology and Religious Studies at King's College London, where she teaches Jewish philosophy. She is the author of *The Twilight of Jewish Philosophy* (1999), and has published articles on Martin Buber, Emmanuel Levinas and post-Holocaust Jewish thought. She was the Stanton Lecturer in Theology at the University of Cambridge for 2008–9.

1

TWENTIETH-CENTURY PHILOSOPHY OF RELIGION: AN INTRODUCTION

Charles Taliaferro

Offering an overview of twentieth-century philosophy of religion is as daunting as offering a unified narrative of twentieth-century art. There is simply too much turbulence and diversity to make for any neat portrait. But one general observation seems secure: philosophical reflection on religion has formed a major, vibrant part of some of the best philosophy in the past century. We now have a virtual library of a hundred years of first-rate, diverse philosophy of religion. At the close of the century there are more societies, institutions, journals, conferences and publishing houses dedicated to philosophy of religion than any other area of philosophical enquiry. The enduring appeal of philosophy of religion may be seen in the fact that many prestigious twentieth-century philosophers whose names are not featured with their own chapter in this volume nonetheless did some work on the philosophy of religion. Selecting figures from the second-half of the twentieth century, Michael Dummett, Robert Nozick, Hilary Putnam and John Rawls are representative of those whose main work is remote from mainstream philosophy of religion, but who nonetheless contributed in different ways to philosophical reflection on God, revelation, the theistic problem of evil, mystical experience and the rationality of religious belief.

There are three sections in what follows. The first takes up what I suggest is the largest theme in twentieth-century philosophy of religion, the second takes up a greater breadth of projects and the third comments on one lesson we might learn from the historical study in this volume.

GODS AND GIANTS

One way to begin building up a picture of twentieth-century philosophy of religion is to invoke Plato's famous depiction of philosophy as a battle between the gods and the giants. In the *Sophist* Plato depicts the gods as trying to account for the world in terms of higher, incorporeal forms, while the giants seek to privilege terrestrial, material reality. If we stretch this metaphor somewhat and depict the gods as idealists and theists and the giants as naturalists, a great deal of twentieth-century philosophy of religion may be seen as taken up in this massive, perhaps perennial, struggle.

The twentieth century in the Anglophone world began with the gods having a modest edge. F. H. Bradley and J. M. E. McTaggart propounded sophisticated idealist systems that were highly influential in philosophy of religion. While McTaggart was an atheist, he defended the view that souls are immortal, destined for a community of love. Bradley's work encouraged monist and theistic models of the divine. Bernard Bosanquet and Andrew Seth Pringle-Patterson also advanced an idealist foundation for religious belief. The assault on idealism by G. E. Moore and especially by Bertrand Russell may be seen as (in part) a movement to more thoroughly secularize the projects of philosophy. In his classic early paper, "The Refutation of Idealism" (1903), Moore explicitly sees himself as refuting a system of philosophy that characterizes reality as spiritual. Neither Moore nor Russell were thoroughgoing lifelong naturalists (indeed, at times both presented powerful arguments against naturalism), but they did tip the scales ever so slightly toward the giants.

Of those philosophers who feature in their own chapters here, the following may be seen as supporting theism, idealism or a religious understanding of the divine that goes beyond secular naturalism: William James, Henri Bergson, Alfred North Whitehead and Charles Hartshorne, Max Scheler, Martin Buber, Jacques Maritain, Karl Jaspers, Karl Barth, William P. Alston, Alvin Plantinga and Richard Swinburne. Others in the camp who flourished in the mid twentieth century include James Baillie, Nikolai Berdyaev, C. A. Campbell, A. C. Ewing, H. H. Farmer, Austin Farrer, Etienne Gilson, C. E. M. Joad, E. L. Mascal, H. H. Price, Hastings Rashdall, William Sorley, John Smith, A. E. Taylor, William Temple and F. R. Tennant. In the last quarter of the twentieth century, philosophical advocates of theism are abundant. The following are representative in addition to Plantinga, Alston and Swinburne: Marilyn McCord Adams, Robert Merrihew Adams, William Lane Craig, Alan Donagan, William Hasker, Brian Hebblethwaite, Norman Kretzmann, John Lucas, George Mavrodes, Basil Mitchell, Philip L. Quinn, James Ross, Eleonore Stump, Charles Taylor, William Wainwright, Merold Westphal, Nicholas Wolferstorff and Linda Zagzebski.

Interestingly, there are not many chapters in this volume arguing for an exclusively secular naturalist position. John Dewey allowed for religious values and was not a reductive or strict naturalist, but he certainly built a strong case against theism based on a broadly conceived naturalism. Russell dedicated serious work against theism along with idealism. And while A. J. Ayer's logical positivism shared with Berkeleyan idealism a high role for mental states, Ayer argued forcefully against the coherence of both theism and Hegelian idealism, along with a case against the cognitive meaningfulness of ethics. The movement that Ayer championed (along with Moritz Schlick and Rudolf Carnap) provided a powerful critique of the metaphysics of religious belief. Using a refined Humean standard of meaning, Ayer, Antony Flew, Sidney Hook and Paul Edwards argued specifically against theism as well as against religious concepts of the soul. While some mid-twentieth-century critics of theism retained some idealist sympathies (Brand Blanshard and C. J. Ducasse), late-twentieth-century critics seem more solidly naturalistic, as is the case with John Mackie, H. J. McCloskey and Kai Nielson. At the close of the century some of the outstanding philosophers who have dedicated important work to the critique of theism and theistic arguments include Paul Draper, Nicholas Everitt, Richard M. Gale, Adolf Grünbaum, Anthony Kenny, Michael Martin, Graham Oppy, William Rowe, J. J. C. Smart and J. H. Sobel.

While the conflict between theistic and non-theistic projects was preoccupied with the meaning of religious belief in the 1950s through to the 1960s, the collapse of positivism has widened the agenda with a great deal of focus on the conditions for justified religious belief (how much, if any, evidence is requisite for religious belief to be rational?), the coherence and character of the divine attributes, and the classical theistic and anti-theistic arguments, from arguments from evil to arguments from religious experience and the contingency of the cosmos.

I offer several general observations about the literature on the problem of evil below, but before doing so I comment briefly on twentieth-century work on the divine attributes and theistic arguments.

Debate over the divine attributes has been massive since the retreat of positivism. Important philosophical work has been deployed in examining the coherence and interrelationship of divine goodness or perfection, omnipotence, omniscience, freedom, eternity, necessity, omnipresence, incorporeality, impassability, moral authority and worship-worthiness. Serious, but somewhat less in quantity, work has focused on God's simplicity and on Christian conceptions of the Trinity and Incarnation. This literature naturally displays the ways in which philosophy of religion has incorporated other subfields of philosophy. So, debate over the eternity of God incorporated work in metaphysics on time, the debate over omniscience incorporated current epistemology, and so on. Not since the late medieval era has there been so much attention on the articulation, critique and reformation of the divine attributes.

Work on the concept of God naturally helped refine and promote arguments about the existence or non-existence of God and the implications of God's existence for human values and practices. Perhaps the greatest beneficiary of the work on divine attributes has been work on the ontological argument. According to some formulations of the argument, if one has reason to believe it is possible God exists, one has reason to believe that God exists. The tenacity of the ontological argument since the end of positivism is extraordinary. Four of the more discussed theistic arguments are arguments from contingency (or cosmological arguments), teleological arguments, moral arguments and arguments from religious experience. The development of cogent defences and reformulations of these arguments, as well as the excellent forceful criticisms these arguments have provoked, has falsified the idea that the Enlightenment (more specifically, David Hume and Immanuel Kant) put an end to philosophical theology. (To appeal to the analogy I employed above about art, the so-called death of natural theology is like the death of painting. At multiple times since the 1960s, painting has been declared dead but, for better or worse, painting in the art world seems as vibrant as ever.)

Two signs of the vibrancy of the theistic debate can be seen in reference books and in other subfields of philosophy. As for reference works, there was a profound shift in the framework of the first edition of the magisterial *Encyclopedia of Philosophy* in 1967 under the editorship of Paul Edwards to the framework of the second edition in 2005. Edwards designed the *Encyclopedia* to address religious issues in the spirit of Hume, Voltaire and Denis Diderot (*see* Vol. 3), namely, relentless criticism. In the second edition there is a shift to critical as well as constructive entries on virtually all areas of philosophy of religion. Quinn, the philosophy of religion editor, launched a far more capacious volume representing naturalism as well as theism and non-theistic religions in a critical but philosophically engaging setting. The same openness to philosophy of religion is evidenced in the competitive multi-volume *Encyclopedia of Philosophy* published by Routledge, with Eleonore Stump working as the philosophy of religion editor. To get some idea of the quantity of work produced, Barry Whitney's annotated bibliography on the problem of evil from 1960 to 1991, published by the Philosophy Documentation Center, has over four thousand entries. Also, one can see significant issues or concepts from the philosophy of religion in play in other subfields of philosophy, from ethics to philosophy of art. Most post-Second World War textbooks introducing philosophy for university and college classes contain some philosophy of religion.

While not represented in this volume, it should also be underscored how a great many theistic themes were taken in up in the twentieth century by continental existentialists and phenomenologists such as Simone de Beauvoir, Nikolai Berdyaev, Albert Camus, Gabriel Marcel and Jean-Paul Sartre. The philosophical exploration of theism was also an abiding interest of some of the best mid- and late-twentieth-century contributors to the history of ideas, such as Ernst Cassirer, F. R. Copleston, Étienne Gilson, Anthony Kenny, Arthur Lovejoy and John Passmore. These historians helped correct the beautifully written but philosophically prejudiced treatment of religion in Bertrand Russell's famous *History of Western Philosophy* (first published in 1945). The philosophical reconstruction of the history of philosophy of religion has also profoundly influenced late-twentieth-century developments. Work by Fred Fredosso and Thomas Flint on Luis de Molina has informed the literature on the divine attributes, as has the work of Brian Davies, Anthony Kenny, Norman Kretzmann, Ralph McInerny and Eleonore Stump on Aquinas. The major philosophers of the past who have received considerable attention in twentieth-century philosophy of religion include Boethius, John Duns Scotus, William Ockham, René Descartes, Blaise Pascal, John Locke, Gottfried Wilhelm Leibniz, Hume, Kant, G. W. F. Hegel and Søren Kierkegaard (*see* Vols 2–4).

A major concern in the naturalism versus theism debate has been the relationship between science and religion. The nineteenth century hosted two dominant positions: on the one hand there were prominent historians such as William Whewell who saw religion and science in conciliatory, complementary terms, while on the other hand John William Draper and Andrew Dickson White construed science and religion in deadly combat. The title of one of White's books says it all: *A History of the Warfare of Science with Theology in Christendom* (1896). Both schools of thought have ample representatives throughout the twentieth century. E. A. Burtt, Whitehead, Ernan McMullin and Ian Barber, among many others, continued the Whewell legacy. Charles Gillispie, John Greene and Alexander Koyré also challenged the sweeping portrait of the Draper–White account of science and religion, which is often referred to now as 'the conflict thesis'. At the close of the twentieth century, proponents of the conflict thesis are well represented by Richard Dawkins, E. O. Wilson and Daniel Dennett.

Apart from the general debate as to whether the practice of science is somehow inimical to the practice of religion, there is little doubt that different scientifically informed philosophies, often described as forms of naturalism, were deeply committed to the critique of theism. In the last quarter of the twentieth century this debate often centred on the prospects of a materialist account of consciousness. Flew, for example, compared the intelligibility of theism to the intelligibility of a dualist, non-reductive account of the mind. He argued that that just as it has become apparent that the human mind is not a non-physical reality, separable from the body, it should be equally apparent that there is no incorporeal, non-physical God. In a way, these naturalists used Gilbert Ryle's critique of dualism, according to which the mind or soul is a ghost in the machine of the body, to argue that God is a mere ghost (and thus merely an object of superstition) in the cosmos. Those arguing against this position often linked their defence of theism with a sustained critique of materialist reductionism. This link between theism and the philosophy of mind is evident in one of the most important works in post-Second World War analytic philosophy of religion: Plantinga's *God and Other Minds* (1967).

The theism and naturalism debate not only ranged over different accounts of the natural sciences and their success or failure in providing a secular view of nature, but also included psychology and sociology. While not philosophers themselves, Max Weber and Sigmund Freud (*see* Vol. 4, Ch. 20) produced philosophically significant accounts of the origin and appeal of religion. This was met with competing, non-reductive accounts such as that of Rudolf Otto and his influential phenomenological study of holiness. Much of the work by Weber, Freud, Otto and others became important reference points on philosophical work on religious experience from the 1970s to the present.

Having described much of philosophy of religion as focusing on theism (either for or against), it needs to be appreciated how many philosophers throughout the century defended idealist positions (e.g. R. G. Collingwood, Benedetto Croce,

John Foster), and that some philosophers advanced models of God that moved away from classic theism. Idealists cited at the outset of this introduction, such as Bradley, did not embrace Christian orthodoxy. Boston Personalism, for example, launched by Borden Parker Bowne, and championed by E. S. Brightman and Peter Bertocci, posited a creator-God but denied God's limitless power or omnipotence. Alternative conceptions of the divine have been central to process philosophers such as Whitehead and Hartshorne, as well as in the uniquely Platonic work of John Leslie.

By way of a final introduction to the theism versus naturalism debate in philosophy of religion over the past hundred years, the focus of attention was often on what counts as a good explanation of phenomena. Theists, generally, have given pride of place to intentional teleological explanations. Naturalists have instead occupied two positions: either recognizing teleological explanations and treating these as emergent, new phenomena or explaining teleology in terms of non-purposive forces. The former faces the challenge of explaining how a naturalist universe can generate radically new types of life and value, while the second threatens to undermine what seems like a common-sense approach to human agency. After all, it appears that I am writing the Introduction and you are reading it in order to meet certain goals and fulfil certain intentions. If the complete explanation of what we are doing makes no reference to goals, purposes and intentions, our ordinary understanding of ourselves appears to be in jeopardy.

If naturalism faces difficulties with accounting for ostensible teleology, the biggest challenge to twentieth-century theism has been the problem of evil. How can one recognize some overriding *telos* or purpose in the suffering and evil in the cosmos?

Several of the chapters will chart the different arguments that have come into play over a theistic account of evil. Some of the twentieth-century literature has consisted in refining the work of earlier centuries. For example, recent work on whether a God who is maximally excellent (or, more modestly, completely good) can or should create a best possible world goes back to Leibniz, and the theistic recourse to appealing to freedom and greater goods has roots in pre-Christian Stoic philosophy. But what is partly distinctive about twentieth-century treatments of evil involves three elements. First, there has been enormous attention given to the twentieth century's most infamous, profound evil: the Holocaust. Reflection on the Holocaust has led to radical movements within Jewish philosophy of religion, some of which retain theism with the explicit incorporation of belief in an afterlife, while others reinterpret the nature of the divine covenant. Secondly, there has been an increasing stress on a passabilist understanding of God, according to which God also suffers with those who suffer. Traditionally, Christians have believed that God incarnate suffers as the Christ, but denied that God the Father suffers (impassabilism). Some Christian philosophical theologians contend that attention to the affective nature of God's presence enables us to make greater sense of how a good God may bring good or redemption out of what appears to us to be a sheer, unmitigated tragedy. Thirdly, Darwinian evolution in the nineteenth century created a challenge for theists in accounting for the cruelty of nature, vividly described by John Stuart Mill for whom nature was no better than a vicious, serial killer. Late twentieth-century theists made use instead of contemporary Western ecology, which stressed the integrated valuable character of ecosystems. Nature still had red teeth and claws, but predation was seen in more amicable terms by later ecologists than their horrified, Victorian forbearers.

BEYOND GODS AND GIANTS

A range of philosophers covered in this volume took philosophy of religion in different directions. Some of these movements were theistic, but the emphasis was not over the metaphysics or epistemology of theism. Martin Heidegger, for example, shifted attention to a phenomenology of our experience of ourselves in the world. In Heidegger's later work we have what may be described as an extended meditation on being. His work defies any easy description; its richness is evidenced, in part, by the way in which it impacted such diverse theologians as Rudolf Bultmann, John Maquarie, Karl Rahner and Paul Tillich. Heidegger's early work inspired philosophers to explore concepts such as authenticity in religious contexts. His later work on being and poetry attracted the attention of many Asian philosophers of religion, especially those in Buddhist studies. Derrida's deconstruction of traditional philosophy inspired a new wave of continental philosophy of religion (leading figures at the end of the twentieth century include John Caputo, Jean-Luc Marion, Paul Ricoeur and Mark C. Taylor). This movement is quite diverse, but it may be seen as united in its promotion of apophatic theology or at least in its critique of cataphatic theology. Apophatic theology (also called the *via negativa*) gives primacy to what cannot be said of God, and resists cataphatic or *via positiva* theologies that reference God univocally or by way of analogy or metaphor. Emmanuel Levinas, a Jewish continental philosopher who rejected cataphatic theology, gave a central role to ethics over and against metaphysics. For Levinas, the heart of Judaism is to be found in ethics and a profound appreciation of the vulnerability of individual persons.

A survey of these other contributors to philosophy of religion makes clear that the field included far more than analytic conceptual analysis or debates in classical metaphysics. If one sees the field as limited to philosophers such as Richard Swinburne and John Mackie, for example, one may well conclude that while the field has shown exciting and substantial progress (the clarity, force, and scope of the arguments have increased over time), it has worked with a similar set of questions going back to Hume and Joseph Butler, or going back even further to the first English-speaking philosophy of the modern era: the Cambridge Platonists Ralph Cudworth and Henry More versus Thomas Hobbes in the seventeenth century (*see* Vol. 3). But when you turn to Simone Weil or Derrida or Levinas or Daly you encounter different methodologies that mix theory and observation, history and ethics, politics and emotion. This is especially true in feminist philosophers of religion such as Pamela Sue Anderson and Sarah Coakley.

I shall risk four further observations here that speak to the fascinating, sprawling field of philosophy of religion.

First, in addition to a general division between what is loosely called continental philosophy (mostly German and French philosophers employing phenomenology in the middle of the century and then existentialism, structuralism and post-structuralism) and analytic philosophy of religion (giving pride of place to conceptual analysis), there has been a division between those philosophers who treat religious beliefs as metaphysically true or false, and those who eschew metaphysics and instead concentrate on religious contexts. The former are customarily considered 'realists' in that they are convinced that religious beliefs are true or false depending on whether the content of these beliefs match reality: for example, the belief that there is a God is true if and only if there is a God. There is no settled term for the opposing party, although some of its members could be said to be 'non-realists' in the sense that they treat religious beliefs as lacking any cognitive content whatsoever. So, in Britain, R. M. Hare and Richard Braithwaite construed religious belief in terms of attitudes (which are neither true nor false) or ethical practices that did not come with claims about what exists that would vex a secular naturalist. More difficult to pin down is the famous Wittgensteinian philosopher of religion, D. Z. Phillips.

From the mid 1960s to his death in 2006, Phillips argued that realist metaphysics as practised by contemporary philosophers of religion was the result of a misunderstanding of the very meaning of religion. For Phillips, and for Rush Rhees, Peter Winch and others, to engage in philosophical debates over whether theism or naturalism or idealism is true is to miss the whole point of religion, which is only to be found in the practices of prayer and other rites, moral action, pilgrimages and the project of living without vanity and in loving regard for one's neighbour. In a way, Phillips rekindled the old controversy over whether there is a division between the God of the philosophers and the God of Abraham, Isaac and Jacob.

It is not obvious, in my view, whether Phillips succeeded in offering a compelling critique of realist metaphysics. But, in general, it can be observed that while the vast bulk of late-twentieth-century philosophy in the Anglophone world, as well as early-twentieth-century continental philosophy, has been metaphysically realist in orientation, challenges to this framework have compelled philosophers (of all stripes) to take more seriously the social, historical and cultural contexts in which religious beliefs and practices have meaning.

Secondly, philosophy of religion in the last quarter of the twentieth century has developed a far greater consciousness of history than in the past. Informed by the work of Alasdair MacIntyre, Hans-Georg Gadamer, Charles Taylor and others, philosophers seem more aware at the end of the twentieth century than at the outset of the historically embedded context of philosophical theories and arguments. This is especially true in philosophy of religion, owing to the historical nature of religion itself. This is not to say that most late-twentieth-century philosophers of religion are historicists. Far from it; yet there is a greater sensitivity to the way ideas can be shaped by economics, politics, gender and so on.

Thirdly, philosphers of religion since the 1970s seem to have developed a great appreciation for how the assessment of a religious worldview is rarely a matter of assessing a single argument, but a wide network of reasons that offer evidential support. This more comprehensive perspective on religion coincides with a move in the philosophy of science in the last half of the twentieth century. Many philosophers came to the conclusion that the assessment of the cognitive meaning of such as Ayer. Ayer regarded religious beliefs (as well as moral beliefs) as non-cognitive because they did not entail empirical verification. In the 1950s Carl Hempel argued forcefully that the meaning of statements had to be determined in light of a comprehensive understanding of the framework in which such statements are made. I cite him at length, for the late-twentieth-century concern for a broader philosophical assessment of religion matches Hempel's successful aim of putting philosophy of science on a better footing:

> But no matter how one might reasonably delimit the class of sentences qualified to introduce empirically significant terms, this new approach [by the positivists] seems to me to lead to the realization that cognitive significance cannot well be construed as a characteristic of individual sentences, but only of more or less comprehensive systems of sentences (corresponding roughly to scientific theories). A closer study of this point suggests strongly that … the idea of cognitive significance, with its suggestion of a sharp distinction between significant and non-significant sentences or systems of such, has lost its promise and fertility … and that it had better be replaced by certain concepts which admit of differences in degree, such as the formal simplicity of a system; its explanatory and predictive power; and theoretical reconstruction of these concepts seems to offer the most promising way of advancing further the clarification of the issues implicit in the idea of cognitive significance. (Hempel 1959: 129)

A parallel appreciation for the systemic way in which religious beliefs form part of comprehensive frameworks has generated a richer philosophy of religion literature at the end of the century than was the case at the beginning. Hand in glove with appreciating the comprehensiveness of worldviews is the appreciation of the role for cumulative arguments in support of religious beliefs.

This more comprehensive approach to philosophy of religion has meant that comparative studies – for example, a contrast between Buddhist and Christian approaches to enlightenment – are less piecemeal and abstract. Broader methods have also brought to light various traditions within religious traditions, thus making it more difficult to reference *the* Buddhist or Christian position on enlightenment.

Fourthly, philosophy of religion since the 1970s has seen a growing concern for religious diversity. A significant body of philosophy of religion has taken up Hindu concepts of Brahman and revelation, reincarnation, karma, Buddhist views of the self, Buddhist epistemology, Daoism, African philosophy of religion and so on. John Hick has championed this expansion. Probably the philosopher who worked the hardest to promote the global study of religion was Ninian Smart, who has left us some superior work on the significance of religious pluralism. The contribution of Sarepalli Radhakrishnan also needs to be acknowledged. As well as being the president of India (1962–7), he was a compelling idealist philosopher who force-fully articulated Hindu philosophy in the English-speaking world. It is partly due to Radhakrishnan's success that his own school of Hinduism, Shankara's Advaita Vedanta, was the most widely discussed in the West during the twentieth century.

Taking seriously the plurality of religious traditions has generated expansive work in the epistemology of religious belief and in political philosophy.

Plural religious traditions created the following puzzles, which exercised late-twentieth-century philosophy of religion: what is the implication of there being two incompatible religious worldviews that appear to be equally well justified to their adherents? If, say, you believe that your religious stance is no more or less justified than an incompatible religious stance, should your confidence in your own beliefs diminish? Or, from the standpoint of a secular enquirer, if one concludes that a pair of incompatible religious worldviews are on a par in terms of evidence and that neither is more justified than remaining secular, is it permissible for the enquirer to accept either religion? These questions fuelled an enormous amount of work on the ethics of belief (should a person always proportion her beliefs to the evidence?), the voluntariness of belief (can I choose what to believe?) and compar-ative accounts of evidence (can what counts as evidence differ between religions?). A major enterprise led by Plantinga and Nicholas Wolterstorff called 'reformed epistemology' has opposed the proposal that religious beliefs require overt eviden-tial justification. Religious beliefs may be warranted as basic beliefs that are gener-ated by God or through God's creation. Debate over reformed epistemology was often framed by questions about religious pluralism: given that we do not know with certainty that Christian theism is true, can we have good reasons for holding that Christian beliefs are warranted as opposed to Buddhist or Hindu beliefs?

In political philosophy, the plurality of religions raised questions about toler-ance and law. In a liberal, pluralistic democracy, is it morally and politically legiti-mate to advance legislation on the basis of religious values that are incompatible with other religious and secular values? Why should legislation not be justified by recourse to religious ethics for the same reason that legislation is sometimes backed by competing, incompatible secular theories of morality and value? To what extent can a secular democratic state legitimately prohibit or curtail the reli-gious practices of its citizens? The debate over such questions at the end of the twentieth century has been especially heated in the literature on political liberalism. Rawls, Thomas Nagel and Robert Audi argued for the primacy of secular values, whereas Wolterstorff, Quinn and Robert Adams argued for a more pluralistic political philosophy that would allow for specific, not universal, religious values to define legislation.

A LESSON OF SORTS

There have been brief periods when philosophy of religion in the twentieth century has been dominated by one school of thought. For a short time, Ludwig Wittgenstein seemed to dominate Cambridge and Oxford, and even as of this writing in Oxford there are still circles of philosophers who regard Wittgenstein's private language argument as irrefutable. At other times, the logical positivists seemed the dominant, unsurpassable paradigm in philosophy of religion. This is not unique to the field. In the late 1970s, nominalism seemed to be the only viable ontology at Harvard while, less than a hundred miles to the south, at Brown University Platonism was the supreme philosophy of the day. The different movements, the ebbing and flowing of competing arguments, give some philosophers reason to be sceptical about the whole enterprise. A different conclusion to consider is that philosophy of religion is not easy. The reasons behind the different methodologies, conclusions and topics of enquiry are complex and cumulative. Rarely is any project in philosophy of religion reliant on a single argument or experience. Rather than scepticism (and scepticism about God, reason, faith, etc. is a part of philosophy of religion, not something set apart from the field), I suggest that twentieth-century philosophy of religion provides some reason for respecting a plurality of methods and conclusions. Undoubtedly, philosophy departments in the future will form a consensus on *the only proper domain of philosophy of religion*. Perhaps the perceived *terminus ad quem* of the field will be naturalism or theism, feminism or Hegelism, idealism, Pyrrhonian Scepticism or rationalism, or any number of other schools of thought. A thorough engagement with the chapters in this volume should caution us, however, in assuming that one's own or one's institution's philosophy of religion is unrivalled as we see how deeply and forcefully competing positions have been advanced, involving many of the best philosophical minds of the twentieth century. This should, I think, cultivate a spirit of respectful openness (a golden rule of sorts may be commendable: treat others' philosophy of religion as you would like your own to be treated) and some humility, lest shortly after you proclaim philosophy of religion has finally come to a rest with your own philosophy, you are called on to admit that the field has moved on to even better positions and arguments. Perhaps the dynamic of this area of philosophy can be summed up in the words attributed to Galileo when he officially retracted his view of the earth's movement: *eppur si muove* (and yet it does move).

2

WILLIAM JAMES

Richard M. Gale

William James (1842–1910) had a peripatetic childhood in which his father, the theologian Henry James, Sr, hustled him and his four younger siblings, among whom was the novelist Henry James, Jr, from one European nation to another in search of an adequate education. After a brief stint as a painting student of William Morris Hunt he entered the Lawrence Scientific School at Harvard in 1861. On graduation in 1864 he enrolled in the Harvard Medical School, completing the MD degree in 1869, with a year off to participate in Louis Agassiz's research expedition to Brazil. After suffering serious ill health and depression from 1869 to 1872, he became an instructor in physiology at Harvard, where he spent his entire career until his retirement in 1907. He rapidly moved up the academic ladder, becoming an instructor in anatomy and physiology in 1873, assistant professor of physiology in 1876, assistant professor of philosophy in 1880 and full professor in 1885, and a professor of psychology in 1889.

The philosophy of William James was an attempt to heal a deep breach within himself. On one level it consisted in an apparent clash between his need to do science and his equally strong need to be religious and lead the morally strenuous life: to be, as he put it, both tough-minded and tender-minded. His pragmatism is advertised as giving us a way to do it all with a clear conscience, thereby serving as a reconciler or mediator, but not a unifier, of these different stances toward the world. It does this by providing a theory of meaning and truth that is common to all these activities, and thus if one of them is legitimate, so are the others; and, since no one wants to deny the legitimacy of science, religion and morality ride its coat-tails to intellectual respectability, being subject to all the consequent privileges and rights. The pragmatic theory of meaning holds that the whole meaning of a belief or proposition is a set of conditionalized predictions specifying what experiences one will have in the future if certain actions are performed, for example, 'If you place this substance in *aqua regia*, then you will have experiences of its dissolving'. A proposition acquires truth when these predictions are actually verified. Pragmatism is based on a Promethean view of human beings as creators of value and meaning through the active control of their environment. By conceiving of things in terms of what we can do with them and what they in turn can do to us, these Promethean endeavours are furthered.

There is, however, a breach within James that occurs on a deeper level, which involves an apparent clash between his Promethean and mystical selves. Whereas the former wants to gain mastery over the surrounding world, ride herd on it, the former wants to penetrate to the inner conscious core of everything, both natural and supernatural, through acts of sympathetic intuition, so as to achieve at least a partial unification with them. To achieve this, the self must abandon its Promethean stance, which requires that it jettison all concepts and become passive. There is an apparently different God for James' mystical self than there is for his Promethean self, and the challenge to the interpreter is to find some way to unify them, which is something that James never succeeded in doing. Each of these Gods will be considered in turn, and then it will be asked whether they can be combined or integrated.

THE GOD OF PROMETHEANISM

This is the God that fits the pragmatic theory of meaning and truth, and it was for this reason that James featured it in the final lecture of his 1907 *Pragmatism*, where it was his purpose to show that his brand of pragmatism was religion friendly. In his earlier essay of 1896, "The Will to Believe", he gave a similar Promethean rendering of the religious hypothesis that begins with the claim that it comprises the following two tenets:

> First, she says that the best things are the more eternal things, the over-
> lapping things, the things in the universe that throw the last stone, so
> to speak, and say the final word ...
>   The second affirmation of religion is that we are better off even now
> if we believe her first affirmation to be true.   (*WB* 29–30)[1]

As a favour to James, the second affirmation will be dropped, since it is not a creedal tenet of any of the major extant religions but instead something that might be claimed by a psychologist of religion about the beneficial effects of religious belief.

James gives a pragmatic analysis of the first affirmation in terms of this condi-tionalized prediction:

---

1. All references to James are to *The Works of William James* (James 1975–) and will be included in the body of the chapter using these abbreviations: *WB*, "The Will to Believe"; *P, Pragmatism; ML, Manuscript Lectures; VRE, The Varieties of Religious Experience; PU, A Pluralistic Universe; ERM, Essays in Religion and Morality.*

R   If we collectively exert our best moral effort, then good will win out over evil in the long run.

This is the pragmatic 'cash value' of the proposition that God exists. It forms the core of his beloved religion of meliorism, which claims that it is a real, existentially grounded possibility that if we make the antecedent of R true by acting in a good-making fashion, the friendly forces within nature will aid us in making R's consequent true. He imagines God offering us this proposal.

> "I am going to make a world not certain to be saved, a world the perfection of which shall be conditional merely, the condition being that each several agent does its own 'level best'. Its safety, you see, is unwarranted. It is a real adventure, with real danger, yet it may win through. It is a social scheme of co-operative work genuinely to be done. Will you join the procession? Will you trust yourself and trust the other agents enough to face the risk?"   (*P* 139)

This conditionalized formulation of the religious hypothesis gets repeated at two places in his lecture notes: "Meanwhile I ask whether a world of hypothetical perfection conditional on each part doing its duty be not as much as can fairly be demanded" (*ML* 319), and pluralism holds that "the world … may be saved, on condition that its parts shall do their best" (*ML* 412).

James claims that a "normally constituted" person would gladly accept this offer (*P* 139). This is the "healthy-minded person", who is contrasted in his 1902 *The Varieties of Religious Experience* with the "sick soul" on the basis of their respective attitudes toward evil. Healthy-minded persons can look evil squarely in the eye because they feel empowered to cope with or even defeat it. In contrast, sick-souled persons are overwhelmed by evil, feeling incapable of coping with it on their own. They favour religions that stress the fallen condition of humanity owing to original sin. Only by undergoing a conversion, which can happen suddenly or gradually, can they acquire the healthy-minded Promethean stance towards evil.

James continually fluctuated back and forth between the healthy-minded and sick-soul stances toward evil. When he was in his healthy-minded moods, he was itching to engage in a Texas death match with evil without any assurance of succeeding. James, however, was also subject to the morbid states of the sick soul, as is amply attested to by his report of one of his own experiences as a medical student of existential angst on seeing a hideous catatonic youth:

> *That shape am I*, I felt, potentially. Nothing that I possess can defend me against that fate, if the hour for it should strike for me as it struck for him. There was such a horror of him, and such a perception of my own merely momentary discrepancy from him, that it was as if

15

> something hitherto solid within my breast gave way entirely, and I
> became a mass of quivering flesh. (*VRE* 134)

The thought that the worst sort of evils can strike any of us at any moment, and that we are helpless to do anything about it, periodically haunted James throughout his adult life.

James, rightfully, claimed that the truth of R could not now be decided on evidential or intellectual grounds; for, it not only makes a conditional prediction concerning the indefinite future, there being no cut-off date for the eventual triumph of good over evil, but depends for its truth on how we shall decide to act. It is impossible that, in advance of her decision, a person can know either what she will decide to do or that an event will occur that depends on what she will decide to do. And the truth of R does depend on how we shall choose to act. What should we now believe with regard to the truth of R, given that its truth or falsity cannot be determined on evidential grounds? There were contemporaries of James, such as W. K. Clifford and T. H. Huxley, who argued that it is morally impermissible to ever believe a proposition on insufficient evidence. This universal moral prohibition requires that we suspend belief, adopt an agnostic stance, with respect to R. In opposition, James developed a doctrine called 'the will to believe' that spelled out the conditions under which one is morally permitted to believe on insufficient evidence and gave the religious hypothesis, R, as a suitable target for a will-to-believe option. This is his most distinctive and influential doctrine and has been the subject of heated debate since it was first presented in 1896, with there being no end in sight.

Basically, the will-to-believe doctrine gives an agent moral permission to believe a proposition on insufficient evidence when doing so will help them to bring about something morally desirable. A standard objection to the will-to-believe doctrine is that one cannot believe at will, voluntarily, intentionally, on purpose. James gets around this objection by pointing out that although in most cases we cannot believe at will, we nevertheless can at will do things that will help to self-induce a belief, such as acting as if we believe. In order to deflect objections that his doctrine licensed wishful thinking and gullibility, he required that the agent lack sufficient evidence for or against the truth of the proposition *after having done their best to discover such evidence.* This would rule out the self-serving ignorance of Clifford's shipowner who believes his ship is seaworthy and sends it on a voyage without properly investigating the matter. Yet another requirement for having a will-to-believe option is that there is a proposition, p, that it is morally desirable that one makes true, and one's chances of making p come true are increased by one's first believing another proposition, q. There are numerous cases in which an agent is aided in helping to make a morally desirable proposition become true by the confidence- and courage-building belief that she has the capacity to do so. A good example is the stranded Alpine climber who must jump across a ravine to get to safety in a storm: she increases the chances of making it become true that this happens by first believing the conditional proposition that if she attempts the jump, she shall succeed. A will-to-believe option is relative to the psychological state of an individual, since people differ with respect to whether they need a prior confidence-building belief that they can succeed in some endeavour before they attempt to do so.

James firmly believed that many persons are so psychologically constituted that their chances of acting in a way that will help make it true that good wins out over evil in the long run, which is the consequent of R, is increased if they first believe R. There admittedly are sick souls for whom a will-to-believe option to believe R is not a real possibility, not a live option. The will-to-believe doctrine can be pressed into service on behalf of believing in the truth of good old-time religion and not James' moralistic substitute for it. For many people, believing that the God of traditional Western theism exists will give them the kind of inspiration and courage to act in a way that will help them to make it true that they become morally better, lead more meaningful lives, and the like.

THE GOD OF MYSTICISM

James begins with a special inward manner in which one person experiences another as a 'Thou' rather than an 'It', and then extends this to the experience of the world at large, even to God and nature. His analysis of the I–Thou experience bears a striking resemblance to that offered by Martin Buber some thirty years later. It is not only persons, both natural and supernatural, that can be I–Thoued, but also nature at large, as nature mystics have traditionally claimed. Clearly, James is personalizing the universe when he writes, "The Universe is no longer a mere *It* to us, but a *Thou*, if we are religious; and any relation that may be possible from person to person might be possible here" (*WB* 31). Taking a religious stance to the world "changes the dead blank *it* of the world into a living *thou*, with whom the whole man may have dealings" (*WB* 101). "Infra-theistic ways of looking on the world leave it in the third person, a mere *it* … [but] theism turns the *it* into a *thou*" (*WB* 106).

Another part of James' account of the I–Thou relation that needs further elaboration is just how unified a person becomes with its Thou, be it another person, God or nature. There are monistic mystics who take the unification to be one of complete numerical identity, but James, being squarely ensconced within the Western theistic mystical tradition, takes it to be something less than that, a case of what he liked to call, using Benjamin Paul Blood's marvellous phrase, "ever not quite" (1874). Throughout his career James was a self-proclaimed 'pluralistic mystic'. In the 1909 *A Pluralistic Universe*, James introduced a strange type of identity, which holds between the I and the Thou. It is strange because it is an identity that is not transitive, thus allowing for *X* to be 'identical' with *Y* and *Y* to be 'identical' with *Z* even though *X* is not 'identical' with *Z*. You might say that *X* is 'identical' with *Y*, only not *that* identical, to paraphrase the punchline of an old shaggy-dog story.

The major thesis of *The Varieties of Religious Experience*, and one that I think is successfully maintained to James' everlasting credit, is that the basis of religion, including its institutional structure, theology and personal religious feelings and beliefs, is rooted in religious experiences of a mystical sort in which the individual has an apparent direct, non-sensory perception of a 'More', an 'Unseen' supernatural or purely spiritual reality into which she is to some extent absorbed and from which spiritual energy flows into her. These 'perceptions' of the 'More' can be viewed as a very heightened and intense form of the I–Thou experience. Through these I–Thou experiences of the More, the subject gets "an assurance of safety and a temper of peace, and, in relation to others, a preponderance of loving affection" (*VRE* 383).

Throughout *The Varieties of Religious Experience* James works with a perceptual model of mystical experiences, likening them to ordinary sense-perceptions in that both involve a direct acquaintance with an object, although only the latter has a sensory content. "Mystical experiences are … direct perceptions … absolutely sensational … face to face presentation of what seems to exist" (*VRE* 336). A perception is 'direct', I assume, if the existential claims made by the subject on the basis of her experience are non-inferential. Another important, and highly controversial, assumption James makes in his likening mystical experiences to sense perceptions is that mystical experiences, like sensory ones, are intentional in the sense that they have an apparent accusative that exists independently of the subject when the experience is veridical. In this respect, they are unlike a feeling of pain, which takes only a cognate or internal accusative, since feeling a pain is nothing but paining or feeling painfully.

James tries to take a neutral stance on whether mystical experiences support a monistic or pluralistic view of the more or unseen reality, in spite of his own strong emotional commitment to the pluralistic version. At one place he seems to come down on the side of the modern-day mystical ecumenists, such as Daisetsu Suzuki, Walter Stace and Thomas Merton, who contend that there is a common phenomenological *monistic* core to all unitive mystical experiences that then gets interpreted by the mystic so as to accord with the underlying culture of her society. "In mystic states we both become one with the Absolute and we become aware of our oneness. This is the everlasting and triumphant mystical tradition, hardly altered by differences of clime or creed" (*VRE* 332). Some of James' major contentions in *The Varieties of Religious Experience*, however, require a dualistic experience. For example, James says that prayer is "the very soul and essence of religion", and then describes prayer as involving two-way interaction between two subjects. James' strong Protestant leanings cause him, for the most part, to give a dualistic interpretation of mystical experiences.

One of the features of mystical experiences, as well as conversion experiences in general, that James stresses is that the subject is passive in respect to them. While persons can take steps, such as following the mystical way, to help induce the experience, its coming is viewed by religious mystics as the free bestowal of a gift on them by the grace of God. Through the experience the subject feels that her conscious will is held in abeyance as she finds absorption in a higher unity. "The mystic feels as if his own will were grasped and held by a superior power" (*VRE* 303). In both cases there must be a cancelling out of the finite so as to open ourselves to the infinite.

James, no doubt with his sick soul's experiences of existential angst in mind, stresses how such mystically based resignation cannot "fail to steady the nerves, to cool the fever, and appease the fret, if one be conscious that, no matter what one's difficulties for the moment may appear to be, one's life as a whole is in the keeping of a power whom one can absolutely trust" (*VRE* 230). The mystical experiences that such submission of the conscious will helps to foster are "reconciling and unifying states" (*VRE* 330) that "tell of the supremacy of the ideal, of vastness, of union, of safety, and of rest" (*VRE* 339). In such mystical union there is a "life not correlated with death, a health not liable to illness, a kind of good that will not perish, a good in fact that flies beyond the Goods of nature" (*VRE* 119). This is just what his Promethean self's beloved religion of meliorism cannot deliver; it cannot help him make it through the dark nights of his soul or face the hideous catatonic epileptic youth. A theme that runs throughout *The Varieties of Religious Experience* is the insufficiency of meliorism. It is condemned as being "the very consecration of forgetfulness and superficiality" (*VRE* 118–19).

James gives a non-pragmatic rendering of the meaning of the mystic's reality-claim in terms of the phenomenological content of her God-type experience, the truth of which depends on whether her experience is objective or cognitive. Meaning now is no longer based solely on future consequences that will be experienced if certain actions are performed. To be sure, the spiritual and moral benefits that the experience occasions become relevant, but only as a means of indirect verification, there now being, as there was not for meliorism, a distinction between direct and indirect verification, with an assertion's meaning being identified primarily with its direct verification. For mystical experiences this is the apparent object, the intentional accusative, of the experience. James seems to recognize this when he says that "the word 'truth' is here taken to mean something additional to bare value for life" (*VRE* 401). Accordingly, James makes the issue of the cognitivity or objectivity of mystical experience a central issue in *The Varieties of Religious Experience*. Concerning experiences of a mystical kind, he asks about their "metaphysical significance" (308), "cognitivity" (*VRE* 324), "authoritativeness" (*VRE* 335), "objective truth" (*VRE* 304), "value for knowledge" (*VRE* 327), "truth" (*VRE* 329), and whether they "furnish any warrant for the truth of the … supernaturality and pantheism which they favor" (*VRE* 335), or are "to be taken as *evidence* … for the actual existence of a higher world with which our world is in relation" (*VRE* 384). James is quite explicit that the answer to the 'objectivity' question is independent of the biological and psychological benefits that accrue from mystical experiences.

James concludes that there is a generic content that is shared by the many different types of mystical experiences that "is literally and objectively true" (*VRE*

405). He gives an argument for this based on an analogy between mystical and sense-experience, which has been ably defended in recent years by many philosophers, most notably William Alston and William Wainwright. First, an overview will be given of a generic version of their arguments, and then an attempt will be made to locate it, or at least the germ of it, in James.

It is an argument from analogy that goes as follows. Mystical and sense-experiences are analogous in cognitively relevant respects; and, since the latter are granted to be cognitive, so should the former. A cognitive type of experience is one that counts, in virtue of some *a priori* presumptive inference rule, as evidence or warrant for believing that the apparent object of the experience, its intentional accusative, objectively exists and is as it appears to be in the experience. For sense-experience, the presumptive inference rule is that if it perceptually appears to be the case that *X* exists, then probably it is the case that *X* exists, unless there are defeating conditions. These defeating conditions consist in tests and checks for the veridicality of the experience that fail on this occasion. Prominent among these tests are agreement among relevant observers, law-like coherence between the experience's content and the content of earlier and later experiences, and being caused in the right way. The presumptive inference rule is said to be *a priori*, because it cannot be justified by appeal to sense-experience without vicious circularity.

If mystical experiences are to be subject to an analogous *a priori* presumptive inference rule, they must be analogous to sense-experiences in having defeating conditions: checks and tests that can fail. All of the contemporary defenders of the cognitivity of mystical experiences argue that the great religious mystical traditions employ a fairly elaborate network of tests for the veridicality of mystical experiences, usually including that the subject, as well as her community, display favourable moral and/or spiritual development as a result of the experience, and that what her experience reveals accords with her religion's holy scriptures and the mystical experiences of past saints and notables, to name some of the more important tests of most of the great religious mystical traditions.

With a little imagination we can find most, but not all, of the elements of this analogical argument in *The Varieties of Religious Experience*. A good case can be made out that James deserves to be credited with being the founding father of this argument. In the first place, James makes a prominent use of a perceptual model of mystical experience, which is the analogical premise of the contemporary argument for cognitivity. He comes right out and says:

> Our own more 'rational' beliefs are based on evidence exactly similar in nature to that which mystics quote for theirs. Our senses, namely, have assured us of certain states of fact; but mystical experiences are as direct perceptions of fact for those who have them as any sensations ever were for us. The records show that even though the five senses be in abeyance in them, they are absolutely sensational in their epistemological quality. (*VRE* 336)

Furthermore, like the contemporary analogical arguers, James goes on to fill out the analogy by showing that there are mystical analogues for some of the tests for the veridicality of sense-experience. What is apparently revealed by mystical experiences "must be sifted and tested, and run the gauntlet of confrontation with the total context of experience just like what comes from the outer world of sense" (*VRE* 338). Mystical experiences are also likened to "windows through which the mind looks out upon a more extensive and inclusive world" than is revealed by our senses, and just as we have checks and tests for mediating between rival sensory-based claims there are analogous ones for mediating between rival mystically based claims. Because of these background defeating conditions, it will be possible for mysticism to have "its valid experiences and its counterfeit ones, just as our world has them ... We should have to use its experiences by selecting and subordinating and substituting just as is our custom in this ordinary naturalistic world; we should be liable to error just as we are now" (*VRE* 339). Further indication of just how close James is to the contemporary analogical arguers is his claim that mystical experiences "establish a presumption" in favour of the thing being as it appears to be in them (*VRE* 336), which sounds very much like their presumptive inference rule.

There is one very important respect in which James differs from contemporary analogical arguers that renders his argument less attractive than theirs, namely, he completely eschews any attempt to place the relevant background tests, which are the overriders or defeaters, within the shared practices of an ongoing religious community. In general, James' failure to see the importance of religious institutions, with their shared beliefs and communal practices, is a significant limitation in the account that is given of religious experience in *The Varieties of Religious Experience*. This is yet another example of James' over-glorification of the isolated individual. His mystic is a lone-gun mystic, cut off from the doxastic practices of a religious community. Where his mystic gets her tests from and how they are enforced remains a mystery. In virtue of being isolated from a community of fellow believers and practitioners, James' mystic must follow her own private tests.

Contemporary analogical arguers are intent on justifying the various ongoing mystical doxastic practices as being reliable for the most part. James, on the other hand, works only on the *retail* level, his concern being exclusively with the justification for an individual mystic taking one of her experiences to be veridical. He fails to see that this justification cannot be cut off from the *wholesale* justification of the shared social practice of basing objective existential claims on mystical experiences. James fails to realize that by eschewing the wholesale level, he significantly weakens the effectiveness of his will-to-believe justification for the lone mystic believing that one of her experiences is veridical. This is a very important application of the will-to-believe, since what she believes in this matter could have the most important consequences for her future moral and spiritual development, that is, for her quest for sanctification. Certainly, she will be aided in her attempt to get herself to believe on will-to-believe grounds that her mystical experience is veridical if she first believes that the general doxastic practice of basing existential claims on mystical experiences is a reliable one that yields true existential beliefs for the most part. This belief also must be based on will-to-believe grounds, since the mystical doxastic practice, like the sensory one, does not admit of any non-circular external justification. James' analogical argument, along with his will-to-believe justification for believing in the veridicality of an individual mystical experience, welcomes supplementation by bringing in the doxastic practice in which his tests are embedded.

With this in mind, a survey can now be made of the different tests he recognized as relevant to determining the veridicality of a mystical experience. Like the contemporary analogical arguers, James recognizes a mystical analogue to the sensory agreement and prediction tests, although he adds a third one: the immediate luminosity test. Here, in brief, is how they work.

James makes a very broad application of the agreement test so that it concerns not only whether there is agreement among the mystics themselves but also whether their reports agree with ordinary sensory-based ones. In regard to the former, he first says that there is a consensus among mystics and that "it would be odd … if such a unanimous type of experience should prove to be altogether wrong" (*VRE* 336). However, he immediately counters that "the appeal to numbers has no logical force" and that there is considerable disagreement among the monistic and pluralistic mystics, not to mention their collective disagreement with demoniacal mysticism. Not only does the agreement test not support the objectivity of mystical experience when only mystical experiences are considered, but it counts against this when the sensory-based experiences are brought in. Mystical experiences "do not come to everyone; and the rest of life makes either no connexion with them, or tends to contradict them more than it confirms them" (*VRE* 22). And, against the claims of monistic mystics, James says that the "eaches" of the pluralists "are at any rate real enough to have made themselves at least appear to everyone, whereas the absolute has as yet appeared immediately to only a few mystics, and indeed to them very ambiguously" (*PU* 62).

James, I believe, tries to soften this clash between mysticism and sense-experience by giving a very understated conclusion concerning what mystical experiences ultimately proclaim:

> As a rule, mystical states merely add a supersenuous meaning to the ordinary outward data of consciousness. They are excitements like the emotions of love or ambition, flights to our spirit by means of which facts already objectively before us fall into a new life. They do not contradict these facts as such, or deny anything that our senses have immediately seized. (*VRE* 338)

The same protective strategy seems operative in James' bizarre initial set of four defining characteristics of a mystical experience – being ineffable, noetic, transitory, and passive (*VRE* 302–3) – in which he fails to include being a unitive experience, which is their most important and distinctive feature, but one that seems to clash with the deliverances of ordinary sense-experience, which presents us with a multiplicity of distinct objects in space and time. This could aptly be called the 'comic book' theory of mystical experiences, since they are supposed to function as do the field of force lines that comic books place around an object that is perceived or thought in a specifically intense manner. This, at best, fits the experiences at the undeveloped end of the mystical spectrum, such as drunkenness, but not those unitive experiences at the developed end, which not only report new facts, James' higher dimensions of reality, but also sometimes seem to contradict our sensory-based beliefs concerning the reality of space, time and multiplicity. James does not want us to have to serve on a jury and decide whether to believe the testimony of the mystics or that of the vast majority of humanity, but he does not map out any effective strategy for preventing the matter from going to trial. He wants to find some common denominator of all mystical experiences that is sufficiently watered down so as not to conflict with the deliverances of sense-experience, but this fails to address the issue of whether the more developed mystical experiences are veridical.

Whereas the agreement test did not offer any support to the objectivity claim of mystics, quite to the contrary according to James, the prediction test does. Because of the passive and transitory nature of mystical experiences, we are not able to predict their occurrence, and to this extent the prediction test counts against their objectivity. But this is more than offset by the fact that so many mystics grow morally and/or spiritually as a result of their experience. In attacking reductionistic causal explanations of mystical experiences, James says that we must "inquire into their fruits for life", rather than their causes (*VRE* 327). This is an ongoing theme in *The Varieties of Religious Experience*, especially in Lectures I, XIV and XV.

Immediate luminosity, the subject's intense feeling of delight and reality, figures prominently in James' network of confirmatory tests, sometimes being accorded pride of place over good consequences (*VRE* 23) and at others taking second place to them (*VRE* 21–2). An interesting question is why James, unlike his contemporary analogical arguers, used this test. The answer might be that *The Principles of Psychology*'s interest-relative account of existence, although not explicitly endorsed in *The Varieties of Religious Experience*, still weighs heavily in James' thinking. This might account for James' seeming relativization of *being evidence for* to persons in his first two conclusions regarding what mystical experiences establish:

(1) Mystical states, when well developed, usually are, and have the right to be, absolutely authoritative over the individuals to whom they come.
(2) No authority emanates from them which should make it a duty for those who stand outside of them to accept their revelations uncritically. (*VRE* 335)

James favours the pluralistic interpretation of mystical experience. A mystical experience is of a surrounding mother-sea of consciousness; however, there is probably more than a single all-encompassing surrounding sea of consciousness, with God merely being the most outstanding of them in terms of power, knowledge and goodness, but still only finite. In a mystical experience, according to the surrounding mother-seas hypothesis, the subject becomes unified with one of these super consciousnesses in a way that falls short of becoming literally numerically one and the same with it but rather in the weaker sense of becoming cognizant that it is a *part* of this enveloping consciousness. This inclusion of one consciousness self within another raises several problems, the least of which is the one that worried James concerning how one conscious state can be a part of another. The surrounding mother-sea of consciousness, be it a single sea or a plurality of seas, is an unseen order said to be "behind the veil" (*ERM* 76, 86, 87) to those of us "here below" (*ERM* 82, 87). It is a "transcendental world" (*ERM* 93, 96) that makes "influx" into a person's ordinary consciousness when the dam or threshold of receptivity is lowered (*ERM* 93).

THE RELATION BETWEEN THE TWO GODS

The clash between the active Promethean self and the passive mystical one, along with their respective Gods, might have been made to appear more formidable than it really is. Even Promethean selves must be permitted to sleep, for they will not amount to much as Promethean agents if they do not. Similarly, they should not be denied some mystical rest and recreation if it should enable them to return to the war zone better equipped to do battle with the forces of evil. For James, mystical emotions and beliefs are valuable and should be cultivated, not just for their own sake, but also for their instrumental value in inducing morally desirable behaviour. James even claimed that for a mystical experience to be veridical or objective its "fruits must be good for Life" (*VRE* 318). But this still leaves us with an apparent clash between the Promethean and mystical Gods.

Here is a textually motivated effort at finding a way to unify them. In *Pragmatism* and "The Will to Believe", that the Promethean God exists is pragmatically reduced to R: if we collectively exert our best moral effort, then good will win out over evil in the long run. But our best moral efforts are not alone sufficient to bring about this victory of good over evil, for they must be supplemented by the friendly forces operating within the world. As James put it, God is "but one helper ... in the midst of all the shapers of the great world's fate" (*P* 143). When James is promoting his melioristic religion based on R, he does not speculate about the nature of these friendly forces. This he does in *The Varieties of Religious Experience*, whose message is that the essence, the lifeblood, of religion is found in mystical experiences. A metaphysical theory about the nature of the apparent object of a mystical experience is called an 'over belief'. James offers a dualistic one that takes it to be an enveloping mother-sea of consciousness, of which there might be and probably are more than one, thereby opening the door to polytheism. The enveloping individual has goals and uses the enveloped individual in realizing them. It would be reasonable for James to identify, although he never explicitly did so, the friendly forces of his melioristic religion with these several mother-seas of consciousness. This would unify his Promethean and mystical Gods.

FURTHER READING

Bishop, J. 2007. *Believing by Faith: An Essay in the Epistemology and Ethics of Religious Belief.* Oxford: Clarendon Press.

Fontinell, E. 1986. *Self, God, and Immortality: A Jamesian Investigation.* Philadelphia, PA: Temple University Press.

Gale, R. M. 1999. *The Divided Self of William James.* Cambridge: Cambridge University Press.

Levinson, H. 1981. *The Religious Investigations of William James.* Chapel Hill, NC: University of North Carolina Press.

Myers, G. 1986. *William James: His Thought and Life.* New Haven, CT: Yale University Press.

Perry, R. 1948. *The Thought and Character of William James.* Cambridge, MA: Harvard University Press.

Sprigge, T. 1993. *James and Bradley: American Truth and British Reality.* Chicago, IL: Open Court.

Suckiel, E. 1996. *Heaven's Champion: William James's Philosophy of Religion.* Notre Dame, IN: University of Notre Dame Press.

On I–THOU relation see also Ch. 8. On MYSTICISIM see also Ch. 3; Vol. 2, Ch. 7. On PRAGMA-TISM see also Ch. 4; Vol. 4, Ch. 17.

3

HENRI BERGSON

John Mullarkey

That the ideas of Henri Bergson (1859–1941) were once associated with the French school of spiritualist philosophy (from Maine de Biran to Teilhard de Chardin); that Bergsonism was, for a time, both commended and rejected as an idealist and idealistic philosophy in reaction against the materialism of its day; that it seemed to deify humanity as the highpoint of evolution (in the face of a century of increasing pessimism regarding the value of human being); and that it urged a concentration on a form of time (*durée*) that transcends space and matter: all this would appear to mark Bergson's thought as one belonging to a transcendental tradition, one with a religious bent at heart, and one with some secretive God residing at its centre. Bergson's embrace of Catholicism and by Catholic thinkers would add to this impression (in 1941 he made a deathbed announcement of his conversion from Judaism to Christianity, although always maintaining its secrecy in favour of a public stance of solidarity with the Jewish community under persecution); so too would the posthumous decline of his philosophical standing under the weight of constant attacks from the more obviously secular thought of Sartrean existentialism and phenomenology, Marxist materialism and Bachelardian epistemology. And yet the connection between Bergson and religion is actually much more complex than either the positive or negative side of these facts would have us believe – and not only because most of his works were placed on the Catholic Church's *Index Librorum Prohibitorum* (List of prohibited books) in 1914, or that he remained an enemy of idealism for all of his philosophical career, or that his so-called spiritualism was in fact an anti-reductionist position and not an immaterialist one.

Rightly or wrongly, Bergson is again of interest today mostly because of the work of Gilles Deleuze, work that is, in essence, a neo-Bergsonian form of thought, and therewith no less ambiguous regarding the place of the divine. Deleuze's central categories of difference, multiplicity, the virtual, life, evolution, problematics, process and empiricism all derive from Bergson more than from any other philosopher. And, consequently, Bergson's contemporary avatar is seemingly no less duplicitous when it comes to God and the transcendental than was his master. Despite Deleuze being the philosopher who has done with 'the judgement of God' like Antonin Artaud, who has embraced the earth like Friedrich Nietzsche (*see* Vol. 4, Ch. 18), and who prioritizes immanence as an absolute like Baruch Spinoza (*see* Vol. 3, Ch. 11), Deleuze can still be seen as a spiritualist thinker, a philosopher 'out of this world' (Hallward 2006), and a transcendentalist, no less than his mentor. For the truth is that Bergson, like Deleuze, is a philosopher of conjunctions, of God *and* nature, of spirit *and* matter, of the transcendent *and* the immanent – each dyad being held together as *tendencies* or *movements*, rather than being either identified as one state or opposed as two.

In this chapter, I shall first set out what Bergson says concerning God in the 'traditional' sense, where he briefly indicates the relation of God to his own metaphysics of *durée* and the *élan vital* (which is basically the cosmic incarnation of *durée*), before turning to the substance of his thought, a substance of movements that outline the immanent emergence from itself of the 'transcendental', the auto-affection of immanence that brings forth both the religious soul (be it either 'static' or 'dynamic') and the image of divinity itself in a process that Bergson dubs, in his final book, *The Two Sources of Morality and Religion* (1932), 'fabulation'. Here we shall see a God that does not stand outside and transcendent to the world, but a world that is itself an indefinite creativity and movement, with no underlying, unmoved mover at its origin.

THE *ÉLAN* OF GOD

In the early texts, *Time and Free Will* (1889) and *Matter and Memory* (1896), works that set out Bergson's metaphysics of time as duration – time as the continual emergence of novelty and the very basis of being – there is little or no mention of God. The final chapter of *Matter and Memory* does talk of consciousnesses greater in duration than our own, but these are clearly plural and immanent to life on earth: they belong to the realm of psychologies existing above and below the human mind, ones that transcend only *human* consciousness rather than consciousness *per se* (hence, to think of Bergson as a humanist in the anthropocentric sense is to misread him badly – the task of philosophy is always to go beyond the human condition, as he clearly states in "An Introduction to Metaphysics" from 1903; Bergson 2007: xx). Given that *Creative Evolution* (1907) does then extend this metaphysics of time to the universe – the *élan* as cosmic principle of change over inertia, of differentiation over repetition – it was perhaps inevitable that Bergson would here at last make some remarks about God. Yet even in *Creative Evolution* he is sparing, stating only that the Absolute 'endures', being nothing less than creativity itself. The holistic and immanent nature of the divine is already clear even here in this barest sketch, for this Absolute, in as much as its essence is creativity, is also said to be 'like us' (Bergson 1911: 262, 315). And what is this *élan*, this all-encompassing principle that subsumes God and us alike? Nothing more or less than novelty itself, the creation of the new, that which is ongoing and completely unpredictable. The *élan* is not a mysterious, immaterial substance, some kind of supernatural *archeus*. It is a kind of time, creative time. Nor is there an abstract, transcendent and infinite *creator* (which would simply be another kind of substance) behind this creativity; there is only this process – a living, immanent and indefinite creativity that does not oppose itself to other finite beings (processes), but is actually on a continuum with them. Indeed, in a related text, Bergson uses the term 'indefinite' to reconcile the infinite and the finite in this continual and continuous process of creativity (Bergson 1946: 211).

THE SOURCE OF THE DIVINE SOUL

With the exception of *Duration and Simultaneity* in 1922 (a technical work in the philosophy of physics, primarily devoted to distancing Bergsonism from Albert Einstein's special theory of relativity, with which it had been compared), Bergson only wrote one other monograph after *Creative Evolution*, but it is the one that finally sets out his ideas on God, morality and religion explicitly: *The Two Sources of Morality and Religion* (hereafter *Two Sources*). It does so, naturally, in immanen-tist terms, explicating the source of the divine image and religious soul in vitalist categories, that is, ones concerning life and consciousness. Indeed, what distinguishes the *Two Sources* from the rest of Bergson's *oeuvre* is that it is primarily a work in sociobiology rather than metaphysics (in fact, it is *the* sociobiological study of religion according to Charles Hartshorne; Hartshorne 1987: 379). For Bergson, we must seek the origin of religion in the biological exigencies of life, placing God back within the "general evolution of life" (*Two Sources* 116, 177).[1]

But we must be cautious here: Bergson's is not at all a reductive sociobiology, for there is no wish here to deflate culture to 'merely' animal, biological or genetic forces. Nor is there any causal agency implied going from some putative biological substratum 'up to' a social superstratum. No, this is an inflationary discourse, for biological influence merits much more worth than we normally give it: "let us then give to the word biology the very wide meaning it should have, and will perhaps have one day" (*ibid*.: 101). Religion (and the divine) are natural, but nature is not inert: it is living creation itself. Hence, Bergson's metaphysics of process and life must be kept in mind when looking at his sociobiology of ethics and religion.

That said, the first manifestation of this redemptive biologism is the religious dualism evident throughout *Two Sources*. There are *two* sources of morality and religion, and both are biological. They can both be biological because there are also two major aspects to Bergson's theory of evolution, namely, on the one hand

---

1. Quotes from *Two Sources* are from Bergson ([1935] 1977).

a tendency towards repetition in the static form of evolved species, and, on the other, a tendency towards differentiation in the evolution of that species into other novel forms of life. Life evolved and life evolving (Spinoza's *natura naturata* and *natura naturans* are not far from here): stasis and dynamism. In religious categories, these tendencies or movements manifest themselves respectively as the 'closed' soul of 'static religion' and the 'open soul' of 'dynamic religion'.

In the former we have a type of social pressure, a centripetal movement of closure, fostering a closed model of society and a static form of religion: groupings maintained through moral laws, social obligations and institutional codes. In the latter we have an outward, dissociative and centrifugal movement, creating open sociability and dynamic spirituality. As against the dogmas of a church, a group, it is instead born through heroic individuals (mystics) whose appeal operates through inspiration rather than law, through the contagion of affect rather than the command of dogma. The closed morality of static religion is a set of rules and balances, pressures and obligations bearing down on the individual by repressing his or her evolutionary alterity. Such a closure tends towards a static form of faith, a codified, institutionalized spirituality that expresses above all the interests of the group rather than a supposedly universal divinity (*ibid.*: 39, 205–7).

Bergson compares this first type of movement to the integrative pressure that maintains the unity of cells within an organism, only in society it is habit that plays the role of the binding force. We should note here that such collectivist thinking as this has often been accused of a romantic organicism, along with the dangerous political implications purportedly attendant to this. It is the totalitarian fantasy *par excellence* to see the body politic literally as an organism. But if there is an organicism in Bergson's sociobiology, it gravitates to political views exactly opposite to those most often repudiated by culturalists. Bergson does not argue for a closed image of the social on the basis of a rigid biological essentialism: rather, because his vitalism is embedded in a process metaphysics, the organic and the social are both left ideally open. Bergson does not believe that organic systems are wholes; rather, they are dynamic, dissociating phenomena that are only *relative* unities (they only appear *as one* by contrast with what they eventually multiply into, but their apparent unity was itself always multiple at heart). Political organicism need only be feared if one's picture of the organic, the biological or the vital is of a particular, totalizing variety. Religiosity, as a form of sociability, *can* be totalitarian (taking the form of a rigid, evolved body), but, ideally for Bergson, it is dynamic and open, being the force that dissolves all forms.

Alongside the force of closure, then, there is another kind of consciousness that responds to the desire for openness, specifically the desire to be open towards openness: a welcome owed to those who are themselves 'opening'. Behind the command to 'love all' lies this other morality – biological too, but in another sense than 'merely' naturalistic (*ibid.*: 17, 33–4). Bergson talks of the 'complete morality' or 'absolute morality' of this 'open soul' and, in a famous passage, describes the 'extreme limit' of its movement as follows:

> The other attitude is that of the open soul. What, in that case, is allowed in? Suppose we say that it embraces all humanity: we should not be going too far, we should hardly be going far enough, since its love may extend to animals, to plants, to all nature. And yet no one of these things which would thus fill it would suffice to define the attitude taken by the soul, for it could, strictly speaking, do without all of them. Its form is not dependent on its content. We have just filled it; we could as easily empty it again. 'Charity' would persist in him who possesses 'charity', though there be no other living creature on earth. (*Ibid.*: 38)

Pure openness sympathizes 'with the whole of nature', but it is also a contact with a principle of nature that expresses itself in quite a different attachment to life than that found in the forces of closure (collective identities and group obligations). It is described as an objectless emotion that loves who or what it does only 'by passing through' rather than aiming for them (*ibid.*: 39, 52, 254–5). The object of dynamic religion is also its source: the generative action of life, which Bergson periodically describes as 'God' (*ibid.*: 53, 252–62).

An example of the difference between the closed and this absolute openness comes in Bergson's discussion of justice. In relative, distributive justice, he argues, there is a perfect mix of closed obligation and genuine, open aspiration: it is a question of distribution, reciprocity and equivalence – a mathematical balancing act of quantity with quantity, quality with quality. Such relative justice creates a form of equality that remains set against the outsider, for the notion of reciprocal freedoms and shared rights still serves the need for *one* social-order opposed to the outside: an immanent order whose operativity relies on keeping the alien, foreigner or stranger at bay, on keeping a transcendent as such (*ibid.*: 69–79). The transition from the idea of this form of justice to that of *absolute* justice is supposedly gradual (ever-increasing enfranchisements), but Bergson regards it as an incommensurable 'leap forward'. Absolute justice has another source altogether from that of inclusion: it refuses to let even one individual suffer for the good of the group. Indeed, it has no object at all that might be included or excluded (be it even an abstraction such as 'death' or 'bare life', as Jean Luc Nancy and Georgio Agamben respectively maintain). While it was the prophets of Israel who gave justice this categorical nature, Bergson argues that it was Christianity that made it genuinely universal, the Judaic form remaining insular.

Now it must be added that both these moral and religious movements, closed and open, are only 'extreme limits' and are never found in any actual society in their pure form (separate from each other), even in Christian society. The forces of openness and closure are present in varying degrees in every society and are inter-mixed in every actual morality. There never has been and neither could there ever be a truly open society and dynamic religion or a fully closed society and static religion. These are limit-ideas. Actual morality encompasses what Bergson describes as a "system of *orders* dictated by *impersonal* social requirements", as well as a "series of *appeals* made to the conscience of each of us by *persons* who represent the best there is in humanity" (*ibid.*: 84): the force of the institution versus the appeal of the mystic. In fact, religious dynamism *needs* static religion for its expression and diffusion, and the two are not at all opposed in their common origin, which Bergson alludes to mysteriously as "some intermediate thing" (*ibid.*: 178, 179). The mystic needs the institution to work within and against; it forms the outline that the action and appeal of the mystic transgresses and, in so doing, broadens. I already observed that the form open morality takes 'is not dependent on its content'; hence, the 'openness' of the mystic soul is also necessarily vague. Fleshing out the vague formulas of openness actually entails an accommodation with its opposite religious and moral tendency towards closure, this fleshing out being the task of the church, the institution. The mystic, therefore, is what is both within and without the institution, immanent and transcendent simultaneously. As such, the mystic also embodies another of the conceptual conjunctions in Bergsonism.

As mentioned, open morality finds its inspiration in the personal appeal of the mystic, and hence some form of direct or indirect interpersonal relationship is required. Where closed morality lies in obedience before the law, open morality lies in an 'appeal', 'attraction' or 'call'. But the call does not come from just anyone: it requires a privileged personality. What is best in our society is bequeathed to us by individuals Bergson calls "heroes", and each hero – living or dead – "exerts on us a virtual attraction" (*ibid.*: 84). But the heroism Bergson describes is fundamentally of a religious variety and mystical: one that is dynamic and wholly active rather than institutional and reified. Bergson's 'mystics' are far from being ascetic contemplatives, however: they are creators, actively transgressing the boundaries of life, mind and society in their inspirational morality. St Paul, like St Theresa or Joan of Arc, were actors first and foremost, sometimes even militantly so.

In crossing all frontiers, mysticism goes "beyond the limits of intelligence" (*ibid.*: 220), the ultimate end of mysticism being to establish a partial coincidence with the creative effort that life manifests. So radical is this inherent creativity, that it *can* appear as mental pathology, and Bergson takes some time to spell out the differences between the symptoms of genuine mental transcendence and those of simple insanity (*ibid.*: 228ff.). What is essentially different is that, while the mystic has travelled the same route as the insane, the mystic has also discovered the way back into society: transcendence and (then) immanence.

So, then, what is the activity of the mystic hero? Curiously enough, what allows the hero to act as a model for others is described as a type of passivity before life. It entails "the complete and mysterious gift of self" (*ibid.*: 225; Bergson is here quoting Soderblom). What is termed 'complete mysticism' is wholly for the other rather than being self-absorbed: "true, complete, active mysticism aspires to radiate, by virtue of the charity which is its essence" (*ibid.*: 309). How it actually radiates is through the contagious properties of a genuinely 'creative' emotion: "for heroism itself is a return to movement, and emanates from an emotion – infectious like all emotions – akin to the creative act" (*ibid.*: 53). But here the etymology of emotion must be taken into account: Bergson is not endorsing some private, spiritual ecstasy so much as a type of movement rich in meaning, a movement of openness. In one fascinating analysis, Bergson describes Socrates as a mystic and religious hero before being a philosophical model. When philosophers constructively engage with society as their Athenian forebear did, they do not merely emulate a Socratic archetype so much as actualize the Socratic-movement and thereby make him (or his essential process) actually live again (*ibid.*: 61–2).

FABULATING GOD

Thus far, we have looked at Bergson's source for religion, *qua* the religious soul, in the moral forces and appeals that emanate from life. But it is also life that is the source of our very idea of God, the idea of a supernatural divine that creates life, is separate from it and even transcends it. The specific origin concerns what the *Two Sources* terms 'fabulation'. The concept of 'fabulation' is vast in its operation, according to Bergson, being a primitive state of mind present in all of us. It is a 'virtual instinct' that works initially by creating rudimentary forms of religion (such as animatism and animism), as well as relating us to the world as such, by anthropomorphizing its processes and activities as events and actions, by creating other personalities, other spirits, in a phrase, 'Other Minds'. It is imprecise to think of fabulation as a species of imagination, still less a form of play, simulation or pretence, for it is far more primitive than all of these and seems to lie at their source (*Two Sources* 110, 107). Most significantly, fabulation also has precise sociobiological origins and, until those origins are fathomed, Bergson tells us, until its source is analysed, we will not see beyond the general similarities it has with other faculties (that tempt us to confuse it with them and thereby generate inaccurate accounts of the origin of our belief in God).

With fabulation, he says that we are dealing with "the reactions of man to his perception of things, of events, of the universe in general" (*ibid.*: 162). So clearly, Bergson's discussion of fabulation concerns more than just religion, for in fact this faculty lies at the origin of fiction and a good deal of our more creative representations of the world; he mentions children's play, writing, theatre and hero-worship in quick succession (*ibid.*: 108). That said, however, all these other forms of representation do come back to fabulation in its *religious* origin.

There are three stages of fabulation (animatism, animism and theism), that can also be seen as three forms of mediation, three forms of creative representation or 'seeing as'. The second form is most interesting as a differential mediation marked by the shift from animatism to animism, the incursion of a dualism in our interpretation of the world, moving us from a vision of the entire universe as animate, to one that divides the universe into that which is animated (with spirits) and that which is inanimate. What spurs this first dissociation in fabulation is what Bergson regards as the ultimate disaster for the mind: *the representation of its death*. The evolution of intelligence brings with it the double-edged sword of the foresight of death. Intelligence can thereby lead to a "disturbance of life" and the "intellectual representation which thus restores the balance to nature's advantage is of a *religious* order" (*ibid.*: 129) concerning the possibility of life *after* death. The traumatic representation of death (and its depressive effects on our animal will to live) must be dampened by the formation of quasi-hallucinations, fictions, myths and ultimately the whole panoply of religious symbolism, which, at its source, is a supplement from nature to compensate for the effects of this shock to thought. Myth, then, when understood in the broadest terms possible, is a refinement of a proto-religious faculty of mind to animate nature with intentions and actions (*ibid.*: 125, 204). It gives life to the inert and thus an afterlife to the dead.

So, there is the shock generated by an intelligent representation (the vision of death), and there is the reply to that shock, which is also generated as a representation, this time of a spiritual world that embodies the promise of *survival* post-mortem. Our intelligence goes beyond its original function by abstracting death from the particular (certain others) to the general (everyone, including itself). In turning its reflective power onto itself, it interferes with its own infinite vision and purpose (to live), refracting it (through this scene of deadly finitude) such that a distorted view of the infinite is generated: the fantasy of *survival*. Death refracts or mediates life into an image *of* life or *sur*-vival, a kind of super-life or meta-life.

This image *of* life is a spectre that comes in various religious forms: anima-tist force, animist spirit, theist person, each one all the more individuated, more integrated, as the felt experience of our body is superseded by its *visual image*. To quote Bergson:

> For contemporary science the body is essentially what it is to the touch; … the visual image of it would in that case be a phenomenon whose variation we must constantly rectify by recourse to the tactile image … But the immediate impression is nothing of the kind. An unwary mind will put the visual and the tactile image in the same category, will attribute to them the same reality, and will assume them to be relatively independent of one another. The 'primitive' man has only to stoop over a pool to see his body just as it really appears, detached from the tactile body. (*Ibid.*: 133)

What Bergson provides here is a specular origin of the spirit-life, one facilitated in part by a kind of *mirror-stage*, whereby we see our reflection in a surface, a false, whole (visual) image that we dissociate from a felt (tactile) image. But what forces the specular dissociation is first the idea of death, the image of our finitude.[2]

---

2. Of course, Jacques Lacan sees the visual image in terms of a false *spatial* continuity (ego identity), where Bergson sees it as the false promise of *temporal* continuity (survival). Bergson himself did believe in the survival of the soul, but for philosophical reasons (at

Fabulation, then, is a 'partial anthropomorphism': an internationalization and vitalization of nature that begins with diffused, impersonal forces; then crystallizes those forces into spirits localized in particular places (animism); before then both imparting increasingly more human personality to those spirits while at the same time detaching them from the world, until we have a full-blown monotheism with a divine that transcends its creatures (*ibid.*: 152, 176). Here is Bergson's depiction of this faculty in operation in the vital second phase, animism, in regard to a water spring (*ibid.*: 180): the meaningful action of giving water was once a "datum provided directly by the senses" with its "own independent existence". But then it became the "spirit of the spring", localized first in a thing and then in a person. It is the "*persistence*" (or repetition) of this *process* of giving water, that "set it [the action] up as the animating spirit of the spring at which we drink, whilst the spring, detached from the function which it performs … *relapse[d] the more completely into the state of a thing pure and simple*" (*ibid.*: 180, emphasis added). This is fabulation somewhere near the beginning of a centripetal process that de-animates matter while (eventually) animating immaterial gods. No longer ourselves being overt animists, of course, we now think of this spirit as an "an abstract idea … extracted from things by an intellectual effort" (*Two Sources* 180), whereas it was originally thought that this spirit *was* that action. It might be truer to say that with the "spirit of the spring" we already have the beginnings of that extraction, and that our conception of this spirit now as merely one abstract idea among others, far from being an innocent description of a tenet of animism, is actually a furtherance of this extractive process (partly effected by our language of 'substance' and 'attributes'). The *activity* of the spring – the *process* of water – has been extracted as an immobile idea, leaving the spring to 'relapse' into a state of inert materiality.

What drives this dissociative process throughout, however, is trauma. Looking through the pages of the *Two Sources* on fabulation, one cannot miss its connection with trauma, especially the trauma of excess novelty, that is, novelty or difference beyond our foresight. As Bergson explains, primitively, we divide reality into that which *in principle* can always be foreseen (the mechanical) and that which cannot: between what we can control and what we cannot. In some circumstances, then, between an intention and its execution there is a gap, leaving room for accident. Fabulation, in these cases, acts as a defence against the "*margin of the unexpected between the initiative taken and the effect desired*" (*ibid.*: 140, emphasis added). The unpredicted events are significant, not so much for what they are in themselves – "earthquakes, floods, tornadoes" (*ibid.*: 153) as well as illness, serious

---

least in published writings such as *Matter and Memory*) to do with the irreducibility of consciousness to the brain, not the ones furnished primitively through refraction. Likewise, Bergson's philosophical argument for God's existence, which just is the argument for the *élan* (that subsumes God and us alike in its novel being) should be kept separate from the social origin of our belief in the divine, which stems from fabulation.

accident, and, of course, "the greatest accident of all", death (*ibid.*: 138) – as for our response to them, *how we see them*. They are given an intentionality, for if the effect has an importance to us, if the effect has meaning for us (*our* death, *our* injury) then the same level of significance must be in the cause (on the basis of a primitive logic of 'like coming from like'). If the event is like something we know, if it is like us, then it is partly domesticated; it seems partly controlled and so less traumatic. This strange tendency is in everyone and not just 'primitives': "a sudden shock arouses the primitive man dormant within us all", Bergson claims (*ibid.*: 142, 145, 146, 164, 176). We may not be overt animists now, but we remain covert ones in our primordial interactions with the world. In this vein, Bergson writes the following of our primitive emotional reaction to domestic collisions, such as when we accidentally bang our leg against a table. Naturally, we blame the table. He continues:

> Between the identification of the table with a person and the perception of the table as an inanimate object, there lies an intermediate representation which is neither that of a thing nor of a person; it is the image of the act accomplished by the striking or, better still, the image of the act of striking … The act of striking is an element of personality, but not yet a complete personality. (*Ibid.*: 125)

Consequently, the representations of mythic, supernatural forces always start or end (even in magical thought) with a *real* trauma of accident, illness or observed death. They stem from 'out-of-the-way experience', excess novelty or a 'sudden shock' that paralyses our superficial psychic life. That such novelties exist (especially the unpredictable but nonetheless inevitable eventuality of our own death) and can be represented by the human mind is what drives fabulation on (given that we know, for instance, both that we are going to die as well as that we will not know how and when we are going to die – at least until it is too late to do anything about it). In one example, Bergson writes from his own experience of a "vague foreboding" of what would be known eventually as the Great War. This was an event much discussed and predicted during the forty-three years after the end of the Franco-Prussian War in 1871, but Bergson describes how, on the announcement of war with Germany in August 1914, he suddenly felt an "invisible *presence*", as what was once only an abstract idea gradually became real. As an idea, it had remained both "probable and impossible", a "contradictory idea", keeping an "abstract character" until the very last moment (*ibid.*: 144, 160), whereupon he had this strange "feeling of admiration for the smoothness of the transition from the abstract to the concrete" (*ibid.*: 176).

Here, finally, we come to the heart of fabulation as something more general than just myth-making, for its own source – in the traumas of illness, natural disaster, war and, pre-eminently, anticipated death – begins with disturbance, with interruption, but one that is *felt* as a presence. And the felt trauma, ultimately the felt presence of the idea of death, is what allows us to *see* anything *as* anything else, to see *x as y*: it creates a faculty (or 'virtual instinct') that can see anger in the dark clouds above, spirits in water springs, and God's presence in the workings of nature. In other words, it lies at the heart of all of our other kinds of representation.

To carve out events from the "continuity of the real" is how fabulation is also described in the *Two Sources* (159), but that is precisely how *all* representation is described throughout Bergson's earlier work, *Matter and Memory*. Representation is born from fabulation, and fabulation is the (immanent and vital) process that creates the (transcendent) image of God. With the theory of fabulation, then, we truly have an important key to Bergson's thought: it is an account of a faculty that not only shows the complex relationship between his metaphysics and religion (being an explanation of how the image of God emerges immanently from natural, vital and psychological processes), but also how central such a vitalizing faculty is to the ultimate purpose of his own philosophy, one that is, in the end, something that provides us with a spiritual image of the cosmos itself as a living, creative, phenomenon.

FURTHER READING

Ansell-Pearson, K. 2002. *Philosophy and the Adventure of the Virtual: Bergson and the Time of Life*. London: Routledge.

Deleuze, G. 1988. *Bergsonism*, H. Tomlinson & B. Habberjam (trans.). New York: Zone Books.

Kolakowski, L. 1985. *Bergson*. Oxford: Oxford University Press.

Lacey, A. 1989. *Bergson*. New York: Routledge.

Lawlor, L. 2002. *The Challenge of Bergsonism*. London: Continuum.

Moore, F. 1996. *Bergson: Thinking Backwards*. Cambridge: Cambridge University Press.

Mullarkey, J. 2002. *Bergson and Philosophy*. Notre Dame, IN: University of Notre Dame Press.

On MYSTICISM see also Ch. 2; Vol. 2, Ch. 7.

4

JOHN DEWEY

Steven C. Rockefeller

John Dewey (1859–1952) was the pre-eminent philosopher in the United States during the first half of the twentieth century, and his thinking has had an ongoing influence in America and in a great diversity of nations and cultures around the world. He is widely recognized as one of the most important philosophers of the twentieth century. Dewey's naturalistic understanding of the religious dimension of experience, his identification of the religious life with the democratic way of life and his concept of piety toward nature constitute a significant contribution to liberal religious thought. An appreciation of Dewey's personal religious faith clarifies his primary concerns and major objectives as a philosopher, educator and social reformer.

John Dewey was born in Burlington, Vermont, in 1859, just before the Civil War in the United States, and he died in 1952 in New York City at the beginning of the cold war. His life spans a period in the United States of extraordinary intellectual, economic and social change driven by scientific enquiry, technological innovation, industrialization, urbanization and the democratic ideal. His career as a philosopher was devoted to reconstructing philosophy in an effort to help society adjust to the modern world and realize the creative possibilities for human development presented by democracy and the scientific method.

Dewey is best known for his contributions in four areas. First, he was a leading proponent of evolutionary naturalism and humanism. He relied on experience and the scientific method as the sole authority in matters of knowledge. He rejected supernaturalism and viewed humanity as part of the one world of nature. Early in his career he accepted Darwinian evolutionary theory. His empirical and naturalistic understanding of nature is a form of process philosophy similar in many respects to the outlook of his contemporary, Alfred North Whitehead. Dewey was a humanist in the sense that he was primarily interested in the problems of people and maintained a basic faith in the capacity of human beings to deal with the challenges of life.

Secondly, together with Charles S. Peirce (*see* Vol. 4, Ch. 17) and William James, Dewey was one of the founders of the North American philosophical school of pragmatism (instrumentalism, or experimentalism). Adopting a Darwinian bio-logical perspective, he viewed the mind as primarily a problem-solving instru-ment and ideas as guides to action. He argued that the meaning of ideas is to be found in their practical consequences and, therefore, knowing involves doing. His career coincides with the rise of the social sciences and, adopting a melioris-tic outlook, he was especially concerned to show how the experimental method of enquiry can be used as a method for cooperative social problem-solving and ethical guidance. He opposed the philosophical quest for certainty and all forms of dogmatism and fundamentalism.

Thirdly, Dewey became a prominent champion of democratic values and social and political liberalism. As an intellectual leader of the Progressive Movement in the United States during the early decades of the twentieth century, he was a tireless defender of freedom and human rights and an outspoken supporter of the labour and women's movements. Following the First World War, he became actively engaged in the movement to outlaw war internationally. Fourthly, in the 1890s he came to believe that the key to enduring social reform is the transfor-mation of the schools. As a result, through groundbreaking research at a labora-tory school, books, essays and public lectures he established himself for over forty years as the foremost leader of the progressive education movement.

Dewey completed his undergraduate studies at the University of Vermont in 1880 and earned a PhD in philosophy at Johns Hopkins University in 1884. His career as a university professor stretched over fifty-five years. He taught at the University of Michigan in Ann Arbor (1884–94), the University of Chicago (1894–1904) and Columbia University in New York City (1905–39). He also travelled and lectured widely, spreading his philosophical, social and educational theories in China, Japan, Mexico, Russia, South Africa and Turkey as well as Europe. His collected works fill thirty-seven volumes. Aspiring throughout his career to develop a comprehensive philosophical vision as a guide to action, Dewey's mature works present an extraordinary breadth of philosophical reflection.

At the start of his career, Dewey embraced neo-Hegelian idealism, and long after he had abandoned the neo-Hegelian system, some of the philosophical vocabulary and many of the insights of the neo-Hegelians continued to influence his thought. For example, using the language of neo-Hegelian idealism, Dewey throughout his career describes the general problem with which philosophy should be concerned as the separation of the real from the ideal in everyday life. In addition, Dewey closely identifies the religious life with the quest for the ideal and its realization.

Dewey was raised in the Protestant Christian tradition and was an active member of the Congregational Church until aged thirty-five. Thereafter, he had little interest in institutional religion. However, Christian values and ideals had an enduring influence on his thought, and he retained a lifelong interest in the reli-gious dimension of experience. As a religious thinker his goal was to work out the full implications of the liberal reconstruction of Christianity initiated in the late eighteenth and early nineteenth centuries by philosophers and theologians who sought to reconcile religion with reason and modern culture. He recognized that the rise of science and the process of secularization had left many people disoriented and confused in their intellectual and spiritual loyalties. He was, therefore, especially concerned to overcome both the conflict between religion and science and the separation of the religious life from everyday life in the secular world. He sought a middle way between monistic idealism and mechanistic materialism, supernaturalism and despairing atheism, and moral absolutism and subjective relativism.

Dewey's thinking on the subject of religion was worked out over a period of six decades in a great variety of books and essays. He never published a comprehensive statement of his views on religion, and he published only one short book, *A Common Faith* (1934), that focuses primarily on religion. Since Dewey arrived at some of his most fundamental convictions regarding religion very early in his career, his thinking is best understood by describing how it evolved, beginning with his early life.

THE EARLY DEWEY: 1859–94

In an autobiographical essay, "From Absolutism to Experimentalism" (1930), Dewey recalls having passed through some stressful emotional problems during his adolescence that generated in him an intense emotional craving for unification. His mother's sentimental brand of evangelical pietism and the New England Calvinism he encountered in the Congregational Church were contributing factors. He describes experiencing "an inward laceration" that involved feelings of sin and guilt and a sense of isolation of self from world and separation of nature from God (LW 5:153).[1] The unification Dewey sought as a young man had three interrelated dimensions involving integration of personality, social adjustment and unity with God, the moral and spiritual ideal. He also was seeking a world characterized by organic unity. The evolution of Dewey's religious life and thought is to a large extent the story of how he pursued his quest for unity and the ideal.

Dewey reports that he found his "spiritual emancipation" during his college years in Samuel Taylor Coleridge's *Aids to Reflection* (1825). Coleridge assured Dewey that faith and reason can and should be harmonized and that he could be both "liberal and pious". It was Dewey's craving for unification and his search for the ideal coupled with the awakening of his powerful intellect that led him into philosophy and to Immanuel Kant (*see* Vol. 3, Ch. 21) and then to G. W. F. Hegel (*see* Vol. 4, Ch. 4), and absolute idealism. In the philosophy classroom of

---

1. In-text references to Dewey's works are from *The Collected Works of John Dewey, 1882–1953*, edited by Jo Ann Boydston, with *EW* referring to *The Early Works of John Dewey, 1882–1898*; *MW*, *The Middle Works of John Dewey, 1899–1924*; and *LW*, *The Later Works of John Dewey, 1925–1953*.

George Sylvester Morris at Johns Hopkins University and in the writings of the British neo-Hegelians T. H. Green, John Caird and Edward Caird, Dewey found the vision of the world as an organic unity for which he was searching. He writes that "Hegel's synthesis of subject and object, matter and spirit, the divine and the human ... operated as an immense release, a liberation" (*LW* 5:153). In Hegel's panentheistic worldview, God is the eternal unity of the ideal and the real and the divine reason immanent in the world, guiding the evolution of civilization toward realization of the ideal.

In his first book, *Psychology* (1887), Dewey endeavours to integrate neo-Hegelian absolutism with experimentalism in the form of the new psychology to which he had been introduced at Johns Hopkins. As a Christian neo-Hegelian, Dewey adopts the view that God is the perfect personality and that the divine purpose in history is the realization of personality in humanity leading to establishment of the kingdom of God on earth. His *Psychology* contains a complex theory of how the ideal or universal self – the perfect personality of God – is reproduced in the individual self. The essence of human nature is defined as self-determining will, and the argument is made that the individual person can progressively realize the universal self in and through a process of intellectual and spiritual growth involving the study of science, philosophy and art, and the development of a moral faith in the ideal and a religious faith in God as the unity of the ideal and the real. Dewey also notes that the act of religious faith gives to experience a distinct religious quality in the form of feelings of dependence, reconciliation, peace and joy.

At the outset of his career, Dewey was especially fascinated with philosophical efforts to unify the ideal and the real with abstract logical arguments and metaphysical speculations. However, under the strong influence of Alice Chipman, an ardent feminist and social activist, whom he married in 1886, Dewey's philosophical interests began to focus on pressing social problems. Early in his career, he arrived at the conviction that the primary task of philosophy is to clarify the major conflicts facing society and to promote progressive social change.

During his years at the University of Michigan (1884–94), Dewey continued to be an active member of the Congregational Church, teaching courses on the Bible, church history and Christian thought, and giving talks before the Student Christian Association at the University. However, it is during this period that Dewey's religious thinking began to move in a radical, liberal direction, and he came to identify the spirit and practical meaning of Christianity in the modern era with the ethics of democracy and the experimental search for knowledge and practical wisdom.

In developing an understanding of the essence of the historical Christian tradition, Dewey adopted the Hegelian theory that biblical stories and Christian theological doctrines involve a mythical and representational apprehension of universal truths that are rationally formulated in philosophical idealism. He argues that the heart of the Christian tradition is not to be identified with a particular religion in the sense of a fixed creed and set of symbols and rites. In the Hegelian vision, the goal of Christianity is unity with God, and God is immanent in history and human social life. These considerations lead Dewey to a conclusion with major implications for his religious thought. He asserts that the healthy religious life knows no separation of religious life and secular life. The individual finds reconciliation with God by identifying his or her self with the shared life of the community and by working for the common good and social justice.

In "The Ethics of Democracy" (1888), Dewey takes a further critical step in his thinking. He had grown up in a culture where Christian ideals and democratic social values were often associated, and he was inspired by Walt Whitman's understanding of the religious meaning of democracy in *Democratic Vistas* (1871). He now argues that in nineteenth-century America, Christianity should be identified closely with the democratic way of life. Democracy, he explains, is much more than a form of government. It is first and foremost a great ethical ideal. It is a personal way of individual life and a form of moral and spiritual association. The ethics of democracy, states Dewey, are entirely consistent with Christian values and constitute "the one, ultimate, ethical ideal of humanity" (*EW* 1:248). Democratic attitudes and values, declares Dewey, should govern all human relations: in the family, school and workplace as well as in the public sphere.

Dewey regards the democratic ideal as a vision of organic unity in which the individual and the community are interdependent. Fundamental to moral democracy are respect for the absolute worth of the individual person, and freedom and opportunity for all, on the one hand, and a high sense of social responsibility and active participation in the life of the community by all, on the other. Each person should be both a sustained and a sustaining member of society. The interests of the community are best served by providing all its members with the educational and occupational opportunities to realize their full potential. The individual finds fulfilment by developing his or her capacities in and through contributing to the life of the community.

In "Christianity and Democracy" (1892), Dewey identifies God with truth and Christianity with the revelation of practical truth and its incarnation in the individual and society. He further argues that democracy involves the freedom to discover, communicate and implement practical truth, leading to the enlightenment, liberation and unification of humanity. "It is in democracy", reasons Dewey, "that the incarnation of God in man ... becomes a living, present thing, having its ordinary and natural sense" (*EW* 4:8–9). In "Reconstruction" (1894), Dewey goes further and links Christianity and the unfolding revelation of practical truth in modern democratic society with the experimental method and cooperative scientific search for truth.

Persuaded by philosophers such as Hermann Lotze and F. H. Bradley, in the early 1890s Dewey adopted the view that the scientific method of enquiry should be regarded as the one intellectual authority on matters of truth. In addition, he was beginning to believe that the social sciences could do for social progress what the physical sciences had done for industrial progress. In the 1890s, reflecting the influence of Auguste Comte (*see* Vol. 4, Ch. 7) and Joseph Ernest Renan, Dewey also began to argue that the experimental method can and should be used in the search for moral truth. In this way he tried to overcome the split in modern culture between science and moral values. Developing an experimental theory of moral valuation became a major focus of his future work as a technical philosopher in the field of logic, which he defined as the theory of enquiry.

EMPIRICAL NATURALISM AND THE DEMOCRATIC FAITH

During the first decade of his career, Dewey steadily advanced his agenda of rationalizing and naturalizing Christian theological doctrines and ideas. Toward the end of this period his writings reveal that he was losing his confidence in the neo-Hegelian system and its concept of God as the ideal self and unity of the ideal and the real. It was William James' revolutionary study *Principles of Psychology* (1891), with its biological account of the development of the self and the function of thought, that was the decisive influence leading to the shift in Dewey's outlook.

As a mature thinker, Dewey asserts that the empirical evidence does not exist to support theism or philosophical idealism. He concludes that the God of both theism and idealism is a creation of the human imagination projected onto the universe. He notes that the idea of God as the unity of the ideal and the real creates an insoluble problem as to why there is so much suffering and evil in the world. He also points out that the belief that the ideal and actual are one on the level of ultimate reality does nothing to help solve the practical problems with which people must contend in their everyday lives except to provide consolation in the face of suffering, tragedy and defeat. The most serious indictment to be brought against transcendentalist philosophies, argues Dewey, is that they have tended to obscure "the potentialities of daily experience for joy and self-regulation" (*LW* 1:41).

After Dewey moved to the University of Chicago in 1894, he terminated his membership in the Congregational Church and began constructing a new naturalistic and humanistic worldview. Even though he had abandoned traditional Christian theology and neo-Hegelian idealism, he retained his faith in progress and he would eventually develop a naturalistic theory of religious experience. He was never inclined to adopt a pessimistic or defiant atheism. On the contrary, Dewey continued to see himself as on the forefront of a great movement involving the evolutionary development of humanity's intellectual, moral and religious consciousness and the transformation of society. His experience and philosophical reflections led him to the firm belief that the fundamental social, psychological and religious problems confronting men and women in modern societies can only be addressed by recognizing the interdependence of the individual and society and by transforming both religious life and social life and fully integrating them. Only commitment to democracy as a moral and spiritual ideal, argues Dewey, will ensure freedom and opportunity for all, unite people in an inclusive and just community, and bring wholeness to the modern psyche.

At the heart of Dewey's understanding of the religious meaning of democracy is his belief in "the ultimate religious value to be found in the normal flow of life itself" (*EW* 4:367). In this regard, he writes in 1933:

> I have found … that all the things which traditional religionists prize and which they connect exclusively with their own conception of God can be had equally well in the ordinary course of human experience in our relations to the natural world and to one another as human beings. (*LW* 9:224)

The meaning, aesthetic enjoyment and spiritual fulfilment that may be found in human relations and in relations with the larger world of nature constitute for Dewey the great religious significance and promise of the democratic way of life.

The foundation for Dewey's philosophy of the democratic life is his empirical and naturalistic theory of the continuity of the ideal and the real. In this regard, he rejects the widespread view in modern philosophy that there is a fundamental conflict between a scientific understanding of the world and belief in the objective validity of human values. It is argued that science conceives the objectively real world of nature to be an indifferent, dead mechanism without purpose or meaning, and humanity's aesthetic, moral and religious values are, therefore, to be understood as purely subjective phenomena existing only in the human mind. What creates this problem, asserts Dewey, is "the great intellectualistic fallacy": the unwarranted assumption that the real is to be identified exclusively with the known (*LW* 4:175, 1:26–9). He rejects this assumption and the idea that scientific knowledge alone provides access to reality.

A sound empirical philosophy, argues Dewey, will recognize that the immediately perceived qualities of things apprehended by the senses and by feeling disclose real qualities of natural objects. Some immediately felt qualities of persons and other things are experienced as of positive value and they are what make life enjoyable, worthwhile and meaningful. Scientific knowledge is concerned with the causal connections among things and is properly understood as instrumental in its function. It enables society to gain control of natural processes and to develop the means for making the immediate qualities of things that are enjoyed in direct experience more secure in existence. As a pragmatist Dewey developed a form of situation ethics in which the experimental method can also be used to distinguish between what appears to be good and what is truly good by exploring the consequences of various choices and actions. He regards moral values as relative to specific situations, but he believed that in concrete situations it is possible to make objective moral value judgements.

Even though nature is not governed by an eternal ideal and final causes, there is continuity between the ideal and the real and "nature is idealizable", explains

Dewey. True ideals are real possibilities resident in nature. Ideals are formed by the human mind. They have their origin in the experience of what people find of positive value in persons, things and events. Natural possibilities become ideals when they are chosen and projected by the human imagination as desirable objectives: ends-in-view. In an open, pluralistic universe intelligent choice and social action can make a difference in the course of events.

As a naturalist and pragmatist with a faith in democracy, Dewey focused his efforts on an "idealism of action" that is concerned with methods and strategies for unifying the ideal and the real in the realm of practical affairs. When imaginative vision and creative intelligence succeed in unifying the ideal and the real, the result is an experience that is a consummation, a fulfilment complete in itself, an end-in-itself. The work of unifying the ideal and the real is art, asserts Dewey, and an experience acquires aesthetic quality when it is valued for its immediate quality as an end-in-itself.

In the books and essays Dewey wrote as an empirical naturalist and democratic humanist, he often closely associates his moral and social faith in the democratic ideal with a faith in experience, intelligence, the experimental method and education. He understood experience to involve the process of interaction between the human organism and its environment. When confronted with problematic situations, experience generates reflection. Reflective thinking is a method of experience by which enquiry into conditions and consequences is conducted. This process is perfected in the method of the experimental sciences. When experience becomes reflective and experimental and is guided by thought, it also becomes educative. With these ideas in mind, Dewey writes in "Creative Democracy – the Task Before Us" (1939) that:

> democracy is belief in the ability of human experience to generate the aims and methods by which further experience will grow in ordered richness. Every other form of moral and social faith rests upon the idea that experience must be subjected at some point or other to some form of external control; to some authority alleged to exist outside the process of experience.   (*LW* 14:229–30)

Since the process of experience is capable of becoming educative, "faith in democracy is all one with faith in experience and education" (*ibid.*).

Among the attitudes and values Dewey considers essential to the democratic spirit are hope, faith in the potentialities of human nature, independence of thought, wonder, open-mindedness, compassion, tolerance, appreciation of diversity, a spirit of amicable cooperation, a commitment to non-violence in managing conflicts and respect for nature. He views a self-seeking individualism as antithetical to the democratic ideal. A person with the democratic spirit is primarily concerned with being, not having. He emphasizes the importance of "intelligent sympathy" as an essential guide to the moral life, because it takes thought out beyond the self, renders vivid the interests and aspirations of others, widens and deepens concern for consequences and humbles the pretensions of the self.

In *Democracy and Education* (1916) and other essays, Dewey asserts that "free and open communication ... is the heart and strength of the American democratic way of living", and it is his conviction that "shared experience is the greatest of human goods" (*MW* 8:443, 9:7; *LW* 1:157–9). Borrowing imagery from William Wordsworth's "Elegiac Stanzas", Dewey writes in *Reconstruction in Philosophy* (1920): "When the emotional force, the mystic force one might say, of communication, of the miracle of shared life and shared experience is spontaneously felt, the hardness and crudeness of contemporary life will be bathed in the light that never was on land or sea" (*MW* 12:201).

THE RELIGIOUS QUALITY OF EXPERIENCE

Dewey did not clearly explain what he meant as an empirical naturalist by his use of the adjective 'religious' or by the term 'faith' until he published *The Quest for Certainty* (1929) and *A Common Faith* (1934). In *The Quest for Certainty*, he argues that a religion consistent with science, naturalism and democracy is a religion devoted to inspiring in people a sense of the ideal possibilities of the actual world, and he defined religious faith as "devotion to the ideal" (*LW* 4:244).

In *A Common Faith*, Dewey makes a clear distinction between religion and the religious quality of experience. He associates religion with the many and diverse institutional religions with their creeds and rituals. Dewey's concept of the religious quality of experience involves a reconstruction of his neo-Hegelian theory of religious experience and religious will set forth in his *Psychology*, and it builds on the early distinction he made between the religious life and religion. It also reflects the influence of William James' empirical approach in his groundbreaking study, *The Varieties of Religious Experience* (1902). However, Dewey was not primarily concerned with the kind of extraordinary mystical experiences that interested James. Dewey's objective is to identify and define the uniquely religious values that can be realized in the everyday life of ordinary people.

Dewey argues that there is no necessary connection between what he means by the religious quality of experience and institutional religion. He emphasizes this point, because in his view the various religions are encumbered with beliefs and practices associated with earlier historical eras and as a consequence they prevent the kind of natural religious experience consistent with present intellectual and social conditions from coming to consciousness and finding expression. Dewey also wants to separate completely his concept of the religious quality of experience from any connection with the supernatural, with which religion is widely associated. The religious quality of experience is not the product of a relationship with some distinctly religious object like a supernatural deity or the numinous.

47

In explaining the nature of the religious quality of experience, Dewey as a pragmatist focuses on the consequences of various experiences rather than on their causes. He argues that many different kinds of experience may have an effect (function or force) that is religious in nature, giving to experience a religious quality. An experience with a religious effect is one that generates "a better, deeper and enduring adjustment in life", leading to a sense of security and inner peace. Dewey associates a deep enduring adjustment with a unification of self and of self and world, and with a sense of the meaning and value of life that can sustain a person during times of loss and despair. In *Art as Experience* (1934), he writes of "a fulfillment that reaches to the depths of our being – one that is an adjustment of our whole being with the conditions of existence" (*LW* 10:23). *A Common Faith* describes the realization of a deep enduring adjustment as an act of the will, but Dewey explains that "an adjustment possesses the will rather than is its express product". It involves "a change of will conceived as the organic plenitude of our being" (*LW* 9:13–14).

Dewey provides a number of examples of different types of experience that can spontaneously generate the quality of experience that he defines as religious. A unification of self and a deep enduring adjustment with the world can be brought about by a moral faith in an inclusive vision of the ideal or by wholehearted devotion to a social cause, a scientific research initiative, or a creative endeavour in the field of the arts. He states: "many a person, inquirer, artist, philanthropist, citizen, men and women in the humble walks of life, have achieved, without presumption and without display ... unification of themselves and of their relations with the conditions of existence" (*LW* 9:19). Dewey also notes that sometimes a passage of poetry or the insight and vision generated by philosophical reflection can have a religious effect.

The primary source of unification of self and self and world in Dewey's personal life experience was his moral faith in the democratic way of life, and he puts special emphasis on the role of faith in the emergence of the religious quality of experience. He defines faith as moral conviction rather than intellectual belief regarding matters of fact. A moral faith involves being possessed in the deeper centre of one's being by an imaginative vision of ideal possibilities. Dewey explains that a moral faith that has a religious effect may be called a religious faith. A moral faith is most likely to have a religious force, and the power to precipitate a deep, enduring adjustment with the world, if it is a faith in an inclusive, unified vision of the ideal that encompasses the interrelationship of the individual, society and the larger world of nature.

When religious faith is defined as a unifying moral faith, it eliminates the possibility of a fundamental conflict between science and faith. From Dewey's perspective, a person with a religious faith is concerned only with discovering the ideal possibilities of existence and striving to realize them. Religious faith involves creation of a future, not propositions about the past. Scientific discoveries may cause people to refine their vision of ideal possibilities, but science presents no basic challenge to the human capacity for wholehearted commitment to a liberating vision of the ideal.

Reflecting his sociological understanding of the origins of religion, Dewey also argues that the core of religious faith in all cultures with a well-developed moral consciousness has always been a moral faith in a unified vision of shared ideals. The ethical values of a people have often been projected onto God or a supernatural realm for safekeeping and sanction. However, a people's values have their source in the natural relationships and social experience of the community. It is devotion to these shared ideals and values that is being expressed in religious faith. With these considerations in mind, Dewey writes:

> Ours is the responsibility of conserving, transmitting, rectifying and expanding the heritage of values we have received that those who come after us may receive it more solid and secure, more widely accessible, and more generously shared than we have received it. Here are all the elements for a religious faith that shall not be confined to sect, class, or race. Such a faith has always been implicitly the common faith of mankind. It remains to make it explicit and militant.   (*LW* 9:57–8)

NATURAL PIETY, MYSTICAL INTUITION AND GOD-LANGUAGE

Throughout his career, Dewey sympathized with the poets of the Romantic movement who rejected a mechanistic and materialistic view of the universe and the idea of a radical separation of human values and nature. As an evolutionary naturalist, he emphasized the continuity of the ideal and the real and the interdependence of humanity and nature. In this regard, he advocated an attitude of natural piety, or piety towards nature, as an essential aspect of a religious faith that aspires to realize the ideal possibilities of nature. Dewey was introduced to the idea of natural piety by Wordsworth's poetry, and his thinking on the subject shows the influence of the discussion of piety and spirituality in George Santayana's *Reason and Religion* (1905).

Dewey defines natural piety as respect for nature growing out of the awareness that humanity and nature share "a common career and destiny" (*MW* 4:176). It includes "the sense of a connection of man, in the way of both dependence and support, with the enveloping world", and it also entails "a chastened sense of our importance" in the larger scheme of things (*LW* 9:36, 1:313–14). Dewey tried to find a middle way between a naive and sentimental idealization of nature and a pessimistic materialism. "Nature may not be worshipped as divine", he argues, "but nature, including humanity, with all its defects and imperfections, may evoke heartfelt piety as the source of ideals, of possibilities, of aspirations in their behalf and as the eventual abode of all attained goods and excellences" (*LW* 4:244). Dewey's sense of interdependence with and piety toward nature guards against an arrogant anthropocentrism and led him to support efforts to conserve natural resources and to protect the environment.

It was Dewey's personal experience that the sense of natural piety and the religious quality of experience can be deepened by poetic intuitions and aesthetic experiences of a mystical nature. In Dewey's process philosophy everything that exists is both a unique individual and interconnected with the surrounding world. The efforts of human beings succeed only in so far as they are supported and sustained by the larger universe in and through an infinite number of interrelations. The larger totality, which includes the continuous human community and the greater evolving world of nature, is present in every experience. Thought cannot grasp this totality of natural events, but the larger whole may be immediately experienced, that is, felt or emotionally intuited and appreciated. Dewey uses the adjective 'mystical' to describe such experiences. As explained in *Art as Experience*, for example, it is a mystical intuition that apprehends the qualitative unity that pervades a work of true art, and intense aesthetic experiences of this nature can awaken a sense of "belonging to the larger, all inclusive whole which is the universe" (*LW* 10:198–9). For this reason, intense aesthetic experiences may acquire a religious quality. Mystical intuitions contribute to the religious quality of experience because they generate feelings of being whole, of connection to the larger whole, and of harmony, cosmic trust, freedom and peace. Dewey states that it is this mystical sense of belonging to the larger inclusive whole that "reconciles us to the events of tragedy" (*LW* 10:198–9).

After Dewey abandoned neo-Hegelian idealism, he ceased employing the idea of God as part of his own philosophical outlook in his published writings. However, his poetry, which he did not publish, and his personal correspondence reveal that the word 'God' continued to hold a certain positive meaning for him and that he was exploring how it could be used within the framework of his humanistic naturalism. In *A Common Faith* he sets out his conclusions on the matter, adopting a position quite similar to that of Edward Scribner Ames, his former colleague in the philosophy department at the University of Chicago, whose naturalistic concept of God is presented in *Religion* (1929). Dewey's intention in *A Common Faith* is to provide a definition of God that is consistent with philosophical naturalism and to explain how God-language may be employed by people who find it helpful and would like to use it. Dewey views use of the word 'God' as optional.

He identifies God or the divine with the ideal. More specifically, he asserts that the term 'God' may be used to refer to the object of a religious faith, that is, a comprehensive, unified vision of ideal possibilities. So defined, this does not reduce God to a mere wish fantasy. Authentic ideals take form in the human imagination, but they are "made out of the hard stuff of the world of physical and social experience," and they shape character and guide action, becoming forces of change (*LW* 9:33–4). In addition, Dewey proposes that the idea of God or the divine may be expanded to encompass all the natural conditions, human capacities and social forces that support and promote realization of the ideal. In this regard, he reconstructs the neo-Hegelian concept of God as the unity of the ideal and the actual and declares that God may be conceived as "the active relation between the ideal and the actual" or the ongoing process of uniting the ideal and actual (*LW* 9:34–5). In defining God in this way, Dewey is careful to point out that God should not be thought of as a person, an existing being or an organically unified process. The collection of conditions and processes that constitute the reality of the divine are unified only in the human mind and through human effort.

Even though Dewey as a mature thinker rejected belief in immortality, the idea of God or the divine clearly retains for him a certain poetic and spiritual power. He believes that its use may help to sustain faith in the ideal, foster natural piety, and focus attention on those forces that make possible and contribute to the process of idealizing the world. He writes: "the function of such a working union of the ideal and actual seems to me to be identical with the force that has in fact been attached to the conception of God in all the religions that have a spiritual content; and a clear idea of that function seems to me urgently needed" (*LW* 9:35).

The publication of *A Common Faith* generated an extended public debate among philosophers and theologians that has continued over the years, engaging a variety of thinkers, including Reinhold Niebuhr, Charles Hartshorne and Richard Rorty. Dewey has been attacked by religious conservatives for promoting secularism and atheism and for failing to address adequately the problem of evil. There are religious liberals as well as conservatives who find his separation of the religious from religion problematical. He has been criticized by some pragmatists and naturalists for preserving a place for the religious dimension of experience and for using God-language within a naturalistic philosophical framework. However, Dewey's philosophy of religious experience has been a source of inspiration for the American tradition of empiricism and naturalism in religious thought and for many religious humanists. A dialogue involving neo-Confucian philosophers in China and American pragmatists in the tradition of Dewey is under way. Dewey's philosophy of religious experience remains profoundly relevant to the twenty-first century. His democratic faith, vision of spiritual democracy, sense of belonging to the universe and call for a common moral faith are of enduring significance as the world struggles to build a just, sustainable and peaceful global society in the midst of great cultural diversity on a small planet with a fragile eco-system.

FURTHER READING

Deneen, P. 2005. *Democratic Faith*. Princeton, NJ: Princeton University Press.

Hickman, L. (ed.) 1998. *Reading Dewey: Interpretations for a Postmodern Generation*. Bloomington, IN: Indiana University Press.

Rockefeller, S. C. 1991. *John Dewey: Religious Faith and Democratic Humanism*. New York: Columbia University Press.

UNIVERSITY OF WINCHESTER
LIBRARY

Rosenbaum, S. (ed.) 2003. *Pragmatism and Religion*. Chicago, IL: University of Illinois Press.
Westbrook, R. 1991. *John Dewey and American Democracy*. Ithaca, NY: Cornell University Press.

On Hegelianism see also Vol. 4, Ch. 10. On NATURE/NATURALISM see also Vol. 3, Chs 20, 21, 22; Vol. 4, Chs 5, 10. On PRAGMATISM see also Ch. 2; Vol. 4, Ch. 17. On SCIENCE see also Ch. 19; Vol. 2, Ch. 12; Vol. 3, Ch. 17; Vol. 4, Chs 7, 11, 12, 15, 17, 19. On SOCIETY see also Vol. 3, Ch. 2; Vol. 4, Chs 14, 21. On TRUTH see also Vol. 1, Ch. 13; Vol. 2, Ch. 17; Vol. 3, Chs 3, 8, 13; Vol. 4, Chs 8, 18.

5

ALFRED NORTH WHITEHEAD
AND CHARLES HARTSHORNE

Lewis S. Ford

Alfred North Whitehead (1861–1947) was an English mathematician and philosopher. He graduated from Trinity College, Cambridge, in 1884, and was a lecturer in mathematics there until 1911. At the University of London he was a lecturer in applied mathematics and mechanics (1911–14) and professor of mathematics (1914–24). From 1924 onwards, he was Professor of Philosophy at Harvard. Whitehead's distinction rests on his contributions to mathematics and logic, the philosophy of science and the study of metaphysics. In the field of mathematics, Whitehead extended the range of algebraic procedures and, in collaboration with Bertrand Russell, wrote *Principia Mathematica* (3 vols, 1910–13), a landmark in the study of logic. His enquiries into the structure of science provided the background for his metaphysical writings. He criticized traditional categories of philosophy for their failure to convey the essential interrelation of matter, space and time. For this reason he invented a special vocabulary to communicate his concept of reality, which he called the philosophy of organism. He formulated a system of ultimate and universal ideas and justified them by their fruitful interpretation of observable experience. His philosophic construction as applied to religion offered a concept of God as interdependent with the world and developing with it; he rejected the notion of a perfect and omnipotent God. In 1945 he received the Order of Merit.

Charles Hartshorne (1897–2000) was born in Kittanning, Pennsylvania. He entered Haverford College in 1915, but completed his college work at Harvard and took his PhD in philosophy there. Awarded a Sheldon Fellowship, Hartshorne studied for two years in Europe, mostly in Germany. On returning to Harvard, he became an assistant to Alfred North Whitehead, whose thought was highly congenial to the vision he had been shaping on his own. In 1928 Hartshorne went to the University of Chicago, where he taught until 1955. He later taught at Emory University, and then at the University of Texas until 1978. Despite his personally irenic spirit, much of his work was polemical. Against classical theism he insisted that its views were neither coherent nor religiously satisfactory. He taught that the idea of divine perfection embodied in the tradition affirmed only one side of what is truly involved in perfection, that is, the element of immutability and absoluteness. But true perfection includes perfect relatedness and thus change. What remains changeless is God's perfect responsiveness to all that is changing.

Hartshorne taught that God creates the conditions that provide the optimum balance of order and freedom. Within the limits set by God, creatures determine the details of what happens. Much that occurs takes place by the chance interactions of diverse decision-making creatures. This, too, expresses the divine perfection. Hartshorne also argued against the widespread loss of confidence in reason, against the abandonment of metaphysics and against fideism. He showed that traditional arguments for the existence of God could be formulated cogently when the idea of God for which they argued was a coherent one. He also maintained from his youth an interest in birds, and on his extensive travels he recorded numerous birdsongs. He taught that birds have a subjective life and are motivated by the enjoyment of singing.

PROCESS PHILOSOPHY

'Process philosophy' takes its name from Whitehead's major work, *Process and Reality* (1929). This book could be more aptly characterized as 'Becoming and Being', or even as 'Concrescence and the Concrete'. 'Concrescence' is Whitehead's term for the process of growing together (*con + crescere*) which produces concrete being. Process theology arises out of the application of the basic categories of process philosophy to the nature of divine perfection. In particular, the nature of divine knowing and divine power are reconceived.

The issue posed by omniscience concerns future contingents, the properties of actualizations to take place in the future. This excludes whatever necessities, either metaphysical or causal, which must be exemplified in future actualizations, for they can be known, especially by a divine knower, beforehand. Classical omniscience affirms the knowledge of future contingents; process omniscience denies it. The reason classical omniscience affirms it has little to do with the special nature of divine knowing, but with divine perfection as classically understood. For on the classical view, God must be immutable, and the only way to have immutable knowledge is to know everything beforehand. In process theism, God's knowledge can be mutable. God's knowing is perfectly contoured to the character of what is known. This is not a self-contradictory limitation on omniscience, for God knows all there is to be known and there are no future contingents to be known. Actualities come into being through a process of self-determination, and are not fully determined until then. Contingent features first arise and have no knowable determinate status beforehand, except as possibilities.

The contrast between these views of omniscience is a contrast between perfect knowability (process) and the knowledge a perfect being could have (classical).

Perfect knowability knows what is to be known according to its mode. It knows the actual as actual and the possible as possible. For classical omniscience a divinely perfect and immutable being can only know immutably. Since nothing new can come to be part of divine knowledge, God must be conceived as already, that is, non-temporally knowing all future contingents, even those in the distant future. How this is to be reconciled with the nature of future actualization, or with whatever freedom exists in the universe, is a secondary consideration as long as divine immutability in being and in knowledge is preserved.

Process omniscience requires that God's experience grows over time. Only as actualizations come to be are they knowable, and they contribute to the divine experience. Classical omniscience is challenged because of its immutabilist assumption, primarily inherited from Greek philosophy. The perfect could only change for the worse. Change meant corruption or instability. In process thought, however, there could be change for the better in the way in which contingents contribute to the enrichment of divine knowing.

Process omniscience safeguards the freedom of actualities, for God's knowledge is dependent on the creatures and not the other way around. This is the general way knowing is understood. It is only in order to safeguard divine immutability that classical omniscience resorts to a reversal in God's case, such that God knows by creating that which God knows.

This would require omnipotence, understood in the sense that God can determine whatever God wills. Literally speaking, omnipotence means that God has all power. If so, we have none. Classical theists protest that 'omnipotence' does not have this meaning in practice. Free-will theism provides a useful way around this problem. God exercised full omnipotence in the creation of the world, particularly in its creation *ex nihilo*, but now limits this power to permit human freedom. At the end of this age God may resume full omnipotence to insure the complete eradication of evil. Thus omnipotence means complete power except in so far as it is restricted by human power.

Process thought rejects omnipotence, whether in its pure or qualified forms. The key issue is the nature of divinely perfect power, which it sees as divine persuasion. Freedom is not merely a feature of human beings, but exists to a degree in all actualities. Creaturely freedom is actualized in response to divine guidance. Omnipotence is usually rejected as 'coercive', but it would be more accurate to describe it as 'determinative'. It is a question of whether things come about through the direct determinative power of God, or by means of God and creatures acting in concert.

Process and free-will theism both affirm human freedom. Process theism, in some quarters, conceives of God as originating the metaphysical principles that both God and the universe exemplify. More often, these principles are taken to be completely natural and uncreated. In any case, if God is thereby limited, it is only in terms of what is perfectly general and necessary. Free-will self-limitation, on the other hand, is contingent. These limitations are temporal, applying to one period of time and not another. At some times divine power was absolute (as before the beginning of the world); at other times it was limited (by the presence of human freedom). Necessary principles, however, apply unrestrictedly to all periods of time. A temporal limitation is such that while it is imposed at one time, it could be withdrawn at another. This could apply to freedom. Freedom may not be such an absolute value that it need be maintained unrestrictedly. If God acts determinately, God could and should restrict the power of tyrants in order to allow the power of others to flourish.

WHITEHEAD'S PROCESS THEISM[1]

Whitehead was not always a process theist. In fact, for much of his mature life, during the years 1898–1925, he was basically atheistic. He was raised a devout Anglican, and at one point was nearly converted to Catholicism. But he drifted away from these moorings. When his eldest son was born, he became concerned about his religious upbringing, and resolved to make an informal study of theology. The young mathematics instructor at Cambridge persisted in this undertaking for some five years, but found no adequate concept of God. His particular objection concerned creation. It appeared that the only way God could create the world would be in terms of unrestricted divine power. Yet omnipotence undercuts human freedom.

Whitehead was also very much impressed with the sceptical conclusions in David Hume's *Dialogues Concerning Natural Religion*, which is in its own way a study of creation. Bracketing all biblical and traditional notions of God, Hume defines God as whatever brings this world into existence, and explores all ways in which creation could occur (*see* Vol. 3, Ch. 19)

Whitehead's atheism was not a rejection of all religious concerns, and these concerns intensified during the First World War. Nevertheless he did not find a suitable concept for God until he worked out his own metaphysics. This process metaphysics replaced enduring things with events. Yet events, as initially conceived, had no firm boundaries. Nor could the countervailing factors, the (eternal) objects, be more than possible forms. Events and objects, sufficient for most purposes, could not account for the concrete determinateness of actuality. So in *Science and the Modern World* (1925) Whitehead introduced the notion of a 'principle of concretion', or as it is usually known, the 'principle of limitation'. It specifies that condition or set of conditions whereby some events are concretely actual. These conditions are not spelled out, but we may suppose them to be the

---

1. This sketch draws heavily on Ford (2006a), which is based on a number of specialized studies cited in that monograph.

all-pervasive metaphysical principles and activity making actuality in general possible. Since all actuality is limited, it constitutes a 'principle of limitation'.

This principle is conceived as God, for it is that cosmic ground that ensures actuality. But God is not conceived of as an omnipotent actuality creating the world. "God is not concrete [i.e. a concrete actuality] but He is the ground for concrete actuality" (Whitehead 1925: 178). God is not a power competing with other powers, but that which makes power possible. It is not even clear whether this God is a being, or what God's relation to the eternal forms should be. Positively, Whitehead's God functions as creator in the sense that, apart from its activity, actualities could not be what they are. Negatively, God thus understood does not entail any conception of omnipotence.

From the claim that 'God is not concrete' it might seem that God is not actual. This is one way of understanding Paul Tillich's claim that God is not a being but the ground of being (Tillich 1951: 235). This may also have been Whitehead's original understanding but, if it was, it was revised in his next book, which proposes three formative elements for each actual occasion: creativity, the realm of eternal objects (here called ideal entities, or forms) and a non-temporal actual entity, God (Whitehead 1926: 90). In place of the one ground of concreteness now three factors are discerned. Each factor is necessary for the existence of every actuality. Without form there would be no pattern, no structure, and without creativity there could be no eventful activity.

Still, God could remain that which is not concrete, if concreteness were interpreted as necessarily finite. In that case God as a non-temporal actual entity could be considered an infinite actuality. This aspect becomes more evident when God is later conceived by Whitehead as the recipient of the infinitude of forms (or eternal objects). That God is considered to be non-temporal, in fact *the* non-temporal actuality, should not be dismissed as some sort of traditional vestige. Although Whitehead was to become a temporal theist, at this stage (and later, even in most of the composition of *Process and Reality*) he was a principled non-temporalist with respect to God. Non-temporality was the primary, necessary difference between the primordial actual entity and the temporal actual occasions. At the same time, however, he rejected the notion of a supreme being having a non-temporal subjectivity. He was convinced that subjectivity was necessarily temporal. It could not be ascribed to a non-temporal actuality although, as we shall see, he made accommodations to his readership.

Non-temporality was central to Whitehead's classification of the formative elements. While the ground of concrete actuality might be thought of dynamically as the underlying substantial activity, creativity is completely temporal and was not to be identified with God. Both creativity and the forms are non-actual as well as non-temporal, while God is non-temporal, so all three differ from the actual occasions they constitute, which are both temporal and actual.

A possible fusion might occur between the forms and God, both of which are non-temporal. Formally they are distinguished in that forms are non-actual and

God is actual. Yet if God is constituted by the set of necessary conditions deter-mining what is actual, that is, the metaphysical principles governing all that is, then God would be a highly complex eternal object, a subset within the realm of forms. If so, it would be a purely immanent formative element, lacking the tran-scendence we associate with God.

This was not Whitehead's intention, I suspect, because his original thinking about creativity and God responded to different issues. He devised the forms or eternal objects by reflection on sense-objects, which were not extremely brief enduring objects, as he previously held, but should be conceived as timeless. This meant that the same object could illustrate different events simultaneously. The ground of concreteness, the principle of limitation, was postulated by Whitehead as a result of his realization that actual occasions could not be fully explained in terms of the activity of creativity (creative activity) and eternal objects, and needed some additional principle to make them actual. This is motivated by a sense that formal explanation is not enough, but if it is, and especially if God is considered to be as non-temporal as the eternal objects are, then it becomes diffi-cult to justify God's transcendence. That justification could be later affirmed once God is conceived as temporal, but this was not yet anticipated.

Some scholars have discerned divine temporality in chapter four of *Religion in the Making*, but I suspect this may require reading later sensibilities into an earlier context. In any case it makes perfect sense to read these passages in terms of strict non-temporality. On the other hand, the fourth chapter does suggest God's personal subjectivity, even though chapter three, implicitly at least, argues that God cannot be both non-temporal and personal. I understand chapter four to explore the implications of Whitehead's metaphysical outlook were we to assume that God should be personal. Nowhere is that assumption justified. This is a huge gap at the very outset of the argument, which is passed over in silence. I believe that Whitehead at that time held that, although God could not be both non-temporal and personal, his principles were such as to also be beneficial in clari-fying the thinking of those committed to a personal God.

His next book, his *magnum opus, Process and Reality*, introduces and elab-orates the basic tenets of process theism. Yet, except for the all-important final chapter and some insertions, most of the book still assumes that God is resolutely and purely non-temporal.[2] This non-temporal actual entity constitutive of most necessary and general features of actual occasions remains in the background. The foreground is taken up with the details of how an actual occasion could come into being. In the end, however, this detailed work has an impact on the background, ushering in process theism.

---

2. There are thirteen passages in the body of the text introducing a contrast between two natures of God, as primordial and as consequent (temporal), which I interpret to be later insertions based on the final chapter.

This development is fascinating, for we get a glimpse of a creative mind at work. *Process and Reality* is an untidy book; it is not rigidly consistent. Whitehead was not afraid to change his mind when he discovered a better idea. Unlike other authors, he left a trail of discarded ideas behind. Most authors reject earlier drafts or seek to harmonize discordant passages. That makes for a straightforward consistent presentation, but then we cannot tell whether the author had it all from the beginning or made it up as he went along. In Whitehead's case, however, it is possible to chart his creative growth (Ford 2006a).

In his process perspective events replace substances. But the notion of an event is too abstract to differentiate between possible and actual events. A possible event subdivided was still a possible event. Events could have the concrete determinateness of actuality only if they could not be subdivided into events that were equally actual. Actual events (termed 'occasions') were indivisible in this sense. Motion and change were understood as the difference between successive occasions, and not within an occasion. Yet each occasion was the embodiment of dynamic creativity. While it could not change, it could become. Thus every occasion has two sides. It is a being in the way it manifests itself to the world, the way we encounter it. But it is also an internal process of becoming, the way in which it comes to be what it is. (This may seem to stray far afield from issues of process theism, but it bears within it the seeds of a novel theory of creation.)

The contrast between being and becoming could also be understood as the contrast between object and subject. As objective being, the occasion causally influences its successors. As subjective becoming, the occasion determines what objective being it will have. Subject and object are not two different kinds of being, but aspects of the same actuality. They contrast as the past and the present aspects of a temporal event.

Whitehead devoted part three of *Process and Reality* to an analysis of the process of becoming, which he called 'concrescence'. Concrescence, as already noted, is the growing together (*concrescere*) of many relations (called 'prehensions') into one concrete whole. The necessary rules governing the process of concrescence (the categorial conditions) resemble Kant's categories in function, if not in content. In both cases they were the subjective means of synthesis. Still, all these factors were insufficient to produce an irreducibly concrete particular actuality.

Whitehead had introduced decision as the mark of actuality. Decision as self-determination is the particular contribution of the occasion to its own actualization. It introduces a telic factor into the process, to be realized in the final result. On further reflection Whitehead recognized that the telic factor needed to be present throughout the whole of a concrescence. It was needed to guide the particular way initial prehensions (the causal relations) had to be perspectivally accepted, and to guide the way all these prehensions should be unified in the final determination. Since it was that which ordered the prehensions, it could not be one of them. This telic factor is called a 'subjective aim', for it is what the concrescing occasion (the subject) aims at. The subject's decision is guided by the aim, while at the same time the subject is capable of modifying the aim. Therein lies its freedom.

Since every (physical) prehension[3] is conditioned by its aim, it cannot be derived from any of these prehensions without circularity. Moreover, since each prehension needs its aim, the aim must be present at the very outset in order to affect all the prehensions. If it cannot come from the past nor wholly from itself, Whitehead proposes that the subjective aim must come from God.

The divine nature must be radically reconceived in order for God to be the source of subjective aims. Originally, as the principle of concretion God constituted each actuality in terms of the necessary metaphysical principles. Later God was conceived as ordering all concepts. Perhaps these included particular concepts and possibilities, although this was left largely open. Now, however, the source of all subjective aims must not only encompass all particular possibilities, but all the possible situations in which these aims could be actualized. Should it also include might-have-beens, that is, unactualized possibilities or even compound might-have-beens, unactualizable 'possibilities' that could have been actualizable only if prior unactualized possibilities were to be somehow actualized? The compounding can go on indefinitely. One such compound, for instance, would be the suicide of the third son of the non-existent Archbishop of Raleigh. This is indeed a tremendous expansion of the possibilities to be entertained by the non-temporal mind.

The requirement that the divine mind provide the particular, contingent aims for every occasion naturally raises the question as to how this could be done. A purely non-temporal being is not so geared to space and time that it can determine how a particular possibility and a particular temporal occasion should be correlated, while the occasion cannot select it for itself out of the vast array of possibilities. Moreover, it must first have the aim to guide it in making any selection. These concerns may have led Whitehead to postulate the second divine nature. He termed this the 'consequent nature', conceived of as an everlasting divine concrescence.

Previously, when God was conceived as only non-temporal, God was considered to have only conceptual prehensions, that is, only concepts of eternal objects (forms). Now, as consequent, God also has physical prehensions of the finite actualities of the world. This is the basis of process theism, for the temporal actualities could only be experienced temporally, given the way prehension works.

Like any other prehension, the prehending is dependent on its datum (object) rather than on the prehender. Since we constitute data for God, we can genuinely contribute to the life of God forever. If we prescind from the future, process and immutabilist omniscience incorporate the same content. They differ with respect to the order of dependence. Process knowing is dependent on the world, whereas

---

3. There are several kinds of prehension. A physical prehension is a causal relation between finite actual occasions. It is to be contrasted with a hybrid prehension, which relates to an actual entity in terms of some eternal object (form).

immutabilist knowing depends on God alone. On immutabilist assumptions we can contribute nothing that God does not already know.

On the other hand, Whitehead did not make explicit any way in which the divine experiencing of the world could affect the specification of aims. Yet it seems easy to show how this could be achieved. As God experiences the array of past actualities which contribute to any nascent occasions, God could correlate that array by means of the one possibility best suited to unify them in actuality. Then there would be no need to entertain irrelevant possibilities, let alone might-have-beens or compound might-have-beens, considerably reducing the domain of possibilities. Only those immediately relevant to the occasion's situation need be entertained. Since the aim is selected for the occasion, the occasion does no initial selecting.

This is such a natural use for the consequent nature that it is astonishing that Whitehead does not avail himself of it. I suspect it lay in his inability to find a way, given his principles, that this could be possible. Acts of becoming (concrescences) were purely private. Only beings could be causally influential. A process that is only now coming into being, such as the consequent nature, did not have the objective status required. How could a purely private divine concrescence influence the determination of other actualities? As long as this problem remained unresolved, Whitehead was not prepared to move forward (Ford 2003).

While it appears to be difficult, if not impossible, to resolve this problem using Whitehead's principles alone, there are several ways of modifying them to account for the causal influence of the consequent nature. Charles Hartshorne (1941) has proposed the most influential suggestion. Since individual occasions causally interact while concrescences cannot, he suggests that Whitehead's everlasting divine concrescence be transformed into an endless series of finite divine occasions. This resolves most problems, although it is open to a rather abstruse objection. Each divine occasion, presumably very brief (as actual occasions are), must fill the entire universe. Such an occasion defines a privileged cosmic simultaneity, which some have thought problematic in the light of relativity physics.

This 'societal' view reduces the everlasting becoming to a series of beings. A contrasting view preserves the endless divine concrescence and seeks to understand the divine–finite connection solely in terms of becoming. It sees finite occasions as localized extensions of the everlasting concrescence. Instead of there being two things, the divine aim for the occasion and its own initial subjective aim, to be related with one another,[4] there is only the one aim (and one localized creativity), which then takes divergent courses. On the divine side, the aim is absorbed into the totality of its life. On the other side, the aim becomes the basis for finite determination. The occasion's decision is the way it separates itself from God to become a finite being. The one extension, having one aim originally, grows into two actualities each having its own aim (Ford 2006b).

---

4. Technically, by a hybrid physical prehension.

However divine aims are communicated, whether in terms of a series of occasions, or by some process of budding, or directly from the non-temporal nature, the important point (as Whitehead himself put it) is that God provides each occasion with the particular aim or impetus for its actualization. This is the basis for the claim that the process God acts persuasively. Such a God is not an omnipotent unilateral creator, for no actuality is brought into being solely through God's action. Rather, God persuades the creature to create itself.

In polemical contexts some process theists contrast divine persuasion with the coercion of traditional doctrines of creation. But this contrast is ill-conceived. Coercion should mean an activity going counter to the will of the individual. Persuasion is activity consonant with, or being made consonant with, the underlying subjective aim (its will). The provision of initial subjective aims is persuasive, but that need not mean that the typical activity of the traditional God is coercive. The traditional God creates by bringing beings into being, which is antecedent to any issue of will.

Along with divine temporalization, the provision of subjective aims is the particular contribution of Whitehead's theism. It in turn rests on a solid basis of inferences. The aim is required to complete the nature of the concrescence as its process of actualization. This act of becoming is needed to express the dynamism of the occasion as an instance of creativity. Because of the indivisibility of the occasion, this dynamism could not be expressed in terms of change but only in terms of becoming. The occasion had to be indivisible to be actual. Whitehead's speculative adventuring generated these ideas, usually in unanticipated ways.

In the process of systematizing his thought, Whitehead postulated two ultimates, creativity, which many distinguish as the metaphysical ultimate, and God, the religious ultimate. Creativity is as ubiquitous and fundamental as being or substance in other philosophies. It is the activity by which every actuality comes into being. A particular advantage of two ultimates is that God is not thought to monopolize the creative act. Creativity is shared by God and creatures. John B. Cobb, Jr, has very effectively used this theory of two ultimates to understand the plurality of religions. Western monotheist religions (Judaism, Christianity and Islam) cluster about the divine pole, while the Eastern religions articulate aspects of creativity (Griffin 2005). Whitehead was one of the first to employ the word 'creativity' (in 1926), although his meaning diverges somewhat from the common usage today, where creativity primarily signifies artistic achievement. The term may well come from 'creative activity', that is, the activity within each occasion whereby it becomes a being. It is both an interior activity and something generalized to all beings, whereas the common meaning today primarily refers only to very highly subjective endeavours. Whitehead may have coined creativity as a substitute for divine creation. At any rate, in so far as God was originally understood as purely non-temporal, creativity and God were thought to be utterly different: one was transcendent and non-temporal, the other immanent and temporal.

Although Whitehead never made this move, it is possible to integrate these two ultimates once God is conceived as an everlasting concrescence. Since creativity infuses all presently concrescing occasions, God can be considered as the source and power behind that creativity. In that sense God is transcendent creativity empowering the creature to exercise its own creative activity. It is important to recognize that this is not a species of efficient causation, the way occasions prehend their past. Past occasions are wholly determinate. They are drained of all creative activity. The activity of relating that is prehension lies in the present occasion, not in the past one. The occasion cannot prehend creativity since it first requires creativity in order to prehend anything. Besides, it can only prehend determinate being while creativity is sheer indeterminate becoming. The past comes to the occasion from without, while creativity wells up from within. Although within the occasion, it is not by the occasion, as if it could author its own creativity.[5]

Both creativity and initial aim are preconditions of the occasion's becoming. If God as transcendent creativity provides initial aims, these two can be integrated. The aim concentrates creativity for this particular occasion, while the creativity thus focused provides the power to achieve the aim as modified by the occasion. Most importantly, creative power is not monopolized by one sole creator. It is shared with creatures as the ontological basis of their freedom. The creative act is not simply God's, but it is completed by the occasion's actualization of itself.

This is a theory of creation, but is rarely called such, and not by Whitehead. The 'self-creation' of occasions is sometimes mentioned, but the notion of 'divine creation' appears only in polemical contexts. Whitehead was opposed to the traditional doctrine of creation *ex nihilo*, which is more the result of a conception of unilateral omnipotence than a derivation from biblical thought. Without using the term 'creation', Whitehead worked out a new interpretation of creation. Instead of being transcendent, non-temporal, purely divine, his theory was mainly immanent and temporal, involving both God and finite occasions. Concrescence charts how actualities come into being, which is how they are created. God's guidance in the form of initial aims contributes to this creative process.

Creation has conflicted with evolution principally because God was considered to be omnipotent. A perfect being creating unilaterally should be able to produce perfect creatures directly, without lengthy intermediate stages. Evolution means to explain this process by random mutation (a form of chance) and natural selection, the perpetuation of those species favourably adapted to their environment. Process thought has no quarrel with natural selection, but it replaces, or at least

---

5. In Ford (2000) I propose that we call this transcendent creativity the future activity of God. This is apt to be misinterpreted, for I emphatically do not mean the ordinary, quite passive, future of beings. It is the activity of a cosmic future, whose activity is bequeathed to the many present occasions. At any rate, this transcendent creativity is neither past nor present in the sense that actual occasions are present, and it is not non-temporal.

supplements, chance by God's provision of initial aims. This gives at least partial directionality to the process.

Process thought quite naturally tends towards considering the universe as having no beginning. Every occasion is the synthesis of many past actualities. They in turn were syntheses of their past, *ad infinitum*. To be sure, when Whitehead wrote he could easily assume that the universe was without beginning. Now we must take seriously the big bang: the claim that thirteen billion years or so ago our universe began in a gigantic explosion, before which there was nothing. Griffin notes that in earlier stages the universe could have occasions, but not yet any enduring things that science could detect (Griffin 2001: 217). This is creation out of chaos, not strictly the nothing that traditional theists insist on.

HARTSHORNE'S PROCESS THEISM

Process theism can be fruitfully considered as the joint product of Whitehead and Hartshorne. Hartshorne's writings are more accessible, as they are largely free of neologisms and have none of the compositional convolutions of Whitehead's. Since Hartshorne is the younger of the two, he is often regarded as Whitehead's disciple. This is not quite accurate. Hartshorne's doctoral thesis of 1923 contains most of the themes he would champion in his life, but he had not really encountered Whitehead until he became his assistant in 1925. Hartshorne has described his early philosophy as a synthesis of Josiah Royce (*see* Vol. 4, Ch. 19) and William James, with an assist from William Ernest Hocking. Nevertheless, most of his characteristic theses were already present in the dissertation, but present in an inverted order. Later he will describe the problem of order in terms of whether the more inclusive category is eternity or time. The dissertation treats eternity as the most inclusive category, under the influence of the reigning absolute idealism. There Hartshorne strives to incorporate as much temporal dynamism (James) as possible, but the end result is confusing on this point. After his encounter with Whitehead, time was reconceived to include 'eternity'.

Whitehead's doctrine of God's two natures revolutionized Hartshorne's philosophy. The non-temporal nature was incorporated within a concrete temporal nature. If the temporal incorporates the eternal, then Hartshorne's categories could be effectively ordered. All else is justification and amplification. Unlike Whitehead's, Hartshorne's philosophy did not undergo significant change over the decades.

This revision, bringing the absolute within the relative, brought the two thinkers close together. Hartshorne found in Whitehead's conceptuality a convenient way of expressing his own ideas, and he became a strong proponent of Whitehead's process philosophy (Hartshorne 1972). This is not to say that he found all of Whitehead's ideas acceptable. He was always critical of 'eternal objects', which like Plato's forms are entirely independent of any temporal instantiation. On this point

Hartshorne is more nominalist. Also he questions the doctrine of the phases of concrescence. These phases are important to Whitehead as a way of spelling out in detail just how there could be any act of becoming. While the idea of becoming or concrescence is central to process philosophy, it is not dependent on any particular account of this act of becoming.

Hartshorne made an early modification in Whitehead's account of God's temporal nature that has won widespread acceptance. Whitehead had conceived of the temporal (consequent) nature as an everlasting, never-ending concrescence. Yet actualities affect one another only when determinate: only when they have become fixed beings. As long as they are concrescing, they have not yet achieved that status. This is no problem for finite acts of becoming, which are all quite brief. But if God is ever-becoming, never achieving determinate being, God as consequent can have no influence on the world.

As noted, Hartshorne substituted for the never-ending process an everlasting series (or society) of finite divine occasions. These divine occasions are patterned after finite occasions: they are brief acts of becoming, which as determinate beings affect subsequent occasions. This transforms unending becoming into a punctuated series of being, which shows how God as consequent could affect the world. Other modifications evading this difficulty have been proposed,[6] but Hartshorne's is the most dominant.

For a time, starting in 1953, he characterized his philosophy as panentheism, the doctrine that the world is included within God, although God is greater than the world. It was intended as a synthesis of theism and pantheism, being both transcendent and immanent, and using the metaphor of the world as God's body. We may understand pantheism as the impersonal life of the cells of the body, while panentheism is the personal individual mind of that body. Hartshorne's panentheism replaces traditional theism with its stress on the creator–creature contrast, which expresses the transcendence of God at the expense of divine immanence. For generations panentheism has been identified with process philosophy, but lately there have been other versions by such thinkers as Jürgen Moltmann, Sallie T. McFague and Grace Janzen. Philip Janzen's version allows for the possibility of creation *ex nihilo*, something Hartshorne clearly rejects (Clayton 1997: 89). Panentheism has certainly broadened its meaning.

Certain features of process philosophy are more evident in Hartshorne's writings, such as process omniscience, which is developed more fully in *The Divine Relativity* (1948). Also, he has intensely explored the nature of the ontological argument and other arguments for the existence of God, something Whitehead hardly touched on.

---

6. If there is a way in which a dominant concrescence can influence a subordinate concrescence, then the divine everlasting concrescence could affect actual occasions without interruption. I propose just such a way, applicable both to the enduring mind and its subordinates, and to God and the enduring mind, in Ford (2006b).

Hartshorne's interest in the ontological argument was given impetus by the discovery that there are two arguments implicit in Anselm's *Proslogion* (*see* Vol. 2, Ch. 6, "Anselm"), one existential and the other modal.[7] While the existential argument is subject to Kant's objection that existence is not a predicate, the modal argument concludes to a proper predicate. Necessary existence, that which exists under all conditions, contrasts with contingent existence, that which exists only under certain conditions. As a perfect being, the mode of God's existence is necessary, either necessary existence or necessary non-existence. Either God must exist under all conditions or God's existence is impossible. This means that if God can possibly exist, God's existence cannot be impossible, and so God must exist.

For contingent beings, possibility of existence is not enough, for further conditions must be met before actualization can take place. Possibility of existence is far less demanding. Usually internal consistency is sufficient to establish possibility. In the case of necessary being, however, establishing possibility requires more stringent criteria. Hartshorne argues for a temporal interpretation of modality. This means that the possible always refers to the future growing out of some past actuality. It is not simply the logical possibility of internal consistency.

The possibility of divine existence can be shown by appealing to process metaphysics: to the nature of God's necessary existence being somehow actualized contingently in each successive divine occasion. Futurity has a real meaning absent from eternal views of God.

Hartshorne appeals to the other arguments for God's existence, seeing each as strengthening the weaknesses of the others. While each may not be sufficiently convincing by itself, combined these arguments make a powerful case for the existence of God.

FURTHER READING

Cobb, J. 2007. *A Christian Natural Theology, Based on the Thought of Alfred North Whitehead*, 2nd edn. Louisville, KY: Westminster John Knox Press.
Dombrowski, D. 1996. *Analytic Theism, Hartshorne, and the Concept of God*. Albany, NY: SUNY Press.
Hartshorne, C. 1948. *The Divine Relativity: A Social Conception of God*. New Haven, CT: Yale University Press.
Hartshorne, C. 1967. *A Natural Theology For Our Time*. La Salle, IL: Open Court.
Hartshorne, C. 1972. *Whitehead's Philosophy: Selected Essays, 1935–1970*. Lincoln, NE: University of Nebraska Press.
Leclerc, I. 1958. *Whitehead's Metaphysics: An Introductory Exposition*. New York: Macmillan.
Viney, D. 1985. *Charles Hartshorne and the Existence of God*. Albany, NY: SUNY Press.
Whitehead, A. N. 1929. *The Function of Reason*. Boston, MA: Beacon.

7. Norman Malcolm is usually credited with this discovery: see Malcolm (1960). Hartshorne had already made the point in Hartshorne & Reese (1953: 96–7).

Whitehead, A. N. 1933. *Adventures of Ideas*. New York: Macmillan.
Whitehead, A. N. 1938. *Modes of Thought*. New York: Free Press.

On CREATION see also Vol. 1, Chs 9, 13, 17; Vol. 3, Ch. 9. On ONTOLOGICAL ARGUMENT see also Ch. 22; Vol. 2, Ch. 6.

6

BERTRAND RUSSELL

A. C. Grayling

Bertrand Russell (1872–1970) wrote much and repeatedly about religion, and an examination of what he had to say yields surprising results for anyone whose knowledge of his views stops at knowing only that he did not believe in the existence of a god or gods, and that he was a trenchant opponent of organized religion and a castigator of what he saw as its harmful effects on human individuals and society. All this is true; but what is even more interesting is that he was deeply concerned to find an alternative to religion as a source of value and a motivator to action aimed at the good. He wrote: "I am constantly asked: What can you, with your cold rationalism, offer to the seeker after salvation that is comparable to the cosy home-like comfort of a fenced-in dogmatic creed?" (1952: 80); and the person who most often asked him this question was himself.

When, in that same passage, he continued, "To this the answer is many-sided" (*ibid.*), he was adverting to the fact that he had tried, and was then in the midst of trying, to find what one might best call a humanistic alternative. This was not an expression he himself used, but it is the closest term in the current lexicon of debate that captures his intentions. The trajectory of his endeavour started with the high-minded sentiments and purple prose of his essay "A Free Man's Worship" (written in 1902–3) and ended long before he described, in his intellectual autobiography *My Philosophical Development* (1959), the conclusion he had reached: that although the desire for an overarching source of value is a powerful and motivating human yearning, it is not a response to anything external to itself.

Before examining these two aspects of Russell on religion – his sharply critical attacks on religion and religious beliefs, and his search for a humanistic alternative – one preliminary must be disposed of. This is Russell's self-description as an 'agnostic' rather than an atheist. His own definition of the terms shows what he meant. In the essay "What is an Agnostic?" he defines the term thus: "An agnostic is a man who thinks that it is impossible to know the truth in the matters such as God and a future life with which the Christian religion and other religions are concerned. Or, if not for ever impossible, at any rate impossible at present" (1999: 41). He then proceeds to define 'atheist' thus:

> Are agnostics atheists? No. An atheist, like a Christian, holds that we *can* know whether or not there is a God. The Christian holds that we can know there is a God, the atheist that we can know there is not. The agnostic suspends judgment, saying that there are not sufficient grounds either for affirmation or for denial. At the same time, an agnostic may hold that the existence of God, though not impossible, is very improbable; he may even hold it so improbable that it is not worth considering in practice. In that case, he is not far removed from atheism. His attitude may be that which a careful philosopher would have towards the gods of ancient Greece. If I were asked to *prove* that Zeus and Poseidon and Hera and the rest of the Olympians do not exist, I should be at a loss to find conclusive arguments. An agnostic may think the Christian God as improbable as the Olympians; in that case, he is, for practical purposes, at one with the atheists.   (1999: 41)

This latter, then, was what Russell meant by calling himself an agnostic: he was "at one with the atheists" but felt bound by logic to admit that he would be at a loss to find arguments to disprove the existence of the Olympian deities. With this reservation, his arguments in criticism of religion and religious beliefs could proceed as if coming from the most trenchant of atheists.

Russell's position in this respect merits challenge. As a logician who in the decades after the publication of *Principia Mathematica* devoted so much effort to showing – in effect, and to use his own earlier terminology – how science, as knowledge by description, can be derived ultimately from knowledge by acquaintance, he should have distinguished between proof in a formal deductive system (demonstrative proof) and proof in the empirical setting (scientific proof). The former consists in deriving a conclusion from premises by rules, and is literally an *explication* in the sense that all the information constituting the conclusion already exists in the premises, so a derivation is in fact a rearrangement. There is no logical novelty in the conclusion, although often enough there is psychological novelty, in the sense that the conclusion can seem unobvious or even surprising if the information constituting it was highly dispersed among the premises.

Demonstrative proof is watertight and conclusive. It is a mechanical matter; computers do it best. Change the rules or axioms of a formal system, and you change the results. Such proof is only to be found in mathematics and logic.

Proof in all other spheres of reasoning, and paradigmatically in science, consists in adducing evidence of the kind and in the quantity that makes it irrational, absurd, irresponsible or even a mark of insanity to reject the conclusion thus being supported. The definitive illustration of what this means, not least for the use that theists would like to make of the myth that 'you cannot prove a negative', is Carl Sagan's dragon-in-the-garage story, where Sagan (1996: 161) poses the question: what's the difference between an invisible, incorporeal, floating dragon who spits heatless fire and no dragon at all? Someone, therefore, who on the basis of evidence and reasoning concludes that it is irrational, absurd, irresponsible or even lunatic to believe that there is such a thing as deity, might further ask whether it is nevertheless none of these things to believe that there *might* be such a thing as deity. Consider an analogy. Suppose someone thinks: 'My belief that rain will wet me if I do not use an umbrella is (only?) inductively justified; therefore I am entitled to believe that it is possible that rain might not wet me next time I do not use an umbrella when it rains.' Is the belief that 'rain might not wet me next time' less irrational or absurd than the belief that rain does not wet at all? Obviously not. For this reason Russell's use of 'agnostic' as functionally equivalent to 'atheist' but with the reservation of a quibble about proof is seen to turn on an assimilation of proof concerning matters of fact to proof of the demonstrative kind – and it is a quibble that does not, *pace* our man with the umbrella, hold water.

Pointing this out matters because misapprehensions about the nature of proof continue to support the apparent plausibility of agnosticism. But agnosticism, as the position that entertains the possibility that there *might be* or *could be* one or more supernatural agencies of some sort, is an irrational position, for precisely the same reason as holding that there *might be* or *could be* fairies or goblins or the Olympian deities or the Norse gods. For this reason, Russell on his own grounds ought to have recognized that he was entitled to declare himself an atheist, just as he was entitled by argument to announce that he was not a Christian. And indeed at times he did describe himself as an atheist, as when, in a wry remark in his autobiography where he talks about nearly having died from pneumonia in China in 1921, he writes: "I was told that the Chinese said that they would bury me by the Western Lake and build a shrine to my memory. I have some slight regret that this did not happen, as I might have become a god, which would have been very *chic* for an atheist" (1975: 364–5).

We can now turn to the two substantive matters involved in Russell's thought about religion – namely, his objections to it, and his quest for an alternative – beginning with the first.

Russell's attack on religious belief took a variety of forms and was expressed in a variety of ways, often in the form of ridiculing the contradictions, absurdities and anthropocentric parochialisms of religions and their sacred texts, practices and ethics, and sometimes in the form of direct argumentation against the claims of either natural theology or revelation. He also argued from more general historical and sociological considerations about the effects of religion – and more generally 'faith' understood as including not just religion but Soviet Communism and the like – on society and human lives. He saw that religions and political tyrannies share in common a monolithic structure that demands subservience and loyalty on pain of punishment, proscribes independence of thought and action, hands down the dogma to be believed and lived by, and issues a one-size-fits-all morality or way of life to which conformity must be absolute. Russell objected both intellectually and morally, and both on principle and in defence of human nature and possibility, to the harm done by this. The tenor of his attacks on religion are explainable accordingly.

The rhetorical technique of refutation by exposing absurdity is by no means an illegitimate one, consisting as it does in focusing attention on claims and their consequences as a way of inspecting their merits. To take just a couple of many examples. In his *History of Western Philosophy* Russell writes that, according to Thomas Aquinas,

> the soul is not transmitted with the semen, but is created afresh with each man. There is, it is true, a difficulty: when a man is born out of wedlock, this seems to make God an accomplice in adultery. This objection, however, is only specious. (There is a grave objection, which troubled St Augustine, and that is as to the transmission of original sin. It is the soul that sins, and if the soul is not transmitted, but created afresh, how can it inherit the sin of Adam? This is not discussed.)
>
> (1961: 449)

Again:

> I am sometimes shocked by the blasphemies of those who think themselves pious – for instance, the nuns who never take a bath without wearing a bathrobe all the time. When asked why, since no man can see them, they reply: "Oh, but you forget the good God". Apparently they conceive of the Deity as a Peeping Tom, whose omnipotence enables Him to see through bathroom walls, but who is foiled by bathrobes. This view strikes me as curious. (1968: 73–4)

The principal objection Russell had to religion concerns its deleterious effect on individuals and society. The harm to individuals was both intellectual and moral, as he respectively points out:

> What I wish to maintain is that all faiths do harm. We may define 'faith' as a firm belief in something for which there is no evidence. When there is evidence, no one speaks of 'faith'. We do not speak of faith that two and two are four or that the earth is round. We only speak of faith when we wish to substitute emotion for evidence.
>
> (1954: 215)

> There is something feeble and a little contemptible about a man who cannot face the perils of life without the help of comfortable myths. Almost inevitably some part of him is aware that they are myths and

that he believes them only because they are comforting. But he dare not face this thought! Moreover, since he is aware, however dimly, that his opinions are not rational, he becomes furious when they are disputed. (*Ibid.*: 219–20)

Pointing out the absurdity of belief and the harm done by its institutionaliza-tion is a more potent way of combating it than by rebutting arguments for the existence of God, which is a major topic of debate in philosophy of religion. But Russell addressed these arguments too, a number of times, although he was satis-fied that Kant had demolished them long before in the *Critique of Pure Reason* (*see* Vol. 3, Ch. 21). He dismissed the first cause argument on the grounds that if the claim that everything must have a cause can only be prevented from collapsing into infinite regress by accepting that there is a self-caused first cause, then there is no reason to invoke the notion of a God since the world could just as well be its own first cause. But in fact, said Russell, the first cause argument is just a version of one that says that the world rests on an elephant and the elephant on a tortoise, and that if you ask what the tortoise rests on, well, let us just change the subject: "The argument is really no better than that" (1999: 79).

Russell was as summary with the argument from design, saying that he found it impossible to believe that omnipotence and omniscience, with all the hundreds of millions of years available to it, should have produced so many imperfections and design flaws as are manifest in the world, or so much cruelty, as any visit to a children's ward in a hospital would show – making Nero 'a saint' in comparison to a deity who could create such a world (*ibid.*: 82). In Russell's view the argument from design was the religious apologist's principal argument, and he repeatedly assaulted and ridiculed it, describing it as "a very poor argument indeed". The design argument, he also repeatedly remarked, was shown by physics to be false because our planet is destined to be destroyed in the natural course of the sun's enlargement and eventual extinction, making nonsense of the idea of a providen-tial creation and design of life (*ibid.*: 82).

Nor could Russell accept the view that the idea of a deity was needed to bring justice into the world, on the grounds that since injustice seems to be so richly rewarded in this life, a next life is required to provide a remedy by giving the just their reward. But if one were thinking scientifically about the evidence, the pres-ence of injustice in this world would be good grounds for inferring that there is as much injustice anywhere else, just as the presence of rotten oranges at the top of a crate makes it probable that there are more rotten oranges deeper down in the crate (*ibid.*: 84).

The somewhat more usual argument to the necessity of God for morality is that without the former you cannot have the latter. The version of this argument that Russell criticized in his essay "Is There A God?" is one popularized by William James. Russell wrote: "The first and greatest objection to this argument is that, at its best, it cannot prove that there is a God but only that politicians and educators ought to try to make people think there is one" (1997b: 545). A second objection is that "Many of the best men known to history have been unbelievers. John Stuart Mill may serve as an instance. And many of the worst men known to history have been believers. Of this there are innumerable instances. Perhaps Henry VIII may serve as typical" (1997b: 546).

For Russell religious belief is not motivated by arguments of the kind just discussed and dismissed, but is the result of being taught in infancy the religion of whatever community one happens to be born into and thereafter being afraid to abandon that belief because of insecurity, anxieties about death and the need for comfort. These are non-rational and often irrational considerations, and are therefore not amenable to argument directed at proof or disproof. The point carries through even to those who putatively offer philosophical support for commitments of faith and its tenets, as Russell shows in criticizing Aquinas, taken to be the greatest of religion's philosophers:

> There is little of the true philosophic spirit in Aquinas. He does not, like the Platonic Socrates, set out to follow wherever the argument may lead. He is not engaged in an enquiry, the result of which it is impossible to know in advance. Before he begins to philosophize, he already knows the truth; it is declared in the Catholic faith. If he can find apparently rational arguments for some parts of the faith, so much the better; if he cannot, he need only fall back on revelation. The finding of arguments for a conclusion given in advance is not philosophy, but special pleading. (1961: 453–4)

For Russell it was close to sufficient to illustrate the action of religion in human affairs to reveal both its implausibility and its unacceptability. The most systematic effort he made in this direction is his book *Religion and Science* (1935). There he took the view that religion and science are direct competitors for the truth about the world, its origin, its nature, whether or not it exhibits purpose, and what can be inferred from it for ethics. One of the chief lessons to emerge, in Russell's view, is the necessity of accepting the deliverances of science and disciplining one's reasoning to its methods. Both here and in the essay "An Outline of Intellectual Rubbish" (written in 1950) Russell contrasted the growth of science with the efforts made by religion to impede that growth:

> Throughout the last 400 years, during which the growth of science has gradually shown men how to acquire knowledge of the ways of nature and mastery over natural forces, the clergy have fought a losing battle against science, in astronomy and geology, in anatomy and physiology, in biology and psychology and sociology. Ousted from one position, they have taken up another. After being worsted in astronomy, they did their best to prevent the rise of geology; they fought against Darwin in

biology, and at the present time they fight against scientific theories of psychology and education. At each stage, they try to make the public forget their earlier obscurantism, in order that their present obscurantism may not be recognized for what it is. (1968: 72)

Such are the kinds of considerations that made Russell an opponent of religions and religious belief. What was equally important to him and even more interesting in itself was his attempt to articulate an alternative vision of the world and value that would do everything for humanity that some people thought or hoped religion would do for it, but without religion's metaphysical irrationality and its moral and social distortions. This is what Russell early called 'a free man's worship', although he came to abandon the high-sounding ambitions for such a thing as his reflections on the matter matured.

To understand what Russell was after in this connection it is important to notice that, in the absence of a ready term to denote what he meant, he gave a second but secular meaning to the term 'religion' to mean a sentiment or feeling that carries individuals out of themselves towards some overarching sense of value or purpose that transcends belittling self-concern. In his essay "The Essence of Religion" (written in 1912) he describes religion in this philosophical sense as a feeling that captures "the quality of infinity" that gives rise to "the selfless, untrammelled life in the whole which frees men from the prison-house of eager wishes and little thoughts" (1999: 57). Throughout his thinking on these matters Russell felt acutely the fact of the universe's indifference and crushingly superior power over the individual, as the blind play of natural forces working according to natural laws unfolded like a juggernaut without consciousness of the pain or pleasure felt by sentient beings, and man's possibility of a small but noble endeavour to sustain a commitment to value in the face of this fact.

In "A Free Man's Worship", Russell had risen to dithyrambic heights in asserting this view:

> Brief and powerless is Man's life; on him and all his race the slow sure doom falls pitiless and dark. Blind to good and evil, reckless of destruction, omnipotent matter rolls on its relentless way; for Man, condemned today to lose his dearest, tomorrow himself to pass through the gate of darkness, it remains only to cherish, ere yet the blow falls, the lofty thoughts that ennoble his little day; disdaining the coward terrors of the slave of Fate, to worship at the shrine that his own hands have built; undismayed by the empire of chance, to preserve a mind free from the wanton tyranny that rules his outward life; proudly defiant of the irresistible forces that tolerate, for a moment, his knowledge and his condemnation, to sustain alone, a weary but unyielding Atlas, the world that his own ideals have fashioned despite the trampling march of unconscious power. (*Ibid.*: 38)

Over thirty years later he was saying much the same thing far more soberly, in *Religion and Science*:

> The man who feels deeply the problems of human destiny, the desire to diminish the sufferings of mankind, and the hope that the future will realize the best possibilities of our species, is nowadays often said to have a religious outlook ... In so far as religion consists in a way of feeling, rather than in a set of beliefs, science cannot touch it.   (1935: 17)

The closest analogy in the history of philosophy that Russell could find to express his view was, he said, Spinoza's idea of 'the intellectual love of God' (*see* Vol. 3, Ch. 11), but where there is no such thing as God, where nature is not substituted for God, and where a sense of the greater value of all things taken together – greater therefore than petty individual self-concern – serves as the target of the self-liberating emotional response Russell yearned for, and yearned to describe.

Indeed, the best account given of this owes itself to Kenneth Blackwell in his *The Spinozistic Ethics of Bertrand Russell*, where he writes: "There is a similarity between Russell's concept, derived from Spinoza, of impersonal self-enlargement and the Buddhist concept of egolessness" (1985: 127). In *The Conquest of Happiness* (1930) Russell had made the idea of self-transcendence – now cast in more prosaic terms as having outward-looking interests and commitments – the key to personal happiness; the insight is a good one, of course, and an obvious one, a fact that has drawn the criticism of banality from those who did not realize that beneath it lay the deepest of Russell's ethical impulses.

The idea of the outward-looking, self-transcending stance expressed itself in two connected ways for Russell. One related to science, the other to personal relationships and the individual's attitude to others in general. In regard to science, the objectivity and scope of science is obviously such as to make individual self-concern a very minor if not indeed nugatory thing. In the essay "The Place of Science in a Liberal Education" Russell wrote: "The kernel of the scientific outlook is the refusal to regard our own desires, tastes and interests as affording a key to the understanding of the world" (1917: 37), and this immediately entails that the disciplines of reason and evidence are the sole legitimate determinants of thinking in general. But in view of the potential that science has, *via* technology, to aggrandize and serve the lust for power that is all too constant a feature of human nature, there has to be a counterbalance, and this Russell identified in another human capacity, this time for love. In *The Impact of Science on Society* (1952), written at a time when the technological threats to human survival were mounting exponentially in the form of weapons of mass destruction, he wrote:

> The root of the matter is a very simple and old-fashioned thing, a thing so simple that I am almost ashamed to mention it, for fear of the derisive smile with which wise cynics will greet my words. The thing

I mean – please forgive me for mentioning it – is love, Christian love, or compassion. (1952: 84)

And he went on to add that if his reader felt such compassion, "you have all that anybody should need in the way of religion" (*ibid.*).

This last statement, written late in Russell's life and in the face of yet another threat – this time an even greater one – than all those that had drawn him to social and political action at various stages of his life, best captures what he desired by way of a practical alternative to religion. It looks far from the objective something-or-other that, because it is independent of individual human desires and weakness, can summon and even command the best from us and be the indisputable ground for action. Rather, it is immanent and as fragile as its source. But it is all there is, and all that is anyway necessary.

After losing his faith as a teenager – an event recorded in an early diary and related in his autobiography – Russell never changed his views about religion, or about the need for an alternative to religion that would be ethically compelling. The absence of a suitable alternative vocabulary for articulating his thoughts in the latter respect made him talk of 'life in the spirit' and 'personal religion', but always in wholly secular terms, and it was in this sense that he once wrote: "I consider some form of personal religion highly desirable, and feel many people unsatisfactory through the lack of it" (1997a: 52).

He also there said that what he regarded as his own best statement of his views on religion, in both the religious and secular senses of the term as he meant them, is the chapter entitled "Religion and the Churches" in his First World War book, *Principles of Social Reconstruction* (1916). In that chapter, after recounting the struggle of both science and individuals to free themselves from the hegemony of the church, Russell states:

> If a religious view of life and the world is ever to reconquer the thoughts and feelings of free-minded men and women, much that we are accustomed to associate with religion will have to be discarded. The first and greatest change that is required is to establish a morality of initiative, not a morality of submission, a morality of hope rather than fear, of things to be done rather than of things to be left undone. It is not the whole duty of man to slip through the world so as to escape the wrath of God. The world is *our* world, and it rests with us to make a heaven or a hell. (1916: 141)

And, adds Russell, the vision that will underwrite the making of a human heaven on human earth

> will not be one of occasional solemnity and superstitious prohibitions, it will not be sad or ascetic, it will concern itself little with rules of

conduct. It will be inspired by a vision of what human life may be, and will be happy with the joy of creation, living in a large free world of initiative and hope. It will love mankind, not for what they are to the outward eye, but for what imagination shows that they have it in them to become. (*Ibid.*)

FURTHER READING

Brightman, E. 1951. "Russell's Philosophy of Religion". In *The Philosophy of Bertrand Russell*, A. Schilpp (ed.), 539–56. New York: Tudor Publishing.

Irvine, A. (ed.) 1999. *Bertrand Russell: Critical Assessments, Vol. 4: History of Philosophy, Ethics, Education, Religion and Politics*. London: Routledge.

Kuntz, P. 1986. *Bertrand Russell*. Boston, MA: Twayne Publishers [esp. ch. 8].

Russell, B. 1935. *Religion and Science*. Oxford: Oxford University Press.

Russell, B. 1999. *Russell On Religion: Selections from the Writings of Bertrand Russell*, L. Greenspan & S. Andersson (eds). London: Routledge.

On AGNOSTICISM see also Vol. 3, Ch. 10; On ATHEISM see also Ch. 17; Vol. 3, Ch. 15; Vol. 4, Chs 2, 10, 20. On HUMANISM see also Vol. 2, Ch. 19; Vol. 3, Chs 5, 16. On MORALITY see also Vol. 2, Ch. 12; Vol. 3, Chs 2, 8, 12, 14, 21, 22; Vol. 4, Chs 4, 12, 18.

7

MAX SCHELER

Quentin Smith

Max Scheler was born in 1874 in Munich, Germany and died at the early age of fifty-four in 1928. During the last fifteen years or so of his life, Scheler was widely regarded as "the most brilliant thinker of his day," according to Bochenski (1961: 140). 'His day' is roughly from 1912 until his death in 1928.

Scheler focused on two main areas in his most influential publications, from 1912 to 1920. One was describing the essence of our emotional consciousness of values, such as a special sort of love: an *act of loving* the holy person, God; a loving act in which *the value of holiness* originally appears. The other is the study of the religious consciousness, or the religious act of 'faith', with faith viewed as a *reactive* response to the self-disclosure of the holy person (God).

Scheler's philosophical writings began with his 1899 doctoral degree under the neo-Kantian Rudolf Eucken, who believed that the nature of the philosopher's task is to discover the eternal realm of values. This view exercised a lifelong influence on Scheler.

The second most important influence on Scheler arose from his meeting 'the father of phenomenology', Edmund Husserl, in 1910. Scheler quickly became the most creative of the many followers of Husserl, and by 1918 or 1920 Scheler was considered by many German phenomenologists to have superseded him.

It was not until he left his first teaching post in 1910, at the University of Munich, and became a freelance writer that Scheler began writing the works that decisively influenced the course of twentieth-century philosophy. In the space of two years he published three of his enduring classics, *Ressentiment* (1912), *The Nature of Sympathy* (1913) and *Formal Ethics and Material Value Ethics* (1913, 1916).[1] This third book, a six-hundred-page work on emotions and values, was

---

1. In order to facilitate comprehension of the history of Scheler's original German publications and their relation to other German publications, I use the date of the original German
publication but use English translations of the title. For example, the date in parenthesis in
'On the Eternal in Man (1920)' is the date of the original German publication and 'On the

completed in 1913; its first part was published in 1913, and the publication of the second part was delayed until 1916. This book is a description of material values (*materialer Wert*). Here the English word 'material' is contrasted with 'formal', somewhat as the English word 'content' is often contrasted with 'form'. Scheler's book title in German, *Der Formalismus in Ethik und die materialer Wertethik*, is translated awkwardly (and inaccurately) by Manfred Frings and Roger Funk as *Formalism in Ethics and Non-Formal Ethics of Values*. I believe a more accurate translation is *Formal Ethics and Material Value Ethics*. Hereafter, I shall abbreviate this work as *Value*. This book on values is considered, by consensus, as Scheler's masterpiece and is a primary focus of the following sections.

The first of these three 'classic' works of Scheler, *Ressentiment*, aims to explain why secularism and subjectivism about values began to take predominance in the late nineteenth and early twentieth centuries (and remain predominant today among most philosophers, despite the renaissance in the 1970s of Christian theism and moral realism among a large minority of philosophers). Scheler reverses Nietzsche's theory that Christianity, objective values and a personal Creator were created by the weak, poor and oppressed, out of envy and *ressentiment* (resentment) of the more powerful types, originally their Roman conquerors (*see* Vol. 4, Ch. 18, "Friedrich Nietzsche"). Scheler follows Nietzsche in using the French word *ressentiment* to emphasize that it is a technical term that is being used. However, Scheler presents an elaborate account of why atheism and value subjectivism emerged. People who are afraid to have their actions and moral beliefs measured against an objective scale of values rejected the notion that there are objective values and reduced values to subjective desires. Christian morality, Scheler maintains, far from expressing the strivings of the morally weak, expresses the attitudes of the morally strong and healthy. The centre of Christian morality is Christian love, a spontaneous overflowing of inner fullness. However, when we feel unable or unwilling to attain the higher values, "value blindness or value delusion may set in. Lowering all values to the level of one's factual desire or ability ... [and] construing an illusory hierarchy of values in accordance with the structure of one's personal goals and wishes" (Scheler [1912] 1961b: 59).[2] The healthy response to recognizing that there are higher values beyond one's reach is 'resignation', which

---

    Eternal in Man' is the English translation of the German title '*Vom Ewigen im Menschen*'. All quotations are from the English translations and the page numbers are given for the English translation. The exception is the English translation of the German title of Scheler's 1913–16 book on ethics, *Der Formalismus in Ethik und die materialer Wertethik*, which I discuss at some length in the text; page numbers from that text are from Scheler (1973a).

2. This quotation is from William Holdheim's (1961) translation of *Das Ressentiment im Aufbau der Moralen*, which was first published in the collection of essays, *Abhanandlugen und Aufsatze* (1915). The 1915 essay, *Das Ressentiment im Aufbau der Moralen*, is an expanded version of the 1912 publication, *Uber Ressentiment under moralalisches Werturteil*. Holdheim and other English writers shorten the title of both versions to the single word *Ressentiment*.

allows one to appreciate the higher values. In old age, if we resign ourselves to our inability to attain or desire the values of youth, we have an ethically mature response to our limitations.

Scheler's 1913 book *The Nature of Sympathy* presents a highly nuanced description of the different feelings he calls 'fellow-feeling', 'benevolence', 'vicarious feeling', 'sympathy', 'pity' and the highest feeling, love of humankind and love of the divine.

Scheler's theory of love includes a special type of love that is a love of God and humankind. Scheler describes this love as participating in God's own love and co-realizing (*mitvollzieght*) the divine acts in which God loves himself and all persons. Scheler leaves these terms undefined, but he is not a pantheist and this way of describing the love of God may be plausibly understood (I suggest) as a metaphor for *imitating* as closely as possible God's love of all persons and God's love of himself.

Scheler's *The Nature of Sympathy* presents the most detailed description of our attitudes to others that can be found, although perhaps part three of Jean-Paul Sartre's *Being and Nothingness* (1943), "Being For Others", matches it. The difference is that Scheler concentrates on our positive feelings towards others, while Sartre concentrates on more negative feelings, finally reducing all feelings and human relations to forms of psychological sadomasochism. It seems a realistic picture is achieved if we take both works into account.

Scheler completed *Value* in 1913, but only part one was published that year and the publication of part two was delayed until 1916. Most of the following sections are about this book and I shall say nothing more about it here.

In 1920 Scheler published what many consider his fourth enduring classic, *On the Eternal in Man*, which is his study of the essence of religious consciousness and its intended object, God, a divine person that essentially possesses the value of holiness discussed in *Value*. *On the Eternal in Man* (hereafter *Eternal*), in addition to *Value*, is one of the two works that will be discussed in detail in later sections.

Shortly after the publication of *Eternal*, Scheler turned away from Christian monotheism to a study of the sociological variations in our apprehensions of objective values. "Problems of the Sociology of Knowledge" (1924) is one of the many essays and books Scheler published after *Eternal*. This work and others shows his movement towards a philosophical anthropology and a pantheistic neo-vitalism; the pantheistic theory is outlined in *On Man's Place in Nature* (1927). Scheler died in 1928, depriving him of the opportunity of developing these theories. Several collections of essays were published posthumously, such as the books *Philosophical Perspectives* (1929) and *Selected Philosophical Essays* (1933), while the translations of various articles or chapters of his earlier books appeared in *On Feeling, Knowing, and Valuing: Selected Writings* (Scheler 1992). Further bibliographical information can be found in the 1973 translation of his 1913–16 book on value ethics, under the title *Formalism in Ethics and Non-Formal Ethics of Values* (see Scheler 1973a: 597–603).

SCHELER'S PLACE IN THE HISTORY OF
TWENTIETH-CENTURY PHILOSOPHY

H. Bershady writes that Scheler "was acclaimed in Europe after the First World War as one of the leading minds of the modern age and Germany's most brilliant thinker" (Scheler 1992: 1). Herbert Spiegelberg is the author of the standard history of phenomenology (a method of describing what is given in our intuition, rather than of constructing theoretical arguments). In *The Phenomenological Movement*, he quotes José Ortega y Gasset as saying, "The first man of genius, the Adam of the new [phenomenological] Paradise … was Max Scheler" (Speigelberg 1971: 227).

Put in a broader context, Scheler was the second of the first three major continental philosophers, a movement that continues to the present day. Continental philosophy, since the 1960s and 1970s, has largely transformed into a 'postmodernism' that stands opposed both to the phenomenological theories of Husserl, Scheler and the early Heidegger, and to analytic philosophy. The phenomenological movement arose in Germany and flourished from 1900 to approximately 1933, when the Nazis banned Husserl's and Scheler's works. In the mid and late 1930s, the movement passed to France with Sartre's early works and lasted until the 1960s and early 1970s with Maurice Merleau-Ponty and Emmanuel Levinas. From the 1960s/70s to the present, the phenomenological movement largely passed into America. It coexists with postmodernism as a dominant form of continental philosophy; however, the precision of description, reminiscent of Husserl and Scheler, makes much of American phenomenology significantly more analogous to current analytic philosophy than to the writings of Jacques Derrida, Michel Foucault or Jean Baudrillard.

Twentieth-century continental philosophy began as phenomenology, with Husserl's *Logical Investigations* (1900–1901), a descriptive study of the *essential nature* of intuitions of logical essences, and of the logical essences themselves, the logical categories and forms of inference, that are immediately given in these intuitions. Scheler succeeded Husserl (approximately from 1918 to 1930) as the primary figure in continental philosophy, and was in turn succeeded by Martin Heidegger, whose 1927 book *Being and Time* was considered by a preponderance of phenomenologists to have 'superseded' Scheler's works (just as Scheler's works were considered by German phenomenologists to have 'superseded' Husserl's works) within two or three years from the publication of Heidegger's work. (Owing to various factors, Scheler's works in English translation never achieved the wide regard accorded to Husserl's and Heidegger's works.)

Scheler, like Husserl, regarded 'the intuitive given' not as sense-data or empirical objects, for example sensory qualities, or things and persons, but as the *a priori* essences that are the material contents of the phenomenological intuitions. An essence is the immediate material content ('material content' here translates *materialie*) of a phenomenological intuition. These *a priori* intuitional material contents are the *phenomena* that phenomenology seeks to describe. Phenomena are not considered to be 'appearances' of something real or 'illusions', but are identified with the *a priori* essences that are the material contents of phenomenological intuitions. The phenomenologists' phrase 'to the things themselves' can be misleading, since Husserl and Scheler had in mind the *a priori essences* immediately given as the material content of phenomenological intuitions. The essence is the content or material (*materialie*) of the intuition. The intuited materials, the essences, are ideal units of meaning or sense that are 'self-given' in the phenomenological intuitions. The 'things themselves', therefore, are not the real things or people we cognitively apprehend in our natural non-intuitive (i.e. mediated by symbols) perceptions of objects. The reality of things and persons are 'bracketed', meaning their reality is neither affirmed nor denied.

Husserl and Scheler are responding to the neo-Kantians, who held that the *a priori* cannot be intuited and are formal rather than material in nature. They are formal truths known in thought or judgement; we think the true *a priori* propositions or deduce them by way of logical argument. The phenomenological intuitions are of *a priori* essences, such as the material value-modalities of the holy and unholy. Phenomenological intuitions are not empirical or *a posteriori* experiences of faith in the divine person (the reality or existence of God cannot be known in phenomenological philosophy). Phenomenology is not only different from traditional deductive philosophy, such as Aristotle's or Descartes', but is also different from inductive generalizations about the characteristics of things or persons.

Scheler's phenomenological intuitions have significant similarities to the 'intuitions of essences' described by Saul Kripke, George Bealer, and others in the field of 'modal epistemology', that is, the field that studies the intuitive knowledge of possibilities and necessities. The phenomenological essences, and essential properties, are necessary to whatever thing or person possesses them. In another analytic tradition, ethical intuitionism, the 'intuitions of synthetic *a priori* values' by G. E. Moore, W. D. Ross and Panayot Butchvarov, are the nearest analogues in analytic philosophy to Scheler's phenomenological intuitions of *a priori* material values. The intuited values and intuited essences of any sort are reported or described in synthetic *a priori* propositions.

These remarks give some indication of the general conception of Scheler's place in the history of philosophy, but as we shall see the revival of interest in the Anselmian ontological arguments by Alvin Plantinga (1974b), Graham Oppy (1996, 2006), Thomas Morris (1987) and other analytic philosophers of religion make Scheler's study of *material values* highly relevant to the 'metaphysical values' at the basis of contemporary 'perfect being theology', particularly in the development of Plantinga's ideas in Morris (1987).

HOLINESS AS THE HIGHEST VALUE

Scheler's substantive philosophy of religion is found mainly in *Value* and in *Eternal*. *Value* includes a study of the different types of religious feelings and the values that belong to the value-modality of the holy. The essential nature of the bearer of the value of holiness, 'the absolute person', is studied in *Eternal*. We begin with Scheler's description of religious values in *Value*, where the value of the holy is the highest value in a rank ordering of values.

Scheler's value hierarchy is an order among the values we experience in everyday life. He presents a detailed outline of this rank ordering and the feelings associated with each of the four levels of values; normally, each act of consciousness we experience includes a *feeling of a value* and a *representation* (thought, judgement, imagination, perception, etc.) *of the bearer* (such as a person or thing) of this value.

The lowest value level includes the values that range from *the agreeable* to *the disagreeable*. These values are apprehended in sensible feelings, which range from enjoying the agreeable to 'suffering' the disagreeable. The feeling-states are the sensations of pleasure and pain. Scheler writes in *Value* that

> the values of the sensibly agreeable are clearly [spatially] extensive in their essence, and their felt experiences occur as localized and as extensive in the body. For example, the agreeableness of sweet, etc., is spread over sugar, and the corresponding sensuous feeling-state [a pleasurable sensation] over the tongue. (*Value* 18)

There is a value-person-type that correlates to the agreeable. This type is a 'pleasure-seeker', a connoisseur of agreeable things, what Scheler usually describes by the French phrase *bon vivant*. This value-person-type is focused on enjoying agreeable things. There is much more to be said about the agreeable and the corresponding feelings and value-person-type, but our interest is in ascending the hierarchy to the holy.

The *vital values* are higher than the values of the agreeable. Vital values include health and illness, strength and weakness, and the values ranging from the 'excellent' to the 'bad' (which is distinct from the moral value of evil). The feeling-states are feelings of health and illness and so on, and this value-modality also correlates to emotional responses such as courage and anxiety. The vital values are Scheler's inclusions of Nietzsche's value-system of the good (in the sense of the excellent and noble) and bad (in the sense of the ignoble, base or vulgar).

The value-person-type correlating to the vital values is 'the hero', a courageous, strong person who realizes things that are 'excellent' and who performs 'noble' deeds. "The value of life, whose personal actualization is the 'hero'" (*Value* 588 n.306), correlates to a higher value-person-type than the type that corresponds to the value of the agreeable, the *bon vivant* or 'pleasure-seeker'. In other words, a hero is a higher value-person-type than a pleasure-seeker.

Higher than vital values are what Scheler calls '*spiritual values*', and they are of three types: *aesthetic values, values of the cognition of truth* and *moral values* such as good and evil. The corresponding emotional reactions correlating to spiritual values include the reactions of approving and disapproving, and respect and disrespect. The feeling-states that correlate to these values include "the feeling-states of spiritual joy and sorrow" (*Value* 108).

The value-person-type correlating to spiritual values is 'the genius'. This includes 'the artistic genius', 'the philosophical genius' and the 'moral genius'.

The values of *the holy* (and the unholy) are higher than aesthetic values, moral values and values of cognition of the truth. The description of this level can be more detailed, since Scheler's description of the values of the holy and the corresponding feelings constitutes his phenomenological theory of religious values and feelings, which will be contrasted in the next section with the religious object (the deity) that has the value of the holy and the cognitive religious act that grasps the religious object. It belongs to the essence of holiness that it can only be a value of the 'absolute being', which is also the highest or infinitely good person. This person's infinite or divine goodness and his 'absolute being' shall be discussed in the ensuing sections.

Corresponding to the value of holiness, the value-person-type is 'the saint', which is a higher value-person-type than the genius, the hero and the pleasure-seeker (or 'connoisseur' of pleasurable things).

One grasps the hierarchy of values in *acts of preferring*, wherein one value is given as preferable to (and thus 'higher' than) another. The vital values are essentially preferable to the values of the agreeable, and preferable to the vital values are the values of aesthetic beauty, of good and evil, and the value of cognition of *a priori* philosophical truths (truths about the essential structure of reality). Scheler interprets science as an instrument for making predictions, and this anti-realism about scientific theories is at the basis of his exclusion of scientific thinking from the category of cognition of truths about reality. Holiness is seen to be the supreme value in acts of preferring holiness to the aesthetic, moral and 'philosophical knowledge' values.

RELIGIOUS FEELINGS THAT CORRELATE TO THE HOLY PERSON

A phenomenology of the *types of feelings* discloses to us further essential properties of holiness that determine the essential nature of the absolute, personal, being. The *feeling-states* range from bliss to despair and they can be regarded as indicators of the nearness or remoteness of the divine in experience.

The *reactive feelings* are different from the feeling-states. Reactions to the holy include awe and adoration, as well as *faith* and lack of faith. The feeling reaction of *faith* has decisive significance in Scheler's theory, for only in reactions of faith in God's reality does God disclose or reveal himself as real or existent. No logical arguments or phenomenological descriptions of essences can show that God exists. This is known only in an emotional reaction of faith. Scheler's precise wording is that "it is of the essence of a religious object that it can attest to its possible reality only through and in an act of faith … the *reality* of the religious object and material … is experienced in real and genuine faith" (*Eternal* 158–9). Scheler notes that phenomenologically we can distinguish the reaction of *faith in the reality of the deity* from the reality of the deity. Faith is the reaction to *the reality of God* that is being disclosed and revealed in that reaction.

The intentional feeling through which we originally apprehend the value of the holy is a special type of love, a love of a person or toward something that has the form of a person. Scheler later describes the love of God, the infinite, holy person. The love of God is a co-loving (with God) of all finite persons "with" God's love of Himself as "the person of persons" (*Value* 498).

There is a threefold distinction among *the value of holiness, the good* and *the person that is the bearer of this value*. This corresponds to Scheler's general distinction between the value, the bearer of the value (the value-bearer is the good) and the thing or person that is the bearer considered in abstraction from its value. There is an intentional *feeling of the value* and an intentional representation (*Vorstellung*) of the person (or thing, in the case of the lowest values). The good, corresponding to the value of holiness, is the supreme good, that is, the *holy person*, and it is apprehended in a religious act, which is a complex of intentional feeling and intentional representation.

A novel idea of Scheler's is that the feeling of the value, for example the feeling of the value of holiness, can occur without a representation of the person that bears this value. In the case of holiness, the feeling of holiness precedes and guides the representation of the person. This can be a value-property only of the highest person.

The intentional feeling of holiness can co-occur with different sorts of representations of the absolute being that has the form of a person; the determination of the specifics of the real nature of the personal absolute cannot be made by a phenomenology of feelings and values. The phenomenology of the value of holiness and the religious feelings gives us a broad outline of the religious good, the divine. Scheler phrases this concisely: the value-modality of holiness "is quite independent of all that has been considered holy by different people at various times … from ideas of fetishism to the purest conceptions of God" (*Value* 109). The problem of the true or real nature of the holy being concerns the "representation of goods within this value-sphere" (*ibid.*). The true essence of the holy being, which is the highest or supreme good (thing or person of value), is described partly in *Value* and partly in *Eternal*. We know from the phenomenological intuition of the essential interconnections between holiness and essences of goods that holiness can only be a property of a *person* and of an *absolute* being. Concerning this absolute person that is the bearer of holiness, we shall separately examine (as does Scheler) the essential attribute of God as the infinitely good *person* and the essential attribute of God as the *absolute being*.

THE INFINITELY GOOD PERSON

There are three senses of 'the person of highest value'. The first involves finite persons and the value-person-type of 'the saint'. The sainthood of the saint is the highest value. Scheler writes about "the highest value, i.e., the *sainthood* of the person, and ... the highest good, i.e., *the salvation of an individual person*" (*Value* 492). Scheler has in mind here the highest value of a human person, a finite person. The second sense is empirically exemplified by Jesus Christ; this is a finite person who is "the only and only holy person" in the sense of being the person to whom God "has imparted his own personal essence and being" (*Value* 162). Scheler claims he is here describing the essential ideas of finite religious persons and is not describing the empirical reality of any natural religion. However, his work was criticized for presupposing a form of Catholic exclusivism as the true *a priori* religion.

The third sense of being the person of the highest value is higher than the other two and applies only to the infinite person, God. He is infinite in the sense that he is infinitely good. All universal value-person-types (apart from those corresponding to the values of the agreeable and the vital values) are co-contained (*mitenethalten*) in the essential goodness of God. In other words, God contains the infinite value that corresponds to the finite value of the value-person-types. This means that God is the all-saintly and all-loving God. He has infinite, unlimited and maximal saintliness and love. This corresponds to the value-person-type of the saint (who is essentially saintly and loving), who is the value-person-type that correlates to the highest value, holiness. Regarding the spiritual value-person-type of the philosophical genius, God is the all-knowing or omniscient God. Corresponding to the value-person-type of the artistic genius, God is the divine artist and the creator. Corresponding to the moral genius, God is the divine lawgiver (an example from a natural religion is the 'Ten Commandments') and the divine judge (judging who shall be saved and who shall not be) (*Value* 588 n.306).

The essential goodness of God also contains individually valid essences of an individual value-person. Scheler comments that this:

> 'co-containing' means the essential goodness of God does not exhaust itself in the infinite exemplariness of the universally and individually valid being of the value-person. It means that the essential goodness of God is primarily infinite as an *indivisible* essential value-quality. It is only through a possible experiential and cognitive relation of a finite person to the infinite person that divine goodness divides into unities of value-essences and value-types and their declining sequence of ranks. (*Value* 588)

THE ABSOLUTE BEING

It is an essence of the value of 'the holy' that it is a value of a person. It is also an essence of this value that it can only belong to what is 'absolute' and not 'relative'. Something is absolute only if it is the supreme, almighty, infinite and independent being, a being that is manifest to us in religious acts as the self-grounded being on which all finite and relative beings are grounded or dependent. A finite thing or person is 'relative' in the sense that it has being only relative to the absolute being, through having the ground of its being in the self-grounded being. The absolute being, in Scheler's words, "is unconditionally superior to all others ... in capacity for sheer 'being'. All other beings are founded on the absolute being and their being 'rests in' the absolute being, but the absolute being is 'founded in and 'resting on itself'" (*Eternal* 163).

The absoluteness of the holy being can be described in terms of the concept of superordination. Being superordinate is the opposite of being subordinate. As subordinate beings, we are dependent on the absolute being, but it is not dependent on us; there is no interdependence relation. The absolute being is independent of us and all other beings.

SCHELER AND CONTEMPORARY PERFECT BEING THEOLOGY

What is the relevance of Scheler's theory of the holy to perfect being theology and the ontological argument that the perfect being exists? Scheler adopts the approach that we determine *what constitutes* the perfect being by examining our intentional feelings of the value of holiness. Holiness is a material value and is a property of God. How does it compare with Plantinga's and Morris' idea of the perfect being as the metaphysically best or 'maximally great' being? Scheler's material value of *holiness* bears similarities to Plantinga's metaphysical value of *maximal metaphysical greatness*. Plantinga states that the property of being maximally great entails having the omniproperties or perfections, and entails having them in every possible world (see the last chapter of Plantinga [1974b] and the summary of his ideas in Smith [1997: 127–37]). On Scheler's theory, the value of holiness is essentially related to a person that has these omniproperties or perfections. Scheler's value of holiness and Plantinga's property of maximal greatness bear significant similarities.

For example, the rank order of metaphysical values, the degree of greatness that certain properties (the great-making properties) confer on a being, share many features in common with Scheler's rank ordering of material values, although Plantinga's and Morris' remarks are comparatively elliptical or sketchy in relation to Scheler's long books and many articles on these value ranks. Metaphysical values, like Scheler's material values, include moral values only as one kind. Metaphysical goodness is *ontological greatness* and there is a ranking of greater beings and less great beings. Greatness is a metaphysical value conferred on a being by certain great-making properties, such as being a person, which confers a degree of ontological greatness on the being, since being a person makes a being *a greater being* than a being that is not a person. The perfect being ('the maximally great being') is the greatest possible being.

Plantinga holds that God has maximal metaphysical worth and since 'metaphysical worth or value' is usually phrased in terms of greatness, the degree of greatness of a being supervenes on its great-making properties. God is the best being, the perfect being, but 'best' does not here have a moral sense. It is better for a being to have consciousness, personhood, free will and knowledge of moral good and evil than not to have these features, all else being equal, but it is false or nonsensical to say that a being ought to strive to acquire the property of being a conscious being, or ought to strive to acquire free will. Rather, a person can freely choose to act in a morally good way, but this presupposes that the person either always or timelessly possesses free will and moral knowledge (in the case of God), or presupposes that the person was generated (whether this means born with the capacity to act and choose freely when the person matures, or was created by God with the essential properties of having free will and some knowledge of good and evil, a 'moral sense' or 'conscience' or, more simply, the capacity to know moral truths). Kindness, altruism, benevolence, generosity and so on are morally good motives or acts, and lead us to say that the person is morally good. But a being having free will, consciousness and the capacity to know moral truths and to act in a way they know is morally good are not themselves morally good features. Many historical figures have these properties, such as Hitler and Stalin (every human person has them), but they are nonetheless disapproved of for acting in morally bad ways.

Scheler went further and developed a systematic ranking of the levels of greatness (or height of material value). On Scheler's theory, it is better to be a being that has the positive material value-property of being sensorily agreeable than sensorily unagreeable, all else being equal. It is better to be a being with positive vital value-properties than a being with negative vital value-properties; for example, it is better to have the material values of being healthy and strong than to be ill and weak. Further, it is better to be a being with positive spiritual values than negative spiritual values; in terms of the three types of spiritual values it is better to be aesthetically pleased than displeased, it is better to know philosophical truths than to be ignorant of them, and it is better to act in a morally right way than a morally wrong way. The material value of being morally good or right indicates how high in the scale of material or metaphysical values the moral value of being morally good is. It is higher than the value of healthiness, equal with the material value of philosophical knowledge and lower than the value of holiness. On the highest level, it is better to be holy than unholy.

Scheler also has a comparison between *the order of rank of the different levels of metaphysical greatness* or positive material value. A being that is *agreeable* and *vital* is of great metaphysical value, of higher material value, than a being that is agreeable (e.g. a cube of sugar) but lacks the capacity to realize vital values. A being that has positive *spiritual* values is greater than a being that has positive vital and agreeable values, but lacks the capacity to bear spiritual values. Finally, a being that is *holy* is a perfect being, the most metaphysically valuable being, the greatest being possible; if one possesses the value of holiness, one also possesses the 'absolute' properties, which is Scheler's term for omnipotence, omniscience, perfect goodness and the personal creator on which all 'relative' or created beings are dependent.

FURTHER READING

Brentano, F. 1969. *The Origin of our Knowledge of Right and Wrong*, R. Chisholm & E. Schneewind (trans.). New York: Humanities Press.

Deeken, A. 1974. *Process and Permanence in Ethics: Max Scheler's Moral Philosophy*. New York: Paulist Press.

Eucken, R. 1916. *The Meaning and Value of Life*, Lucy Judge Gibson & W. R. Boyce Gibson (trans.). London: Black.

Hartmann, N. 1932. *Ethics*, S. Colt (trans.). New York: Macmillan.

Heidegger, M. 1962. *Being and Time*, J. Macquarie & E. Robinson (trans.). New York: Harper & Row.

Smith, Q. 1986. *The Felt Meanings of the World: A Metaphysics of Feeling*. West Lafayette, IN: Purdue University Press.

Smith, Q. 1988. "An Analysis of Holiness". *Religious Studies* **24**: 511–27.

Staude, J. 1969. *Max Scheler*. New York: Free Press.

On BEING see also Chs 10, 11, 14. On FAITH see also Ch. 18; Vol. 1, Ch. 13; Vol. 2, Chs 6, 12, 16, 18; Vol. 3, Ch. 8; Vol. 4, Chs 8, 10, 13.

8

MARTIN BUBER

Tamra Wright

Martin Buber (1878–1965) is best known in philosophical and theological circles for his dialogical philosophy of the I–thou relation, and within Jewish studies for his collections of Hasidic tales. These seemingly disparate writings are linked, together with Buber's mature work on the Bible, philosophical anthropology, Zionism and other subjects, by his central concern: the relationship between human beings and God or the 'Eternal Thou'.

Buber was born in February 1878 in Vienna. His parents separated when he was a young child and he went to live with his paternal grandparents in Galicia. Initially, he assumed that he was only there temporarily and that his mother would return for him. In his "Autobiographical Fragments", Buber describes the moment when he realized that she was never coming back, and says that everything he subsequently wrote about 'genuine meeting' had its origin in that moment (1967a: 3–4).

Buber's grandfather, Solomon Buber, was a respected scholar who published the first modern editions of Midrash. During the years that Buber spent with his grandparents he participated in Jewish religious life. However, when he returned to his father's house in Vienna at the age of fourteen, he abandoned Jewish observance and became interested in philosophy. At the universities of Vienna, Leipzig, Berlin and Zurich, between 1896 and 1899, he studied philosophy together with history of art, German literature and psychology.

Towards the end of his student years, Buber re-engaged with Judaism by joining the Zionist movement. He advocated a form of Zionism that would foster a cultural and spiritual renaissance of the Jewish people. He also developed a scholarly interest in mysticism and turned his attention to Hasidism, publishing collections of Hasidic tales in 1906 and 1908 (see Buber 1956, 1969).

Buber worked closely with Franz Rosenzweig from 1921 until Rosenzweig's death in 1929. He taught at the Frankfurt Freies Jüdisches Lehrhaus (the well-known centre for Jewish adult education that Rosenzweig ran) from 1922, and collaborated with Rosenzweig on a translation of the Hebrew Bible into German, which he completed after Rosenzweig's death. Buber also held a lectureship in Jewish religious studies and ethics at Frankfurt University.

Under the Nazi regime, Buber was banned from teaching publicly. He moved from Germany to Jerusalem in 1938, where he held a professorship at the Hebrew University. He lived and taught in Jerusalem until his death in 1965.

Although Buber was a prolific writer, *I and Thou*, published in 1923, remains his best-known philosophical work. It marks the transition from his mystically inspired early works to his mature philosophy of dialogue. Buber's subsequent philosophical works build on this foundation. In *The Knowledge of Man* (1965a), Buber develops an epistemology based on the I–thou relation. *Paths in Utopia* (1949a) presents his vision of utopian socialism. His last major work, *Eclipse of God* (1952), argues that God is not dead but is temporarily hidden. However, Buber's final writings intimated that he had begun to perceive "a speaking through the silence" (1967b: 716).

THE TRANSITION TO DIALOGICAL PHILOSOPHY

Buber's early work reflects his immersion in the study of different mystical traditions and their emphasis on the quest for unity. The romantic hermeneutic at work in his early collections of Hasidic tales focuses on the unity of the reader or writer and the teller of the original tale. Similarly, Buber's early philosophical writings emphasize the quest for unity. In *Daniel: Dialogues on Realization* (1965b), Buber describes two ways of being in the world. 'Orientation' refers to the world of ordinary experiences, whereas 'realization' refers to "that enhanced meaning of life which springs from moments of intensified existence and intensified perception" (Friedman 1991: 36). The path of realization is that of unifying one's subjectivity with the other. To enter into true relation with a tree, one must "receive the tree; surrender yourself to it, until you feel its bark as your skin, and the force of a branch spring from its trunk like the striving in your muscles" (Buber 1965b: 54).

In Buber's mature writing, from the period of *I and Thou* onwards, this emphasis on unifying the self and the other is replaced with a dialogical account of relation, in which the distinction between self and other is always maintained. Different explanations have been offered for this radical change in Buber's thinking. In his "Autobiographical Fragments", Buber relates an episode that may have contributed to this shift. After spending a morning in religious contemplation, Buber was visited at his home by a young man. Although Buber received him warmly, devoted time to him and answered all of the questions he asked, he realized later that he had not been fully engaged in the conversation and, therefore, had been unable to discern that his visitor had sought out his company because of some deep existential need that went unmet:

> Later, not long after, I learned from one of his friends – he was no
> longer alive – the essential content of these questions; I learned that
> he had come to me not casually but borne by destiny, not for a chat
> but for a decision ... What do we expect when we are in despair and
> yet go to a man? Surely a presence by means of which we are told that
> nevertheless there is meaning.   (1967a: 26)

The young man had not committed suicide; rather, he was killed at the front in
the First World War (Friedman 1991: 80). Buber's point in the fragment is that he
was absent in spirit when his full presence was required. From this experience, he
derived a lesson about 'religious experience'. "Since then I have given up the 'religious' which is nothing but the exception, extraction, exaltation, ecstasy; or it has
given me up" (1967a: 26). In place of the pursuit of mystical experience, Buber
relates, he was 'converted' to a religiosity of the everyday: "I possess nothing but
the everyday out of which I am never taken ... I know no fullness but each mortal
hour's fullness of claim and responsibility" (*ibid.*).

Buber's new sense of the dangers of mystical pursuits and the desire for union
may also have been triggered by his friend Gustav Landauer's critique of Buber's
initial enthusiasm for the First World War. Buber at first thought that the heroic
mood in Germany had "initiated an epoch of unconditioned action in which
one realizes one's *Erlebnisse* in their fullness and thereby gains 'a connectedness
with the Absolute'" (Mendes-Flohr 1989: 18). He initially saw the tragedy of war
as being of "marginal import compared to the war's metaphysical significance"
(Mendes-Flohr 1989: 18).

In May 1916, Landauer wrote to Buber, criticizing both his "perverse" politics
and the asocial metaphysics from which they were derived. All of Buber's public
statements subsequently show him to be completely opposed to the war (Mendes-
Flohr 1989: 102). Buber also began to address one of the key themes in Landauer's
own teaching, the insistence that transformation of inter-human relations is
needed prior to any attempt to change the quality of spiritual life (*ibid.*: 19).

Rivka Horwitz offers a different explanation of Buber's shift from the mystical
quest for unity to the philosophy of dialogue. According to Horwitz, the key factor
was the influence of Rosenzweig. Rosenzweig's influence can be demonstrated
through a comparison of the text of Buber's "Religion as Presence" lectures,
delivered at the Frankfurt Lehrhaus in 1922, to the different drafts of *I and Thou*
(Horowitz 1988: 193–205). On the basis of this comparison, Horwitz argues that
the dialogical basis of the I–thou was a late addition to a pre-existing structure
(*ibid.*: 194) and that many of the inconsistencies and puzzling formulations of *I
and Thou* can be explained, at least in part, as arising from the imperfect fusion of
two different approaches (*ibid.*).

In *I and Thou* Buber relies on a simple binary distinction to form the foundation of a multifaceted philosophy. The two terms, which he introduces on the
first page of his poetical book, are I–it and the more famous I–thou (Buber 1970:

53).[1] I–it refers to our ordinary mode of engaging with things in the world. We treat them as means to our own ends; we engage with them only on a superficial level; and our knowledge of them is mediated by concepts and categories. There is nothing inherently wrong with this way of relating to objects, and even human beings must often be related to in the mode of I–it rather than that of I–thou. Indeed, Buber acknowledges the absolute necessity of I–it. However, it is of paramount importance for Buber that when I relate to an object or person in the mode of I–it, I am not fully engaged in the world. The self that engages in I–it relations is the 'limited I'.

Buber contrasts this mode of being with the I–thou relation, in which I relate to the other with my whole being. In this encounter, I open myself to the other. I relinquish any thought of objectives or desired outcomes; and the limited, indirect knowledge of the I–it mode of experience is replaced with a deeper, unmediated knowledge. Most importantly, for Buber, I emerge from the encounter with a sense of confirmation of my being and an affirmation that existence itself is meaningful.

Although the I–it/I–thou distinction parallels Buber's earlier distinction between 'orientation' and 'realization', the crucial difference between 'realization' and I–thou is that, in the latter, unification of self and other is no longer the aim of the relation. Buber does, however, see mutuality as a key feature of the fully actualized dialogical relation: just as I address the other as my thou, the other says thou to me. Both parties to the encounter emerge from it with a sense of confirmation of their being and the affirmation that existence is meaningful.

Buber understands I–thou as potentially functioning in three spheres of relation: our life with nature; our engagement with fellow human beings; and our connection with 'forms of spirit', including religious and artistic inspiration as well as God or the 'Eternal Thou'. He acknowledges that the I–thou with nature cannot be fully reciprocal; unlike the relation with human beings, the thou spoken to plants and animals "remains at the threshold of language" (1970: 56).

THE ETERNAL THOU

Buber's aim in writing *I and Thou* was to help overcome the 'sickness of the age' by awakening his readers to the potential for I–thou relation. He believed that the dominance of the I–it mode of being in modern life had nearly destroyed individuals' awareness of, and therefore their capacity for, I–thou encounter. Part I of *I and Thou*, with its highly poetic descriptions of I–thou, is designed to invoke the reader's recollection of their own experience of encounter, and to provoke a desire

---

1. All quotations use Walter Kaufmann's translation of *I and Thou* (Buber 1970). However, for the sake of consistency I have followed Ronald Gregor Smith in translating '*du*' as 'thou' rather than 'you'.

for future I–thou. The book is divided into three parts. In the third part, Buber introduces a concept that is central to his dialogical philosophy, but only alluded to briefly earlier on: the idea of the Eternal Thou. Part one states simply that in each thou "we address the eternal Thou" (1970: 57). In part three Buber makes it clear that this is not an added extra of I–thou relationships, but is constitutive of them. "The mediatorship of the Thou of all beings accounts for the fullness of our relationships to them" (*ibid.*: 123). In other words, to overcome the 'sickness of the age', we need to not only open ourselves to mutually affirming encounters with others but at the same time be prepared to address, and be addressed by, the Eternal Thou.

The Eternal Thou cannot be equated with the God of philosophy or even the God of much theological discourse. Buber emphatically denied that he was a theologian. He insisted that there can be no *logos* of God: God can only be 'addressed', never 'asserted' or 'expressed'. He refers to God as the 'Eternal Thou' because, unlike every other thou, God can never become an it (1970: 147). This is one of the central claims of Buber's philosophy of religion. In order to understand it, we must remember that 'I–it' and 'I–thou' are 'word pairs', rather than a simple combination of the constituent terms. According to Buber, we do not really know what 'I', 'it' and 'thou' are in themselves, we know 'I', 'it' or 'thou' only as we experience them in the moment of either I–it relation or I–thou encounter (Kohanski 1982: 108). As stated earlier, one of the key characteristics of I–thou encounter is that one engages in such a relation with one's whole being, that is, by gathering within oneself all of one's cognitive, volitional and affective experiences and conjoining them into a oneness in one's own essence (*ibid.*: 106). Buber argues that it is only possible to relate to the Absolute or the Eternal Thou with such wholeness of being, and therefore an I–it relation with God is not possible (Kohanski 1982: 108).

According to Buber, God cannot be deduced from either nature or history. Rather, the God of whom Buber speaks is "what confronts us immediately and first and always" (Buber 1970: 129). As such, even a self-proclaimed atheist can be in relation with the Eternal Thou: "whoever abhors the name and fancies that he is godless – when he addresses with his whole devoted being the Thou of his life that cannot be restricted by any other, he addresses God" (*ibid.*: 124).

Whereas in his earlier writings Buber had presented unity of self and other as the ideal form of relation, in *I and Thou* he explicitly rejects the ideal of renouncing the ego, insisting that "the I is indispensable for any relation, including the highest, which always presupposes an I and a Thou" (*ibid.*: 126). He does, however, distinguish between unification of the soul – in which "all forces are concentrated into the core" of the self and distractions are eliminated – and unification with the other. The former is a necessary stage of preparation for a full spiritual life; the latter is a dangerous distraction from the I–thou encounter in the world of the everyday (*ibid.*: 134–5). He also rejects renunciation of the world. According to his dialogical philosophy, one actualizes the relation with the Eternal Thou, not by turning away from the world, but by learning to see the world in the Thou (*ibid.*: 126).

In the concluding pages of *I and Thou* Buber elaborates his vision of a fully actualized person and society. The ideal would not be to refrain from I–it relations, which is impossible in any case, but to allow the relation with the Eternal Thou to imbue all of life with meaning. Each person's life should be so permeated with true I–thou relation that moments of encounter are not transient, like "flashes of lightning in the dark"; rather, they should be like "a rising moon in a clear starry night" (*ibid.*: 163). Individuals who experience their life in this way would form an ideal community, whose centre is the Eternal Thou. For Buber, it is the lines of relation between each person and the Eternal Thou that create true community (*ibid.*: 163).

I–thou encounter does not simply provide individuals and communities with a general affirmation that existence is meaningful. In the moment of encounter there is also revelation of a commandment. In part one, Buber discusses the process of artistic inspiration: a work of art arises when "a human being confronts a form that wants to become a work through him" (*ibid.*: 60). Buber sees both religiosity and ethical action as similarly originating in a response to the thou. Encounter is a form of revelation, where what is revealed is both the general affirmation of the meaningfulness of life, and a more specific commandment to the particular individual. In the same way that the artist cannot express in words the form that presents itself in encounter, but can only attempt to create the artwork itself, the person who receives revelation cannot articulate its content to others, but can only strive to fulfil the commanded deed.

For Buber, the ethical and religious spheres merge in the individual's spontaneous encounter with the Eternal Thou (Kohanski 1982: 93). His ethics is ultimately based on the self's relation to the Eternal Thou. Buber presents his approach to responsibility as the transcendence of normative ethics. "Duties and obligations one has only towards the stranger", he writes. But someone who "always has God before him" will be kind and loving towards others, and able – indeed, required – to leave the third-person dictates of ethics behind (Buber 1970: 157). Buber acknowledges that inherited precepts can be helpful (1967b: 718), but argues that a universally valid systematic ethics, which could dictate in advance the correct response in a given situation, is impossible (*ibid.*: 717). According to his philosophy, there is no way of knowing in advance when it will be sufficient to act in accordance with traditional moral prescriptions and when one will need to forge one's own response to a unique situation. For Buber, the key point is that whether I choose to follow traditional teachings or to create my own response, I am equally responsible for the course of action I choose. My task is to discern the correct course of behaviour as a response to the relation with the Eternal Thou. Although his emphasis on spontaneity has led some critics to suggest that his ethics is relativistic, Buber strenuously denied the charge: "I have never made a secret of the fact that I cannot hold the decision of a man … as to what is right and wrong in a certain situation to be a decision valid *in itself*. In my view, rather, he must understand himself as standing every moment under the judgment of God" (*ibid.*: 719).

Buber's insistence that revelation is without expressible content differentiates him from mainstream Jewish theology. However, he does not deny that Judaism has content in the form of dogmas. On the contrary, the notions of revelation, monotheism and human freedom are central to his understanding of Judaism (Breslauer 1980: 119). Emil Fackenheim explains the philosophical reasoning that allows Buber both to describe revelation as 'without expressible content' and to maintain concepts such as revelation and monotheism. According to Fackenheim, Buber is able to reject doctrinal statements about God and still know that God is eternal and infinite, because these attributes are not known through speculation but through I–Thou[2] encounter itself (Fackenheim 1967: 287). God's eternity and infinity are, in effect, the minimum content of any revelation. Similarly, human freedom for Buber is not a postulate of reason but something that is concretely revealed in the I–Thou encounter: one discovers one's own freedom to respond.

At the same time as revealing God's eternity and human freedom, the moment of encounter also includes specific content. Fackenheim explains that this is possible because in each encounter there remains an independent human I and the I, of course, is finite and temporal. The Eternal Thou speaks to the human I in its concrete situation. The specific content of the revelation is thus a mixture of the divine speech and human response (*ibid.*: 287–8). This idea is similar to a traditional Jewish view of prophecy: according to Moses Maimonides (*see* Vol. 2, Ch. 11), all of the prophets, with the exception of Moses, transformed the word of God even as they transmitted it.[3]

For Buber, every human being is in this sense potentially a prophet: able to enter into I–Thou relation with the Eternal Thou and receive a specific commandment through revelation. Buber, however, insists that the revelation is 'without expressible content' because he is convinced of the impossibility of ascertaining precisely which elements of the revelation constitute, as it were, the pure word of God, and which aspects are contributed by the human being. This is true of ethical decision-making, religious responsiveness and biblical interpretation.

REVELATION AND INTERPRETATION

Buber's concern about biblical interpretation in particular is emphasized in one of the episodes of his "Autobiographical Fragments". In "Samuel and Agag", Buber recounts a journey with an acquaintance, an observant Jew. They found themselves

---

2. I have reserved the use of capitalization of the word 'Thou' in 'I–Thou' for contexts that refer specifically to the encounter with the 'Eternal Thou'.
3. Moses Maimonides, *Mishne Torah, Hilkhot Yesodey HaTorah* 7:6.

discussing the Book of Samuel and, within it, the episode in which King Saul is told by the prophet that he will be punished for having spared the life of Agag, the conquered prince of the Amalekites. Agag protested to Samuel, "Surely the bitterness of death is past" (1 Samuel 15:32), but was nevertheless hewn to pieces by the prophet. Buber told his companion, "I have never been able to believe that this is a message of God". Questioned by his interlocutor, Buber went on to explain his belief that Samuel had misunderstood God and, much to his relief, his companion concurred with this idea. Commenting on this exchange, Buber reflects at length on the difficulty of separating God's word from human additions and distortions:

> Man is so created that he can understand, but does not have to understand, what God says to him … Already in hearing he blends together command of heaven and statute of earth, revelation to the existing being and the orientation that he arranges himself. Even the holy scriptures of man are not excluded, not even the Bible. (1967a: 32)

The passage presents Buber's explanation of how Saul could make such a grave error. But the continuation of the passage complicates matters further. Although Buber asserts that nothing could make him "believe in a God who punishes Saul because he has not murdered his enemy",[4] he nevertheless qualifies the statement:

> And yet even today I still cannot read the passage that tells this otherwise than with fear and trembling. But not it alone. Always when I have to translate or to interpret a biblical text, I do so with fear and trembling, in an inescapable tension between the word of God and the words of Man. (*Ibid.*: 33)

If Buber was so certain that God would not punish Saul for refraining from murder, why did he read the passage with fear and trembling? Although this seems paradoxical, it fits with Buber's account of ethics and his general dialogical philosophy. As discussed above, Buber sees ethics as being absolute, because in every situation one's actions are subject to divine judgement, yet at the same time, there is no universal law or code of ethics that can be consulted and simply followed. The agent is fully responsible for their choice of action, but has no way of knowing for sure that the choice is the correct one. Similarly, Buber's awareness that human beings mix their own ideas with divine revelation, in such a way that it is difficult to know how to separate the two, entails an understanding that any

---

4. This is perhaps one of the statements that led Emmanuel Levinas to charge that Buber sometimes "reads the Bible as if he possessed the entire Holy Spirit all by himself" (Levinas 1994: 13).

human interpretation of Scripture is potentially mistaken or distorted – including Buber's own.

Buber's view that divine revelation can never enter the world in an undistorted form leads him to be critical of organized religion. He distinguishes between 'religiosity' – the spontaneous response to the unconditioned or the Eternal Thou – and 'religion', that is, formal systems of laws, rituals and ceremonies (Kohanski 1982: 157). According to Buber's understanding, religions emerge from genuine, spontaneous encounters with the Eternal Thou. However, the I–Thou relation is by its nature fleeting, lacking continuity in both time and space. Human beings tend to try to overcome this; they turn God into an 'object of faith' to fill the gaps between moments of encounter, and they create cultic practices to represent the community's relationship to God. Over time, communal prayer and an objectified faith first supplement, and then eventually replace, genuine relation with God (Buber 1970: 162). As a reaction to this, reformers arise who try to reintroduce spontaneity and genuine encounter to religious life.

Given this understanding of the development of religions, it is not surprising that Buber's approach to Judaism focuses on biblical texts (representing moments of genuine encounter) and Hasidism (an attempt at reintroducing spontaneity and genuine encounter) rather than on rabbinic texts and *halacha* (Jewish law). Buber sees a unifying theme in the different books and genres of the Bible: it is concerned with I–Thou encounters with God, or in the words of his 1926 essay "The Man of Today and the Jewish Bible", with "the encounter between a group of people and the Lord of the world in the course of history" (1982: 1). According to to Buber, despite their differences, all genres of biblical writing engage with this theme:

> Either openly or by implication, the stories are reports of encounters. The songs lament the denial of the grace of encounter, plead that it may be repeated, or give thanks because it has been vouchsafed. The prophecies summon man who has gone astray to turn, to return to the region where the encounter took place, promising him that the torn bond shall once more be made whole. (*Ibid.*: 1)

The Bible is therefore able to speak to readers of all generations because it deals with a timeless concern: the yearning for encounter with the Eternal Thou.

Buber was, however, less enthusiastic in his assessment of rabbinic literature. Although he found much of religious value in the *aggadic* (non-legal) portions of the Talmud, the rabbinic emphasis on study and obedience of *halacha* (Jewish law) is clearly in tension with Buber's own emphasis on spontaneity and openness in the religious and moral sphere. He was frustrated by both the legalism of the ancient rabbis and the rationalism of much subsequent Jewish philosophy, and felt the need to "extricate the unique character of Jewish religiosity from the rubble with which rabbinism and rationalism have covered it" (1967c: 81). Buber saw in the *aggadic* portions of the Talmud, including stories about the lives and teachings of the sages, a truer expression of the authentic religious spirit of Judaism. He was particularly interested in the 'teaching' to which the texts bear witness. Buber's concept of such teaching involves a person who is a living model of religiosity, whose teaching cannot be reduced to a set of ideas that can be transmitted in verbal form (Breslauer 1980: 50). This concept of 'teaching' is a sort of human analogue of the revelation 'without expressible content' that results from the encounter with the Eternal Thou.

Unlike his contemporary Leo Baeck, who saw rabbinic Judaism as a harmonious blend of law and folklore, Buber believed that the tension between *halacha* and *aggadah* meant that rabbinic Judaism was not unified and therefore could not provide a healthy model of Jewish religiosity (*ibid.*: 51). Instead, he turned to Hasidism as a contemporary model of authentic Judaism. He thought that Hasidism succeeded where rabbinic Judaism had failed; it integrated structure and spirituality and "cultivated the growth of the religious ideal – a life lived in the categories of 'teaching'" (*ibid.*: 53). Hasidism was not "a teaching which was realized by its adherents in this or that measure, but a way of life" (Buber 1958: 41).

Gershom Scholem and other scholars have criticized Buber's collections of Hasidic tales and his understanding of Hasidism. However, scholarly concerns as to the historic accuracy of Buber's presentation need not detain us. Hasidism represents, for Buber, a concrete example of a community that embodies true religiosity. Buber's (admittedly idealized) Hasidic community has God, or the Eternal Thou, at its centre. Its members do not see their religion as simply a body of laws and dogmas, but as a holistic way of life. Their teachers, the *tzaddikim* (saintly, righteous people), are examples of righteous living, whose teaching cannot be separated from their own individual personalities and life stories, and their *rebbes* (teachers and spiritual leaders) do not allow legalism and tradition to stifle the drive towards religious innovation that results from selfless attention to the address of the Eternal Thou (Breslauer 1980: 60). Buber himself never became a Hasid, nor did he expect his readers to do so. But he saw himself as a true disciple of the Hasidic masters, in that he was able to transmit the religious teaching of Hasidism in a new age and context.

THE ECLIPSE OF GOD

Buber's own writings, however, open the possibility that neither his general philosophy of religion nor his renewal of Hasidic teaching is entirely adequate in a post-Holocaust age. As noted above, part three of *I and Thou* shows that Buber saw a relationship with the Eternal Thou as essential to ethics, to authentic communal life and to providing the individual with confirmation that human life is meaningful. Yet the possibility of such a relationship in a post-Holocaust age is called into question by many Jewish thinkers, not least by Buber himself.

Buber's use of the phrase 'eclipse of God' to describe the contemporary age is well known. The phrase evokes the traditional Jewish notion of *hester panim* ('the hiding of the face') and may sound as though it were used by Buber specifically to describe the silence, or absence, of God during the Holocaust. In fact, Buber used the phrase to refer to the entire twentieth century, which he saw as a time of spiritual and moral decline. The closing pages of *Eclipse of God* repeat an idea first presented in *I and Thou*: the contemporary age is 'sick', and its sickness consists in the ever-increasing preponderance of I–it:

> The I of this relation, an I that possesses all, makes all, succeeds with all, this I that is unable to say Thou, unable to meet a being essentially, is the lord of the hour. This selfhood that has become omnipotent, with all the It around it, can naturally acknowledge neither God nor any genuine absolute which manifests itself to men as of non-human origin. It steps in between and shuts off from us the light of heaven.
>
> (1952: 167)

It is interesting to note, however, that Buber did not end the book with this image of despair. Indeed, as Fackenheim observed (1970: 61), the impermanence of an eclipse means that it is, in a sense, a hopeful image. Buber himself wrote, "The eclipse of the light of God is no extinction; even tomorrow that which has stepped in between may give way" (1952: 167).

The image of an 'eclipse of God' is consonant with a major theme of Buber's biblical hermeneutics: that of the alternation between the presence and absence of God in the history of Israel. In his 1949 work *The Prophetic Faith*, Buber traces the changing nature of the relationship between God and Israel. He emphasizes the intimacy of God with the patriarchs and with Moses, and explores the distancing that occurs at other times, such as when the Israelites sin by worshipping the golden calf (Exodus 32). Moses and subsequent prophets attempt to overcome this distance by bringing the people back to the true service of God. Much of *The Prophetic Faith* emphasizes the role of human decision-making in bringing the Messiah, and as such fails to address the issues raised by the Holocaust. However, Buber does discuss the suffering of the innocent in the final chapter. He focuses on the 'suffering Messiah' of Deutero-Isaiah, and also draws on the Book of Job and the Psalms to further develop the theme. Buber does not explicitly link these texts to the Shoah; nevertheless, it seems likely that Buber concluded the work with images of human suffering as a way of struggling with the theological issues raised by the Holocaust (Kepnes 1992: 136).

Nevertheless, in *The Prophetic Faith* Buber's reading of Job emphasizes not the antitheodic moment of protest, but the eventual re-establishment of Job's relationship with God. At the end of the story, Job experiences God only "through suffering and contradiction, but even in this way he does experience God" (Buber 1949b: 192). Buber presents the Book of Job as a tale that "narrates the man of suffering, who by his suffering attained the vision of God" (*ibid.*: 197). Ultimately, this reading of Job focuses more on the conditions that make religious encounter possible than it does on the problem of evil (Braiterman 1998: 64).

By contrast, his 1952 essay "The Dialogue between Heaven and Earth", which also comments on Job, explicitly addresses the post-Holocaust situation and reaches a very different conclusion. Buber asks, "how is life with God still possible in a time in which there is an Auschwitz?" (1967c: 224). He understands that a person might still 'believe in' a God who permitted the Shoah to happen, but he questions the possibility of encounter with the Eternal Thou in the aftermath of the Holocaust.

> Can one still hear His word? Can one still, as an individual and as a people, enter at all into a dialogical relationship with Him? Dare we recommend to the survivors of Auschwitz, the Job of the gas chambers: 'Give thanks unto the Lord, for He is good; for His mercy endureth forever'?   (1967c: 224)[5]

By raising the question as to the possibility of dialogical relationship with God, Buber implicitly acknowledges that the basis of his entire philosophy of religion may be called into question by the Shoah. A central claim of *I and Thou* was that God is always present: it is human beings who absent themselves from the relationship (1970: 147). In "Dialogue between Heaven and Earth", Buber does not suggest that the 'eclipse of God' is the fault of human beings; the corollary of this lack of responsibility is that we do not have the power to bring about the end of the 'eclipse'. The concluding paragraph of the essay suggests that the most that can be expected of the Jewish people is that they await God's reappearance, in a stance that combines faithfulness with the willingness to 'contend' with God and to recognize his cruelty:

> And we? We – by this is meant all those who have not got over what happened and will not get over it. Do we stand overcome before the hidden face of God like the tragic hero of the Greeks before faceless fate? No, rather even now we contend, we too, with God, even with Him, the Lord of Being, whom we once chose for our Lord. We do not put up with earthly being, we struggle for its redemption, and struggling we appeal to the help of the Lord, who is again and still a hiding one. In such a state we await His voice, whether it comes out of the storm or out of a stillness that follows it. Though His coming

---

5. Buber is quoting a verse from Psalms that is one of the refrains of *Hallel* (a liturgical expression of praise of God the Redeemer).

appearance resembles no earlier one, we shall recognize again our
cruel and merciful Lord.   (1967c: 225)

Despite the antitheodic tone of these remarks and his recognition that "a time in
which there is an Auschwitz" is a fundamentally altered reality, Buber never revised
his dialogical thought to accord more fully with this changed reality. He consistently maintained that the teaching of the I–thou relation was the most important
insight in his life's work, and he eventually argued that the eclipse of God was not
something that "breaks off the divine revelation"; rather, it was an event "*between*
God and man*" (Friedman 1986: 173). In his final words on the eclipse of God,
Buber cautiously intimated that he himself had begun to perceive "a revelation
through the hiding of the face, a speaking through the silence" (Buber 1967b:
716). However, in keeping with his own teaching that the revelation of I–Thou is
one without expressible content, Buber did not elaborate; instead, he warned the
reader: "He, however, who today knows nothing other to say than 'See, there, it
grows lighter!' he leads into error" (*ibid.*: 716).

FURTHER READING

Atterton, P., M. Calarco & M. Friedman (eds) 2004. *Levinas and Buber: Dialogue and Difference.*
    Pittsburgh, PA: Duquesne University Press.
Breslauer, S. 1980. *The Chrysalis of Religion.* Nashville, TN: Abingdon.
Buber, M. 1970. *I and Thou*, W. Kaufmann (trans.). New York: Scribner's.
Kepnes, S. 1992. *The Text as Thou: Martin Buber's Dialogical Hermeneutics and Narrative
    Theology.* Bloomington, IN: Indiana University Press.

On I–THOU relation see also Ch. 2. On JUDAISM see also Ch. 15; Vol 1, Chs 9, 10; Vol. 2, Ch. 8;
Vol. 3, Ch. 15. On REVELATION see also Ch. 23; Vol. 1, Ch. 14; Vol. 2, Ch. 11; Vol. 3, Chs 7, 11,
16; Vol. 4, Chs 5, 11.

9

JACQUES MARITAIN

Peter A. Redpath

Jacques Maritain (1882–1973), maternal grandson of Jules Favre, a leading architect of the Third French Republic, was the only son of a divorced, virulently anti-Catholic, Protestant, rationalist mother, Geneviève Favre and her lawyer husband, Paul Maritain. Maritain spent 1898–9 studying at the Lycée Henri IV, where he became friends with Ernest Renan's grandson Ernest Psichari. In 1900 Maritain began studies at the Sorbonne, where he met his Jewish girlfriend and later wife, Raïssa Oumançoff, as well as Étienne Gilson and Charles Péguy, who took Jacques and Raïssa to attend Henri Bergson's course at the Collège de France. In 1905 he met his spiritual godfather, Léon Bloy. An early and outspoken opponent of anti-Semitism before the Second World War, Maritain was later appointed by Charles de Gaulle as leader of the Free French in the United States and as his representative to President Franklin D. Roosevelt during the war. A political liberal, turned conservative, turned again liberal, maybe turned again conservative, Maritain was actively involved in major political issues of his day. He was a personal friend, among others, of Mortimer J. Adler, Saul Alinsky, Marc Chagall, Paul Claudel, Jean Cocteau, Dorothea Day, Caroline Gordon, Julien Green, John Howard Griffin, Robert M. Hutchins, Walter Lippmann, Gabriel Marcel, Thomas Merton, Pope Paul VI, Yves R. Simon and Allen Tate. After the Second World War, de Gaulle appointed Maritain French ambassador to the Vatican. Together with Gilson, Maritain was a major architect in designing and founding the United Nations and UNESCO, and was a chief author of the UN Declaration on Human Rights. He was recipient of Pope Paul's "Message to Intellectuals" at the close of Vatican Council II, probably the chief influence on the development of post-Second World War Christian democratic movements throughout Europe and Latin America, and a main architect of the recent worldwide reconciliation between Catholics and Jews. Mortimer J. Adler has called him one of the three great philosophers of the twentieth century, Gilson and Bergson being the other two. Maritain's major writings include: *Antisemitism, Approaches to God, Bergsonian Philosophy and Thomism, Art and Scholasticism, A Christian Looks at the Jewish Question, Creative Intuition in Art and Poetry, The Dream of Descartes, Distinguish to Unite or the Degrees of Knowledge, Education at the Crossroads, Existence and the Existent, The Peasant of the Garonne, The Person and the Common Good, A Preface to Metaphysics: Seven Lectures on Being, The Range of Reason, Scholasticism and Politics, Reflections on America, The Twilight of Civilization* and *Science and Wisdom.*

Some readers of a book on the philosophy of religion might find startling the claim that Jacques Maritain never composed a work devoted to the philosophy of religion considered as such. Sometimes, the truth startles. A simple glance at the contents of the University of Notre Dame Jacques Maritain Center's *Collected Works of Jacques Maritain* or the sixteen-volume Fribourg (Switzerland) edition entitled *Oeuvres complètes de Jacques et Raïssa Maritain* (The complete works of Jacques and Raïssa Maritain; 1982–) reveals no title that Maritain devoted precisely to a study of the philosophy of religion. And some leading Maritain scholars readily admit that Maritain never wrote a work chiefly concerned with the philosophy of religion.

Since Maritain apparently never wrote an article or book specifically devoted to the philosophy of religion, anyone studying his works will have to compose such a philosophy from Maritain's existing writings. For many reasons, doing so is a difficult task.

To some extent Maritain had no philosophy of religion because (i) his life was his philosophy of religion and (ii) he never adequately distinguished his understanding of philosophy from his understanding of Christian theology. Ralph M. McInerny says, "Maritain was a philosopher who metamorphosed into a theologian" (2003: 3). Whether or not McInerny's claim is precisely true, there is no disputing his observation that the only way we can correctly understand Maritain's life is in terms of "the quest for Christian perfection, for sanctity" (*ibid.*: 210).

There is also no disputing that, from his mid twenties onwards, Maritain consciously considered himself to philosophize as a Thomist philosopher (*see* Vol. 2, Ch. 13, "Thomas Aquinas"). In 1908, shortly after his 1906 conversion to Catholicism, he reported experiencing an "irreducible conflict between the 'conceptual pronouncements'" of his newly acquired faith and the Bergsonian philosophical doctrine that freed him "from the idols of materialism" of the Sorbonne and had helped save him and Raïssa from committing suicide (cited in Raïssa Maritain 1945: 198–210).

At that time, Maritain reported, he had not yet become acquainted with the teachings of Thomas Aquinas:

> My philosophical reflection leaned upon the indestructible truth of objects presented by faith in order to restore the natural order of the intelligence to being, and to recognize the ontological bearing of the work of reason. Thenceforth, in affirming to myself, without chicanery or diminution, the authentic value as reality of our human instruments of knowledge, I was already a Thomist without knowing it. When,

> several months later, I was to meet the *Summa Theologica*, I would
> erect no obstacle to its luminous flood.   (cited *ibid.*: 210)

From that time on, in short, we may correctly state that, consciously aware of it or not, Maritain sought to philosophize *sub illuminatione Sancti Thomae* (under the illumination of St Thomas).

WHAT MARITAIN'S PHILOSOPHY OF RELIGION COULD NOT HAVE BEEN

This way of philosophizing constitutes part of the complexity of Maritain's thought for contemporary students. Today, in popular speech, we often identify 'religion' with 'God-talk'. We tend to think that all talk about God is a sort of religious speech. As a student of ancient philosophy and Aquinas, and a Catholic, Maritain would not make this sort of identification. All these traditions maintain, as many people still do today, that a person can talk about God, can accept God's existence, and not be religious.

Among other disciplines, ancient philosophers talked about gods in what they called 'theology', or as a branch of 'metaphysics', and in ethics. During the Middle Ages, Christian theologians started to distinguish the 'theology' of the ancient philosophers from the 'revealed theology' of Jews and Christians. They called 'natural theology' the philosophical theology, or theodicy, that investigated questions such as the possibility of proving God's existence by human reason unaided by grace-inspired faith. They called 'revealed theology' the supernatural theology that used faith-inspired reason to investigate God's revelation concerning human salvation.

When Maritain philosophized he consciously turned to Aquinas' revealed theological teaching (a teaching richly influenced by ancient philosophy). Aquinas well knew that for ancient philosophers such as Socrates, Plato and Aristotle (*see* Vol. 1, Chs 4, 5), every art or science presupposes, it does not prove, the existence of its subject. The science of dentistry, for example, does not prove the existence of teeth nor the science of medicine the existence of unhealthy people. Since Maritain well knew that, to some extent, God is the subject of revealed theology and philosophy of religion, he well knew that no science of theology or philosophy of religion can prove God's existence.

Nonetheless, Maritain maintained that human beings had many ways of knowing God's existence. Philosophically, we could demonstrate God's existence from a knowledge that starts in observing the behaviour of sensible things. Maritain thought that this is the way philosophers start to demonstrate everything. Maritain recognized that Aquinas' famous 'five ways' of reasoning from effect to cause (*demonstratio quia*) to God's existence proceeded in this way. He thought that all philosophical knowledge must, in some way, trace its origin to original sense knowledge.

But Maritain also recognized that other ways existed to come to a knowledge of God's existence unaided by supernatural faith. For example, he maintained that we can have a pre-philosophical, rational, "*virtually metaphysical*" knowledge of God's existence. This reportedly comes to us through a "primordial intuition" that we experience when we realize that the existence of other things threatens our existence by revealing to us our liability to death and nothingness. Simultaneously, and analogously, it reveals to us the utter independence of absolute existence over ourselves and other things (1967: 18–19).

Maritain also proposed a 'sixth way' of demonstrating God's existence from an intellectual intuition that we experience when we are able to raise our minds above sense and imagination and are concerned "with intelligible objects alone" (Maritain 1967: 70). In this act of contemplation, the spiritual operation of thought, Maritain maintains, we raise ourselves above time and experience ourselves as always existing, as existing in our cause. The self-as-thinking exists in the immediate present, in a spiritual way, devoid of movement, with no knowledge of past or future, superior to time (*ibid.*: 70–76).

WHAT MARITAIN'S PHILOSOPHY OF RELIGION SHOULD HAVE BEEN

Given Aquinas' heavy influence on Maritain, if we wish to understand Maritain's philosophy of religion, prudence dictates that we first turn to Aquinas to get a general understanding of how Aquinas considered the nature of religion. When we do so, we find Aquinas in the *Summa theologiae* (II.2.80.1) initially considering religion as a moral virtue, as "a potential part" (that is, species) of justice because the Roman rhetorician Marcus Tullius Cicero (*see* Vol. 1, Ch. 8) stated that religion "consists in conducting devotions and ceremonies to some superior nature, which people call divine" (*ibid.*).

The Catholic theologian Aquinas cited the pagan rhetorician Cicero to start to make intelligible the nature of religion because (i) Aquinas understood the theologian's job to involve the use of philosophy as a handmaiden to theology, and (ii) as he indicates in his *Commentary on the Metaphysics of Aristotle* (5.1.22), he well understood that philosophy, as the ancient Greeks and the Romans who followed them practised it, studied real relations and proper acts (essential accidents, or properties) of proximate acting subjects, of real beings causing real, universal, actions. For example, the acting subject 'Socrates the musician' is the universal, proximate, acting subject and generic cause of all the many specific musical acts (effects) that the habit of music enables Socrates to produce. These effects are different in kind from those that the proximate acting subject 'Socrates the mathematician' or the proximate acting subject 'Socrates the physician' produces because they arise from different habits and manifest different properties. While Socrates as Socrates is not essentially a mathematician, musician or physician, if Socrates happens to be a mathematician, musician or physician, he has properties that result from possessing these respective habits, properties that necessarily – that is, of *their* nature – make him a generically different acting subject.

Religion is an act, an act that free (moral) agents produce. Through their moral habits or virtues, free agents are the proximate acting subjects, the concrete causes (universal, or generic, causes) of specific religious acts just as the sun is the individually existing, concrete universal, or generic, cause of all the effects (species) it produces in the things it heats (Owens 1981: 148–65); and these effects analogously relate to the sun as their common cause or principle. No sun: no effects that the sun's heat produces. No individual free agents: no many, specific, analogously related religious acts. Hence, since philosophy studies concrete universals, cause–effect relations of substances as acting natures, real, proximate, generic, proper causes of many specific real actions (effects) that exist in these effects as their subject causes and first principles, the philosophical study of religion involves studying religious acts in light of their proximate, real, or concrete, generic, proper, or universal first principles and causes.

Aquinas' *Commentary on the Metaphysics of Aristotle* (7.1.22) indicates that he clearly understood philosophy to be the study of acting natures, of the concrete one and many, concrete genera, single causal natures naturally existing, in analogous ways, through their causal efficacy, in their many effects. Philosophy is not the study of abstract natures or essences. Logicians, not philosophers, study abstract essences. Philosophers chiefly study acting natures, not abstract essences. Hence, as Armand A. Maurer correctly notes (1963: 75), logicians chiefly talk in a univocal way. Their job is to refer one definition to many subjects in identically the same way, or according to the same relationship. But the philosopher's job is more nuanced. It demands the ability to refer one definition to many subjects in somewhat the same, somewhat different ways, or according to different relationships.

Hence, Aquinas tells us (*Summa theologiae* II.2.80.1) that the demands of a morally virtuous life give rise to, or cause, many specific kinds of just acts that we refer to an acting subject in many different ways (analogously). The moral virtue of justice necessarily inclines its possessor to perform many acts, such as to pay debts of one sort or another to render another person his or her due. A moral debt is one we have to satisfy to fulfil the demands of living a morally virtuous life, but we fulfil it in many ways. Hence we have to talk about religious activities in many different ways while referring to one chief definition that expresses religious action.

Because we can consider a debt from the perspective of the person owing or the person to whom something is owed (*ibid.*), Aquinas distinguishes the many species of justice that the virtue of religion involves by considering diverse kinds of human relationships (for example, to our parents, the state, God) and the demands these sorts of relationships place on us. By so doing, he concludes that, properly considered, "religion imports a relation to God" (*ibid.*).

Since, for Aquinas, religion imports a relation to God, and since Aquinas states (*Summa theologiae* II.2.81.5) that religion is a part of justice, religion is a moral, not a theological or intellectual, virtue. As such, strictly speaking, the subject matter of a Maritainian philosophy of religion should not be revelation, or revealed theology. Nor should it properly consider the relationship between faith and reason.

The subject matter of the virtue of religion is fitting worship of God. Such being the case, fitting worship of God, not God's existence, or the problem of the relation of faith and reason, is the proper subject matter of a genuine Maritainian philosophy of religion.

Since we are physical and psychological beings, Aquinas says (*Summa theologiae* II.2.81.7) that we fittingly worship God through internal and external acts. We do so for our own, not God's, perfection, because subjection to a legitimate superior perfects every inferior being. Consequently, the philosophy of religion should be the practical philosophical study of the proper internal and external human acts (the effects of the virtue of religion) that befit God the creator and governor of the universe. In short, Aquinas says (*Summa theologiae* II.2.82–91) religion is identical with sanctity, or holiness: with that principle of internal and external acts that dispose us properly to reverence God, such as devotion, prayer, adoration, sacrifice, offerings, tithes, vows, oaths and invocations.

NECESSARY POINTS OF CONSIDERATION

We cannot possibly do justice to any philosopher's teaching unless we first know what that philosopher thinks philosophy to be. Hence, we cannot possibly do justice to constructing a Maritainian philosophy of religion unless we first know what Maritain thought philosophy to be. By this point, I have established beyond reasonable doubt what, as Thomistic, a Maritainian philosophy of religion should be: a practical study, the ethical study, of the causes of sanctity or holiness and the internal and external acts that are proper to such a life. Maritain would concur with McInerny that, "A religious person is one whose life is devoted to the acquisition of perfection, of holiness" (2003: 49).

Having determined the subject matter of a Maritainian philosophy of religion (sanctity), what remains for me at this point is to: discuss Maritain's understanding of philosophy; explain why Maritain's failure to understand classical philosophy makes it difficult for us to construct a Maritainian philosophy of religion; and summarize the contents of a Maritainian philosophy of religion.

MARITAIN'S UNDERSTANDING OF PHILOSOPHY

Maritain's understanding of philosophy is identical with his understanding of ancient Greek philosophy. Maritain rightly understood (1959: 100–108; 1968: 100) that, in some way, sense-knowledge constituted the first principle of philosophy for all the leading ancient Greek philosophers.

The reason for this is simple. First principles are starting-points. And the starting-point of philosophy is something that, in some way, we know. If we know nothing we can ask no questions; and if we can question nothing, we can never do philosophy. Since the things we know through our senses and the senses through which we know them (not logical premises, Cartesian doubt, faith, impossible dreams of pure reason, or anything else) are the starting-points of all human knowledge, sensible beings and human sense faculties are philosophy's remote first principles. Since sensory knowledge is the starting-point of all human knowledge, and philosophy's starting-point is human knowledge and human experience, sensory knowledge to some extent must be a remote first principle of philosophy for everyone, everywhere, for all time.

Maritain maintained this simple philosophical truth with unswerving zeal. At the same time, he realized that philosophy is more than a sensing being and a being sensed. These first principles of human knowledge are necessary, not sufficient, conditions of philosophical activity.

Maritain nominally defined philosophy as "human wisdom" or "wisdom insofar as it is accessible to human nature" (1959: xiii). By wisdom accessible to human nature he understood philosophy to be "the scientific study of purely rational truths" (*ibid.*: 33). As a "science" Maritain understood philosophy to be "certain knowledge of causes" (*ibid.*: 76). As human knowledge of purely rational truths, he understood philosophy to be knowing the evidence of its object (objective formal principles, essences, or "first causes or highest principles *in the natural order*") by the natural faculty of the human intellect (*ibid.*: 77–8).

Hence, Maritain said "that the philosopher does not seek the explanation nearest to the phenomena perceived by our senses, but the explanation most remote from them, the ultimate explanation" (*ibid.*: 78). Philosophy concerns "*first causes*, highest principles, or ultimate explanations" (*ibid.*: 78). Maritain maintained that philosophy's material object, or subject matter, is everything. Its formal object, or aspect under which it studies everything, "is the *first causes* or highest principles of things in so far as these causes or principles belong to the natural order" (*ibid.*: 79). (By natural order, he did not mean the physical order. He meant a non-supernatural order.)

Strictly considered, Maritain maintained that philosophy is metaphysics, or wisdom, because "it is the province of wisdom to study the highest causes" (*ibid.*: 80). Thus, philosophy "grasps the entire universe in a small number of principles and enriches the intellect without burdening it" (*ibid.*). Considering philosophy in general to be a body, and metaphysics to be its head, Maritain defined "philosophy in general as a universal body of sciences whose formal standpoint is first causes (whether absolutely first causes or principles, the formal object of metaphysics, or the first causes in a particular order, the formal object of the other branches of philosophy)" (*ibid.*: 80). Given this definition, he maintained "that metaphysics alone deserves the name *wisdom* absolutely speaking (*simpliciter*), the remaining branches of philosophy only relatively or from a particular point of view (*secundum quid*)" (*ibid.*: 80).

MARITAIN'S MISUNDERSTANDING OF CLASSICAL PHILOSOPHY

In defining philosophy in general as a universal body of sciences, Maritain mistakenly thought he was following "the ancients". He said, "The ancients understood by the term *philosophy* the sum-total of the main branches of scientific study (*physics*, or the science of nature; *mathematics*, or the science of being as such; *logic*; and *ethics*)" (1959: 80 n.1). Maritain often used the term 'ancients' in an eccentric way to refer to classical thinkers, such as ancient Greeks and Romans, and/or to medieval thinkers. If by 'ancients' he meant ancient Greek philosophers, his claim is false.

None of the leading ancient Greek philosophers understood philosophy in this sort of nominalistic and logically and metaphysically reductionistic fashion. Socrates, Plato and Aristotle did not think of philosophy as a universal body of sciences. They thought of philosophy in terms of a habit of soul, as did Maritain's mentor, Aquinas. Maurer (1974) has established beyond reasonable doubt that, in the tradition of the ancients, (i) Aquinas chiefly understood philosophy to be a human habit, not a system or body of knowledge, and (ii) the notion of philosophy as a 'system' or body of knowledge arose with William Ockham (*see* Vol. 2, Ch. 15).

Maritain's misunderstanding of the nature of classical philosophy caused him to make several other mistakes regarding the nature of philosophy. He maintained that: (i) we find philosophy's basis in "common sense considered as the understanding of self-evident first principles"; (ii) philosophy's "matter is experience, and its facts the simplest and most obvious facts – the starting-point from which it rises to the causes and grounds which constitute the ultimate explanation"; and (iii) philosophy's "formal principles are the first principles apprehended in the concept of being, whose cogency consists wholly in their evidence for the intellect" (1959: 106).

Strictly speaking, Maritain was wrong about philosophy's basis, matter and formal principles. Philosophy's remote basis is philosophical knowers and beings capable of being philosophically known. Philosophy's proximate basis is its subject matter, and philosophy's subject matter contains philosophy's formal principles, which include the way of knowing of the philosophical knower. Philosophy's subject matter is not experience: it is 'wondrous experience', something philosophers, poets, theologians and many others share. For the ancient Greeks and for all time, philosophy begins in wonder, not in faith seeking understanding, universal methodic doubt or impossible dreams of pure reason.

Strictly speaking, philosophy's formal principles are not the first principles apprehended in the concept of being, metaphysical principles most remote from sensation. Philosophy's first principles are the proper causes of wonder, the acts of things and acts of human habits that give rise to wonder. While all these principles have their remote root in metaphysical principles and evident principles of common sense, as proper causes of wonder that generate different sciences such as physics and mathematics, not all these principles are metaphysical or commonsensical. How close these principles are to sensation depends on the subject matter, including the acting subject of philosophical wonder. Hence, the principles about which mathematicians wonder are more remote from sensation than are those about which a classical physicist wonders; and those of metaphysics are more remote from sensation than are those of mathematics.

In book 7 of his *Republic* (515b–531c), Plato makes clear that philosophical experience arises from conflicting, contrary, reports from our perception of specific subjects that cause our intellectual faculty immediately to start to consider whether our opposing communication arises from one perceived subject and perception or from two. *Experience of contrary opposition related to the same acting subject* (wonder) that we intellectually desire to put to rest, what Plato called 'provocative' thought, is the material principle of all philosophy. The causes of such provocative thought that put our wonder to rest are philosophy's formal principles. Philosophy studies subjects susceptible to contrary opposition in action in an attempt to discover the causes of the contrariety we experience in them.

Maritain understood philosophy's formal principles to be "a solid kernel of genuine *certainties*" that exist in ordinary human knowledge. Among these certainties that the philosopher recognizes he included: (i) "data of the senses (for example, that *bodies possess length, breadth, and height*)"; (ii) "self-evident axioms (for example, *the whole is greater than the part, every event has a cause*, etc.)"; and (iii) consequences immediately deducible from these axioms (proximate conclusions) (1959: 101).

Maritain maintained that these certainties spontaneously arise in the human mind "when we first come to the use of reason". Consequently, he called them "the work of nature in us", or "an endowment of nature as proceeding from the natural perception, consent, instinct, or natural sense of the intellect". Because human nature is the source of these evident first principles, Maritain stated that we could say they "belong to the common perception, consent, or instinct, or to the *common sense* of mankind" (*ibid.*: 101).

Maritain thought that, prior to Aristotle, we could consider philosophy as existing in a sort of "embryonic stage and in the process of coming to birth" (*ibid.*: 62). After Aristotle, he held, "its formation complete, it was capable of indefinite development, knew no bounds" (*ibid.*: 62). Along the path of this development, he said, "Socrates had shown that what we must seek and attain at all costs are the essences of things which the mind apprehends and expresses in a definition" (*ibid.*: 56). Maritain understood this to mean that philosophy must attain abstract universals, essences abstractly considered, abstracting from any particular, such as "*triangle*, abstracting from any particular triangle" (*ibid.*: 56–7).

Aquinas, on the contrary, held that the universal (genus) the philosopher studies primarily refers to the acting subject: the immediate, proximate, first or proper subject of different properties or necessary *per se* accidents. Hence, while Socrates the human being need not be a musician, if he is a musician his actions will display specific properties necessary to all musicians. The art of music studies this acting subject in terms of these properties. It does not study the abstractly considered essence studied by the logician. It studies the concretely existing nature, the essence considered as a concrete principle of action existing in a prox-imate acting subject (*Commentary on the Metaphysics of Aristotle* 5.1.22).

Surface is the proximate subject of all colours and plane figures. As such, it is the proximate subject of all surface accidents, such as colour and texture. Surface body, the subject of geometry, acts as the proximate subject of all figures subjec-tified in a quantified substance just as the musically habituated person acts as the proximate subject of all his or her musical acts. Hence, when we define a musical activity (a human accident, or property) philosophically, not logically, we have to define it as the proper or proximate effect that a musical person produces through musical habits just as we define geometrical activity in terms of the way we put together and take apart geometrical bodies. In so doing, analogously, the way we define resembles the way logicians define. In both instances, we include the genus in the definition of the species.

In both cases the definition of the species refers to its subject genus, its substance, for its intelligibility. But, philosophically considered, the musical substance or subject is a musically habituated person: the substantial body that acts as the subject genus, the proximate cause, of the acts of the musician. It is not the subject genus, or abstract essence, of the logician: the genus as an abstractly considered universal.

Aquinas added (*Commentary on the Metaphysics of Aristotle* 7.1.22) that the natural scientist and metaphysician consider and talk about a genus as the first, or proximate, subject of accidents, not as what we say of different categories of being (the abstract way a logician considers and talks about generic diversity). Clearly, these two ways of thinking and talking about a genus are radically different. In the case of the abstract way of considering essences of the logician, we must abstract from, separate our thought from considering, the existence of the acting subject (from the way natures act as proximate causes in reality) to grasp the principles according to which we must reason logically. In the case of the natural scientist and metaphysician, failure to consider the existence of the acting subject, the way natures act as proximate causes in reality, makes the principles of the subject's action philosophically or scientifically unintelligible. For this reason, Aquinas thought that univocal predication is the proper way of predicating terms for a logician and analogous predication of terms is the proper way of predicating for a philosopher (such as a physicist, geometrician, or metaphysician).

Apparently, Maritain was unaware of this distinction in Aquinas. For this reason, among others perhaps, I think he made a specious distinction between philosophy considered in its pure, or absolute, nature (philosophy as a body or system of knowledge) and philosophy existing in some state (philosophy as an existing habit). He said:

Considered in its pure *nature*, or essence, philosophy, which is spec-ified by an object naturally knowable to reason, depends on the evidence and criteria of natural reason. But here we are considering its absolute nature. Taken concretely, in the sense of being a *habitus* or group of *habitus* existing in the human soul, philosophy is in a certain state, in either pre-Christian or Christian or a-Christian, which has a decisive influence on the way it exists and develops.   (1938: 79)

Unhappily, philosophy as a pure nature or essence specified by an object naturally knowable to reason, philosophy as a system or body of knowledge, exists nowhere. It is a spectre of the abstractly considered essence of the logician. Strictly speaking, philosophy is the act of a human habit. It exists in philosophical activity, in the rational investigation of the causes of contrary opposition existing within the acts of a multitude of natural agents. For example, political philosophy exists in the political philosopher's investigation of the causes of war and peace within the acts of political bodies. And, philosophical consideration of medicine investigates the causes of health and disease within the actions of human bodies ranging from the sickliest to the healthiest.

Because Maritain failed at times to recognize this distinction, he reduced the principles of philosophy to metaphysical premises. He compounded this mistake by conflating metaphysical knowledge with theoretical, or speculative, thinking. Hence, he said, "Philosophy in the strictest sense is theoretical philosophy" (1959: 112). Then he conflated theoretical thinking with logic.

Having reduced all philosophy to theoretical philosophy, speculative logic, Maritain had boxed himself into a corner in which he was forced to conclude that, as a science, ethics is theoretical, not practical (*ibid.*: 111–12). Clearly, this contradicts the well-known teachings of Aristotle and Aquinas, for whom ethics is a practical, not theoretical, science. Worse, from the standpoint of constructing a philosophy of religion as a species of justice, as a Thomist should, it is incoherent.

Strictly speaking, if all philosophy is speculative, philosophy of religion as a species of justice cannot be practical. Justice, however, is a moral virtue. It must be practical.

Clearly, Maritain has a problem understanding how to explain practical philosophy. As I have said elsewhere, Maritain maintained that "speculative philosophy is *truly* philosophy, is *truly* scientific, because it looks at things from the perspective, or 'eidetic visualization,' of abstract universal essences; because it looks at things according to their 'intelligible values' rather than according to their 'actual conditions of contingence and singularity'" (Redpath 1987: 108). In short, Maritain thought that speculative philosophy is truly philosophy, is truly scientific, because it looks at things from the perspective of the logician. "Practical philosophy, on the other hand, considers things according to their actual conditions, and, in so doing, precludes itself from being scientific qua practical" (*ibid.*: 108).

Maritain attempted to resolve his misunderstanding of practical philosophy by maintaining that ethics can only become a practical science through subalternation to theology. Apart from theology, Maritain maintained that the practical science of ethics cannot know its proper object because understanding this object involves knowing the existential condition in which we exist towards our end. Since only theology, through grace, can know this end, can grasp theoretical and practical objects with all their detail, we need its mediation to transform the speculative essence of ethics into a concrete essence that we can apprehend in a fittingly scientific way. In so doing, Maritain nonetheless claimed that revealed theology and philosophical ethics remained formally distinct in their own objects and procedures (1938: 107–9; 1955a: 12, 68, 71, 86, 103 n.13; Redpath 1987: 107–9).

A SUMMARY OF THE MARITAINIAN PHILOSOPHY OF RELIGION

I maintain that Maritain could not, and cannot, give us a coherent philosophical account of the philosophy of religion because he never adequately understood philosophy's nature or how properly to distinguish philosophical universals from logical universals. The net result of this failure was that he could never adequately distinguish philosophy from theology. Consequently, while I agree with many of his conclusions and respect his intellectual genius, I reject Maritain's claim that he separated ethics as a philosophy from theology. Strictly speaking, Maritain maintained that philosophy is a science. Apart from theology, however, he claimed that ethics was no science. As such, it could be no philosophy, even as theoretical.

Such being the case, if we want to find a philosophy of religion in the work of Jacques Maritain we can only do so by benignly interpreting Maritain's mystical theology of religion to be philosophy. Maritain's philosophy of religion is his mystical theology of the life of holiness. From his spiritual godfather Léon Bloy, Maritain had learned every day to study Scripture, read the liturgy, the lives of the saints, and the writings of the mystics, and to have a special devotion to the Blessed Mother (McInerny 2003: 35). In one such work, *The Primacy of the Spiritual*, Maritain states, "Contemplation alone discovers the prize of charity … [O]nly contemplation makes the universal real for us, makes the soul Catholic in spirit and truth" (cited *ibid.*: 188).

Liturgy, worship, as McInerny tells us (*ibid.*: 189), is an act of religion. Like all acts of religion, it calls us to contemplation. Maritain thought that contemplation is philosophy's goal, its *telos*, and the goal, *telos*, of the Christian life. Maritain maintained that ethics as theoretical philosophy drives us toward contemplation by driving us toward scientific moral action. It does this because philosophical ethics is theoretically inadequate to provide us with a scientific awareness of the end of our action.

This means that ethics drives us towards liturgy and prayer to move us towards contemplation. According to Maritain, "Contemplation is a silent prayer which comes about in recollection in the secret of the heart and is directly ordered to union with God" (cited *ibid.*: 189). As such, McInerny rightly notes, "it is a gift".

For this reason, Maritain thought that "religion is ordered to the further end of the theological virtues and the gifts" (*ibid.*). As McInerny, quoting Maritain, says:

> What the liturgy "asks of the soul, and to which it incites, the liturgy of itself does not suffice to give. There is need of a personal ascetic effort, the personal practice of mental prayer, aspiration to personal union with God and personal docility to the Gifts of the Holy Spirit".
>
> (*Ibid.*: 189)

Maritain's philosophy of religion, then, consists in religious activity as handmaiden to mystical contemplation. In the end, for Maritain, the be-all and end-all of religion and the philosophy of religion is a call to the life of mystical theology through private and public prayer and sanctity.

FURTHER READING

Dougherty, J. 2003. *Jacques Maritain: An Intellectual Profile*. Washington, DC: Catholic University of America Press.

Maritain, J. 1931. *Religion and Culture*. London: Sheed & Ward.

Maritain, J. 1931. *The Things That Are Not Caesar's*. New York: Scribner's.

Maritain, J. 1959. *Distinguish to Unite; or, The Degrees of Knowledge*, G. B. Phelan (supervision of trans.). New York: Scribner's.

Maritain, J. 1964. *Moral Philosophy*. New York: Scribner's.

Maritain, J. 1968. *Integral Humanism*. New York: Scribner's.

Maritain, J. 1972. *On the Church of Christ*. Notre Dame, IN: University of Notre Dame Press.

Ollivant, D. (ed.) 2002. *Jacques Maritain and the Many Ways of Knowing*. Washington, DC: Catholic University of America Press.

Redpath, P. A. (ed.) 1990. *From Twilight to Dawn: The Cultural Vision of Jacques Maritain*. Notre Dame, IN: University of Notre Dame Press, for the American Maritain Association.

Schall, J. 1998. *Jacques Maritain: The Philosopher in Society*. Lanham, MD: Rowman & Littlefield.

On THOMISM see also Ch. 20; Vol. 2, Ch. 13.

10

KARL JASPERS

Kurt Salamun

Jaspers was born in the city of Oldenburg in the northern part of Germany in 1883. He studied medicine at the universities of Munich, Göttingen and Heidelberg. Early in his youth he had to recognize that he was inflicted with an incurable lung disease that significantly influenced his daily physical activities. Jaspers did not begin his academic career as a professional philosopher. He wrote his doctoral thesis (1909) on a psychiatric problem and worked for some years as a voluntary research assistant at the Heidelberg psychiatric hospital, before becoming a professor of psychology at the University of Heidelberg in 1916. It was not until 1920 that he became a professor of philosophy at the same university. His first major work, *General Psychopathology* (1913), is a study in the methodology of psychiatry. He developed his existentialism in the three *Philosophy* volumes published in 1932. After the Nazis came to power in Germany in 1933, Jaspers was excluded from all administrative duties at the University of Heidelberg. In 1937 he was denied the right to teach, and a year later he was forbidden to publish. Until the very end of the Second World War, Jaspers and his wife, who was of Jewish origin, were in constant danger of being deported to an extermination camp. In 1948 Jaspers moved from Heidelberg to Switzerland where he earned a professorship at the University of Basel. There he wrote *The Origin and Goal of History* (1950) as well as his major contribution to political philosophy, *The Atom Bomb and the Future of Man* (1958). During this period, Jaspers also published his main works in philosophy of religion and began developing a new and original conception of world-philosophy. When he died in 1969 only a single volume of his history of world-philosophy had been published.

Jaspers is generally known as a representative of German existential philosophy. A closer look at his extensive philosophical writings indicates that to view Jaspers as an existentialist only would be highly reductionist. His philosophy covers a broad range of problems involving different fields of philosophy. Four primary concepts relate to his philosophy of religion: (i) transcendence, (ii) experiencing transcendence by specific acts of human self-realization, (iii) the encompassing in relation to ciphers of transcendence, and (iv) philosophical faith as a counterpart to religious faith, or more precisely to 'revelational faith'.

THE CONCEPT OF TRANSCENDENCE

For Jaspers, the question concerning being is the fundamental problem of all philosophical reflection, and many philosophers have developed ontological systems of categories, ranges, modes or stages of being. In contrast, Jaspers rejects every philosophical approach that attempts to formulate a doctrine or system of being. Such approaches give the false impression that all being can be known in objective categories of thought, and they ignore the fact that being can become manifest only in the dichotomy of the subject and object relationship. The epistemological fact of a subject–object split implies the consequence that:

> being is always defined in reference to something else. Being and the knowledge of being, the existent and what we say of it, are accordingly a texture of diverse interpretations … no being that we know is being in itself and as a whole. The phenomenality of the empirical world was made fully clear by Kant.   (Jaspers 1973: 78–9)

Jaspers' position concerning the question of being is very different from that of Martin Heidegger. Whereas Heidegger's intention is to construct a fundamental ontology of being by means of phenomenological method and to highlight some fundamental features of human-being (*Dasein*) in his book *Being and Time*, Jaspers refuses every kind of ontology. His philosophizing maintains that there exists a transcendent source of all objective being, and in this source lies the unity and truth of all being. The role of metaphysics, then, is not to categorize and describe any dimension of being, but rather to appeal to every individual to get in touch with transcendence in an indirect way. Metaphysical speculation provides us with an impulse to undertake intensive self-reflection, by which we become aware of transcendence in the process of realizing our unique and authentic selfhood in existential situations.

TRANSCENDENCE AS ABSOLUTE BEING, THE ALL-ENCOMPASSING, DEITY AND GOD

A closer look at various contexts wherein Jaspers speaks of the transcendent source of all being makes clear that he also uses other expressions for this source, for example 'absolute Being', 'ultimate Being', 'absolute Reality', 'Being as such', 'Being-in-itself', the 'All-Encompassing', 'God' and the 'Deity'. For Jaspers, transcendence is a meta-empirical reality that cannot be researched by scientific approaches or proved by rational arguments. It cannot be grasped in the categories of thinking and resists objectivization in cognitive knowledge. Transcendence can be neither naturalized nor anthropomorphized. Every attempt to rationalize and embody the reality of transcendence must necessarily founder. In response to the question of how human beings can become aware of a non-cognitive 'ultimate Being', Jaspers focuses on two possibilities, which he expounds in his main existentialist work, *Philosophy* (especially in volume two, entitled "Existential Elucidation", and in volume three, entitled "Metaphysics"), in several chapters of later works concerning the doctrine of the encompassing, and especially in *The Perennial Scope of Philosophy* and *Philosophical Faith and Revelation*. The two possibilities of gaining an awareness of transcendence are: (i) the method of transcending philosophizing that enables a human being as "possible Existenz" to read the "Cipher-script of Transcendence" in the world; and (ii) the encounter with transcendence by means of acts of existential self-realization.

FORMAL TRANSCENDING TO TRANSCENDENCE AND 'READING' THE CIPHERS OF TRANSCENDENCE

Jaspers' basic intention in his conception of 'transcending philosophizing' is to ascend from the objective to the non-objective, from the thinkable to the non-thinkable, and from the immanent to the transcendent. His metaphysical reflections in the third volume of *Philosophy* highlight possibilities for transforming objective thinking to a type of thinking that transcends the objective reality given in our usual way of thinking. The crucial idea is that human beings become aware of transcendence when they experience principle boundaries or limits to their rational capacities. When human beings founder in all categories of thought and rationality, the possibility is open for them to face transcendence as the unconceivable being and totally other. "Transcendence is located neither in this world nor in another. Its location is a boundary" (1971: 13). Because of the 'antinomial structure' of all being – a central metaphysical presupposition of Jaspers' – human beings inevitably have experiences of foundering time and again. In 'world-orientation', we founder in searching for a definite unity of knowledge because we can grasp only particularities of being in the world. Scientific thinking founders when we demand a definite answer from the sciences about their own meaning for our lives. We also founder when we demand from the sciences a complete explanation of our own individual humanity. A human being is "fundamentally more than it can know about itself" (1973: 63). For Jaspers, human beings may have a transcendent dimension of authentic self-being that he calls 'Existenz'. The task of metaphysical thinking is to initiate a shift in our whole consciousness of being so far as we come to think that "*It is conceivable that there are things which are not conceivable*" (1971: 35). The method employed by Jaspers to reach this aim lies in what he calls 'formal transcending' to transcendence. By means of reflection on antitheses, contradictions, oppositions and polarities – subject and object, being and nothingness, unity and duality, form and material, universal and individual, time and timelessness – the thinker may become aware of absolute being or transcendence.

A critical analysis of Jaspers' methodological intention of formal transcending raises a serious problem. Because the concept of transcending philosophizing is highly ambiguous, it entails the danger of philosophical mysticism accompanied by the rupture of every philosophical discourse. This becomes evident in those contexts where Jaspers proposes to introduce contradictory statements in order to accept such statements only as 'signposts' pointing to the non-objective dimension of being. He demands that we should relativize the descriptive meanings and informative contents of such statements. But if sentences have the sole function of signposts to transcendence, then their cognitive and descriptive content becomes absolutely irrelevant. Whether or not they can fulfil their function cannot be examined or proved because the dimension to which they point as signposts is non-objective and cannot be verbally communicated. As a consequence, we must not follow Jaspers in his demand to transcend or relativize the descriptive contents of his sentences; otherwise we would not be allowed to give any interpretation to them. This deconstructive consequence of Jaspers' methodological idea of transcending all thought contents can be avoided only by not accepting his demands for transcending and relativizing the content of his philosophical sentences in a *strict* sense. The best way to interpret him is to see his methodological demand as an appeal to philosophical open-mindedness that does not reduce all being to that which can be objectively articulated.

The concept of 'cipher' plays a prominent role in Jaspers' metaphysics. A cipher is not a mere symbol in the common sense use of the term 'symbol'. While a symbol represents an objective reality, a cipher points beyond it to a transcendent reality. A symbol can always be interpreted in reference to a certain object or subject, and its meaning is open for rational discussion. In contrast, a cipher does not refer to any being that can be objectified by categories of thought. Ciphers refer to the unknowable transcendence, they are the non-cognitive "language of Transcendence" and are not interpretable at all (Jaspers 1967: 93–5). The non-objective "meaning" of a cipher can only be "felt" or "viewed" within a non-cognitive, intuitive act by a singular human being who is open to the dimension of a non-conceivable being. Because a cipher is neither a sign nor a cognitive interpretable symbol, we may call it an 'intuitive symbol'. A cipher always remains open-ended in meaning, and functions as a signpost to transcendence. Every person may be touched emotionally by a cipher in different ways because of the genuine and incomparable subjectivity and historicity of being human. Jaspers asserts that anything in the world can become a cipher of transcendence, and he explicitly mentions the ciphers of nature, history, creations in the arts, metaphysical systems, myths and religions, and most importantly the human being itself in its unique existential situation (1967: 92–255).

Here, again, we may critique Jaspers' cipher concept. For if he holds the thesis that a cipher is a non-interpretable symbol of transcendent being and that the subjective 'experience' of a cipher in an intuitive moment of an individual cannot be communicated by descriptive language, then he is again very near to a mystical position that denies every possibility of verbal communication about the transcendent experience of 'cipher-reading'. These experiences cannot be verbally articulated, are not comparable, and one cannot speak or write about their content, implications and consequences. Such experiences remain a secret of the individual consciousness that encounters transcendence through ciphers.

EXISTENTIAL ENCOUNTERS WITH TRANSCENDENCE BY REALIZING ONE'S OWN EXISTENZ

A basic presupposition of Jaspers' philosophy is the anthropological thesis that all human beings have the potential to undertake a genuine or true act of self-becoming and self-realization. By appropriating ideas from Kant and Kierkegaard (*see* Vol. 3, Ch. 21, "Immanuel Kant" and Vol. 4, Ch. 13, "Søren Kierkegaard"), Jaspers understands a human being as both an empirical and a non-empirical phenomenon. While the empirical dimension of humanity can be researched by the sciences (e.g. biology, psychology, sociology), the non-empirical dimension of human-being cannot be described and explained in scientific terms. Jaspers calls this non-empirical dimension of subjective being 'Existenz'. Existenz stands for the authentic ground of human-being: the dimension of personal autonomy, existential freedom, undetermined moral decision; the non-objective actuality of self-being, authenticity and true selfhood. No empirical studies or doctrines of anthropology and ontology can give an adequate understanding of this intimate dimension of subjectivity. Such an understanding is possible only by realizing the 'true' or 'genuine selfhood' in one's own life, and/or by elucidating its possibility by the method of transcending philosophizing. In the non-cognitive act of realizing its Existenz, a human being becomes aware not only of his or her historic singularity, but also:

> feels dependent on a Transcendence that has willed what seems to be the utmost possibility: a free, self-originating self-being. It feels a transcendent will that this being appear to itself in the transiency of temporal existence. Without cause, therefore, I am conscious of my Existenz only in relation to the Transcendence without which I slide into void. (Jaspers 1970: 46)

Despite a strong liberal tendency in Jaspers' philosophy, he stands in opposition to any kind of liberal fundamentalism that tends to absolutize individual freedom and the human capacity of independent self-realization. This fundamentalist

123

tendency often implies dangerous consequences of arrogance, over-estimation of oneself, arbitrariness and so on. Jaspers guards against such negative consequences by arguing that in the act of human self-realization as Existenz and unconditioned freedom, we become aware that this act is not only a product of our own efforts, but is also a gift of transcendence. We have to accept the limits of our human capacities and to see that the human being is, despite his or her autonomy and freedom, not the absolute ground or foundation of being. Some interpreters of Jaspers argue that the idea of a gift of transcendence may be merely a secularized version of the theological idea that human beings depend on the grace of God for self-realization.

Human beings may become aware of transcendence in existential reflections and through paradoxical experiences when confronted by existential antinomies in their own subjectivity, such as defiance and surrender, rise and fall, the "diurnal law" (order of the day) and the "nocturnal passion" (passion of the night), and the "wealth of diversity" and "the one" (Jaspers 1971: 63–111). The antinomies that every individual experiences in life are inevitable elements of the human condition. The antinomial structure of human existence is responsible for the permanent foundering of human beings to satisfy an elementary impetus deeply rooted in the human condition; namely, to reach a state of unity, totality or absolute certainty in the processes of living, thinking, feeling and so on. In this context, 'foundering' implies the antinomial structure of all existence. On the one hand, foundering can lead to frustration, resignation and despair; on the other hand, foundering can be the origin of the 'leap' to Existenz and the experience of transcendence.

The idea of a subjective, intuitive act of gaining awareness of transcendence is closely connected to two key concepts of Jaspers' existentialism: (i) 'boundary situation' (*Grenzsituation*), also translated in English as 'ultimate situation', 'limit situation' or 'borderline situation'; and (ii) 'existential communication'.

ENCOUNTER WITH TRANSCENDENCE IN BOUNDARY SITUATIONS

Jaspers agrees with other existentialists (e.g. Jean-Paul Sartre) that every human being is constantly involved in situations. To exist means to be in situations. What Jaspers calls a 'boundary situation' is a special type of situation that confronts human beings in the process of living. Jaspers philosophizes about boundary situations in the second volume of his *Philosophy*: "They are like a wall we run into, a wall on which we founder. We cannot modify them; all that we can do is to make them lucid, but without explaining or deducing them from something else. They go with existence itself" (1970: 178).

Boundary situations cannot be handled by cognitive knowledge that we use to solve problems in everyday life. If we try to escape boundary situations by managing them with rationality we must necessarily founder. Instead, boundary situations require a radical change in attitude and in one's common way of thinking. The adequate way to react within boundary situations "is not by planning and calculating to overcome them" (*ibid*.: 179), but by the very different activity of becoming the Existenz we potentially are. In this context, close affinities between Jaspers and Kierkegaard are evident. Like Kierkegaard, Jaspers maintains that the subjective experience of boundary situations is necessarily bound to an intensive process of self-reflection. This process is a non-empirical and non-objective relationship to one's own self; it elucidates one's existential possibilities and leads to an awareness of one's possible Existenz and to an act of self-acceptance in the face of the boundary situation.

Which situations are actual boundary situations? Such situations are evident in the inevitable fact that we are always in situations and cannot escape the historicity of our existence. We cannot live without *struggling* and *suffering*. We cannot avoid *guilt*. We must all die and have to come to terms with our own *death*. It is in these specific situations that we either open our being to the transcendent dimension of our humanity, or else close ourselves off from the truth and authenticity of our Existenz. "We become ourselves by entering with open eyes into the boundary situations", writes Jaspers. "We can know them only externally, and their reality can only be felt by Existenz. To experience boundary situations is the same as Existenz" (*ibid*.: 179). In short, to experience boundary situations is at the same time to experience the radical foundering of all our usual means of handling situations, rational problem-solving capacities and common ways of thinking. Boundary situations can initiate true human self-realization as Existenz, and within the autonomous act of self-realization we become aware of transcendence and of our individual freedom and personal authenticity as a gift of an absolute being. Although only implicit in his writings, Jaspers links the idea of existential self-realization in boundary situations with a set of moral attitudes that can be interpreted as necessary (not sufficient) preconditions of realizing Existenz, such as courage, truthfulness, serenity, composure, dignity, patience and personal responsibility.

ENCOUNTER WITH TRANSCENDENCE IN
INTERPERSONAL COMMUNICATION

Jaspers stresses the relevance of interpersonal relations for human self-realization. He distinguishes four types of communication that are correlative to the four dimensions of self-realization that are prominent in his philosophical anthropology. These communicative dimensions will be discussed later in the context of the concept of the encompassing. One type of communication concerns human beings in their naive vitality and spontaneous instinctive life. Persons use others only to reach vital ends, for example to satisfy the basic needs of sexuality, power, desire, and so on. On the material dimension of existence, the underlying motives of communication are egocentric. In Kant's terms, persons are treated only as means to an end, and not as an end in themselves. Another type of communication is based on the capacity of human rationality and its formal rules and categories. A typical model for such a communication is an intellectual discussion with the aim of solving a technical problem. It is not the irreplaceable individuality of the participants that constitutes communication, but rather the cognitive competence for problem-solving. A third mode of communication goes further than the first two modes. Jaspers gives a characterization of it when he writes that "community in the idea of a whole – of this state, this society, this family, this university, this profession of mine – is what puts me for the first time into substantial communication" (1970: 49–50).

While the foregoing types of communication take objective form in human interaction, the highest and most valuable form of communication, whereby human beings realize Existenz, cannot be adequately described in an objectifying language. Jaspers calls the highest form 'existential communication'. It can be elucidated only by philosophical reflection and experienced only in one's own life. In existential communication there exists an intimate personal relationship between two human beings such as friends, lovers, husband and wife, father or mother and child, teacher and student.

The crucial point in relation to Jaspers' philosophy of religion is the fact that he again links the act of self-realization as Existenz with an intuitive encounter of transcendence. He argues that, during the non-temporal act of existential communication, which lasts for only short moments in temporal objectivity, the two communication partners experience the other self, one's own self, their own autonomy and existential freedom, and the intimate relation to the partner as a gift from a transcendent source or transcendence (1970: 4; 1960: 21).

THE CONCEPT OF THE ENCOMPASSING

The concept of the encompassing (*Das Umgreifende*) – or as translated by Ralph Mannheim, 'the Comprehensive' – is another way in which Jaspers points indirectly to transcendence or an infinite unity of being. The doctrine of the encompassing that Jaspers developed after his early period of existentialism must not be understood as an ontological conception. Jaspers interprets the doctrine as a 'periechontology' (from *periechon*, a principle that holds the world together), and he deduces the doctrine from the epistemological fact of the subject–object dichotomy.

> Whatever becomes an object lies in the Encompassing which is itself not an object. The Encompassing comprises subject and object and is accordingly neither … As we think of the Encompassing we cannot help making an object of it for a moment, because we cannot get out of the subject–object dichotomy. The very thought puts us back into it.
> (1967: 71)

Philosophical thinking can never recognize the encompassing in its unity and totality, but only distinguish among certain modes of the encompassing. The all-encompassing is the ground of all modes of the encompassing, it is transcendence as the non-thinkable source and infinite ground of all being, or, in some contexts, God or deity.

FROM EXISTENTIAL ANTHROPOLOGY TO METAPHYSICS OF THE ENCOMPASSING

In Jaspers' existential philosophy, reflections have priority that revolve around the aim of human "self-becoming", "self-being" and authentic "selfhood" (1970: 25–46). His philosophizing appeals to every human being to realize his or her genuine existential possibilities. In this context we may see the influence of Kant, Nietzsche and Kierkegaard in so far as the crucial feature of Jaspers' existential anthropological framework is the idea that the human being is a dual self-realization project: an empirical being, on the one hand, and a non-empirical being, on the other hand. While the empirical dimension of humanity can be researched by the sciences (e.g. life sciences, cognitive sciences, social sciences), the non-empirical dimension cannot be described and explained in cognitive terms. Jaspers distinguishes three stages of the empirical dimension of existence. One stage of human self-realization is "mere existence" (*blosses Dasein*), that is, naive vitality or vital existence. This stage of human life is without self-reflection and self-consciousness (*ibid.*: 28–9).

The second stage is "consciousness in general" or "consciousness at large" (*Bewusstsein überhaupt*), by which Jaspers refers to the human dimension of logical thinking and rationality. This type of consciousness is the universal medium for the attainment of generally valid, objectively compelling knowledge.

The third stage of human self-being is the dimension of "spirit", "mind" or "reason" (*Geist*). Its specific capacity is the creation of ideas that become manifest in personal ideals, principles of religion, moral worldviews, political ideologies and creative conceptions of the arts.

These three stages of self-being represent humanity only as an empirical phenomenon. All human beings, however, have the potential to surpass the empirical dimension of their selves, thus transcending to the highest mode of self-realization as Existenz. This mode is meta-empirical and has no duration in time. As Existenz we can experience timelessness and eternity. The continuity of time ceases. Only the immediate presence is relevant, and there exists no past and future for the non-cognitive existential experience. In his existentialism Jaspers conceives of these three stages from a bottom-up perspective. There is an explicit ranking of the three lower stages to the highest stage of Existenz. In his doctrine of the encompassing, Jaspers transforms those ideas into a transcendental and metaphysical framework by introducing different modes of the encompassing that are equal in ranking.

MODES OF THE ENCOMPASSING AND THEIR FUNCTION

The modes of the encompassing are open 'spaces' or 'horizons' for the appearance of being. By methodically transcending reflection on the nature of the subject–object split, we become aware that the appearance of Being is "either the *Being in itself* that surrounds us or the *Being that we are*" (1960: 17; 1986: 140–77). Being in itself implies an immanent and a transcendent dimension to the encompassing, that is, the world and transcendence. The immanent mode is the world as such or the world as a whole, which can never be an object of cognition, but is rather a regulative idea of reason (Kant). The world is the open 'space' for us to experience and recognize an infinite number of particular objects. The being that we are as subjects has an immanent and a transcendent dimension. The immanent dimension includes the three modes of encompassing that correspond to the three stages of self-realization within the anthropological framework, that is, mere existence, consciousness in general and spirit. These modes are the open spaces where human beings constitute themselves as empirical phenomena. The transcendent mode of the Encompassing of the being that we are is Existenz. Jaspers introduces the notion of reason to the subjective modes of the encompassing. Reason is the bond or glue that holds all of the other modes of the encompassing in a "tensive unity" (1967: 73). Reason has the dynamic function of stimulating impulses for acts of self-being in every mode of the encompassing (biological, rational, etc.). Reason also serves to unify exclusive and irreconcilable acts of self-being by giving impulses for mutual communication. The concept of the Encompassing includes the idea of living within the various modes of being without absolutizing one mode over another. Reason thus exercises a balance within and among these various modes.

Two other important features connected to the doctrine of the encompassing that may be relevant to understanding Jaspers' philosophy of religion are: (i) Jaspers makes a distinction between two concepts of transcendence; and (ii) he links the doctrine of the encompassing to the philosophical question concerning truth. Jaspers speaks of Transcendence as one of the modes of the encompassing that is present in all the other modes. In all the other modes, human beings can become aware of a transcendent dimension of being at the boundaries or *aporias* of human action and of objective and cognitive being. In action and cognition, the experience of transcendence at the boundaries must be seen only as a cipher of that kind of transcendence that Jaspers calls the "Transcendence of Transcendence" or "Transcendence ... as the Other, the Encompassing of all encompassing" (1967: 69). The link Jaspers draws between the doctrine of the encompassing and the philosophical question concerning truth has a similar argumentative structure. He distinguishes between specific kinds of truth in each mode of the encompassing.

> In consciousness at large truth means cogent general validity for every thinking person. In existence it means the fulfillment of life ... In the mind (spirit) it means the flow of comprehension ... In Existenz

it means identification with the source, the unconditional historic resolve out of infinitely deepened repetition of love and reason.

(*Ibid.*: 70)

But the "common source" of the different kinds of truth in the modes of the Encompassing lies in "Transcendence, the Encompassing of all encompassing". Transcendence is, then, the ground of absolute truth, which is non-definable because the attainment of the absolute unity of truth lies beyond the categories of human thinking and finite human temporality.

PHILOSOPHY IN RELATION TO THEOLOGY AND RELIGION

In *The Perennial Scope of Philosophy* and *Philosophical Faith and Revelation*, Jaspers distinguishes between his own philosophical faith and what he calls religious faith or 'revelational faith'. The crucial difference is that philosophical faith is a faith in transcendence, the encompassing and the non-objectifiable deity or God, whereas religious faith is faith in a revealed God who is objectified in the contents of revealed religion.

> Religion has a cult, is bound up with a peculiar community of men, arising from the cult, and is inseparable from the myth. Religion always embodies man's practical relation to the transcendent, in the shape of something holy in the world, as delimited from the profane or unholy ... What religion localizes in a specific place, can for philosophy be present everywhere and always. Philosophy is a product of an individual's freedom, not of socially determined conditions, and it does not carry the sanctions of a collectivity.   (1960: 78–9)

THE CRITIQUE OF RELIGIOUS FAITH GROUNDED IN REVELATION

Jaspers' discussion of religious faith is in some respects ambivalent because he severely criticizes religious positions, and yet he appreciates them in relation to possible Existenz. His critical analysis of religions focuses primarily on the implications and consequences of the idea of revelation. 'Revelation' is defined as "the immediate utterance of God, localized in time and valid for all men, through word, commandment, action, event" (1960: 83). One argument against this idea of revelation is that it is impossible to make a clear distinction between an original content of a revelation of God, and the interpretive elements that are added by priests, ministers, gurus, imams and so on, as interpreters who project their own wishes and ideas onto the hidden Godhead. Another argument Jaspers develops concerns the role of authority and the authoritarian elements of biblical religion, especially the claim to an exclusive, absolute truth. Authoritative claims are present in the Christian faith, "in the Jewish doctrine of law, in the various forms of national religion, and in Islam" (*ibid.*: 95). With respect to Christianity, claims to absoluteness and exclusivity have led to the claim that only those people who believe in Christ will have eternal life, or to evoking false fears and illusions of torments of the soul, as well as the persecution of others' beliefs and claims to absolute authority in religious affairs by priests.

In accordance with Jaspers' philosophical position, no dogma or message about God or God's will can be grounded in religious creeds and religious institutions. God, as transcendence, is forever hidden to humanity (*Deus absconditus*). Jaspers denies two basic elements of the Christian faith: (i) the possibility of having a personal relationship with God through prayer; and (ii) the incarnation of God in a human being, Jesus Christ. Despite his criticisms of revelational or religious faith, Jaspers appreciates the Bible and the tradition of Western biblical religion as indispensable in the history of humanity. The Bible and biblical religion are not only a foundation of Western philosophy and culture, but they are also

> the deposit of a thousand years of borderline (boundary) experience. Through these experiences the mind of man was illuminated, he achieved certainty of God and thus of himself. In the Bible we see man in his fundamental modes of failure. But in such a way that existential experience, and realization, are manifested precisely in his failure.
>
> (*Ibid.*: 101)

The Bible positively articulates the idea of the one God, and expresses polarities that are characteristic of the lives of human beings throughout history. Besides hatred and force, we can find appeals to love and peace; besides illusions of totality and exclusivity we are reminded of the incompleteness of the created world and its antinomial structure. In fact, in the context of the crisis of modernity and the two world wars in Europe, Jaspers concludes that the positive elements of the Bible and biblical religion must be appropriated again. But the necessary presupposition of any reappropriation of biblical faith is the elimination of all claims to exclusivity, and the purification of biblical religion from any fixation in dogmas, such as the idea that God can be manifest in the world in a temporal act of revelation, and the idea of the God-man, Jesus Christ (*ibid.*: 104). For Jaspers, Jesus is not the son of God but a "paradigmatic individual" (along with Socrates, Buddha and Confucius). Because of the paradigmatic way in which Jesus realized the existential possibilities in his life, especially the ability to love and the capacity of suffering, he is relevant for human beings at all times. The myth of Jesus Christ can become a cipher of transcendence, but it does not say anything about transcendence as such. God remains hidden to humanity.

Jaspers sees a positive function for every religion and every myth in the fact that all of them can become ciphers of transcendence. In this case, they are signposts to God without giving any descriptive information about absolute being. It is precisely for this reason that Jaspers criticizes the demythologization of biblical myths proposed by the German Protestant theologian Rudolf Bultmann (Jaspers & Bultmann 1958: 3–56). Biblical stories can only become ciphers of transcendence for individuals if they are understood as myths to live by in one's historicity and existential truth. Religious narratives and myths, however, must not be reduced to cognitive knowledge about certain historical events in the past.

Jaspers' mistrust of religions that are grounded on claims to absolute revelation is also articulated in his political philosophy. As long as the world religions seek to justify their faith claims on the grounds of an exclusive divine proclamation of a generally valid absolute truth, they will founder in their efforts to prepare the field for a unification of humanity in a permanent world peace. Absolutist and authoritarian religious faith claims breed intolerance, restrict individual freedom in a variety of ways and hinder the capacity for genuine mutual communication with persons of other religious faiths. Claims for an exclusive absolute truth must be replaced by a non-dogmatic, open-minded, philosophical faith (1963: 251–61).

THE CONCEPT OF PHILOSOPHICAL FAITH

In contrast to religious faith, philosophical faith has no objectively guaranteed proof of the existence of God or transcendence, and it is not bound to rituals, churches, priests or theologians who pretend to be interpreters of God's revelation or will. Philosophical faith believes that transcendence or God exists, but without constructing any personal image of absolute being. This faith is a kind of optimistic credo and confidence in humanity, in the possibility of freedom and in the existence of a meta-empirical dimension of being. From the perspective of philosophical faith, personalist religions, and even atheism or pantheism, are understood as possible ciphers of transcendence. As ciphers, they are highly subjective and depend for their truth and authenticity on individual acts of existential self-realization. Jaspers' concept of philosophical faith is closely connected to basic elements in his understanding of philosophy as a whole. From the perspective of philosophical faith, the kinds of dogmatism and fundamentalism that obstruct the realization of true humanity have to be unmasked and criticized, including every form of the "deification of man", demonology as well as nihilism, and superstitious beliefs or pseudo-sciences masking themselves as good science (1960: 128–41). The sciences are an indispensable basis of philosophical faith, but a clear separation between the methods and capacities of the sciences and those of philosophy must be drawn. Reductionist views that restrict philosophy to a science have to be rejected, as well as philosophical positions that ignore the cognitive knowledge produced by the sciences.

The concept of philosophical faith is also intimately connected to Jaspers' understanding of reason and communication. Reason is a necessary component of philosophical faith because it stimulates multiple activities of world-orientation and projects of authentic self-realization in all dimensions of the encompassing. Reason also makes clear that authentic humanity "implies unreserved communication among men". "Philosophical faith", Jaspers writes, "is inseparable from complete openness to communication" (*ibid.*: 172–3).

To conclude, philosophical faith cannot accept the idea of an objectified God. It has a restricted understanding of religious rituals. It is suspicious of organized religions and confessions because of the harm they may bring to the freedom and authentic self-realization of the autonomous individual. Philosophical faith criticizes claims to absolute and exclusive religious truth because of the dangers of fanaticism and the coercive missionary implications it entails. On the other hand, philosophical faith is always open to dialogue with religious faith. Philosophers cannot pray with religious believers, but they should always be able to communicate with them. Religious faiths have a positive function for philosophical faith because they can be seen as ciphers of the ever-unknowable dimension of absolute being. Religions and religious faiths are indirect signposts to transcendence or God.

FURTHER READING

Ehrlich, L. 1975. *Philosophy as Faith*. Amherst, MA: University of Massachusetts Press.

Kirkbright, S. 2004. *Karl Jaspers: A Biography: Navigations in Truth*. New Haven, CT: Yale University Press.

Long, E. 1968. *Jaspers and Bultmann: A Dialogue between Philosophy and Theology in the Existentialist Tradition*. Durham, NC: Duke University Press.

Olson, A. 1979. *Transcendence and Hermeneutics: An Interpretation of Karl Jaspers*. The Hague: Martinus Nijhoff.

Salamun, K. & G. Walters (eds) 2008. *Karl Jaspers' Philosophy: Expositions and Interpretations*. Amherst, MA: Humanity Press.

Schilpp, P. (ed.) 1957. *The Philosophy of Karl Jaspers*. La Salle, IL: Open Court.

Schrag, O. 1971. *Existence, Existenz, and Transcendence: An Introduction to the Philosophy of Karl Jaspers*. Pittsburgh, PA: Duquesne University Press.

Thornhill, C. 2002. *Karl Jaspers: Politics and Metaphysics*. London: Routledge.

On BEING see also Chs 7, 11, 14. On EXISTENTIALISM see also Chs 11, 14. On TRANSCENDENCE see also Ch. 14; Vol. 4, Ch. 2.

11

PAUL TILLICH

William L. Rowe

Paul Tillich (1886–1965) was born and raised in Germany. He received his PhD in 1910 and in 1912 was ordained in the ministry. From 1914 to 1918 he served as a chaplain in the First World War. Returning from the war, he taught both philosophy and theology at several universities. In 1933 the Nazi government suspended Tillich's position at the University of Frankfurt. He then went to the United States where, until 1937, he was Visiting Professor of Philosophy of Religion and Systematic Theology at Union Theological Seminary. He served at Union as Associate Professor of Philosophical Theology (1937–40) and Professor (1941–55). From 1955 to 1962, he was a University Professor at Harvard, and during his last three years he was the Nuveen Professor of Theology in the Divinity School of the University of Chicago. He was buried in New Harmony, Indiana. Tillich wrote a number of books among which are the following: *Systematic Theology* (3 vols, 1951–63), *The Courage to Be* (1952), *Biblical Religion and the Search for Ultimate Reality* (1955) and *Dynamics of Faith* (1957).

In his writings Tillich describes certain basic questions (he calls them 'existential questions') that arise out of the human situation. These questions cannot be answered within that situation. Their answers, he claims, are found in the great symbols of the Christian message. In his writings he endeavours to analyse the human situation and to interpret the traditional Christian symbols as answers to this situation.

The concept of non-being is fundamental in Tillich's existentialist view of human existence, as well as in existentialist literature generally. Indeed, the basic human problem, as Tillich sees it, is the threat of non-being. In *The Courage to Be* he suggests three ways in which non-being is experienced as a threat to one's being:

> Non-being threatens man's ontic self-affirmation, relatively in terms of fate, absolutely in terms of death. It threatens man's spiritual self-affirmation, relatively in terms of emptiness, absolutely in terms of meaninglessness. It threatens man's moral self-affirmation, relatively

in terms of guilt, absolutely in terms of condemnation. The awareness of this threefold threat is anxiety appearing in three forms, that
of fate and death (briefly, the anxiety of death), that of emptiness and
loss of meaning (briefly, the anxiety of meaninglessness), that of guilt
and condemnation (briefly, the anxiety of condemnation). In all three
forms anxiety is existential in the sense that it belongs to existence
as such and not to an abnormal state of mind as in neurotic (and
psychotic) anxiety.   (1952: 49)

This anxiety or concern about one's own being produces a quest or longing for
that which is not subject to the threat of non-being. Since only being-itself is,
on Tillich's view, not subject to the threat of non-being, he views our concern
about our own being as resulting in a quest or longing for being-itself. Being-itself,
however, is not directly accessible. Human beings seek it only through something
concrete through which the power of being is mediated. In step-by-step fashion,
Tillich's view may be represented as follows:

1. Human beings are infinitely concerned (anxious) about their being.[1]
2. The source of this anxiety is non-being, for non-being is what threatens our
    being.
3. This infinite concern (anxiousness) about our being produces an infinite quest
    or longing for that which can overcome this threat to our being.
4. That which can overcome the threat of non-being is being-itself, for only
    being-itself is not exposed to that threat.
5. Human beings, therefore, are searching for being-itself, for some vital contact
    with that reality which possesses the power of overcoming the existential
    threat of non-being.
6. Since humans can encounter being-itself only through the concrete, their
    infinite quest for being is focused on something concrete through which the
    power of being is experienced.

The picture suggested by these six propositions is that God and the metaphysical
ultimate (being-itself) are *literally* one and the same. And this does seem to be
Tillich's mature view. In an early essay, however, he apparently denied the identification of God with being-itself: "The thing referred to in the mythical symbol is
the unconditioned transcendent, the source of both existence and meaning, which
transcends being-in-itself as well as being-for-us" (1940: 26). Since some of Tillich's
critics took being-itself to be what is metaphysically ultimate, they naturally rejected
the idea that there might be something (God, the unconditioned transcendent) that

---

1. By a human person's 'being' Tillich does not mean just their existence. He means primarily
   "the meaning, and the aim of man's existence". See Tillich (1951: 14).

transcends being-itself (see Aubrey 1941: 202). In volume one of his *Systematic Theology*, Tillich appears to have sided with his critics and explicitly accepted the view that the statement 'God is being-itself' is not itself a symbolic statement:

> The statement that God is being-itself is a non-symbolic statement. It does not point beyond itself. It means what it says directly and prop- erly; if we speak of the actuality of God, we first assert that he is not God if he is not being-itself. Other assertions about God can be made theologically only on this basis. (1951: 238–9)

However, in the introduction to volume two of his *Systematic Theology*, after asserting that "everything that religion has to say about God, including his quali- ties, action, and manifestation, has a symbolic character" (Tillich 1957b: 9), Tillich again raises the question of whether there is a point at which a non-symbolic statement must be made, and says: "There is such a point, namely, the statement that everything we say about God is symbolic. Such a statement is an assertion about God which itself is not symbolic. Otherwise we would fall into a circular argument" (*ibid.*). But if everything we say about God is symbolic, then when we say that God is being-itself we are not really making the non-symbolic state- ment that Tillich professed it to be in volume one. Moreover, Tillich's assertion in volume two, "everything we say about God is symbolic", is not in fact what Tillich claims it is: a statement *about* God. It is in fact a statement about *statements* about God, namely, that all of them are symbolic, which is Tillich's original position. What it tells us is that God is *incomprehensible* in the sense that no literal positive predicate can be meaningfully applied to God. Despite this apparent confusion, the position he takes in volume one – that 'God is being-itself' is a literal, non- symbolic identity statement – will be accepted as his settled view.

Following Tillich, a distinction must be made between his philosophical iden- tification of God with being-itself and the way in which 'God' is defined in reli- gious discourse:

> A phenomenological description of the meaning of 'God' in every religion, including the Christian, offers the following definition of the term 'god'. Gods are beings who transcend the realm of ordinary experience in power and meaning, with whom men have relations which surpass ordinary relations in intensity and significance. (Tillich 1951: 211–12)

As religious people use the expression 'God', it refers to a being who exhibits human- like qualities (knowledge, power, love, etc.), appears at various times and places, brings about extraordinary events in human history and so on. It is features like these that Tillich has in mind when he speaks of the 'tendency towards concrete- ness' in the idea of God. But there is also a strong 'tendency towards ultimacy' in the idea of God. In speaking of God, religious people also deny that God is subject to limitations, bound by space or time, had a beginning or will have an end. God is said to be immortal, invisible, eternal, possessed of unlimited power and perfect knowledge and beyond human comprehension. Any tenable view of God, Tillich believes, must strive to accommodate both of these tendencies. Since a being can exist only by virtue of participating in ultimate reality, being-itself, Tillich believes that by identifying God with being-itself he can accommodate both tendencies. For unlike particular beings, being-itself is beyond all limitations, and thus may be said to be what is 'ultimate' in reality. And since every being exists only by virtue of participating in being-itself, being-itself may also be said to manifest the tendency toward concreteness in the human picture of God.

Tillich makes two important assertions concerning being-itself. The first is that although every being is subject to limitations, *being-itself is beyond all limitations.* The second is that *every being participates in being-itself (ibid.:* 237). The first assertion accounts for the aspect of ultimacy in the idea of God. Tillich's reasoning is that since every being is subject to limitations, only being-itself can adequately represent God's ultimacy. The second assertion is used to account for the element of concreteness in the idea of God. His point is that the relationship of participation between every being and being-itself makes it possible for a particular being to become a focal point through which God is disclosed. In this way, Tillich seeks to explain sacred objects and religious symbols.

It is reasonably clear *why* Tillich rejects the common view that God is a particular being among other beings, even if God is taken to be the greatest and best of all such beings. He rejects any such view because he takes it to imply that God, along with every other being, depends for his existence on a reality beyond himself: being-itself. What is less clear is why Tillich thinks that there *is* such a reality as being-itself on which every particular being is dependent for its existence. But putting this question aside, after noting that being-itself (God) cannot be finite or temporal, what is especially perplexing is Tillich's tendency to then go on to question whether God (being-itself) can be infinite or eternal. As Charles Hartshorne notes:

> Professor Tillich often speaks, indeed, almost as though 'absolute', 'unconditioned', 'infinite', 'eternal', were synonyms for 'being-itself', and equally literal in application to deity; but he also insists that being-itself, or God, is "beyond finitude and infinity" (144), and implies the same with respect to "relative" and "absolute" (cf. 138), "temporal" and "eternal", and even "spatial" and "spaceless" (184, 186).
> (Hartshorne 1961: 164–5, quoting Tillich 1951)

I believe Hartshorne's observation is correct. Moreover, its implications for our understanding of Tillich's view are important and far-reaching. As Hartshorne points out, for the classical theologians:

To say that God is being-itself used to mean that He had no aspect of becoming. And God was held not to be separated from anything only in the sense that he is cause of all and conscious of all. Scarcely even symbolically would the classical theologians, as a rule, allow the substance-accident schema, or potentiality, or becoming, to be used to describe God. But Tillich accepts all of them as symbols. The doctrine of pure actuality is declared to be mistaken, since God is (symbolically speaking) living, and "life is actualization, not actuality" (84, 153).

(*Ibid.*: 165–6)

The main difficulty in trying to understand Tillich's concept of God may be expressed as follows: (i) to explicate his concept of God we must first understand what being-itself is; (ii) being-itself is ineffable. Two points follow from (i) and (ii). First, there is something wrong with Tillich's proposed elucidation of our admittedly analogical or symbolic discourse about God in terms of ontological statements about being-itself. For on his own account, being-itself is ineffable. Consequently, any statement that purports to ascribe a positive, intrinsic property to God (being-itself) must be understood to be either false or, at best, a way of expressing something that cannot be said. And what this means is that Tillich's concept of God as being-itself simply cannot be explicated except by saying what it is not. The difficulty with this conclusion, of course, is that it conflicts with two fundamental claims about God that Tillich affirms: (i) God is the supreme object of all desire and aspiration; and (ii) God is the creative and sustaining ground of everything that exists. For these two claims ascribe positive properties to God and, therefore, given that God simply is being-itself, the positive properties must also be properties of being-itself. Despite this apparent confusion in Tillich's view of God as being-itself, the following claims do seem to express his settled view of the matter:

1. Being-itself is not an essence or universal – it transcends the distinction between essence and existence.
2. Being-itself is not *a* being.
3. We can have no positive, literal knowledge of being-itself.
4. Everything participates in being-itself and depends on it for its existence – it is the source or ground of everything that is.
5. Being-itself is the ultimate object of all desire and aspiration.
6. Being-itself is absolutely unconditioned, beyond any distinction or division.

Perhaps the most disturbing feature of Tillich's theology is his claim that "God does not exist" (1951: 237). If we ask what Tillich has to say in support of the existence of God, it appears that he is bent on denying it:

It would be a great victory for Christian apologetic if the words 'God' and 'existence' were very definitely separated … God does not exist.

He is being-itself beyond essence and existence. Therefore to argue
that God exists is to deny him.   (*Ibid.*: 205)

Thus the question of the existence of God can be neither asked nor
answered. If asked, it is a question about that which by its very nature
is above existence, and therefore the answer – whether negative or
affirmative – implicitly denies the nature of God. It is as atheistic to
affirm the existence of God as it is to deny it.   (*Ibid.*: 237)

Consider two statements: 'God exists' and 'God does not exist'. The second passage
quoted above makes it clear that Tillich is not saying that the first of these statements is false and the second true. He regards both assertions as mistaken. For
both suggest that God is the sort of entity that *could* exist. And it is this view that
he believes is mistaken. Normally, when one asserts a sentence of the form '*x* is
not *y*' it is conceivable that '*x* is *y*'. Only in extraordinary circumstances would one
have a need to assert, for example, that the number two is not red or not larger
than the number three. For the number two could not conceivably be red or larger
than the number three. So too, for Tillich, it is misleading to assert that 'God does
not exist', for to do so suggests that God is the sort of being that could exist. But
since theists generally claim that God exists, whereas atheists assert that God does
not exist, Tillich regards it necessary to assert that God (as he understands this
term) is beyond both existence and non-existence:

However it is defined, 'the existence of God' contradicts the idea of a
creative ground of essence and existence. The ground of being cannot
be found within the totality of beings, nor can the ground of essence
and existence participate in the tensions and disruptions characteristic
of the transition from essence to existence.   (*Ibid.*: 204–5)

There are two reasons given here for why the notion of 'existence' is incompatible
with the nature of God. The first reason is that God cannot be found in the totality
of beings: God is not *a* being. The second reason is that God does not participate in the disruptions of existence. By the 'disruptions of existence' Tillich means
the conditions of finitude: time, space, causality and substance. What this second
reason reveals is that 'exists' and 'existence' are used by Tillich in a technical sense.
When the classical theologians asserted the existence of God they did not mean
to imply, nor were they taken to imply, that God is subject to the conditions of
finitude: time, space and so on. Be this as it may, given Tillich's view of the limitations implied by the concept of existence, it is understandable why he rejects its
application to God as being-itself.

As we have seen, by identifying God with being-itself, Tillich believes he can
account both for the aspect of ultimacy and the aspect of concreteness in the idea
of God. For the ontological claim that being-itself is beyond all limitations satisfies

the aspect of ultimacy, and the claim that every being participates in being-itself makes possible, Tillich believes, a theory of religious symbols that adequately accounts for the element of concreteness in the idea of God. He distinguishes signs from symbols as follows: if x is a sign then x points beyond itself but does not participate in the reality of that to which it points; whereas if x is a symbol then x points beyond itself and participates in the reality of that to which it points. Tillich speaks of certain words as signs and other words as symbols. Religious and poetic language is, he claims, largely symbolic language. Words such as 'God' and 'Christ' are symbols. However, most words are merely signs. The distinction we must bear in mind is between *linguistic* and *non-linguistic* signs and symbols. The flag and the crucifix are examples for Tillich of non-linguistic symbols. The road sign and the red traffic light are examples of non-linguistic signs. Finally, it should be noted that Tillich ascribes several features to symbols, and sometimes uses one or more of these features to distinguish symbols from signs. Thus, in addition to the basic claim that symbols participate in the reality of that to which they point, Tillich claims that symbols: (i) open up levels of reality which are otherwise closed to us; (ii) unlock dimensions and elements of our soul that correspond to the dimensions and elements of reality; (iii) cannot be produced or replaced intentionally; and (iv) grow and die.

There is, I believe, an important distinction between two classes of signs, a distinction that is not accounted for in Tillich's theory. Signs, he insists, are always *conventional*. "A red light and the stopping of cars have essentially no relation to each other, but conventionally they are united as long as the conventions lasts" (1957b: 41); "signs can be replaced for reason of expediency or convention, while symbols cannot" (*ibid.*: 42); "signs are consciously invented and removed" (*ibid.*: 58). However, there are *natural* as well as conventional signs. Nimbus clouds are a sign of rain. Smoke is a sign of fire. But the relation between nimbus clouds and rain, as between smoke and fire, was not devised or decreed by human beings, it was discovered by them. A red light and the stopping of cars, as Tillich remarks, have essentially no relation to each other. But nimbus clouds and rain do have a natural relation to each other. So, it appears that what I have called 'natural signs' are not really signs at all in Tillich's theory. However, unless nimbus clouds and smoke are symbols for Tillich, it follows that on his theory not all entities that point to (signify) something else are either signs or symbols. Moreover, it is fairly clear that Tillich would not regard nimbus clouds and other natural 'signs' as symbols since they lack some of the essential characteristics he ascribes to symbols. For example, he says that a symbol "opens up levels of reality which otherwise are closed for us" (*ibid.*: 42). We would be hard put to imagine a level of reality revealed to us by nimbus clouds that we could not get at in any other way. It may make sense to think of a great painting as doing this, but hardly a nimbus cloud. Therefore, we should conclude that although signification (pointing to) is a necessary condition for x being a sign or symbol, it is not a sufficient condition. 'Natural signs' signify what they are signs of, but they fail to satisfy Tillich's requirements for a sign or a symbol. Thus some modification of his theory of signs is necessary in order for it to embrace natural, as well as conventional, signs.

As we have seen, Tillich claims that the fundamental difference between signs and symbols is that symbols, unlike signs, participate in the reality of that to which they point. He sometimes expresses this by saying that symbols participate in the meaning and power of the reality to which they point. But just what is this relationship of participation, setting symbols apart from signs that signify but do not participate in that which they signify? One possibility is that the relationship of participation between the symbol and what it signifies consists in the way human beings respond to and treat the symbol. We respond to, feel towards, and treat the symbol in ways essentially similar to the ways we respond to, feel towards, and treat that for which the symbol stands. Consider the example of the flag, which, according to Tillich, we accept as a symbol of our nation. The suggestion is that the flag participates in the nation in the sense that it shares in the dignity we attribute to the nation. Thus, in America, if we come upon a man washing his car using the American flag as a washrag, this act would be considered an attack on the dignity of the nation. 'The man has absolutely no respect for his country!', might be the appropriate thing to say. Thus there seems to be a similarity between the flag and the nation in the sense that many of the appropriate ways of responding to the nation are the appropriate ways of responding to the flag. It is also clear that religious symbols have this character. Ordinary elements such as bread or wine, when viewed as symbols of Christ's body, are treated with the sort of reverence and awe one might feel towards that which the symbol signifies.[2] Perhaps, then, this is what Tillich has in mind when he says that symbols *participate* in the reality that is symbolized. That is, x participates in y means that x is similar to y in the sense that human beings feel towards and treat x in the same way they do y. Of course, simply by virtue of the fact that x and y are different sorts of things there always will be modes of treatment appropriate to the one but not to the other. Thus we *fold* the flag; we do not fold the nation. We *raise* the flag; we do not, at least in the same sense, raise the nation. But what is required is that in certain important ways we feel towards and view the symbol in much the same way as we do that which it symbolizes.

Tillich's identification of God with being-itself should be viewed as an attempt to provide a doctrine of God that adequately accounts for a basic tension in the religious idea of God: a tension between 'a tendency toward ultimacy' and 'a tendency toward concreteness'. Since being-itself is beyond all limitations, it is not difficult to see how the identification of God with being-itself satisfies the tendency towards ultimacy in the idea of God. But on the surface it would appear that the identification of God with being-itself renders it impossible to accommodate the tendency toward concreteness, a tendency that is reflected in the religious person's conception

---

2. One other possibility is the view of orthodox Catholicism that the bread and wine, when consecrated, actually become the body of Christ.

of God and experience of God. For as Tillich notes, God is conceived by the religious person as a more or less *concrete* being – Yahweh, Baal, Zeus, Odin and so on – and experienced as *personal*. Once God is identified with the ultimate of Tillich's ontology (being-itself), how is it possible to adequately account for the tendency toward concreteness in the idea of God? Tillich puts the problem as follows:

> Is not God in the religious encounter *a* person among others, related to them as an *I* to a *thou*, and vice versa? And, if so, is he not *a* being, while the ontological question asks the question of being-itself, of the power of being in and above all beings? In the ontological question, is not God himself transcended? (1955a: 27–8)

As we have seen, his effort to resolve this problem rests on his theory of religious symbols. His central point is this:

> The religious symbol has a special character in that it points to the ultimate level of being, to ultimate reality, to being itself, to meaning itself … Religious experience is the experience of that which concerns us ultimately. The content of this experience is expressed in religious symbols. (1955b: 109–10)

What this passage reveals is that Tillich's theory of religious experience embraces three distinct points: (i) religious symbols point to being-itself; (ii) being-itself is that which is of ultimate concern for us; and (iii) the concrete content of our ultimate concern is a religious symbol. In a significant religious experience, its immediate content is never being-itself, it is something more or less concrete, a burning bush perhaps, that Tillich takes to be the concrete content of the experience (a religious symbol). He then *interprets* the profound experience involving the burning bush as somehow representing what is ultimate in his metaphysics, being-itself, and attaches to this the claim that the person who has the religious experience on seeing the burning bush is in reality experiencing, *via* the burning bush, that which concerns us ultimately, being-itself. Thus we find Tillich providing somewhat complicated interpretations of what is actually going on in acts of religious devotion: "Devotion to the crucifix is really directed to the crucifixion on Golgotha, and devotion to the latter is in reality intended for the redemptive action of God, which is itself a symbolic expression for an experience of what concerns us ultimately" (1961: 301). Presumably, Tillich is interpreting the crucifix as a symbol pointing beyond itself to the crucifixion on Golgotha, which itself is symbolic for the redemptive action of God, which itself is symbolic for an experience of what concerns us ultimately: being-itself. Of course, no one directly experiences being-itself. Indeed, only Tillich and his followers, or those who have read his writings, have even the concept of being-itself. The focus of a religious experience, Tillich would claim, is always something concrete that serves as a symbol of the ultimate: being-itself. And provided one can experience *x* via experiencing something concrete that in some way expresses *x*, one can be said to have experienced *x*, even if one lacks a concept of *x*. Thus Tillich can say that devotion for the redemptive action of God "is itself a symbolic expression for an experience of what concerns us ultimately": being-itself. This is, of course, Tillich's philosophical interpretation of what occurs in religious experience. And whether it is correct or not logically depends on whether his philosophical view that there is such a reality as being-itself on which all existing things depend for their existence is true. If it is not true, his entire ontological theory of religious symbols is a failure. Of course, so long as we cannot discover anything contradictory in his ontology, we will have to allow that for all we know his theory could be correct. And given that there is little to be said about being-itself – other than what it is not – the task of discovering a contradiction either in his account of being-itself or in its relation to whatever we know to exist would be extraordinarily difficult.

What is perhaps worth pursuing is the question of whether there are any good or convincing reasons to think that there is such a reality as being-itself. And on this matter we can do no more than examine Tillich's argument for his view that it is necessarily true that there is such a reality as being-itself:

> The ontological question, the question of being-itself, arises in something like a 'metaphysical shock' – the shock of possible non-being. This shock often has been expressed in the question, 'Why is there something: why not nothing?' But in this form the question is meaningless, for every possible answer would be subject to the same question in an infinite regression. Thought must start with being. It cannot go behind it, as the form of the question itself shows. If one asks why there *is* not nothing, one attributes being even to nothing. Thought is based on being, and it cannot leave this basis; but thought can imagine the negation of everything that *is*, and it can describe the nature and structure of being which give everything that is the power of resisting non-being. (1951: 163–4)

Tillich argues that there is something seriously wrong with the question 'Why is there something; why not nothing?' In this passage he presents two distinct reasons for rejecting this question. The first is simply that it is impossible to answer the question, for whatever *thing* we refer to in our explanation of why something exists will be such that the very same question can be asked about it. To endeavour to answer this question is to initiate an infinite regress of question and answer. And because it is impossible to answer the question, Tillich concludes that the question is *meaningless*.

It is doubtful that the reason Tillich mentions really justifies his conclusion that the question 'Why is there something, why not nothing?' is meaningless. For it is not at all clear that the question cannot be answered. Indeed, the notion of a *necessary being* – a being whose nature entails its existence, a being that does exist and logically could not fail to exist – is precisely what, for many advocates of the ontological argument and for some advocates of a version of the cosmological argument, does answer the question. For the answer tells us that it is impossible for there to be nothing since it is necessarily the case that God exists.

Tillich does offer a second reason for taking the question 'Why is there something, why not nothing?' to be meaningless. "If one asks why there *is* not nothing, one attributes being even to nothing" (1951: 163). What he means is that the possibility that one endeavours to envisage when one asks 'Why is there not nothing?' is not a possibility at all. For the proposition 'Nothing exists' or 'Nothing is' attributes being even to nothing. Hence, the question must be rejected because it asks why something is not so – that is, that nothing exists – which could not conceivably be so. It could not conceivably be so because it involves the contradiction of predicating being of non-existence (nothing). It is difficult to assess this argument. For the argument to be successful, '*x* has being' must entail '*x* exists'. Otherwise something could have being even though nothing exists. But if '*x* has being' does entail '*x* exists', there does appear to be a contradiction in attributing being to something that does not exist. But if that is so, it simply would be a mistake for anyone, including Tillich, to think that the proposition 'Nothing exists' or 'Nothing is' attributes being even to nothing. The proposition 'Nothing exists' does not assert that some very mysterious entity, 'Nothing', itself has the property of existing. What it asserts is that should there be a proposition that asserts or entails the existence of anything whatever, that proposition would be false. Therefore, it is difficult to credit Tillich's claim that "If one asks why there *is* not nothing, one attributes being even to nothing". And apart from accepting that claim, Tillich appears to have no sufficient reason for claiming that the question 'Why is there something, why not nothing?' is meaningless.

Tillich has developed a philosophical theology that is important in contemporary culture. By rejecting the view that God is an existing being in favour of the view that God is being-itself he has managed to avoid many of the critical arguments in opposition to traditional theism. Moreover, his interpretation of religious symbols is both profound and enlightening. If there is a weakness in his philosophical theology, it lies in his reasons and arguments for the view that there is such a reality as being-itself.[3]

FURTHER READING

Heywood, T. 1963. *Paul Tillich: An Appraisal*. Philadelphia, PA: Westminster.
McKelway, A. 1964. *The Systematic Theology of Paul Tillich: A Review and Analysis*. Richmond: John Knox Press.

3. Parts of this essay are taken from my book on Tillich: Rowe (1968).

Tavard, G. 1962. *Paul Tillich and the Christian Message.* New York: Scribner's.
Wheat, L. 1970. *Paul Tillich's Dialectical Humanism: Unmasking the God Above God.* Baltimore, MD: The Johns Hopkins Press.

On BEING see also Chs 7, 10, 14. On EXISTENCE OF GOD see also Ch. 16; Vol. 1, Chs 18, 19; Vol. 2, Chs 5, 6, 13, 14; Vol. 3, Chs 6, 12, 13, 14, 15, 21. On EXISTENTIALISM see also Chs 10, 14. On SYMBOLS see also Vol. 1, Ch. 16.

12

KARL BARTH

Paul Dafydd Jones

Writing to a close friend in 1922, Karl Barth (1886–1968) confessed bewilderment at the work of John Calvin, the sixteenth-century Protestant Reformer (*see* Vol. 3, Ch. 4). "Calvin is a cataract, a primeval forest, a demonic power", he wrote. "I lack completely the means, the suction cups, even to assimilate this phenomenon, not to speak of presenting it adequately" (Barth 1964: 101). While such flourishes of rhetorical creativity may be in short supply at present, comparable reactions to Barth – arguably the greatest Protestant thinker of the twentieth century – are fairly common. Dismay at finding most interpretive paradigms inadequate; perplexity in face of a prose style accessible, yet stretched to conceptual breaking-point; astonishment at a 'Christological concentration' that inhibits freewheeling speculation, but enables doctrinal innovation on a grand scale: these are common responses among those who come newly to Barth. While few read without sensing a formidable intellect at work, many find themselves overcome by the scope and drift of Barth's thought.

This chapter obviously cannot provide the 'suction cups' needed to gain purchase on Barth. Such appendages must be self-grown; their development requires a sustained engagement with the original texts. My aim is rather to orient readers to key features of Barth's thought, focusing primarily on the multi-volume *Church Dogmatics*.[1]

The eldest child of Anna Katharina and Johann Friedrich Barth, Karl was born in the northern Swiss city of Basle in 1886. His childhood, spent mostly in Berne, was distinguished by a solid education, an atmosphere of moderately conservative piety and a fondness for rough-and-tumble. He commenced university studies in Berne in 1904, having decided on theology as a course of study and ministry as a vocation. He subsequently spent time in Berlin and Marburg, delighting in the

---

1. Barth (1956–77). When I cite this work in the main body of text, the notation *CD* is followed by the relevant volume and part number.

thought of Protestant liberals such as Adolf von Harnack (1851–1930), Wilhelm Herrmann (1846–1922) and Martin Rade (1857–1940). In 1911 he took a parish in Safenwil, a small industrial town in the Aargau region in the north of Switzerland. In this year he also became engaged to Nelly Hoffmann. The couple married in 1913.

Pastoral responsibilities put Barth's commitment to Protestant liberalism under tremendous strain. Key tenets of the theological outlook he had embraced at university – specifically, the presumption that historical-critical reflection ought to govern scriptural interpretation, a positive appraisal of religious experience and bourgeois morality, a concern to coordinate theological reflection and cultural affirmation, and the marginalization of eschatology – began to lose their lustre. This became acutely evident when Barth's sermons were "forced out with terrible birth-pangs" (Busch 1976: 61).[2] Concomitantly, social and political issues weighed heavily on Barth's mind. Locally, Barth recognized the necessity of resisting the exploitation of working-class parishioners. He therefore worked hard to understand the complex material conditions that engendered economic oppression and campaigned for Christianized forms of socialism. Nationally, Barth was appalled by various intellectuals' endorsement of Germany's foreign policy at the outbreak of the First World War, not least because a number of his former teachers were signatories of a manifesto supporting armed conflict. Barth would later cite this symbol of *Kriegstheologie* (war theology) as a pivotal moment in his disillusionment with liberalism, claiming that it disclosed a theological posture that could neither identify nor effectively oppose state-sponsored militarism.

Barth's pastoral experiences, in conjunction with some intense interpersonal and religious encounters, had a tremendous effect on him. Negatively, it led to a loss of faith in Protestant liberalism. He began to view this modulation of Christian thought as a disastrous legitimization of bourgeois complacency, evasive of the foundational truths of the gospel. Positively, Barth discovered in himself a compulsive urge to promulgate a theological viewpoint of his own, a viewpoint that, while cognizant of the philosophical, cultural and political conditions of Western modernity, was also passionately committed to the vital claims of Christian faith. In close conversation with his friend and confidant Eduard Thurneysen, Barth began to expound this new perspective in sermons, in numerous essays and speeches and in *The Epistle to the Romans* (hereafter *Romans*) – arguably the most important biblical commentary of the twentieth century.

While the first edition of *Romans* holds interest for scholars, the second edition, published in 1922, shows most vividly the cast of Barth's early thought. There is, first of all, an uncompromising commitment to reading the Bible theologically. While Barth did not deny the utility of historical-critical insights, his primary

---

2. This is a phrase used in one of Barth's letters to Eduard Thurneysen, dated 1 April 1917. For the letter see Barth (1973: 187–90).

concern is to recover a mode of exegesis alert to the possibility of divine revelation. He therefore adopts a theological posture reminiscent of the *sola scriptura* principle championed by Martin Luther and John Calvin (*see* Vol. 3, Chs 3, 4). He construes the Bible as a discursive realm through which God reveals Godself; he places Scripture, in all of its threatening and unusual complexity, at the centre of theological reflection. This does not mean, however, that Barth favours anything akin to the scriptural 'inerrantism' propounded by some contemporary evangelical Christians. Barth's version of the "old doctrine of Verbal Inspiration" (1968: 18) turns on the postulation of an *indirect* identity between the word of God and the words of Scripture. "The Strange New World Within the Bible"[3] becomes vital and inhabitable through God's gracious action, which alone renders Scripture revelatory. Thus the task for the biblical exegete is to encounter God's address today: to hear the divine word that sounds, now, in the human words of Scripture.

Secondly, in *Romans* Barth insists on the objectivity and otherness of God. The insistence on 'objectivity' is an insistence that the sheer reality of God's being and action is a dominant concern in theological discourse. A simple tautology – "God is God" (1968: 11) – has inexhaustible importance, for it is the irreducible fact of God's being, above all else, that grounds faith and provides Christian theology with its principal theme. The insistence on 'otherness' is an insistence that God's reality ought not to be equated with any created reality. The second edition of *Romans* upholds, often ruthlessly, an "infinite qualitative distinction"[4] between God and humanity, God and culture, God and world. Barth hereby contests an implication of much Protestant liberal thought, namely, that God is continuous with, or at the very least akin to, bourgeois European religiosity, experience and morality. The opposite is the case. God is the "divine contradiction" (*ibid.*: 40); the "Holy One, the altogether Other" (*ibid.*: 42); the Lord who is *otherwise* than the world and humankind.

This brings us to the third aspect of Barth's thought at this time: a description of Christian existence that makes existential unrest a constitutive element of faith. The term *krisis*, heavy with connotation in the chaotic aftermath of the First World War, pervades *Romans*: it signals that the Christian finds herself buffeted between an awareness of sin and an encounter with God's saving love. While faith is properly described in terms of the Christian being *simul iustus et peccator* (simultaneously justified and sinful), the *simul* – or, to dialectize Friedrich Schleiermacher (*see* Vol. 4, Ch. 3), the "*antithesis* of sin and grace"[5] – fascinates Barth to the point at which any pietistic construal of faith *qua* assurance drops away. Certainly, God's grace outbids sin. Barth's emphasis on divine objectivity and otherness does not make God a metaphysical brute fact; God cannot be thought aright unless the *saving* activity of Christ and the Holy Spirit norms theological reflection. But Barth

---

3. This is the title of an address Barth delivered in 1916. See Barth (1978: 28–50).
4. Barth takes this phrase from Søren Kierkegaard (*see* Vol. 4, Ch. 13).
5. This is a key phrase in Schleiermacher's *Christian Faith* (1999).

maintains, nevertheless, a decidedly un-pietistic sense that existential disquiet is basic to Christian life. God's saving action causes acute unease, both with respect to the sufficiency of 'religion' as it mediates the relationship between God and the human and with respect to the challenges of Christian existence. Thus a trio of striking sentences at the heart of *Romans*:

> In God I am what I am; I cannot therefore wait to be what I am. Under grace, and aware of the message of Christ, I am exposed to the full and unavoidable earnestness of His demand, claim, and promise; I am subjected to a vast and vehement pressure. To be a Christian is to be under this pressure.   (1968: 229)

Barth expresses exactly this existential unrest on each and every page of *Romans*. Since human language cannot do justice to God's reality and action, since the human being can only hope to be what she ought to be, given that she dashes God's hopes at every moment, so then must theology move between affirmation and negation, comedy and tragedy, time and eternity.

These comments, of course, only skim the surface of a text at once monstrous, beautiful and baffling. *Romans* can be read in various ways: a compelling alternative to Harnack's liberal manifesto *Das Wesen des Christentums* (The essence of Christianity; 1900);[6] a modulation of Herrmannian liberalism, with an outsized affirmation of divine reality accompanying a marginalization of historical-critical reflection; a competitor to the provocations of Ernst Troeltsch and the 'history of religions' school; an outburst of *avant garde* literary expressionism; a problematic swansong for the religious socialisms of Hermann Kutter and Leonhard Ragaz; an initial step towards a genuinely post-Kantian project that recognizes Christian theology to be grounded in God's self-revelatory and salvific action. Whichever evaluative tack is preferred (the options above are not mutually exclusive), one point stands beyond dispute: *Romans* represents the first move in a theological project that would dominate the next four decades of Barth's life.

Barth's employment at several German universities followed on the heels of the success of *Romans*: he held posts at Göttingen, Münster and Bonn in fairly quick succession. At each institution, he worked furiously to accredit himself academically, spending considerable time on biblical exegesis, the history of Christian thought and the interpretation of theological giants such as Calvin, Schleiermacher and Anselm. He also offered lecture cycles on dogmatics and in 1927 produced the initial volume of an aborted systematic theology, *Die christliche Dogmatik* (Christian dogmatics; see Barth 1982). The question of how Barth's work in the 1920s and early 1930s relates to his later theology has sparked some debate. Influentially, Hans Urs von Balthasar (1992) viewed Barth's study of

---

6. For the English translation, see Harnack (1978).

Anselm, published in 1930, as the point of decisive maturation. It was at this juncture, Balthasar argued, that Barth finally transitioned from a 'dialectical' position that depended, in part, on existentialist philosophy, to an 'analogical' posture, whereby Christian discourse is responsive to God's revelation and God's formation of Christian faith. More recently, Bruce McCormack (1995) has contested this reading, arguing that Barth's first series of lectures on dogmatics held pivotal importance for his intellectual formation. For McCormack, Barth's immersion in Protestant scholasticism enabled him to tie a neo-Kantian construal of revelation to the 'Christological concentration' that characterizes his later work. Whatever interpretation one ultimately favours, there is at least clarity about Barth's theological ambition in the 1920s. Moving beyond a critique of liberalism and the rhetorical flamboyance of *Romans*, Barth now aimed to formulate an expansive and conceptually precise statement of Christian belief. And from the mid-1930s until his death, this ambition found fulfilment in the *Church Dogmatics*.

Before considering this remarkable text more closely, mention must be made of Barth's resistance to National Socialism. Although Barth steered clear of politics in the 1920s, Hitler's seizure of power spurred him to action. An initial public statement against Nazism was *Theological Existence Today* (1933); in 1934, Barth also penned much of the 'Barmen Declaration' issued by the 'Confessing Church' (a Protestant coalition whose members opposed Nazi policies, especially as they impinged on the ecclesial sphere). At first sight, neither text seems particularly political. *Theological Existence Today*, for instance, opens with the striking claim that scholars ought to do "theology and only theology ... as though nothing had happened" (1933: 9). Yet with these and other texts Barth invented a new kind of political theology, distinguished by its radical content and indirect rhetoric. This theology showed only secondary interest in the specifics of Hitler's political programme, hideous as these were. Its principal goal was to expose the fundamentally idolatrous character of Nazism, given that this ideology comprehensively evaded the fact that the only genuine 'authority' is God, Godself, the One revealed in the Hebrew Bible and New Testament. Divine authority, in other words, invalidates every totalitarian political claim. For if "we reject the false doctrine, as though there were areas of our life in which we would not belong to Jesus Christ, but to other lords" (Cochrane 1976: 240), what choice does the Christian have but to protest against fascism in all of its forms?

This is not to say that Barth's resistance should be blithely lauded. It can be argued that he did too little, too late; that the theological idiom employed was overly subtle, in face of the Nazi threat; that, along with other members of the 'Confessing Church', a concern for ecclesial autonomy forestalled a more forthright denunciation of anti-Semitism. Whatever the case, the powers-that-be viewed Barth's activity with consternation. *Theological Existence Today* was banned in July 1934; Barth's public lectures, sermons and critiques of Christians sympathetic to Nazism were disparaged; his refusal to sign an oath of loyalty to Hitler led to a tribunal and monetary fine; and the Gestapo banned his speaking in public in

March 1935. In June 1935 the Minster of Cultural Affairs dismissed Barth from his post at Bonn. Barth therefore left Germany and returned to Switzerland, taking up a university post in his hometown of Basle.

THE *CHURCH DOGMATICS*

While the size of the *Church Dogmatics* – an unfinished work of twelve hefty part-volumes, amounting to around nine thousand pages – makes summary difficult, broad interpretive judgements can be formulated with relative ease. There are two reasons for this fortunate state of affairs.

On one level, Barth was a highly disciplined author, fascinated with the order and form of doctrinal reflection. Although the word 'system' would occasion protest (it could signal an evasion of revelation under cover of intellectual tidiness), Barth's mature work depended on stable assumptions, recognizable argumentative patterns and an interlocking clutch of motifs. Furthermore, he organized the *Dogmatics* according to a clear sequence of topics: "The Doctrine of the Word of God", "The Doctrine of God", "The Doctrine of Creation" and "The Doctrine of Reconciliation" (volumes one to four, respectively; Barth died before the fifth volume on redemption could be written). This structure allowed Barth to offer a progressively thickening description of Christian thought, with claims explicated, anticipated, recapitulated and refined from various angles. The total effect is a dense but mappable discursive world, the intelligibility of which goes hand in hand with particular landscapes of startling nuance and novelty.

On another level, Barth believed that Christian faith, by virtue of its internal dynamics, engenders a comprehensible account of itself. Scripture witnesses to God's self-presentation in Christ by way of the 'anticipations' and 'recollections' of the Old and New Testaments; at the same time, God's conferral of faith carries with it an ordered intellectual apprehension of these anticipations and recollections. Christian theology, as Anselm suggested (*see* Vol. 2, Ch. 6), is therefore a matter of 'faith seeking understanding'. The dogmatician 'follows up' God's self-revelation, disclosed in the Bible, gifted in faith and embodied in the Christian community.

THE CHURCH AND CHRISTIAN THEOLOGY

With the title *Church Dogmatics*, Barth suggests that theology ought to derive from and pertain to the Christian community. In *deriving* from the church, theology provides an account of the Christian community's encounter with revelation. This does not mean that dogmatics must be reckoned a subset of historical theology, with the 'affections' of a specific community supplying the point of departure for theological reflection. Against Schleiermacher, Barth insists that the primary 'data' with which the theologian works are not ecclesial, but rather biblical. Past wisdom (creeds, major theological works, controversies, etc.) might assist the theologian in the execution of her task, but her starting-point is never other than the Bible's continuing witness of God's self-revelation. In *pertaining* to the church, theology aims to guide the thought and practice of actual Christian communities. Barth's preference for the word 'dogmatics', over and against less assuming phrases (such as 'systematic theology'), ought therefore to be taken seriously. His is a discourse of unabashedly didactic proportions. He ventures claims boldly and unapologetically; he aims to instruct. None of this is to say, of course, that Barth presumes to speak *sub specie aeterni* (i.e. from a God's-eye view). Despite an occasionally forbidding tone, he considers theological statements to be provisional, fallible and very much open to criticism. It does mean, though, that Barth eschews tentativeness when writing about God, creation, reconciliation and so on. Because faith participates in God's self-knowledge, a cognitively significant understanding of God's being, intentions and action is always being made available to the Christian. And the theologian, in his or her own way, has a role in helping the Christian community to understand the God that it knows and worships.

The dogmatician will, of course, draw on resources external to the Christian tradition when considering the 'understanding' ingredient to faith. Barth is unperturbed by this prospect. He is certainly not antipathetic towards a positive relationship between theology and philosophy. Indeed, in order to present doctrinal claims in a maximally precise way, the *Dogmatics* freely appropriates conceptual patterns from Kant, Hegel and various other European thinkers. What Barth does oppose is a fixed relationship between dogmatics and philosophy. Why so? Well, once again, Barth insists that it is God's revelation, witnessed in the Hebrew Bible and New Testament, that constitutes the material basis of dogmatic reflection. This revelation does not require supplement. God speaks fully, sufficiently and definitively through the words of Scripture. Accordingly, at no point may the theologian allow philosophical claims to shape substantively her deliberations. The relationship between philosophy and theology must be administered on terms determined by Christian faith. While the theologian may talk with whomsoever she chooses (and the *Dogmatics*, at its best, converses freely with all manner of thinkers), attention must be fixed on the word of God.

GOD AS TRINITY, AND THE DOCTRINE OF ELECTION

Barth is a thoroughly Trinitarian thinker, insistent that the one God be identified as Father, Son and Holy Spirit. In contrast to Schleiermacher's somewhat hesitant suggestion that the doctrine of the Trinity summarizes, at a remove, the Christian community's self-consciousness, Barth considers a frank acclamation of divine triunity to be the proper starting-point for theological reflection. Thus *Church Dogmatics* I/1 outlines the doctrine of the Trinity via an analysis of the structure of revelation. It is not quite that the Trinity is "an immediate utterance concerning the Christian self-consciousness" (the claim resisted by Schleiermacher [1999: 738–42]); rather, the doctrine arises when Christians begin to think about faith, which meditates on the basic fact that God presents himself as "Revealer, Revelation, and Revealedness" (*CD* I/1, §8). At the same time, Barth critiques the classical description of God as 'three persons in one essence'. To his mind, the word 'person' connotes a distinct centre of consciousness, and thereby imperils a robust affirmation of God's unity and simplicity. Talking about God's three 'ways or modes of being' is therefore preferable. Such phraseology maintains an Augustinian emphasis on divine unity (*see* Vol. 1, Ch. 18, "Augustine") while also highlighting God's triune self-differentiation.

Although *Church Dogmatics* I advances a prolegomenal statement that spells out certain 'rules' for talking about God's triunity (I/2, incidentally, adds important remarks on Christology, Scripture and the nature of the Christian community), it is the second volume of the *Dogmatics* that shows Barth to be a thinker of startling creativity. *Church Dogmatics* II/1 advances the striking claim that God is "the One who loves in freedom", because God is *free*, God is Lord of God's own being, determining exclusively God's identity and activity. God certainly stands under no external constraints with respect to God's relationship with creation and humankind: Barth remarks often that God *could* have been 'satisfied' with God's own life, rich as it is in its triune relating. How much more significant, then, that God does move towards humankind! Thus, correlative to a declaration of divine freedom, Barth emphasizes divine *love*. God's freedom is put in service of God's decision to exist in companionship with humankind. There is no part of God that does not intend fellowship with each and every human being. God's objectivity and otherness, not to mention God's 'perfections' (omnipotence, omniscience, etc.) must be understood in light of God's decision to be *pro nobis*.

Church Dogmatics II/2 intensifies this line of thought by way of an audacious re-conceptualization of the doctrine of election. Many classical Reformed thinkers, following Calvin's suggestions (which were uncompromisingly codified by the Synod of Dort in 1618/19), tended to view election in terms of the post-mortem standing of the individual. Those whom God deems to be 'elect' profit from unmerited grace and will enjoy a future of blessedness; those whom God renders 'reprobate', in contrast, will suffer judgement and condemnation for their sins. Barth baulks at this line of thought. Not only is it incompatible with his account of God – for what manner of love expresses itself in this way? – but, more particularly, it makes election external to God's being. Barth's response is to position election within the doctrine of God. Election specifies how God loves in freedom. It describes God's eternal decision to assign Godself *qua* Son the identity of Jesus Christ, 'electing God' and 'elected human'. In light of this decision, it becomes impossible for Christian theology to think of the being and action of God as generically *pro nobis*. God's love for humanity works itself out in utterly particular terms. God involves Godself intimately in the salvation of humankind, organizing God's own being around the person of Jesus Christ. By way of the doctrine of election, then, the programmatic Trinitarianism of *Church Dogmatics* I is conjoined to a 'Christological concentration' of startling force. One cannot think about God's triunity without reference to the Incarnation; one cannot think about the Incarnation without reference to God's being Father, Son and Holy Spirit.

Two further points about *Church Dogmatics* II require mention. First, in II/1 and II/2 Barth's 'actualistic' ontology gains vivid expression. As the word suggests, discussions of God's reality require a description of God's being-in-*act*. God is not akin to an object apprehended by human beings; God, in fact, is often not usefully described with conventional terms such as essence, substance or nature. For God is an *event*, a rich dynamic process, a life distinguished by vitality and exuberance. Secondly, in connecting the doctrines of election and God, Barth departs significantly from what is sometimes called 'classical theism': a perspective that presents God as ontologically impervious to events transpiring in the finite sphere. Although Barth does not believe the divine is adventitiously qualified by such events (he would vigorously reject 'process' perspectives), he does claim that God freely determines Godself *qua* Son in terms of the person of Jesus Christ. By dint of God's free elective decision, the principal event by which God manifests God's unwavering love for and solidarity with humankind – the life, death and resurrection of Jesus Christ – is always being applied to God's life, just as God applies this event to the life of humanity as such. Because of God's unceasing and jealous love for humankind, God wills that God *qua* Son be 'humanized' in this way, with the concrete life of the 'electing God' and 'elected human' becoming a part of God's identity for all eternity.

HUMANITY AND CREATION

As should already be evident, Barth's concern to stick close to the biblical texts and to focus attention on the person of Christ does not constrain his thinking. While metaphysical flights of fancy may be suppressed, Barth's 'particularism' enables a theological vision of unusual precision, range and audacity. These qualities are in ample supply throughout *Church Dogmatics* III, a four-part volume that considers, among other things, humanity, ethics, creation and the nature of evil.

Barth's theological anthropology is grounded in his understanding of election and incarnation. Because the Son takes on the identity of Jesus Christ, all human-kind has been made and remade: 'made' in that each human being is defined by Christ's life of free obedience to God; 'remade' in that each human being's sin has been cancelled and forgiven by way of Christ's death and resurrection. Accordingly, Barth's description of the human being sounds a consistently posi-tive, even cheerful, note. Since humanity exists 'in Christ', sin cannot be a leading theme of dogmatics. Sin refers rather to the state from which the human being has been rescued: an 'unnatural' condition from which we have been liberated.

Barth therefore discusses human-being with categories such as gratitude, responsibility and freedom. The *imago dei* definitive of each person bears a Christic, not
an Adamic, face.

A distinguishing feature of this outlook is Barth's rich understanding of human
agency. Integral to the *Dogmatics* is a "moral ontology" (Webster 1995: 1, and
passim): an expansive account of human action before and with God. In many
cases, divine action is not exclusive of human action, but is rather inclusive of
human action. Grace, one might say, *capacitates*. It is an event in which God
gives human beings the opportunity to share in God's work. A crucial term here
is 'correspondence' (*Entsprechung*). It signals that genuine human agency occurs
in light of, and in accordance with, God's prevenient advance. Indeed, when the
human being corresponds herself to God's directive address, she realizes the
imago dei to be not only a gift, but also a task. The task is possible because of a
gracious initiative: God constantly approaches human beings, asking that we take
up our covenantal commitments. The task is achievable in light of God's conferral
of ability: God gives us the strength to realize God's intentions, to be 'co-rulers'
(which means 'co-*lovers*') in the created realm.

In detailing this viewpoint, Barth's ethical reflections roam far and wide. He
comments on prayer, political responsibility, work, the nature of the state, the
responsibility of parents to their children and numerous other matters. At points, his
outlook seems painfully outdated. His remarks on gender and sexuality, for example,
betray a problematic embrace of patriarchal norms and have prompted concern
among those who aim to connect Christian theology with the struggle for the rights
of women, gay men and lesbians. At its best, though, the *Dogmatics* offers ethical
insights of abiding importance. For example, Barth's opposition to a Kantian codifi-
cation of ethical principles and his preference for a 'command ethic' (introduced in
Church Dogmatics II/2) does not disallow a 'shaped' Christian ethic; it rather ensures
that discussions of Christian conduct take their bearings from a living relationship
with God, mediated by Scripture. Equally, Barth's insistence on the practical import
of theology and his sharp critiques of self-serving religiosity have inspired various
forms of liberation theology. Since dogmatics "has the problem of ethics in view
from the very first" (*CD* III/4, 3), the theologian cannot but be keenly interested in
Christian conduct, in human suffering and in questions of social justice.

Accompanying Barth's theological anthropology is a broader doctrine of
creation, laid out primarily in *Church Dogmatics* III/1 and III/3. Central here is
the proposal that covenant and creation are correlative loci: covenant being the
"*internal* basis of creation" and creation being "the *external* basis of the covenant".
This intriguing pairing raises more issues than can be considered here, not least
the difficult matter of Barth's attitude towards scientific insights about cosmology
and evolution. Most basically, though, the connection of covenant and creation
indicates Barth's belief that God's redemptive intentions affect the *entirety* of finite
reality. As such, the whole non-human world – animals and plants, human society
and culture, angels and demons, and the like – must be considered in light of

God's action, in Christ through the Spirit, to bring humanity into companionship with God. Genesis 1 and 2, equally, ought to be read as cosmological 'sagas' that recount God's primordial commitment to relate graciously to humankind. And the doctrine of providence ought to do no less than attest to the inherent goodness of creation (a point of no small import, given that Barth wrote after the horrors of the Second World War and at the beginning of the cold war). To use Eberhard Busch's rich formulation: throughout his treatment of creation, Barth draws attention to "God's constant yes to his creature" (Busch 2004: 186–91).

An important bridge to Barth's doctrine of reconciliation comes with his discussion of evil. Summarizing suggestions ventured in earlier volumes, §50 of *Church Dogmatics* III/3 foregrounds the category of *das Nichtige*, roughly translatable as 'nothingness'. This term identifies evil as both genuinely inexplicable and genuinely threatening. It is inexplicable because theology must herewith confess its 'brokenness' (for how can the evil that God does *not* will be comprehensible?); it is threatening because, by dint of human sinfulness, a rogue dynamic haunts the created order, imperiling God's plan of salvation. Only God's gracious intervention in human affairs, specifically in the person of Christ, can re-establish the covenantal relationship that God wishes to enjoy with each and every human being.

RECONCILIATION: JESUS CHRIST, SIN AND THE CHRISTIAN LIFE

Barth's doctrine of reconciliation, articulated throughout *Church Dogmatics* IV, is noteworthy both for its size and for its intricate structure. Barth maintains and nuances further the 'Christological concentration' of previous volumes by using the *munus triplex* (Christ's 'threefold office') to pattern his remarks. Volume IV/1 considers Christ's identity as the humiliated 'priest', IV/2 describes Christ as the exalted 'king', and IV/3 focuses on Christ as 'prophet'. (The incomplete IV/4, incidentally, tackles baptism, putting forward the controversial suggestion that Christian communities eschew infant baptism and practise adult baptism.) Atop this Christological foundation, Barth lays further topics: justification, sin as pride and fall, the gathering of the community and Christian faith (IV/1); sanctification, sin as sloth and misery, the upbuilding of the community and Christian love (IV/2); and vocation, sin as falsehood and condemnation, the sending of the community and Christian hope (IV/3). Such architectonic virtuosity prevents any constriction of the dogmatic account of reconciliation, a problem Barth perceives to be endemic to Protestant scholasticism. It also ensures that his own 'Christological concentration' flows into expansive discussions of sin, the Holy Spirit and the church.

Church Dogmatics IV begins in earnest with Barth's famous discussion of "The Way of God into the Far Country" (IV/1, §59). Barth's focus in this paragraph is the divinity of Christ: he aims to describe how the Son responds to the Father's call that humanity be brought into fellowship with God. This leads to the daring suggestion that there is obedience within the life of God. For if God *qua* Son determines in terms of the Incarnation, and Christ lives according to the will of the Father, how can one describe the relationship between the first and second 'persons' of the Trinity *other* than in terms of obedience? Concomitantly, Barth advances a model of atonement that recalls the juridical mindset of many of his Reformed forebears, identifying Christ as the "judge judged in our place" (IV/1, §59.2). Justification, on this reckoning, entails the restorative (not retributive) 'punishment' of sinful humanity in the person of Christ. Volume IV/2 switches the angle of vision, focusing on the kingship of Christ and the sanctification of humankind effected by his life and death. By way of conversations with Protestant scholasticism and some brilliant exegetical moves, Barth's affirmation of Christ's divinity is now complemented by a sophisticated account of Christ's humanity and human agency. Making full use of the idea of 'correspondence', Barth suggests that Christ's humanity has a pivotal, though secondary, role in God's realization of reconciliation. Finally, IV/3 considers the luminous unity of Christ's divinity and Christ's humanity. Christ's identity as 'prophet' is elucidated in terms of his being the definitive witness to God, the "light of the world" (John 8:12), who discloses truth abundantly and perfectly.

As suggested above, discussions of human sinfulness follow the Christological foundation of each part-volume. Barth's aim here is to show that dogmatic descriptions of human corruption should be shaped by the scriptural accounts of Christ's life and passion, as opposed to generic assumptions about wickedness. Thus IV/1's account of Christ's exinanition – the Son's 'humiliation', as he incarnates and bears human sin – leads to a naming of sin as pride: human beings' refusal to acknowledge and conduct themselves as obedient servants of God. The presentation of the Son's exaltation in IV/2, which focuses on Christ's human correspondence to the divine will, exposes sin as sloth and misery. Sin is not merely disdain for divine Lordship; it is also a pitiful kind of lethargy that leads the human being to take up her assigned covenantal role. In IV/3, the treatments of sin as pride, fall, sloth and misery are complemented by an exposition of sin as falsehood. Each human being, not least the Christian, evades and distorts the truth; each human being, sinfully, obscures God's gracious revelation.

At the end of each part-volume of *Church Dogmatics* IV one finds Barth's descriptions of Christian life in community. This life is lived by a redeemed people: a people that enjoys, with and for the world, the Holy Spirit's application of God's reconciling love. Indeed, it is only by way of the operations of the Spirit that Christ's 'past' history is made real in the present. Barth amplifies the *filioque* clause of the Niceno-Constantinopolitan Creed (381 CE) in dramatic fashion, suggesting that the *filioque* 'goes both ways' in a manner that recalls the third book of Calvin's *Institutes of the Christian Religion* (2006).[7] As the Spirit proceeds from

---

7. This clause of the Niceno-Constantinopolitan Creed, favoured by many Western Christians, affirms that the Spirit 'proceeds' from the Father *and* the Son.

the Father and the Son, the Spirit also moves back towards the Father and the Son. And with this movement, the Spirit draws human beings into a vital companionship with God. Thus the 'procession' of the Spirit *from* the Father and the Son is honoured and complemented by the Spirit's offering humanity *to* the Son and the Father: humanity, that is, as it is (re)made in Jesus Christ. The Spirit, now and in the future, creates and rules over a church that is less an 'institution' and more an ongoing project: a distinctive time and space in which human beings, uplifted by the resurrection, learn to live and grow in fellowship with "the One who loves in freedom".

KARL BARTH TODAY

Although Barth has often been dubbed 'neo-orthodox', this chapter has assiduously avoided such a characterization. If 'orthodox' means upholding established doctrine, with the qualifier 'neo' suggesting only modest modification, then Barth cannot be defined in this way. While his work shows unflagging interest in established doctrinal *loci*, Barth sets his own stamp on every theological issue he tackles. As such, revelation is figured in terms of God's triune self-presentation, traditional terminology for the divine persons is jettisoned, the doctrine of election is radically reconceived, the relationship between divine and human action receives fresh and unusual attention, the *munus triplex* shapes the entire doctrine of reconciliation, and infant baptism is effectively rejected. Indeed, further innovations have come into view throughout this chapter. Barth's 'politics' involves a novel form of theological rhetoric; his doctrine of creation entails an exceptionally positive account of humanity and the natural world, interrupted only by an admission of 'inexplicable' evil (which, incidentally, echoes Kant's *Religion within the Boundaries of Mere Reason* [1996]); and his actualistic ecclesiology intimates a fascinating account of Christian life in community, superintended by the Spirit. The moral? Reliance on the category of 'neo-orthodoxy' inhibits appreciation of the *Church Dogmatics* and does Barth a terrible disservice. One must take Barth on his own terms: as a highly idiosyncratic thinker who will surprise, delight and sometimes antagonize his readers at every turn. The aim of this chapter has been to introduce some of Barth's central provocations; I encourage interested readers now to turn directly to Barth's own writings.

A final question: what meaning does Barth hold for Western philosophy of religion and Christian theology today? Rather than moving back into the *Dogmatics*, I want to conclude by identifying two issues that merit close attention in the coming years. The first issue concerns the political import of Barth's thought. Barth obviously sought to move beyond debates about 'church and state' and 'religion and public life'; with but a little attention, one detects political concerns woven into the thick textual fabric of the *Dogmatics*. Barth's overwhelmingly positive view of creation and humanity, for example, involves a direct response to post-war pessimism and the apocalyptic stupidity of nuclear stockpiling. And Barth's denunciation of sinful pride and sloth (which might well manifest itself in a disengagement from the 'world') carries a critique of bourgeois complacency just as devastating as anything in *Romans*. But can those issues that preoccupy many contemporary thinkers – globalization and the (literally) mortifying misdistribution of wealth, the rights of women and looming ecological collapse, to name but a few – be adequately treated with an indirection similar to that which characterizes the *Dogmatics*? More generally, given that Barth has inspired various forms of liberation theology (see e.g. Cone 1990), what future impact might his work have on politically progressive theological perspectives?

A second issue will perhaps have been looming in various readers' minds. What should the philosopher of religion or Christian theologian make of Barth's seemingly boundless confidence in theological discourse? The *Church Dogmatics* is arguably one of the most utopian theological works of the last few centuries. It presents Christian faith in a remarkably ideal form; it betrays an impatience with ambiguity and doctrinal half-measures; it manifests an unwavering faith in the propriety and referentiality of Christian declarations about God. But such theological derring-do seems hard to sustain in the present day. Despite the rise of fundamentalist religious options at home and abroad, many in the late-modern West despair of committing to a particular religious tradition and feel inclined towards various kinds of epistemological humility when it comes to claims about God, the world, Jesus Christ and the like. And in this context one may well feel utterly perplexed by the faith and thought of Karl Barth. What ought one to do in this situation? Without falsely dichotomizing a 'traditional' faith reared on nostalgia and the transitory bluster of some postmodern thinkers, one can at least conjecture as to Barth's response. "The decision", he might say, "is not in your hands. Rely instead on God's free love. And, since all else fails, simply cry out: *Veni Creator Spiritus*".

FURTHER READING

Barth, K. 1956–77. *Church Dogmatics*, 13 vols, G. Bromiley & T. Torrance (eds). Edinburgh: T&T Clark.

Barth, K. 1960. *The Humanity of God*. Richmond, VA: John Knox.

Barth, K. 1968. *The Epistle to the Romans*, E. Hoskyns (trans.). Oxford: Oxford University Press.

Busch, E. 1976. *Karl Barth*, J. Bowden (trans.). Philadelphia, PA: Fortress.

Gorringe, T. 1999. *Against Hegemony*. New York: Oxford University Press.

Hunsinger, G. 1991. *How to Read Karl Barth: The Shape of his Theology*. New York: Oxford University Press.

Jüngel, E. 2001. *God's Being is in Becoming: The Trinitarian Being of God in the Theology of Karl Barth: A Paraphrase*, J. Webster (trans.). Edinburgh: T&T Clark.

McCormack, B. 1995. *Karl Barth's Critically Realistic Dialectical Theology: Its Genesis and Development 1909-1936*. New York: Oxford University Press.

Webster, J. 1995. *Barth's Ethics of Reconciliation*. Cambridge: Cambridge University Press.

Webster, J. (ed.) 2000. *The Cambridge Companion to Karl Barth*. Cambridge: Cambridge University Press.

On CHRISTIANITY see also Vol. 1, Chs 10, 14, 17, 18. On ETHICS see also Chs 15, 21; Vol. 1, Ch. 11; Vol. 2, Chs 4, 8; Vol. 3, Ch. 9; Vol. 4, Chs 13, 19. On SCRIPTURE see also Vol. 1, Chs 9, 13, 17; Vol. 2, Ch. 19; Vol. 3, Chs 3, 4, 15; Vol. 4, Ch. 3. On THE TRINITY see also Ch. 23; Vol. 1, Chs 14, 17, 20; Vol. 2, Chs 2, 8, 15; Vol. 3, Chs 3, 9, 17; Vol. 4, Ch. 4.

13

LUDWIG WITTGENSTEIN

Genia Schoenbaumsfeld

"Tell them I've had a wonderful life." These were Wittgenstein's last words, spoken on his deathbed in 1951 (Monk 1991: 579). Certainly, Wittgenstein had a remarkable life: one devoted not just to philosophy, but to a relentless pursuit of truthfulness, to a purity of heart and mind. Right until the very end Wittgenstein was working on remarks that have come to be known as *On Certainty*, but the only piece of writing completed and published during his lifetime remains his early masterpiece, the *Tractatus Logico-Philosophicus* (hereafter *Tractatus*). It fell to his literary executors to prepare his immense *Nachlass* for publication.

The life that ended at Storeys End, Cambridge, began in *fin de siècle* Vienna on 26 April 1889. Ludwig Josef Johann was the eighth and youngest child of a prominent and wealthy Austrian family of Jewish extraction. The Wittgenstein children grew up in an extraordinary environment: not only did the family itself display considerable musical talent, but their grand home in the Alleegasse was frequented by an assortment of the time's greatest artistic figures, among them Johannes Brahms, Pablo Casals, Gustav Mahler and Bruno Walter. Wittgenstein's sister Margarete was painted by Gustav Klimt, and his brother Paul became a celebrated concert pianist, for whom Ravel, Prokofieff and Strauss wrote concertos. But Ludwig's early life was also overshadowed by tragedy: two of his brothers committed suicide before Ludwig was out of his teens.

Until he discovered philosophy by happening upon the work of Bertrand Russell while a research student in aeronautics at Manchester, Ludwig seemed the least promising of the Wittgenstein siblings, with more of a technical, practical bent than an artistic or intellectual one. But once taken on as Russell's student at Cambridge, Wittgenstein's great talent immediately became apparent, much to the surprise of his sister Hermine, to whom Russell said: "We expect the next big step in philosophy to be taken by your brother" (Monk 1991: 55). 'The next big step' turned out to be, according to the preface of the *Tractatus*, "the final solution of the problems" (Wittgenstein 2002: 4) that had been bedevilling Gottlob Frege and Russell, or so Wittgenstein thought in 1918.

Written during the First World War, while Wittgenstein was a volunteer in the Austrian Army, the *Tractatus* is perhaps best known for its last words: "What we cannot speak about we must pass over in silence" (Wittgenstein 2002: 89). For ten years after completing his book Wittgenstein himself remained true to this line, abandoning philosophy, and retraining to become a schoolteacher in an out-of-the-way Austrian village called Trattenbach.

It was the philosophy of mathematics that reeled Wittgenstein in again: in 1928 he heard Brouwer lecture in Vienna, and this may have served to convince him that there was, perhaps, more to say on the subject after all (Monk 1991: 251). Wittgenstein duly returned to Cambridge in January 1929, or, as Keynes put it: "God has arrived. I met him on the 5.15 train" (*ibid.*: 255).

In the subsequent years, Wittgenstein's philosophy changed dramatically. He dismantled the logical atomism of the *Tractatus* and got rid of the idea that language functions in only one way: to convey pictures of the facts. Just as, throughout his life, he had striven to rid himself of sin, so Wittgenstein now tried to purge his thought of metaphysical dogmatism, in keeping with his conception of philosophy as work on oneself.

A year after Nazi Germany's annexation of Austria, Wittgenstein succeeded G. E. Moore as Professor of Philosophy at Cambridge and became a natural-ized British citizen. The outbreak of the Second World War temporarily put paid to Wittgenstein's academic duties, and he took up war work at Guy's Hospital in London. He resumed his position at Cambridge in 1944 only to resign it for good three years later, a reflection of his view that Cambridge academic life was a kind of living death. Wittgenstein spent the last years of his life trying to get the *Philosophical Investigations* into publishable form. He died at a friend's house in Cambridge three days after his sixty-second birthday, "one of the greatest and most influential philosophers of our time" (von Wright, in Malcolm 2001: 3).

WITTGENSTEIN AND RELIGIOUS BELIEF

Wittgenstein published next to nothing on the philosophy of religion and yet his conception of religious belief has been immensely influential. While the concluding, 'mystical' remarks in his early work, the *Tractatus*, are notorious, we find only a single allusion to theology in his *magnum opus*, the *Philosophical Investigations* (hereafter *PI*), posthumously published in 1953. Wittgenstein's mature views on the nature of religious belief must therefore be pieced together from scattered remarks made in his notebooks from the 1930s, the *Lectures and Conversations on Religious Belief* (compiled from lecture notes), the *Remarks on Frazer's "Golden Bough"* and from what has come to be known as *Culture and Value* (hereafter *CV*). All of the above, as well as recorded conversations with friends, testify to Wittgenstein's lifelong involvement with religious issues, so it is not readily explicable why Wittgenstein remained silent about them in his most important work. But then Wittgenstein once said to his friend Maurice Drury, "It is impossible for me to say in my book one word about all that music has meant in my life. How then can I hope to be understood?" (Rhees 1984: 79). This remark might equally well apply to religion.

Wittgenstein's reflections about religious belief are inspired by a number of thinkers, such as Tolstoy, Dostoevsky, William James and, most notably perhaps, the Danish philosopher, Søren Kierkegaard (*see* Vol. 4, Ch. 13).[1] With the latter he shares the view that Christianity is not a theory about the behaviour of supernatural entities, but an existence-communication, whose demands are primarily ethical, not intellectual. The believer, on this conception, is supposed to transform himself, not his ontological commitments; he is called to exist in the truth as lived out by Christ, the paradigm or pattern, not to engage in speculation about the metaphysical compatibility of the 'two natures' of Christ, say.

Wittgenstein once wrote: "If Christianity is the truth then all the philosophy that is written about it is false" (*CV* 83e).[2] If this is indeed apt, it would seem to confine pretty much everything that goes on in philosophy of religion and theology departments to the scrapheap. Small wonder, therefore, that Wittgenstein's views about the nature of religious belief continue to engender the fiercest opposition, both in those who are sympathetic to religion and in those who are not. In this chapter I shall concentrate solely on Wittgenstein's later conception of religious belief and shall leave his *Tractatus* views to one side.

Unsurprisingly, Wittgenstein's conception of religious belief in many ways mirrors his philosophical concerns more generally. Just as Wittgenstein rejects the idea that philosophy is a theoretical exercise whose purpose consists in developing explanatory hypotheses about the hidden workings of language and the world – "we must do away with all *explanation*, and description alone must take its place" (*PI* §109)[3] – so, too, he jettisons the thought that Christianity offers us a philosophical theory about what goes on in a celestial realm. Instead, he shares Kierkegaard's insight that truth "in the sense in which Christ is the truth is not a sum of statements, not a definition etc., but a life" (Kierkegaard 1991: 205). Christianity, according to Kierkegaard, provides a 'radical cure' for the problem of life and hence requires something much more fundamental than assent to a sum of tenets. This is already shown, as Wittgenstein points out in the *Lectures and Conversations* (hereafter *LC*), by this "extraordinary use of the word 'believe'. One talks of believing and at the same time one doesn't use 'believe' as one does ordinarily. You might say (in the normal use): 'You only believe – oh well ...'" (*LC* 59–60).[4] But in the religious case it makes no sense to say 'oh well', for, as the Bible

---

1. For a detailed analysis of Wittgenstein's relation to Kierkegaard, see Schönbaumsfeld (2007).
2. References to *Culture and Value* are to Wittgenstein (1977).
3. References to the *Philosophical Investigations* are to Wittgenstein (1953).
4. References to the *Lectures and Conversations* are to Wittgenstein (1966).

UNIVERSITY OF WINCHESTER
LIBRARY

tells us: Thou *shalt* believe. This, it would seem, is an ethical injunction – it is a call to become a certain kind of person (one, say, capable of acknowledging his need for redemption) – it is not the demand to force intellectual assent to a proposition about some kind of 'master of the universe' figure.

One does not, Wittgenstein thinks, come to Christianity through argument and intellectual deliberation; it is rather the shape of one's life and experiences that will (or will not) teach one a use for the Christian concepts. The exigencies of life may, as it were, thrust these concepts upon one. It is for this reason that Wittgenstein says: "It strikes me that a religious belief could only be something like a passionate commitment to a system of reference. Hence, although it's *belief,* it's really a way of living, or a way of assessing life. It's passionately seizing hold of *this* interpretation" (*CV* 64e).

The implications of Wittgenstein's conception are complex and have not always been understood correctly. So, for example, it has often been thought, by believers and unbelievers alike, that by emphasizing faith's 'existential' dimension – that is to say, its embeddedness in religious *practice* – Wittgenstein has thrown out the baby with the bathwater: once all the philosophy that is written about Christianity is put aside, we would seem to be left with nothing more than adherence to a 'doctrineless' form of life. If true, this would indeed be a serious objection. But the matter is much more complicated than this criticism would suggest. As in his philosophical practice more generally, the point of Wittgenstein's remarks is to challenge the very terms in which the debate is cast. That is to say, Wittgenstein wants to show that it is itself an illusion to suppose that we are confronted by two exhaustive alternatives here: either adherence to a set of metaphysical beliefs (with certain ways of acting following from these beliefs) or passionate commitment to a way of life; there is no third way.

The thought that there cannot be any middle ground here is fuelled by the fact that we are naturally prone to suppose that it is possible neatly to separate the meaning of words from their use – "here the word, there the meaning. The money and the cow you can buy with it (But contrast: money, and its use)" (*PI* §121) – and so we might be tempted to believe, as many commentators do, that it is possible to inspect the words alone in order to find out whether they make sense or not. This conception has fairly disastrous consequences for the meaning of religious language, as Kai Nielsen, for example, has shown:

> It is not ... that I think that God is an object among objects, but I do think ... that he must – in some very unclear sense – be taken to be a particular existent among existents though, of course, 'the king' among existents, and a very special and mysterious existent, but not an object, not a kind of object, not just a categorical or classificatory notion, but not a non-particular either. Though he is said to be infinite, he is also said to be a person, and these two elements when put together seem at least to yield a glaringly incoherent notion. He cannot be an object

– a spatio-temporal entity but he is also a he – a funny kind of he to be sure – who is also said to be a person – again a funny kind of person – who is taken to be a person without a body: a purely *spiritual* being. This makes him out to be a 'peculiar reality' indeed. He gets to be even more peculiar when we are told he is an *infinite* person as well. But now language has really gone on a holiday.

(Nielsen & Phillips 2005: 123)

What Nielsen seems to be assuming in this passage is that owing to the fact that I can understand what 'person' and 'infinite' mean in ordinary contexts, I am also able to understand the religious expression 'God is infinite', as if this were just a matter of combining the two linguistic 'atoms', 'person' and 'infinite', into a 'peculiar' complex whose sense, to put it mildly, is elusive. But if this were in fact a good model for understanding what goes on here, we would be similarly stumped as regards ethical and aesthetic language use; that is to say, we would have to conclude that it, too, is a partner in the crime of perpetual holidaying. For example, we would be just as much at a loss about how it is possible to apply emotive language to music, say. That is, if Nielsen's analysis of 'God-talk' is anything to go by, we would be confronted by the following dilemma: either we understand sentences such as 'the music of the string quartet is tearful' because it makes sense for sounds or bits of marks on a page to be sad – an analogue to Nielsen's strictly literal rendering of religious language – or such sentences are, as Nielsen is fond of emphasizing, purely 'symbolic', that is, the 'tearful' is merely a fancy way of saying something like 'arousing feelings of sadness in most perceivers' – a correlate of Nielsen's claim that if religious language cannot be construed literally, then it reduces to "morality touched by emotion" (Nielsen & Phillips 2005: 314). But, although philosophers have at one time or another held such views (e.g. Mackie 1982: 219–22), the options that Nielsen is presenting us with here do not strike me as exhaustive. It would be rash just to write-off religious, moral and aesthetic language simply because it does not fit nicely into either of Nielsen's preconceived moulds.

So let us look instead at the alternative that Wittgenstein proposes:

Actually I should like to say that … the *words* you utter or what you think as you utter them are not what matters, so much as the difference they make at various points in your life. How do I know that two people mean the same when each says he believes in God? … *Practice* gives the words their sense.

(*CV* 85e)

In passages such as these Wittgenstein is not saying anything different than when he is, for example, tackling the philosophical (or logical) problem of what it is to mean something in the *Philosophical Investigations*: "For a *large* class of cases – though not for all – in which we employ the word 'meaning' it can be defined thus: the meaning of a word is its use in the language" (*PI* §43).

This view has the following implications for understanding the meaning of religious expressions. In order to be able to grasp their sense, you not only need to understand what the 'atoms' – that is, the individual words constituting the utterance – mean in *other* contexts (in contexts, say, in which you have first learnt the uses of these words), but what the sentence as a whole means, and for this to be possible, you must understand how the words are functioning in *this* specific context (you must, that is, understand their technique of application *here*); something that cannot be accomplished by, for example, simply hazarding a guess about what the words composing the sentence might or might not be 'referring' to. This is why Wittgenstein says (*LC* 55) that in one sense he understands all that the religious person who believes in a Last Judgement says, because he understands, for example, the ordinary words 'God' or 'separate',[5] but that, in another sense, he does not understand the sentence *at all* for, in this particular context, he has no grasp of how these familiar words are used: "my normal technique of language leaves me" (*ibid.*).

Wittgenstein's case, to borrow an example of Cora Diamond's, is similar to someone who understands the ordinary use of the word 'beautiful', say, but who is at a loss when someone applies it to a person like George Eliot, for example. For according to the habitual criteria Eliot obviously is not beautiful. If I am therefore to understand this new application of a familiar concept, my ordinary vision must, as it were, first be transformed. In Diamond's words:

> She [George Eliot], that magnificently ugly woman, gives a totally transformed meaning to 'beauty'. Beauty itself becomes something entirely new for one, as one comes to see (to one's own amazement, perhaps) a powerful beauty residing in this woman … In such a case, she is not judged by a norm available through the concept of beauty; she shows the concept up, she moves one to use the words 'beauty' and 'beautiful' almost as new words, or as renewed words. She gives one a new vocabulary, a new way of taking the world in in one's words, and of speaking about it to others. (2005: 125)

That is to say, a "conceptual reorientation" (*ibid.*) must take place if I am to understand the application of the word 'beautiful' to Eliot, a reorientation that, as Diamond says, makes possible new ways of speaking about the world. And something similar, if Wittgenstein is right, happens in religious contexts, when I am, for instance, suddenly brought to understand, perhaps through certain kinds of

---

5. It is unclear why Wittgenstein speaks of 'separate' in connection with a discussion of the Last Judgement, but I presume he is thinking of sentences such as 'the soul is separate from the body' or some such thing; of course, this is only a guess. What exactly Wittgenstein meant, however, is irrelevant to our discussion.

experiences of dependence and dependability,[6] what it means to call God 'Father'. In this respect, just as Eliot "moves one to use the words 'beauty' and 'beautiful' almost as new words", so, it could be said, does God move the religious believer to use the words 'father' or 'fatherly love' almost as new words.

Consequently, one could now say that for someone for whom this 'conceptual reorientation' does not occur, no real understanding of the sentence (or words) in question is possible. That is to say, someone like Wittgenstein, who does not know what to make of the 'after death man's'[7] words, can be said only to 'understand' such sentences in the sense that he recognizes, for example, the ordinary English words 'scrutiny', 'soul' and so on that might constitute them, but without being able to understand, to speak with Diamond, the 'renewed use' of these words. This would be similar to someone who knows that the sun is a star located at the centre of our solar system, but who fails to see the aptness of the phrase 'Juliet is the sun'. And such a failure of understanding cannot be remedied by, say, pointing at Juliet and at the sun and saying, 'she is like that', but rather by drawing attention to aspects of the sun that make the comparison with Juliet meaningful. If this still does not help, then perhaps getting the person to read more poetry will gradually make understanding dawn.[8]

It is ironic that in most philosophical domains it is fairly commonplace nowadays to appeal to context and practice when it comes to the question of effecting an understanding of something; indeed, as regards understanding ethical and aesthetic concepts, for example, one even speaks of cultivating certain virtues of character said to be necessary for making such understanding possible. But when it comes to understanding religious language, these lessons are generally forgotten and it is assumed that here the only pertinent question to ask is whether religious language 'refers', as if there were only *one* thing referring could be, as if what constitutes 'referring' does not itself, in many ways, depend on *context*. Noticing a 'religious fact', if one wants to talk that way, requires an understanding of theological concepts – such as, for example, seeing the point of calling God 'Father' – just as understanding a 'mathematical fact' needs the established practice of mathematics.

So when Wittgenstein is, for example, saying that Christianity is not a doctrine, he does not mean that it has no conceptual content. Rather, what he is suggesting is that being able, say, to recite the Creeds or statements of Catholic dogma is not sufficient for having any real understanding of religious concepts at all. For the kind of understanding that is required here is being able to see religious utterances non-instrumentally, that is to say, being able to see their *point* and aptness rather than their ability, as it were, to convey 'information' about God. And being

---

6. Compare Wittgenstein's talk of 'feeling absolutely safe' in the *Lecture on Ethics*.
7. This phrase is Diamond's.
8. Of course it is possible that, regardless of what one tries, understanding will never occur. In such cases one may want to speak, like Wittgenstein, of a kind of 'aspect blindness'.

able to see this is not possible, if Wittgenstein is right, independently of having some familiarity and grasp of the Christian form of life and the phenomenology of experience that gave rise to it. Hence, when Wittgenstein says that the important thing with regard to the Christian 'doctrine' is to understand "that you have to change your life" (*CV* 53e) or "the *direction* of your life" (*CV* 53e), he is not implying that it is somehow possible to do this *without* committing oneself to the Christian claims. For to say that much more than rote-reciting is required is not to say that therefore the 'doctrine' – the Christian claims – are irrelevant, as this would be as absurd as thinking that because a song can be sung both with and without expression, you could have the expression without the song (*LC* 29).

This also helps us to understand what Wittgenstein means when he says that

> in religion every level of devoutness must have its appropriate form of expression which has no sense at a lower level. This doctrine, which means something at a higher level, is null and void for someone who is still at the lower level; he *can* only understand it *wrongly* and so these words are *not* valid for such a person. (*CV* 32e)

Here Wittgenstein is suggesting that there are different levels of understanding as regards religious doctrines corresponding to the relative depth of devoutness and spiritual development of the person concerned. So, for example, someone who thinks that the expression "the Lord has given, the Lord has taken away, blessed be the name of the Lord" is a cheap attempt at trying to justify the caprice of the deity, is at a lower level of religious understanding than someone who sees it as a trusting acceptance of God's sovereignty. If the idea that spiritual development is necessary for a proper understanding of religious expressions to occur strikes us as implausible, it may again be useful to remind ourselves of what goes on in aesthetic contexts. Someone, for instance, who lacks a musical education and does not possess a 'musical ear' will not be able to contradict the judgement of a connoisseur, as such a person will not have sufficient (musical) sensibility even to understand what the connoisseur is saying. In other words, such a person will neither possess the vocabulary nor have the appropriate concepts that would enable them to say anything genuinely meaningful about a musical work, short perhaps of finding it 'pleasurable' or 'relaxing'. For exactly analogous reasons, Wittgenstein feels that he cannot contradict what the religious person is saying, since he, as yet, lacks a real grasp of the concepts involved. That is to say, just as there is musical sensibility and tone deafness (and, to be sure, much in between), there is also religious sensibility and blindness for religion, and neither musical nor religious sensibility is acquired by learning a set of theses, doctrines, by heart – about who the great composers were, about the laws of counterpoint or about transubstantiation – since this would only bring about a purely intellectual understanding of the subject comparable to having learnt a code. But what is required here is the kind of understanding that makes the musical work or the prayer (the religious words) *live* for me, not the kind that allows me to parrot a form of words. And such an understanding can only be brought about by immersing oneself in the culture or practice that has given rise to these phenomena. This is why Wittgenstein says in the *Lectures on Aesthetics*, "In order to get clear about aesthetic words you have to describe ways of living" (*LC* 11). If we understand that this is so in the case of aesthetics, it is only prejudice that prevents us from seeing that this applies in exactly the same way to religion. Hence Wittgenstein's remark that he could only utter the word 'Lord' with meaning if he lived *completely* differently (*CV* 33e).

Now one might think that if this account is correct, it effectively seals off religious belief from any form of rational criticism. For if I have to immerse myself in religious practice if I am to have any hope of understanding religious expressions, then I cannot just criticize them from a detached, philosophical viewpoint by, for instance, showing that they fall short of commonly accepted criteria of rationality. But if so, then are we not just espousing, as Nielsen has forcefully argued, a form of fideism? Many philosophers inspired by Wittgenstein's remarks on religious belief have been tarred with Nielsen's fideistic brush, most notably D. Z. Phillips, Peter Winch and Rush Rhees. I shall not here be reopening the debate as to the accuracy of labelling these philosophers thus; this has been done to death, I think, in the recent exchange between Phillips and Nielsen entitled *Wittgensteinian Fideism?* (2005). What I propose instead is to bite the bullet as regards this criticism.

As I have already argued, if criticizing religious beliefs comes down to trying to determine on paper, as it were – by inspecting the words alone – whether they make sense or not (or whether religious expressions 'refer' or not), then this is indeed something we cannot do. But nor can we do this as regards *any* form of discourse. For example, someone who has not been trained in philosophy will not be able to understand the works of Immanuel Kant, even if he understands – knows the habitual use of – all the words contained in those works. Indeed, as should be obvious to anyone who has ever tried to teach students philosophy, even paraphrasing and explaining Kant in your own words to them will very often not effect understanding either. The path to understanding is long and arduous here: it involves years of studying the thought of other philosophers, of seeing the point of asking certain kinds of question, and so on. If Nielsen were right about religion, then we would analogously have to conclude that there is something wrong with philosophy if people cannot understand it, rather than that the fault lies with them and their lack of training. As Wittgenstein says: "Are you a bad philosopher, then, if what you write is hard to understand? If you were better you would make what's difficult easy to understand. – But who says that's possible?!" (*CV* 76e).

In other words, Wittgenstein's conception rules out the possibility of constructing a 'neutral set of criteria' – what Nielsen seems to be hankering after – against which individual practices can be assessed and found wanting. But this should not worry us, for it implies neither that philosophy can have nothing to say to religion nor that religious beliefs cannot be criticized. All it prevents us from doing is taking Nielsen's all too short line here: religious beliefs are just plain incoherent.

In fact, if Wittgenstein is right, philosophy has quite a lot to say to religion. For Wittgenstein's grammatical investigations not only show that Nielsen's approach cannot be right, but also reveal that much of what religious believers say about their beliefs may not be an accurate reflection of what is really going on. For example, the kind of believer who, like a certain Father O'Hara in Wittgenstein's *Lectures and Conversations*, thinks that religious belief is a 'question of science' is called 'unreasonable' by Wittgenstein:

> I would definitely call O'Hara unreasonable. I would say, if this is religious belief, then it's all superstition. But I would ridicule it, not by saying it is based on insufficient evidence. I would say: here is a man who is cheating himself. You can say: this man is ridiculous because he believes, and bases it on weak reasons. (*LC* 59)

The error that Wittgenstein is seeking to expose here consists in taking the existence of God to be on a par with the existence of some super-empirical object or entity that one could, in principle, encounter if only one possessed the relevant faculties. That is to say, the conception that Wittgenstein has within his sights is of the kind exhibited by the Soviet astronaut Yuri Gagarin's remark that God is an object he would have observed, had it existed, during his first space flight (Nielsen & Phillips 2005: 48). But such a view, according to Wittgenstein, is absurd, since "the way you use the word 'God' does not show *whom* you mean – but, rather, what you mean" (*CV* 50e).

On Wittgenstein's conception, in other words, 'God' does not denote some *thing* that one could encounter independently of having the concept in the sense that one could, for example, encounter a unicorn or the Loch Ness monster, if there happened to be such things. For although, as Wittgenstein says in *Lectures and Conversations*, the word 'God' is among the earliest learnt, I did not learn the word 'God' by being shown a picture of him (*LC* 59). That is to say, even though the word is used like a word representing a person (God sees, rewards, etc.), "it plays an entirely different role to that of the existence of any person or object I ever heard of" (*LC* 59). In the later Wittgenstein's parlance, the surface grammar of the word 'God' functions in many ways analogously to that of an outlandish person while its depth grammar is actually quite different. This is shown, for example, by the fact that it is impossible, even in principle, to paint a picture of God[9] or to hear

---

9. And Michelangelo's painting of God creating Adam is not a 'picture of God' in the relevant sense. As Winch says in his illuminating essay, "Wittgenstein, Picture and Representation":

> In other words, what makes the picture a religious picture is not its pictorial relationship to some event. If it is said that it is a relationship to a *supernatural* event, that of course makes a difference: but the chances are that in this context the speaker will be conceiving the 'supernatural' event as a weird sort of *natural* event.

Him speak to someone else. Neither of these features are *contingent* descriptions of God as they would be if, *per impossibile*, they happened to apply to a human person. Rather, they serve to constitute (aspects of) the meaning of the word 'God'. Perhaps this is why Wittgenstein cites theology as his first example when he says in one of the most famous passages from the *Philosophical Investigations*: "Grammar tells what kind of object anything is. (Theology as grammar.)" (*PI* §373). Hence, if Wittgenstein is right, it is a *grammatical* (conceptual/logical) feature of the concept 'God' that you cannot hear him talk to someone else: it is not because of the fact that God is a person with an impossibly low voice (or, indeed, a disembodied one).

However, none of this implies, as those who are all too readily persuaded by Nielsen's account believe, that what Wittgenstein *really* means when he says that 'God' is not the name of an entity, or that what is at issue is not the existence of some thing, is that actually there is no God. Rather, what he is trying to show is that it makes no sense to construe God's existence as meaning something like 'a white elephant exists'. In other words, the grammar of the concept 'God' does not function, *pace* Nielsen, like the grammar of *eine Existenz* (of an entity). This is also the reason why Wittgenstein says that it is possible to describe what it would be like if there were gods on Mount Olympus, but not "what it would be like if there were such a thing as God" (*CV* 82e). For in pagan religions the deities are conceived as on a par with other empirical objects, only vastly more powerful. There is therefore no grammatical difference between talk of Poseidon, say, and talk of an ordinary human being, except that Poseidon happens to have superhuman powers. But this is not qualitatively different from encountering a new species of beings from a distant planet who have powers surpassing our own or, indeed, from encountering the Loch Ness monster. In Christianity, however, talk of God is not like that. Consequently, it is possible to give an account of what would have to be the case if there were a Poseidon or if there were a Loch Ness monster – since the opposite of these scenarios can also be imagined and described – but not how it would be if there were a God, or how it would be if God existed, for in these cases there simply is no such thing as imagining or describing 'the opposite'; the 'phenomena' in the world remain the same whether there is a God or not. To become aware of God's presence is therefore nothing like becoming aware of the existence of some esoteric object whose presence had hitherto escaped one's notice. This is the significance of Wittgenstein's remark:

> Life can educate one to a belief in God. And *experiences* too are what bring this about; but I don't mean visions and other forms of sense

---

So it is best to leave aside talk about 'a relationship to an event' altogether … let us not overlook the fact that what makes the picture a representation of God the Father (rather than of a man in a queer blanket) is not itself something pictorial.
(Winch 1987: 79–80)

experience which show us 'the existence of this being', but, e.g., suffer-
ings of various sorts. These neither show us God in the way a sense
impression shows us an object, nor do they give rise to *conjectures*
about him. Experiences, thoughts – life can force this concept on us.
So perhaps it is similar to the concept of 'object'.   (*CV* 86e)

What Wittgenstein is trying to bring out here is that, just as we cannot infer the
proposition 'there are objects' from the proposition 'here is a hand', so too in the
case of religious belief it is not a matter of making inferences from certain sense-
perceptions. For religious experiences do not stand to the proposition 'there is a
God' as, say, satellite pictures of the earth (or of Loch Ness monsters, black holes
or what have you) stand to the proposition 'the earth is round' (as Wittgenstein
says, we did not learn the concept 'God' by being shown pictures of him, nor
'could' we be shown pictures of him, and the nature of this 'could' is logical). There
simply is nothing that we would ordinarily call an 'evidential basis' here.

It is for these reasons that Wittgenstein believes that it is a mistake to want
to demonstrate God's existence. For instance, say I wanted to go about demonstrating Napoleon's existence from Napoleon's works, to use one of Kierkegaard's
examples. This is only possible if I assume from the outset that Napoleon's works
are 'his' works, that is, if I already assume that Napoleon exists. For, if I do not do
this, all I can demonstrate is that the works in question have been accomplished
by a great general, but this in itself is not sufficient to demonstrate *Napoleon's*
existence (as opposed to someone else's), as another person could have accomplished the same works (Kierkegaard 1985: 40). And the same, of course, applies
to demonstrating God's existence from his 'works', that is, from the existence of the
universe: I cannot infer the existence of God from the existence of the universe,
since God's works do not exist immediately and directly in the way that tables and
chairs do. Hence, even if we assume that nature is the work of God, only nature is
directly present, not God. Therefore, just as in Napoleon's case, I can demonstrate
God's existence from these works (nature/the universe) only if I already regard
them ideally as *God's*, that is, if I already assume what is to be proved, namely, that
the universe is ordered according to providential or divine principles.

That I cannot, just as in the case of the ontological argument, get beyond a
petitio principii here – I can only see divine governance in nature or the universe
if I already believe in divine governance (and vice versa) – shows that what is at
issue is not something that could, even in principle, be amenable to empirical
or philosophical investigation. Hence, if I am not religious already nothing will
count as 'evidence for the existence of God' for me. Given that there is no such
thing as a self-validating experience or a self-interpreting rule, the way I perceive
certain events will itself already be shaped by my world-picture. I can therefore
go on examining nature *ad infinitum* in order to find traces of God in it, but such
an investigation will never be able to tell me whether nature is the work of God or
the product of chance, just as a historical investigation of the New Testament will

never be able to tell me whether Christ was God. For the very idea of attempting to 'calculate the odds' for something as absolutely extraordinary as that God became man is incoherent, as it betrays the qualitative (grammatical) confusion that the claims of Christianity are on a par with *secular* claims to which it is possible to assign probability values. But this – to borrow again from Kierkegaard – is not only as confused as "assuming that the kingdom of *heaven* is a kingdom along with all other kingdoms on *earth* and that one would look for information about it in a geography book" (1992: 391), it is also, in Kierkegaard's eyes, *blasphemous* (1991: 29), since it presupposes that we are in a position to tell what it is probable for *God* to do – the height of philosophical *hubris* – and according to which criteria should we ever be in a position to tell whether it is probable, for example, that Christ was God or that he rose from the dead?

Consequently, if Wittgenstein is right, then, *pace* Blaise Pascal (*see* Vol. 3, Ch. 10) and Father O'Hara, there is no such thing as 'quantifying' oneself into faith. Rather, it is a grammatical confusion – a kind of category mistake – to believe that a scientific or probabilistic investigation of religious claims is possible. In this respect, Wittgenstein's philosophical reflections on religious faith are clearly critical; Wittgenstein is showing us how *not* to construe religious beliefs and this, it seems to me, assigns to philosophy an extremely important role. So, although philosophy in one sense "leaves everything as it is" (*PI* §124) – that is to say, it does not interfere with our actual practices – in another sense it changes everything, for it clears away the conceptual confusions and obstacles that cause us to misinterpret these practices.

In conclusion, I regard it as Wittgenstein's greatest achievement in this area to have shown how a religion without metaphysics might be possible. And this means that, if Wittgenstein is right, there is a third way of understanding religious practice and we no longer have to come down on either side of Nielsen's unappetizing dichotomy: either incoherent metaphysics or 'morality touched by emotion'. Of course, this also means that we can no longer just confidently assert that "the whole of mankind does all that [i.e. engages in religious practice] out of sheer stupidity" (Wittgenstein 1993: 119), but this, it seems to me, is all to the good. Wittgenstein must surely be right, to speak anachronistically, to apply Donald Davidson's 'principle of charity' here: "when others think differently from us, no general principle, or appeal to evidence, can force us to decide that the difference lies in our beliefs rather than in our concepts" (Davidson 2001: 197). That is to say, rather than plumping for the option, like James George Frazer, of simply attributing a whole host of false or incoherent beliefs to religious believers, it would seem more sensible to look, like Wittgenstein, "for an entirely different interpretation altogether" (*LC* 62). Once sufficient attention is paid to the grammar of religious concepts – to how these concepts actually function within the religious form of life – it should become clear that something *different*, rather than something irrational, is going on there. As Wittgenstein said in discussion with Rhees: "the grammar of our language about God has holes in it IF YOU LOOK AT IT AS BEING

THE GRAMMAR OF STATEMENTS ABOUT A HUMAN BEING" (Rhees 2005: 414). So, rather than attempting to patch up the holes, as it were, with implausible theories about the antics of persons without bodies, say, the presence of the holes should rather alert us to the fact that a new form of understanding is needed here: the kind, if Wittgenstein is right, that is both the result of conceptual reorientation and personal transformation.

FURTHER READING

Arrington, R. & M. Addis (eds) 2001. *Wittgenstein and Philosophy of Religion*. London: Routledge.

Kerr, F. 1986. *Theology after Wittgenstein*. Oxford: SPCK Press.

Malcolm, N. 1993. *Wittgenstein: A Religious Point of View?* Ithaca, NY: Cornell University Press.

Phillips, D. Z. 1988. *Faith after Foundationalism*. London: Routledge.

Phillips, D. Z. 1993. *Wittgenstein and Religion*. London: Macmillan.

On FIDEISM see also Vol. 3, Ch. 5. On LANGUAGE see also Ch. 20; Vol. 2, Chs 4, 11, 12; Vol. 3, Ch. 14; Vol. 4, Chs 3, 8.

14

MARTIN HEIDEGGER

Laurence Paul Hemming

It would be difficult to argue that Martin Heidegger (1889–1976) is in any way a philosopher of religion and yet, as I have found myself writing on other occasions, Heidegger 'reeks of God', and rarely in reading him is it possible to pass more than a few pages without a mention of God, the gods or the divine. If the great majority of the interpreters of Heidegger overlook or merely ignore the question of divinity in Heidegger's work, at the same time few of those who do not have been able to see through to Heidegger's relation to religion as a whole. In this Heidegger himself provides no easy signposts or assistance. When confronted with the question of religion directly he is more often than not elusive or cryptic: "difficult to catch", as Socrates remarks of the nature of the Sophist in Plato's dialogue of that name. When asked privately by a distinguished German theologian what he thought of God, Heidegger is said to have remarked in a way full of the cunning he brings to the question: "das ist die Fragwürdigste …". This can translate variously as "that is the most questionable thing to ask", or (more literally) "that is what is most worthy of questioning", or even "that is where the question really lies". In no way is the answer straightforward, even if we can secure for ourselves what the *question* is, or whether it is a question addressed to the philosopher or thrown back to the theologian, or to whom else it might refer.

If Heidegger thought of salvation, he referred to it in a way consistent with this elusive trail. Interviewed in September 1966 by the German weekly *Der Spiegel* for an article that was only published immediately after Heidegger's death, the philosopher's verdict is "only a god can save us now": a sardonic, sharp verdict, but on what? On the planet's pitching itself headlong into an apocalyptic destruction precipitated by an intoxication with technology, cybernetics and atomic destruction? On the political situation of the West? On that of thinking, philosophically, theologically, religiously? All Heidegger will say on this occasion is "we cannot think [the god] into attending us. We might at best prepare the readiness of expectation" (Heidegger 2000: 672).[1] Is this any different from the outlook towards the gods and divinity itself of Homer's epic poems?

HEIDEGGER'S RELIGIOUS ORIGINS

Elsewhere, and in the midst of equally cryptic remarks, Heidegger says – refusing once again, to be drawn easily – "some of you perhaps know that I came out of theology" (2005: 437), and indeed he did. He was born in 1889 in a remote Schwabian village in the south-east of Germany, close to the French and Swiss borders, into a family whose lives were intertwined with the Catholic Church, given that his father was the sexton of the parish at which he was registered from birth until he was buried in its churchyard in 1976. The sexton was the man responsible for the upkeep of the fabric of the building, the digging of graves, the ringing of the bells and many of the parish records. The family were evicted from their home (tied to the church) for several years when distant controversies in Rome touched their village as almost the entire community except the Heidegger family broke from the Catholic Church over questions of papal infallibility and the dogmatic formulations of the First Vatican Council (1869–70). The family was not rich, and the promising scholar Martin Heidegger was educated by Catholic charitable monies right up until he completed his habilitation thesis (the thesis written after the doctoral thesis to this day in Germany, without which he could not have taught at a German university) in 1916.

Heidegger prepared for Catholic priesthood in the seminary throughout his university studies, flirting briefly with the Jesuits (but never studying with them, departing after only two weeks) and even after his habilitation pursued the possibility of a chair in medieval Catholic thought. Intellectually the Catholicism of Heidegger's youth is best understood by the name 'neo-scholasticism': the attempt to interpret the texts of the high middle ages, above all those of Thomas Aquinas (*see* Vol. 2, Ch. 13), as primarily philosophical works providing a rational underpinning for Christian faith. The young Heidegger was sympathetic to this orthodoxy, publishing a number of journalistic articles and reports in conservative Catholic journals of his time.

Heidegger was in confrontation with the Catholic Church at various times in his life. In 1919 he announced to Engelbert Krebs, the priest who had married him to the Protestant Elfride Petri two years earlier, that "the system of Catholicism [is] problematic and unacceptable to me, but not Christianity *per se* or metaphysics" (Ott 1993: 106). Yet in 1976 he was buried according to the rites of the Catholic Church, with a funeral oration by Bernhard Welte, himself a family friend and Catholic priest. If he was a close and careful scholar of Martin Luther (so that Rudolf Bultmann

---

1. Translations throughout are my own.

described Heidegger as having an extraordinary knowledge of Luther [letter to Hans von Soden, 23 December 1923; in Lemke 1984: 202]), and if he is reputed to have thrown Jesuit priests out of his seminars in the 1930s (because they were Jesuit priests), nonetheless he himself wrote in a letter as late as 1968, "I am from the outset Catholic" (letter to W. D. Zimmermann, 4 July 1968, author's collection).

The breadth of Heidegger's education was vast, benefiting from the study of Latin and Greek that was a part of the German *Gymnasium* school system (until the Nazis largely dismantled the teaching of classics in the 1930s): from the very beginning he was steeped in the classical texts; in Aquinas, Bonaventure and the breadth of Catholic medieval thought; as well as the whole history of German idealism up to and including the works of Friedrich Nietzsche. He was therefore extraordinarily well placed to understand the whole breadth and depth of the Western tradition while having at first hand the three languages most precious to acquiring that strength. Heidegger taught almost all his life at the University of Freiburg, initially from 1919 to 1923. He was briefly appointed to lecture at the Protestant University of Marburg, and then returned to Freiburg (replacing Edmund Husserl in the prestigious chair of philosophy) in 1928 until his retirement. He was suspended from teaching between 1946 and 1951 under the denazification process undertaken by the Western allied powers (in his case overseen by the French), although the chaos of the war brought his lectures to a close by the summer of 1944.

We should struggle in vain to identify psychological or personal motives for Heidegger's philosophy, let alone philosophy of religion, in his personal piety, his background or the decisions made in his early life regarding Christian faith. Heidegger's piety, like his politics, are uneasy places to look for easy explanations of what he writes. Heidegger was no more a Vatican apologist than he was committed to the biologist racism of Nazism (despite his capacity for occasional anti-Semitic asides), and yet in as much as he was a Catholic all his life, he was also a Nazi from 1933 until it was no longer possible to be so (in 1945). We can no more erase his religion than his politics (nor should we do so with either, for to do so falsifies not just the man but the history to which he belongs), and yet neither explain his philosophy. And Heidegger is that philosopher who most potently said in 1925 in his lectures on the history of time, "phenomenological research is, and remains, atheistic" (Heidegger 1988: 109), in a direct reference to Nietzsche's work *The Gay Science* (where Nietzsche expressly proclaims the death of God); and at the very beginning of his introductory lectures to metaphysics in 1935 he adds, "a Christian philosophy is a square circle and a misunderstanding" (Heidegger 1983: 9).[2] To understand Heidegger's philosophy of religion one must attend first and foremost to Heidegger as a philosophical thinker. That is, we must attend not to what Heidegger *thinks*, but to what he attempts to direct us think *about*.

---

2. The term he used was "Ein hölzernes Eisen", literally, 'a wooden iron'.

BEING AND TIME AND HEIDEGGER'S
BASIC UNDERSTANDING OF PHILOSOPHY

Martin Heidegger, the philosopher of being whose 'collected works' (*Gesamtausgabe*) will eventually comprise 102 volumes, more than half of which are edited transcripts of his lecture courses, wrote in effect only one real book in his life, and even that was incomplete. *Sein und Zeit* (Being and time) was published in 1927, having been written under extreme pressure (in order to enable Heidegger to be a candidate for a junior professorial position at Marburg), much of it in Heidegger's mountain hut in Todtnauberg. The plan for the book can be found at §8, and describes a book of three divisions, the latter two each in three parts. Only the first division, and the first two parts of the second division ever appeared. The other 'books' are more often than not either reworked versions of his lecture courses (for instance, his lectures on Kant, Schelling and Nietzsche), or unedited notes (as in his *Contributions to Philosophy* and *Mindfulness*). Heidegger refers to *Being and Time* repeatedly in many other places, and every attempt to show that he changed direction or adopted a different course in his later work fails because it is possible to identify the seeds of that change, or even its plan, in *Being and Time* itself. Although the language of the later Heidegger is often markedly different from that of *Being and Time*, even this difference deceives. In the reports of his *Zollikon Seminars* with the psychologist and psychotherapist Medard Boss, which took place over ten years between 1959 and 1969, the language of *Being and Time* repeatedly returns afresh as if it had never been let go.

It is essential, therefore, if we are to understand Heidegger's relation to the philosophy of religion, to turn to *Being and Time*, where in outline (if not explicitly) an answer is already given to a question Heidegger posed only in the 1950s (2006b: 64): how did God get into philosophy? An answer to this question is only possible, Heidegger believes, because another even more fundamental question is examined by *Being and Time* itself: the *Seinsfrage* or 'question of being' itself. And yet *this* latter and more basic question is itself only possible *not* because God has entered philosophy, but because God is, and the gods are, in flight, in flight from philosophy as such.

Being and Time speaks constantly of *Dasein*, a German term that both the English versions of the book leave untranslated (although Joan Stambaugh changes the German *Dasein* to *Da-sein* in her English text). In German *Dasein* means, at its simplest, 'existence'; this is the sense in which Kant first employed the term philosophically. Literally translated it means 'here-to-be' or 'here-being'. It does not mean 'being-there' (a possibility of translation Heidegger himself expressly rejected). As 'existence' it has all the ambiguity in German that the word has in English: it can mean a particular existence (mine, yours, that person's); or it can mean a kind of existence – Heidegger often speaks of 'human *Dasein*' or on occasion 'Christian *Dasein*'; or it can mean existence in general, the whole of being. In each case, for Heidegger, attention is drawn to the 'here' of the German word *da*.

Da can also mean 'there', as in 'here and there' but it cannot mean 'over there', which in German would be *dort*. The reason for this is that Plato had employed a word that has the same force as 'over there' (*epekeina*) when speaking of being as such. Being, as Plato has been interpreted, is itself divine, and unchanging, and 'beyond' every particular, changeable 'here': it is expressly 'over there' and absolutely other with respect to human life. If there is no direct discussion of anything like a philosophy of religion in *Being and Time*, already it is possible to see that in the very term *Dasein* Heidegger introduces a critique of metaphysical transcendence. Existence, being as such, is in each case being with respect to some place, 'here and there', but not *beyond* and so 'over there' with respect to the 'here' of the world. Being is always concerned with the being of being-human: human-being, as we currently and presently know it, is not determined with respect to any understanding of being that is 'beyond' and divine.

Far more provocatively, Heidegger says in *Being and Time* that [human] "*Dasein's essence lies in its existence*" (1977: 56). The provocation implied in this phrase cannot be underestimated: it is in flat contradiction to a principle enshrined in the work of Aquinas that had been elevated by philosophy since the middle ages to a formal axiom in all philosophy of religion – 'God's essence is to exist'. It is a form of this principle that Anselm had relied on for his so-called 'ontological proof' of the existence of God (*see* Vol. 2, Ch. 6, "Anselm"), and which René Descartes also makes much of (*see* Vol. 3, Ch. 8). Because it is so much part of the essence of God to *be*, it is impossible to conceive that God is *not*. As the one whose essence most 'is', the being of every other being is derived from this necessary principle and origin of existence. If God *is*, God *must be*, God's being is necessary; the being of any other thing, however, is merely contingent – it is possible for it not to be, or for it to cease its being – it has a beginning and an end, so that there is something before and after it itself *is*.

Heidegger reverses this, by pointing out that in as much as I am, I am that being whose being is, *must be*, a concern for myself. I can *imagine* myself not existing, but I can never *know* non-existence *except* through the existence that I am (this is the only way I can even imagine not being 'here' – during my being-here, I project my imagination to a before or an after to the 'here' that I am). It is of my essence to exist and to know that I do. Heidegger does not argue that this makes human-being equivalent to God; indeed, later he says "never can man put himself in the place of God because the essence of man never reaches the essential realm belonging to God" (2003a: 255). Heidegger's argument is that no *philosophical* causal relationship is to be traced between the gods, or divinity, or God, and the being of being human. However, the consequences of this go even further: in as much as any philosopher has declared God to be dead, or has interpreted religion as a pantheism, or panentheism, these philosophical outlooks cannot (by evacuating the place of God) put the being of being-human in divinity's place. In *Contributions to Philosophy* and in the *Letter on Humanism*, Heidegger interprets even liberal atheism as well as Marxism and any form of theism as all stemming from the same ground, and so as making a formal connection between God and being.

HEIDEGGER'S LATER THOUGHT

Heidegger does not argue that God formally, and on philosophical grounds, cannot be the creator of the heavens and the earth. Quite the reverse: he argues in at least one place that this is a perfectly tenable view to hold, in faith. We may believe that God created the heavens and the earth in as much as God has revealed this to be the case, but we may not hold this as a philosophical 'truth' and then claim to be entering genuinely into the philosophical enquiry that pursues the question of being. Philosophy does not ever *know* in certainty the things that faith (in revelation) can make principles of its very possibility.

The whole of *Being and Time*, and indeed Heidegger's earlier mature work from 1919 onwards (at least), is argued from this position. Yet it is also clear that Heidegger understands this breaking of the (philosophical) causal relationship between God and *Dasein* to be a matter of historical possibility. It is only because of Nietzsche's declaration 'God is dead' that philosophy can return to a more genuine and originary understanding of the gods, divinity and God. Here again we must attend to what Heidegger believes philosophy to be doing. Philosophers do not 'create' thinking, even if their response to what is to be thought *through* is itself the deepest and most profound confrontation with being itself. It is not that Nietzsche 'causes' the death of God (nor does Descartes 'invent' the statement 'cogito, ergo sum'). Nietzsche describes the essence of existence itself, here taking existence (*Dasein*) in its most general sense. This sense is not *my* existence, nor a specific region of existence, but how *my* existence, how every *particular* region of existence, is drawn off from, and determined by, what it means to exist in the present age *at all*. Existence, being-historical, opens up and closes off possibilities of being for the whole world as such.

For Heidegger, if God is, then every declaration that 'God is dead' touches God, or divinity, or the gods, not at all. The declaration 'God is dead' rather speaks of how humanity itself *lets itself* 'be' with respect to God, and divinity, and the gods. In as much as God is, and existence is determined by the death of God, then existence is deaf to every manifestation of divinity since it has decided in advance that God is dead. Yet the very declaration 'God is dead' has prepared the way for the recovery of the question of being, because it has been reopened in human, historical, existence, so that the question of being has become a question only for that being whose being is its own concern, human *Dasein*. At the same time, the question of being opens up the question of the nothing, which reveals itself in the phenomenologically and ontologically negative mood of anxiety (*Angst*) and in the recovery of the sense of human finitude in 'being-towards-death' (*Sein zum Tode*).

To understand how this relates to Heidegger's philosophy of religion one would have to turn to a series of lectures given by Heidegger at Marburg in 1927, immediately after the completion of *Being and Time*, although they are among the very last of his lectures to have been made available in published form. Entitled the *History of Philosophy from Thomas Aquinas to Kant*, they sum up in the most succinct form Heidegger's whole position, while making one new and extraordinary claim: that the philosophy of subjectivity has its roots not in Descartes and his period, but in the thought of the Paris of the thirteenth century. In §16, entitled "The God-lessness of Philosophy", Heidegger says:

> Strongly stated nothing philosophical can be expressed concerning the eternity of God, because God is never an object of philosophy. What one uncovers with the help of the concept of God is an idol, which only has the philosophical meaning, and which becomes thereby visible, where the idea of 'summum ens' and being in general is leading. Philosophy is, if it is correctly understood, god-less … If God is, he allows himself to be discovered in the least possible way through philosophy. [God is] only discoverable, insofar as he himself reveals himself.   (Heidegger 2006a: 77)

Heidegger's fundamental position on the godlessness of philosophy, well encapsulated here, did not change at any point later in his life. He recapitulated what is said here in similar, if more Delphic, words in a seminar of 1951, when he said, "if I were to undertake a theology … then the word 'being' would not need to appear in it" (2005: 437).

Philosophy provides no access to God because God is not an object of philosophy. This does not mean that philosophy cannot discuss God or the gods; Heidegger's own work is a case in point, Nietzsche's another. They both, in very different ways, discuss divinity from the negative position of showing the limits of what can be said of God in what is said philosophically. This is critically important. What is said philosophically is always *human* speaking; philosophy is a wisdom concerning the being of being *human*, it concerns human self-transparency, human self-understanding.

However, philosophy has since late antiquity, and above all in the medieval period, become a discussion governed by the attempt to describe the divine essence and the relation of human-being to the divine essence (even if it wants to argue that this essence 'does not exist'). In this sense a philosophical construction has been placed on the kind of claim made by Aquinas, for instance, that only God is transparent to God. Because God is construed as the plenitude of self-presence to self, and so the plenitude of presence *as such*, God as *pure* presence is understood as the abolition of all nothingness, all privation. Privation, nothingness, absence are given an explicitly moral construction – by Augustine (*see* Vol. 1, Ch. 18), and above all by Aquinas. All of this is unproblematic (for philosophy at least) if it is confined to an understanding given through faith in what God has revealed to be true about God. At this point it becomes God's address *to* humanity, a form of speech received by human ears but said itself not to be human. However, as constructive, human thinking it becomes what Heidegger will come to call 'ontotheology', where philosophy and (especially Christian) theology are fused together as if they were one and the same thing, and in respect to the extreme position arrived at by Hegel, where the self, the world and God are resolved in absolute subjectivity as, Heidegger says, 'onto-ego-theo-logy'.

If existence, as that place from which every particular existence, *Dasein*, draws its own existence, and in which its self-knowledge and self-transparency is discovered (or not), has become godless, what are the consequences, both for the philosophy of religion and for this as a *historically particular* situation, one that occurs only now, only, as Heidegger says, when metaphysics is fulfilled and completed and at an end?

THE DEATH OF GOD AND BEGINNING WITH THE GODS

In the first place, the historical situation after Nietzsche's proclamation of the death of God is that *philosophically* God is no longer understood as the ground of all being and the ground of every particular being. Leibniz's argument that God is the underlying 'reason for being' of every being (*see* Vol. 3, Ch. 13) – "nothing *is* without a *reason*" – has come to a close. The situation that now pertains, Heidegger argues in his last ever lecture course, is that *nothing* is *without* a reason, so that *the* nothing can at last be spoken of again, beyond every attempt to rationalize it, to calculate or destroy it: this is at one and the same time the triumph of absolute nihilism as Nietzsche described it, and a return to the proper place of *the* nothing in thinking.

In the second place, the death of God and the end of the 'principle of reason' means that the texts employed to give a philosophical justification to claims made historically by theologians with regard to faith can and must be re-read all over again. For the early Heidegger this is the entire motor and driving force to re-read Aristotle, Plato, and then later Parmenides and Heraclitus. No longer need they be read in relation to the Christian God, as prophetically prefiguring a religion yet to come; now they can be read in an entirely different way. Aristotle's 'first mover' turns out not to be a personal God; indeed, far from Aristotle and Plato arguing that 'God is (absolute) being' (as medieval metaphysics had ended up claiming), it becomes possible to see how for them 'being itself is divine' (*see* Vol. 1, Ch. 4, "Socrates and Plato", and Ch. 5, "Aristotle"). The word for divinity here functions as an adjective, not as a noun. In this way Heidegger 'dismantles' the history of the way in which Plato's 'over there' of being had been read as a way of removing the possibility of the meaning and understanding of being from *here*, from the world, to *there*, to what Kant and Nietzsche (one positively, one derogatively) call the 'super-sensible', the 'real' world beyond the world in which we actually dwell.

In the third place, it becomes possible to see how the Greeks understood divinity at all, so that we too can understand the gods, divinity and even the theistic (and Christian) God. Heidegger's remarks about this are scattered across his works, but where he concentrates most clearly on this is in his lectures on the pre-Socratic philosopher Parmenides and in relation to the poet and contemporary (and university room-mate) of Hegel's and Schelling's, Friedrich Hölderlin. Heidegger argues that the fragments of Parmenides' didactic poem "Truth" show how the Greeks were bound to being in such a way that, poetically, they understand the 'before' and 'after' to being as an encircling place of concealment. Concealment and 'the' nothing are here to be understood in the same way. 'The' nothing is therefore not a mere absence, or the annihilation of what *is*, but rather (the other way round) what is concealed from mortals in their existence, either individually, or in regions of existence, or in existence as a whole, and from out of which all that *is* springs forth. Concealment and *the* nothing are now to be understood ontologically, from the 'here' of the being of being human, and not metaphysically, from a 'universal perspective' and total vantage point of either reason, or God, or mathematics. The concealed and the nothing, as the before and after to mortals, therefore both reveal its finitude to whatever is *in* existence and disclose the meaning of time, as the future and the past. In existence, mortals look out to the future while forgetting, or remembering, the past. It becomes clear from this how important Heidegger's understanding of truth is. The Greek word for concealment is *lēthē*, and the Greek word for truth is *alētheia*. The 'a' of *a-lētheia* is a privative, so that truth is 'that which is drawn out from concealment': *un*-concealment. Existence as what is extant and stands out for mortals is the true, as what is surrounded by, and drawn out from, and falls back into, the concealed.

Heidegger shows how from this understanding of the nothing and concealment the Greeks understand the gods to be *sunistores*, a word usually translated as 'witnesses', but which Heidegger translates as 'ones seeing alongside'. The Greek understanding of the gods is of those who see *into* the concealed. Coupled with this is the fact that, even seeing into what mortals cannot see, the gods cannot necessarily change what they see: the gods, as much as mortals, are bound to what is fated, what is allotted to 'be'. Unlike the God of theism, the gods do not have an omnipotent will, the way things are is not merely at their disposal. Nevertheless humanity is entrusted to the gods (and the gods to humanity) for the sake of the relation of the concealed to unconcealment and so truth. No mortal can predict what a god will do or say, nor how he or she will appear; the gods address men and women for the sake of allowing them to enter into the concealed and unconceal it (and so see into its truth). Every attempt to pre-empt the gods therefore attempts to evacuate their entering into being and so puts the gods to flight. In this sense Heidegger shows how rationalism, as that which knows what anything is by calculating what it is to be in advance, by knowing it even before it encounters it, destroys the relation to the gods.

The ones above all who let what the gods see be known are the poets, and here is Heidegger's interest in Hölderlin. The poets speak from out of the essence of the holy, "the holy as the fire that inflames the poet" (Heidegger 1993: 193). In perhaps one of the best known of Heidegger's discussions, in *The Origin of the Work of Art*, he elaborates the setting and character of a Greek temple as what "encloses the form of the god" and "first gives to things their look, and to men their outlook on themselves ... as long as the god has not fled from it". Heidegger adds that "this presence of the god is in itself the extension and delimiting of the precinct as one which is holy" (2003b: 27, 29).

It would be possible to misunderstand the interpretation of the temple as a mere description of a house for a god. Heidegger is well aware that nothing can house the god, for God and the gods exceed the being of being human in every way, and yet the god comes to presence in this work that is at the same time a house. The temple has therefore always to be understood ontologically, which means as the way the god can appear (in so far as the god does) to mortals within being. For Heidegger to interpret the temple ontologically is to understand it with respect to man, as that being whose existence is a concern for him (*Dasein*). Understood like this, the building does not house the god, but houses our betrothal *to* the god. The temple is the house of *our* openness to the god so that the god can address us, as well as being the place allotted to us to be the place of the god's deigning to address mortals. It is for this reason that the temple has guardians, ones who stand in between the god and everything that pedestrianizes the god and the sacred dimension in which the god appears. The guardians are the ones who protect the holiness that lets the god come into being and come to presence: but above all the guardians of the temple are the poets, those inflamed by the holy.

CONCLUSION: THE LAST GOD

Heidegger says "in poetry ... man is gathered upon the ground of his existence" (1996: 45), while (again in the context of a discussion of Hölderlin, in the *Letter on Humanism*) he adds that the holy "alone is the essential place of divinity, which in turn alone affords a dimension for the gods and for God" (1976: 338). Heidegger argues that Hölderlin was so steeped in an understanding of the mythic and of the gods that what was known to the Greeks by means of the gods is able to speak in Hölderlin's poetry all over again. Hölderlin, as any true poet does, lets being speak. This is because "the founding of being is bound to the god's hints" (1996: 46). This is not quite as romantic as it sounds; if the true is the unconcealed, and the poet's genuine work is to speak the being of beings, then the poet *is* the place of uncon-cealment in his speaking. We see immediately here the parallel between the work of the poet and the work of the philosopher. You will recall the philosopher is the one who genuinely speaks what existence means and shows how existence really *is*; he does not 'invent' the understanding of existence, but speaks about it in the deepest way. The philosopher's work is the work of the poet: they speak what the gods give them to speak. So when the gods are in flight, the philosopher will speak of the flight of the gods: either, in Descartes' case, of the last strenuous attempt to secure the existence and being of God metaphysically (so witnessing to this flight by seeking to arrest it) or, in Nietzsche's case, to make the declaration that God is dead.

If space permitted, and if it were necessary for the fullest understanding of Heidegger's philosophy of religion, we could dwell on Heidegger's confrontation with theology, especially in his earlier work. Here we would speak of his extraordinary interpretation of Paul's first Letter to the Thessalonians from his lectures on *The Phenomenology of Religious Life*, of the time of primitive Christianity as *kairological* or 'crisis' time; of his readings of Augustine in these same lectures and in key passages of *Being and Time*. We might add discussion of Heidegger's interpretation of theology in his lecture on *Theology and Phenomenology* as an 'ontic' science, whose object is not 'God', but 'faith', or the way in which, in interpreting Plato's dialogue the *Sophist*, Heidegger entirely overlooks and refuses to discuss the references to divinity at the end of that text. We could examine the successive theologians who have claimed Heidegger as a teacher (such as Karl Rahner) or whose work so influenced their own (Rudolf Bultmann, Eberhard Jüngel, Heinrich Ott, John Macquarrie), or who drew attention to what they understood to be the entirely pagan character of Heidegger's religious thought (Hugo Ott, who nevertheless reminds us, in the light of Heidegger's own remarks to a private circle in 1954, that "it was always the Christian God" with whom Heidegger had to do [Ott 1995: 154]). None of this is central, however, to Heidegger's philosophy of religion, which is always a philosophical affair, whatever his personal pieties may have been. Nevertheless, Heidegger understood that by freeing theology from philosophy, and vice versa, each could enter a proper relationship one with the other, above all so that God, divinity and the gods could once again speak and address humanity, through philosopher, poet or priest.

And here one must not underestimate Heidegger's own self-understanding as the one who speaks of the 'Last God', of the understanding of the God to come (both the God and the understanding of the God). Early on in Heidegger's *Contributions to Philosophy* we find that "the flight of the gods must be experienced and endured" (1989: 27). Such an endurance and experience prepares for the nearness of the last god, against the "prolonged Christianizing of God" (*ibid.*: 24), so that "the nearness to the last God is the keeping of silence. This must be set into work and word in the style of reservedness" (*ibid.*: 12). The penultimate section of *Contributions to Philosophy* is itself entitled *The Last God*. 'Last' here means final, and newest, and latest: that understanding of divinity to which we are to be turned out towards, *after* we have understood that in Nietzsche's declaration 'God is dead' it is (in Nietzsche's own words) "only the moral God who has died" (Nietzsche 1999: vol. 12, 213). It is for this reason that we *await* what God has to say, not decide in advance what God *could* and so *should* or *must* say (as if we already knew God before God deigns to appear) in God's address to humanity. The manifestation of God and what God has for the sake of addressing humanity, for

Heidegger, is always surprising. Perhaps after attempting to understand what it is Heidegger has to say of God, we might attempt a better translation of Heidegger's most heralded phrase, more faithful to any philosophy of religion he might have had – the phrase he dictated be spoken only at the moment of his death, and which appeared in the *Spiegel* magazine: '*Nur kann ein Gott uns rettenden!*' – 'Only *now* can a God save us'.

FURTHER READING

Heidegger, M. 1977. "The Word of Nietzsche: 'God Is Dead'". In M. Heidegger, *The Question Concerning Technology and Other Essays*, W. Lovitt (trans.), 53–112. New York: Garland.

Heidegger, M. 2004. *The Phenomenology of Religious Life*, M. Fritsch & J. Gosetti-Ferencei (trans.). Bloomington, IN: Indiana University Press.

Hemming, L. 2002. *Heidegger's Atheism: The Refusal of a Theological Voice*. Notre Dame, IN: University of Notre Dame Press.

Kovacs, G. 1990. *The Question of God in Heidegger's Phenomenology*. Evanston, IL: Northwestern University Press.

Prudhomme, J. 1997. *God and Being: Heidegger's Relation to Theology*. Atlantic Highlands, NJ: Humanities Press.

Safranski, R. 1998. *Martin Heidegger: Between Good and Evil*, E. Osers (trans.). Cambridge, MA: Harvard University Press.

Vedder, B. 2007. *Heidegger's Philosophy of Religion: From God to the Gods*. Pittsburgh, PA: Duquesne University Press.

Vycinas, V. 1961. *Earth and Gods: An Introduction to the Philosophy of Martin Heidegger*. The Hague: Martinus Nijhoff.

On BEING see also Chs 7, 10, 11. On EXISTENTIALISM see also Chs 10, 11. On TRANSCENDENCE see also Ch. 10; Vol. 4, Ch. 2.

15

EMMANUEL LEVINAS

Jeffrey L. Kosky

Emmanuel Levinas (1906–95) is best known for his insistence that 'ethics is first philosophy'. While the majority of critics of the so-called postmodern or post-metaphysical philosophy condemned its passage beyond good and evil, and the majority of its devotees celebrated this same liberty, Levinas sought a position that cut across these options. He stood almost alone, until perhaps the last decade and a half of the twentieth century, in insisting that postmodernity and the end of onto-theological metaphysics were not incompatible with morality and ethics, but in fact offered a unique opportunity for awakening our ethical regard for the Other. After the Nietzschean diagnosis of the death of God (*see* Vol. 4, Ch. 18, "Friedrich Nietzsche") and after the end of metaphysics had put an end to transcendental grounds for moral obligation, Levinas found an injunction whose source survived. This was the face of the Other. The face of the human other issued an undeniable obligation, which Levinas often formulated in the ethical injunction 'thou shalt not murder', and the hearing of this command altered the very subjectivity of man, leaving behind the self-grounding, autonomous subject of onto-theological metaphysics for a relational subject not determined by representational consciousness.

While this might represent the most important reception of Levinas, one could, with perhaps a bit more precision, also consider Levinas as the third of the great twentieth-century phenomenologists. Thanks to Levinas, phenomenology pushed beyond the limits of its historical practice in Edmund Husserl and Martin Heidegger to discover things heretofore passed over in silence: at least one enigmatic phenomenon or phenomenal enigma that, Levinas claimed, phenomenology had failed spectacularly to constitute – namely, the Other. Levinas' discovery of the Other, described in his phenomenology of the human face, called for a revision of key phenomenological concepts and theories. Following Husserl's reduction to the transcendental ego, and after Heidegger's reduction to *Dasein* or Being, Levinas practised a reduction to the interpersonal or ethical relation. The source or opening of meaningfulness or appearance lay not in the intentional openness of consciousness nor in anxious projection towards death, Levinas claimed, but in the approach of the Other met in ethics. The phenomenology of the ethical relation thus describes not only a particular region of phenomenal experience, but, according to Levinas, the ultimate to which all experience must be reduced in order to be seen in its originary source of meaningfulness. The revision of phenomenological concepts and theories that this called for would prove decisive for subsequent philosophical movements, such as the deconstruction practised by Jacques Derrida and the phenomenology of givenness developed by Jean-Luc Marion. Even if these movements did not stress the ethical horizon, they did develop theories of signification and phenomenality that appear heavily indebted to Levinas.[1]

In the last two decades of the twentieth century, Levinas was also made popular among students and scholars as the philosopher who confronts philosophy with its 'Jewish other'. As Judaism became a privileged marker of difference and otherness in those decades dominated by a concern to recover and revalue repressed voices, Levinas was held up as a paradigmatic case of how "Judaism can again reorient philosophy" (Gibbs 1992: 4). What this reorientation means most frequently is that philosophy abandon its speculative mode of devotion to the knowledge or truth of being and adopt a mode of questioning devoted to justice, the good or the face of the Other. It is recognition of Jewish thought, tradition and experience, the argument goes, that teaches philosophy the importance of this reorientation. Catherine Chalier writes,

> a mind not educated by the Book, with eyes not opened thanks to its teaching, would remain unskilled in the perception of the face trans-mitted by philosophy. This perception does not impose itself evidently or spontaneously; it is undeniably guided by the reading of the Torah, preceded by the idea of man fashioned in the image of his Creator.
> (Chalier 1993: 96, my trans.)

Others, looking chiefly at the Jewish experience of the Holocaust, see Levinas as a philosopher who takes seriously the demands placed on philosophy by this deci-sive Jewish experience. In the wake of the Nazi genocide and extermination of the Jews, philosophy must make the question of ethics and justice its primary concern, and it cannot think justice without starting from the primacy of others, justice always being due to the Other and never something that can be stated starting from the I. Levinas' almost single-minded focus on ethics provides a unique

---

1. Even Jean-Paul Sartre, whose atheism, humanism, and existentialism all stand at a marked distance from Levinas' own mode of thinking, remarked that it was Levinas who intro-duced him to the phenomenological movement that would have so profound an impact on his own philosophy.

opportunity for reorienting philosophical concepts and categories in accordance with this demand to respond to the experience of the Holocaust.

ANOTHER OPTION: LEVINAS AS PHILOSOPHER OF RELIGION

Given these standard interpretations of Levinas, it is clear that he is not often read in the context proposed by this volume: namely, within the history of the philosophy of religion in the West. He is either a postmodern ethicist (paradox of paradoxes!), a radical phenomenologist (so radical that many orthodox phenomenologists see him as more of an anti- or non-phenomenologist), or a Jewish philosopher (for better or worse), and most often some combination of these. Each of these approaches is well founded. Indeed, they are so well founded that the reasons in favour of including Levinas in a history of philosophy of religion are not immediately obvious, for one finds little in his writings that would be recognized as belonging to traditional forms of philosophy of religion. With few exceptions, Levinas makes no assertions regarding the existence of the entities of religious belief; he does not analyse any propositions regarding the immortality of the soul, the reality of mystical experience, the existence of God, or other subjects commonly considered in philosophy of religion.

His departure from the most common forms of philosophy of religion can be made clear by considering his dismissal of the fundamental consideration of classical philosophy of religion: the arguments for the existence of God. According to Levinas, these say more about the operations of human consciousness and its mode of knowing than about God. That is, deciding about the existence or non-existence of God, Levinas argues, "translates perhaps the logical necessity of fixing the object of religion in conformity with the immanence of a thinking that aims at the world" (Levinas 1998b: 105). To assume that God must first be and be affirmed conceptually if the word 'God' is to have any meaning whatsoever assumes the primacy of knowledge, and moreover of a knowledge that is always and only knowledge of beings within the world. This "ensures the efficacy of God in the world, but sacrifices transcendence" (Levinas 1991: 191), reducing God to the ranks of a being whose existence could be demonstrated like all the others.

Against the ultimacy of being or the world as a totality that admits no beyond or transcendence, Levinas' phenomenology of the interpersonal will claim that the face of the Other met in ethics is not a being like the beings of the world. When phenomenology is re-established according to the primacy of ethics as first philosophy, therefore, a whole new realm of meaning and meaningful experience (or even rationality and intelligibility) opens beyond that whose limits are set by intentional consciousness, representational knowledge and the ultimacy of worldly signification. This new realm of meaningfulness and intelligibility, Levinas suggests, might include meanings often classified as religious, which, when reduced to the interpersonal ethical situation, are now assured of their intelligibility and guaranteed in their possibility. This would open the prospect of a philosophy of religion that does not proceed through the analysis of propositions, but that, following the phenomenological insight, seeks to return concepts to the situation that gives them meaning. In Husserl, this situation was the intentionality of consciousness. In Heidegger, it was *Dasein* as experience of Being. In Levinas, it is the interpersonal situation of ethics. When philosophy adopts the mode of signification, intelligibility and rationality promoted by ethical phenomenology, then phenomena that heretofore were consigned to the irrationality of madness or a deluded faith take on meaning.

This prospect of using a revised phenomenology to guarantee the possibility or secure the intelligibility of religious language and experience is pursued most explicitly in the essay "God and Philosophy", appearing in the collection *Of God Who Comes to Mind*, and it is also the aim of the essay "The Idea of the Infinite in Us", reprinted in the collection *Entre Nous*. In both these essays, Levinas' stated aim is to articulate the intelligibility of divine transcendence. The starting-point for his reflection is the idea of infinity, which he claims "conserves for reflection the paradoxical knot which is already tied in religious revelation … knowledge of a God who while offering himself within this openness, also remains absolutely other or transcendent" (Levinas 1998c: 219). God, who appears for religion in the paradox of a revelation of that which transcends knowledge, is kept for philosophical thought by the idea of the infinite, since this idea is precisely an idea of what cannot be included in any idea, an idea whose *ideatum* exceeds or transcends the *idea* by which philosophy touches on it. By means of an explication of the idea of the infinite (one that is not without a profound debt to René Descartes, the father of a philosophy of consciousness that many would think to be most antithetical to Levinas' ethics), both essays then proceed to elaborate the philosophical intelligibility of a God that nevertheless transcends knowledge.

Interestingly enough, both essays move from this starting-point to arrive at a description of responsible subjectivity. Desire for the Infinite leads me to the Other as my desire is turned from the Good it seeks precisely because this Good does not want for itself, but for the Other. This movement from the Infinite to the Other has led some commentators to claim that a theological relation is the condition for the ethical. While this might be true, this procedure could also be read as the practice of phenomenological method, wherein philosophical reflection starts from a given (here the word 'God') and returns (by means of a reduction) to the situation in which these words take on significance (the ethical situation in which subjectivity is summoned to an infinite responsibility). While speculation on the idea of the infinite can elaborate the meaning of transcendence (the idea of Infinity analysed in the first part of each essay), such a God will seem abstract, a mere play on words, or the pretence of a not yet fully rational thought, if it is not returned to an originary experience in which this meaning takes on signification (responsibility for the Other described in the second part of each essay). Hence each of these essays will repeat the description of transcendence. After the speculative articulation of the meaning of transcendence by means of an abstract explanation of the mere word 'God', Levinas then claims that "the exposition of the ethical meaning of transcendence, and of the infinite, can be carried out starting from the proximity of the neighbor and my responsibility for the other" (Levinas 1998a: 70).

In elaborating the philosophical intelligibility of divine transcendence, a Levinasian philosophy of religion wants to stand outside the modern distinction between faith and reason, the God of revelation and the God of knowledge, or, as Levinas himself puts it, it is "implicitly to doubt the formal opposition ... between, on the one hand, the God of Abraham, Isaac, and Jacob, invoked without philosophy in faith, and on the other the god of the philosophers. It is to doubt that this opposition constitutes an alternative" (*ibid.*: 57) – precisely because it does not let divine transcendence lapse into the silence or supposed irrationality of faith while at the same time it seeks to introduce such transcendence into a rationality that does not sacrifice transcendence and unconditionality to full and total knowledge.

A significant objection to Levinas' thought of divine transcendence was raised by the philosopher Dominique Janicaud in *Le Tournant théologique de la phénoménologie française* (published in English as *Phenomenology and the "Theological Turn"*), where he claimed that, in the case of Levinas and others such as Marion, Paul Ricoeur and Michel Henry, "phenomenology was taken hostage by a theology that does not want to say its name" (Janicaud 2000: 31). According to Janicaud, the phenomenological status of Levinas' work was compromised by an unstated prior commitment to "nothing less than the God of the biblical tradition" (*ibid.*: 16). Far from discovering responsible subjectivity and divine transcendence through phenomenological practice, Levinas supposed them from the outset, making his work more properly speaking a dogmatic or theological work than a phenomenological practice of ethical description. Now, as I have tried to suggest, Levinas would reject the idea that his philosophy supposes religious events or experience and would therefore reject the claim that his work would not qualify as phenomenological. Although Levinas never responded directly to Janicaud, he did address a similar objection made by Jean-François Lyotard. Against Lyotard's claim that "Revelation is necessarily inscribed in your thought, in contradistinction to Husserl – who is a true phenomenologist, if I might dare say so, someone for whom Revelation is *not* proposed for recognition" (Levinas 1988: 80, my trans.), Levinas stated that the inverse is the case: "[Husserl] would not consider the way to the other as original, and because of that he did not have Revelation. This relation to the other [responsibility] is so extraordinary ... that it can bring us to the problem of Revelation in the religious sense of the term" (*ibid.*). What this means is that the phenomenology of responsibility brings philosophy back (according to a method that must be understood as a form of the phenomenological reduction) to an originary situation (interpersonal relation with the Other) in which it becomes possible to give meaning to the concepts by which religious experience has been understood.

RELIGION, RELIGIONS, THE RELIGIOUS:
THE HISTORICAL AND THE PHILOSOPHICAL

Another way to understand the task of philosophy of religion, besides analysis of propositions, is that made popular by Immanuel Kant and the Kantians: namely, as a critical analysis of the relation between historical religions and some supposed ideal of religion, be it Kant's religion of reason, Friedrich Schleiermacher's intuition of the whole, and so on (*see* Vol. 3, Ch. 21, "Immanuel Kant", and Vol. 4, Ch. 3, "Friedrich Schleiermacher"). This method would prove decisive for much post-Enlightenment philosophical reflection on religion. Here again one finds little in Levinas' philosophical work that seems to assume the task of reflecting on historical religion and its relation to an ideal.

And yet it is apparent to even the least religiously informed reader that there is something of the religious operative in this ethical phenomenology and its description of human subjectivity as responsibility. Those with ears to hear will indeed find religious themes clearly identifiable in Levinas' ethical phenomenology to the point that the articulation of responsibility proves impossible to conceive without the contribution of religion. In *Otherwise than Being*, Levinas himself admits that "In the prehistory of the ego posited for itself there speaks a responsibility ... Beyond egoism and altruism, [what is at stake in responsibility] is the religiosity of the self" (1991: 117). And in *Of God Who Comes to Mind*, he claims that overcoming the primacy of the I "signifies the ethical, but probably also the very spirituality of the soul" (1998c: 177). Theses such as these suggest that even if we do not find a philosophy of religion in Levinas, neither as analytic of propositions nor as critical reflection on historical religions, nevertheless responsibility is bound up with a certain form of religiosity. And even if Levinas would disavow the status of a theologian, his description of responsibility produces a discourse that speaks with a religious vocabulary and even syntax.

A few examples, by no means exhaustive, can illustrate the religious dimensions of this account of subjectivity as responsibility.

- *Election.* In responsibility, the self is elect or the chosen one. Levinas writes:

> The identity aroused behind identification is an identity by pure election. Election traverses the concept of the ego to summon me as me through the inordinateness of the other ... Obligation calls for a unique response not inscribed in universal thought, the unforeseeable response of the chosen one. (1991: 145)

Just as the theological (Jewish and Christian) notion of election means that I am, or a people is, chosen to receive its identity before having done anything to merit its choice, so too, Levinas claims, in responsibility the self is summoned to itself as responsible before being free to choose or commit itself to this responsibility, summoned even without regard for its capacity to respond adequately. In this sense, its identity cannot be described apart from the notion of election.

- *Here I am!* In so far as the identity of the self is one given to it by its election in responsibility, the first words of the self are those uttered by the prophets: "Here I am! Send me!" (Isaiah 6:8, cited in Levinas 1991: 199 n.11). In other words, in responsibility, the I does not precede its summons, but comes after it, emerging only in response to it. "Here I am" is the response in which the responsible self first appears. In the "Here I am", at least when said in French (*me voici*) or in Hebrew (*hinneni*), the self appears in the accusative, not nominative, case. The summons summons me before I am there, so the first words in which subjectivity is stated are those uttered by the prophet: *me voici*. As Levinas writes, "the word *I* means *here I am*, answering for everything and everyone" (1991: 114).

- *Expiation.* The responsible self is an expiation in so far as it sacrifices all concern for itself in responsibility for every other, to the point of expiating even for the faults of others. In one of his most challenging and oft-criticized declarations, Levinas claims that responsibility goes so far that in it the self passes "from the outrage undergone to the responsibility for the persecutor and in this sense from suffering to expiation for the other" (*ibid.*: 111). Assuming responsibility even for the crimes for which others are responsible, "the self is goodness … It is an expiating for being" (*ibid.*: 118) by which being and the world are redeemed or made good. The notion of expiation is thus tied to an order of intelligibility in which the Good is beyond Being and the world is not self-sufficient but stands in need of justification beyond its mere existence. Existence or Being, Levinas claims, is inevitably unjust in so far as the positing of existence requires taking a position or assuming 'my place under the sun', an assumption with which the usurpation of the place of others begins. Beyond being, a justification for existence is provided by the expiation for others that is responsibility.

- *Witnessing, inspiration and prophecy: à-dieu.* Even if Levinas avoids arguments for the existence of God, he nevertheless claims that the *me voici* of responsibility does testify to the transcendence of God, to such a point that he calls the responsible self a prophet, inspired by the infinite, and develops an important account of the face of the Other in terms of the *à-dieu*. The face as *à-dieu* must be distinguished from a representation that presents God in the way that a trace that marks absence must be distinguished from a sign that synchronizes signifier with signified and so makes both co-present. For Levinas, the transcendence of God is not revealed by being put before the I, present to it in an experience I have. This would be to reduce divine transcendence to the immanence of an object constituted by the intentional activity of my consciousness. Rather, divine transcendence is revealed in the saying of *me voici* to the Other who summons me *à-dieu* in responsibility. "I am the witnessing or the trace or the glory of the Infinite … The infinite is not 'in front of' me; it is I who

JEFFREY L. KOSKY

express it …: *me voici* … The sentence in which God comes to be involved in words is not 'I believe in God'" (Levinas 1998a: 75). Responsibility itself, *me*, is thus the revelation of God. It testifies to God without affirming a concept of God, without even stating the word 'God', and without encountering this God in the present of an experience. The face thus summons me to God (*à-dieu*), but to a God who appears only in the trace left by his forever departing, bidding *adieu*, from the face that presents itself to me.

What these few brief illustrations are meant to convey is the way in which Levinas' ethical phenomenology develops a fundamental religiosity of the subject that is inseparable from its articulation in and as responsibility. Even if Levinas' phenomenology of responsible subjectivity does not always reflect on religious experience, it remains the case that this subjectivity as responsibility is articulated in a recognizably religious discourse. The question then arises as to how we are to interpret this religious language. Where does it come from, and what meaning are we to assign to the fact that it proves operative? Is it optional or is it necessary to the account of responsibility? If optional, then why did Levinas choose to employ such language and what commitments or presuppositions does it indicate? Does the religious language used to describe responsibility compromise the philosophical status of the phenomenology of intersubjectivity (this would be the objection of Janicaud noted above), or does it alter our understanding of philosophical intelligibility and rationality? What does such language tell us about the relation between the religiosity of responsibility and actual, historical religion and religious tradition?

One option has been to claim that such language be read as evidence that Levinas' philosophy is "committed to the Jewish tradition, to a properly Jewish conception of God" (Cohen 1994: 173). It has even led some to claim what amounts very nearly to an equation between postmodern ethics and Judaism, an equation suggested by Robert Gibbs' apposition "this Jewish other of philosophy, this radical subject" (1992: 4). There is much to be said for such interpretations. But such claims must be reconciled with Levinas' own apparent insistence that his work be divided into a philosophical side and a confessional side. The philosophical side presents itself as a revision of phenomenology that reconsiders questions and concepts raised in the history and practice of phenomenology in light of a reduction to the ethical or interpersonal, while the confessional side takes up political, theological and even philosophical problems in the history of Judaism by commenting on the authoritative texts of this tradition.[2] While one need not

2. The major philosophical books include *Totality and Infinity*, *Otherwise than Being, or, Beyond Essence* and *Of God Who Comes to Mind*. These were preceded by two earlier works (*Existence and Existents* and *Time and the Other*) in which one finds a presentiment of the major insights into the ethical, but where Levinas' ethical phenomenology has not reached its maturity. The confessional side comprises occasional pieces delivered to Jewish audiences or printed in publications with largely Jewish readership, and Talmudic lectures with

194

always take an author at his word, this asserted division of his work is enough, in my opinion, to cause serious trouble for those who claim that Levinas' chief contribution to twentieth-century philosophy was made as a 'Jewish philosopher' or that his philosophy is "committed to the Jewish tradition, to a properly Jewish conception of God". With such a division of his work, he would explicitly disavow the authority of Jewish tradition over the philosophical work and would seem to assign consideration of explicitly Jewish experience to another body of his own work. In fact, when Lyotard presented to Levinas his own interpretation of Levinas' philosophy as thought of the Old Testament God, Levinas responded, "I am not for all that an especially Jewish thinker; I am a thinker, *tout court*" (Levinas 1988: 83, my trans.). Lyotard even remembers Levinas claiming, "It is not under the authority of the Bible that my thought is placed, but under the authority of phenomenology … You make of me a Jewish thinker" (*ibid.*: 78–9). Such claims suggest that we cannot collapse the philosophical and the religious in Levinas.

Even if Levinas disavows the authority of Judaism and Jewish tradition over his philosophical work, it remains the case that his philosophy does indeed invoke religious, even particularly Jewish, themes and language in its account of the responsible subject. Religious themes are clearly identifiable in Levinas' ethical phenomenology and yet this discourse does not belong to a religious tradition or place itself under the authority of a particular religion. Everything happens as if the analysis of responsibility alone, without reference to the authority of religious tradition, institutions, or historical events experienced by myself or others, was sufficient to reach the religiosity of human subjectivity. Derrida has noted a similar sort of religious discourse in the Czech phenomenologist Jan Patočka:

> What engenders all these meanings and links them, internally and necessarily, is a logic that at bottom … has no need of *the event of revelation or the revelation of an event*. It needs to think the possibility of such an event but not the event itself. This is a major point of difference, permitting such a discourse to be developed without reference to religion as institutional dogma and proposing a genealogy of thinking concerning the possibility and essence of the religious that doesn't amount to an article of faith. (Derrida 1995b: 49)

Levinas, like Patočka, belongs to a philosophical "tradition that consists of proposing a nondogmatic doublet of dogma, a philosophical and metaphysical doublet, in any case a *thinking* that 'repeats' the possibility of religion without religion" (*ibid.*: 49). This tradition of philosophy of religion includes at least, I

---

a similar, although often more academic, audience. They are collected in *Difficult Freedom, Nine Talmudic Readings, Beyond the Verse* and *In the Time of the Nations*.

would argue, Kant's deduction of the religion of reason from the principles of practical reason (not the same as his assessment of historical religion in light of the religion of reason) and Hegel's deduction of Christianity from the speculative concept of God in *The Lectures on the Philosophy of Religion* or from the experience of consciousness in *Phenomenology of Spirit*. Both these might parallel Levinas' own production of the religiosity of the subject strictly through an analysis of the possibilities latent in responsible subjectivity. Even if the religiosity produced in each case is different in content (Kant's practical reason is, of course, not Levinas' responsibility, for instance, and so the former's religion of reason is different from the latter's religiosity of the responsible self), the formal or structural similarities in the relation of the religious and the philosophical remain.

At the same time, as Derrida again observes in regard to Patočka, "one might as well conclude, conversely, that this concept of responsibility is Christian [in Levinas' case Jewish or, if one wants, Judaeo-Christian] through and through and is produced by the event of Christianity [or Judaism]" (*ibid.*: 50). What Derrida suggests here about the relation between responsibility and historical religion and religious tradition could be said of Levinas: namely, the concept of responsibility that Levinas explores first appears historically in the event known as Judaism (or, if one wants, Judaeo-Christian tradition) such that this religion or this religious tradition has endowed our own historicity with the notion of responsibility whose philosophical analysis in Levinas produces a religiosity that dispenses with the need for reference to history and tradition. The circle is patent: the phenomenology of responsibility, without reference to historical religion or the authority of religious tradition, produces a religiosity that repeats an actual historical religion precisely because responsibility was originally given by this religious tradition, whose possibility it has established.

Such a circle might give us occasion to reflect on the necessarily ambiguous 'of' in philosophy *of* religion. In some cases, this *of* means that philosophy masters religion, submits it to its own standards of evidence and rationality. In other cases, it means that philosophy belongs to religion, moving without questioning entirely within the conceptuality and assumptions of a religious mode of thinking. In each case, philosophy fears religion as much as religion fears philosophy. The ambiguous *of* in Levinas' philosophy of religion might provide occasion for each, overcoming its fear, to recognize the inescapability of the other.

FURTHER READING

Calin, R. & F.-D. Sebbah 2002. *Le Vocabulaire de Levinas*. Paris: Ellipses.

Calin, R. 2005. *Levinas et l'exception du soi*. Paris: Presses Universitaires de France.

Chalier, C. 1995. "The Philosophy of Emmanuel Levinas and the Hebraic Tradition". In *Ethics as First Philosophy: The Significance of Emmanuel Levinas for Philosophy, Literature, and Religion*, A. Peperzak (ed.), 3–12. New York: Routledge.

Gibbs, R. 1995. "Height and Nearness: Jewish Dimensions of Radical Ethics". In *Ethics as First Philosophy: The Significance of Emmanuel Levinas for Philosophy, Literature, and Religion*, A. Peperzak (ed.), 13–23. New York: Routledge.

Hart, K. & M. Signer (eds) 2009. *The Exorbitant: Emmanuel Levinas between Jews and Christians*. New York: Fordham University Press.

Kosky, J. 2001. *Levinas and the Philosophy of Religion*. Bloomington, IN: Indiana University Press.

Levinas, E. 1969. *Totality and Infinity*, A. Lingis (trans.). Pittsburgh, PA: Duquesne University Press.

Levinas, E. 1990. *Difficult Freedom: Essays on Judaism*, S. Hand (trans.). Baltimore, MD: Johns Hopkins University Press.

Levinas, E. 1990. *Nine Talmudic Readings*, A. Aronowicz (trans.). Bloomington, IN: Indiana University Press.

Levinas, E. 1994. *Beyond the Verse*, G. Mole (trans.). Bloomington, IN: Indiana University Press.

Levinas, E. 1994. *In the Time of the Nations*, M. Smith (trans.). Bloomington, IN: Indiana University Press.

On ETHICS see also Chs 12, 21; Vol. 1, Ch. 11; Vol. 2, Chs 4, 8; Vol. 3, Ch. 9; Vol. 4, Chs 13, 19. On JUDAISM see also Ch. 8; Vol. 1, Chs 9, 10; Vol. 2, Ch. 8; Vol. 3, Ch. 15. On PHENOMENALISM see also Ch. 17.

16

SIMONE WEIL

Stephen Plant

Those who write about Simone Weil (1909–43) use strikingly similar vocabulary, describing her as ascetic, brilliant, enigmatic, a genius, heretical, mad, mercurial, an outsider, passionate, prophetic, revolutionary, spiritual and troubled. The list of frequently used terms is longer, but not by much. Aside from what these terms tell us about those who comment on her life and thought, they suggest how hard it can be to classify Weil's thought or locate her in a history of ideas. Weil simply does not fit snugly into a tradition or belong neatly to a school of thought. She admired Plato, but her interpretation of him is shot through with idiosyncrasies. Indebted to Karl Marx, she came to reject revolution. Enraptured by Catholic religion and in love with Jesus Christ, she saw in the Catholic Church an embodiment of the "Great Beast ... the object of idolatry ... an *ersatz* God" (Weil 2002: 164). A religious mystic, she thought atheism purified religion. Her writings, moreover, are fragmentary by comparison with those of other major modern thinkers. She published little, and what she did publish tended (with one exception, the 1934 political essay *Oppression and Liberty*) to be in the form of short articles in obscure journals. Her inclination to unfold her thinking by means of short *pensées* in the style of Blaise Pascal was fostered by her teacher, Alain (Emile Chartier), and later necessitated by the exigencies of the Second World War. The notebooks, in which Weil's thoughts appear in the sequence in which they occurred, were left in the hands of friends. When they were published posthumously either they were printed in an unedited form lacking an obvious systematic coherence or, for example in the case of *Gravity and Grace*, were sifted by an editor who arranged a few selected individual aphorisms under headings of his own devising and for his own purposes (in that particular instance, Weil's friend Gustave Thibon seems to have been intent to set her thought out in the pose of a Catholic saint). Weil's natural inclination to the aphorism rather than the monograph as a medium for philosophical thought was also fostered by external circumstances beyond her control. She was a woman in a society not naturally welcoming to women's participation in politics, philosophy or theology. She died young and the last years of her life were disrupted by war. The consequence is that not only in form, but also in content, her trains of thought are sometimes unfinished or improperly developed; sometimes placed in the interrogative mood rather than something more assured and final. The form allowed her to pursue a natural intellectual eclecticism such that she proves hard to keep up with as she leaps like a mountain goat across the boulders of Western thought, from philosophy to geometry, from the causes of Nazism to Sophocles' *Antigone*, from quantum theory to the love of God, and from aesthetics to the nature of work. Sometimes she asserts truths rather than arguing towards them. Her views can be quite uncompromising, and occasionally they were bizarre.

WEIL'S LIFE

Weil was born in 1909 in Paris, the younger of two children. Growing up she compared herself unfavourably to her brother, a mathematical prodigy. Her parents were secularized Jews in a France in which anti-Semitism was a living reality. Weil's subsequent hysterical and uncharacteristically prejudiced rejection of most of the Hebrew Scriptures and of what she considered to be the worship of power in Judaism is a serious flaw, but its origin might charitably be laid at the door of early twentieth-century French anti-Semitism. Weil's home was happy, although her relationship with her mother was unusually intense. During the First World War, Simone's father worked as an army doctor, and the family moved frequently, settling in Paris after the cessation of hostilities. The war had profound and complex consequences for French society. A generation of Frenchmen was decimated, killed in the trenches or left physically or psychologically scarred. One consequence of this missing generation was that French social and political institutions tended to be run by a gerontocracy. Young Frenchmen and women growing up in the 1920s and 1930s typically felt excluded and driven towards social and political extremism. Many regarded revolutionary politics, now flourishing in the Soviet Union, as a franchise on which the French had a moral copyright. Nonetheless, in spite of these undercurrents, mid-1920s France was blithely confident; it had been victorious in the First World War and was now insulated by the flow of reparations payments from Germany and by trade with its extensive colonies. This stability began to be undermined following the Wall Street Crash of 1929 and then, from 1936, by the outbreak of a politically motivated civil war in Spain across France's western border.

In 1925 Weil enrolled at the Lycée Henri IV, where she was taught philosophy by Alain. Alain was, by common consent, a very fine teacher. Anti-clerical but not insensible to the power of religious myths, not socialist but sympathetic to the plight of the poor, his students found him inspirational. They included Maurice Merleau-Ponty, André Maurois and Maurice Schumann (who became Weil's friend, and who was later de Gaulle's foreign minister). Alain prized intellectual rigour and independence of thought, and found both in Weil, whom he affectionately called 'the Martian' to indicate how distinctive she was. In his termly reports on her, he predicted "brilliant success" but noted a tendency to abstruseness in her thoughts (Pétrement 1976: 41–2). One of Alain's contributions to Weil's intellectual formation was to encourage in her an admiration for the writings of Plato, who became a key element in her own philosophy. In 1927 Weil topped the list of philosophy students at the Sorbonne, but failed the broader and highly competitive entry requirements for the École Normale Supérieure. After a further year she succeeded and in 1930 was ranked seventh of the 107 candidates in the final *agrégation*. At the École Normale, Weil's most substantive academic product was a dissertation on science and perception in the work of René Descartes. The first part of the dissertation (published in English in a volume of her *Formative Writings 1929–1941*) is a fairly standard exegesis of Descartes' *Discourse on Method*. Even here, however, she departed from the mainstream of interpretation by arguing that real (i.e. practical) science was, for Descartes, the correct use of reason. The second part of the dissertation turned to the capacity of a reasoning individual to direct their own reason. The dissertation concludes with reflections on work, which was to become a key theme in her later writings.

During the years she was a student at the École Normale Supérieure, Weil was active in several social and political arenas. She taught evening classes for workers; she raised funds; she campaigned. This made her unusual and unpopular with some of her teachers, one of whom called her 'the Red Virgin'. This possibly had a bearing on her appointment in 1931 to the first of a succession of teaching posts in the relatively obscure town of Le Puy. In Le Puy, and in the schools to which she was transferred on a roughly annual basis, Weil continued to be active in trade unionism as a teacher and campaigner. As a schoolteacher she was popular, although by conventional standards she was not very successful. Judging by student notes from her lectures (published in English as *Lectures in Philosophy*, 1978) she took students into philosophy at a more fundamental level than they were prepared for, encouraging in them the same independence of thought and intellectual rigour that Alain had valued in her. In 1934 she took a year's leave, in the first instance to write the political essay *Oppression and Liberty*, and then to work as a labourer in several factories in Paris: the two are related. In the book, Weil argued that Marx had given "a first-rate account of the mechanism of capitalist oppression" by showing that the exploitation of workers was driven not so much by the greed of capitalists as by the necessity to expand rapidly in order to compete with rivals (Weil 1988: 39). Marx had shown, according to Weil, that this social and economic mechanism was not something random. That meant that careful study and reflection might lead to actions that would genuinely improve the functioning of capitalism for workers. Yet although, for Weil, Marx was the first seriously to reflect on capitalist societies, he failed to realize the potential of what he had begun:

> The materialistic method – that instrument which Marx bequeathed
> us – is an untried instrument; no Marxist has ever really used it,

201

beginning with Marx himself. The only really valuable idea to be found in Marx's writings is also the only one that has been completely neglected.   (*Ibid.*: 44)

This conclusion was consistent with the basically syndicalist (rather than communist or simply socialist) outlook of Weil's politics. It was on this basis that Weil took the decision to work 'anonymously' as a factory hand in order to experience what most communist theorists knew little of, namely, the world of work. Her intention was better to grasp the situation of workers in order to reflect on ways in which capitalist systems could be transformed. But the experience of working in a factory had unanticipated outcomes. Factory work proved physically and psychologically tough for her. A factory journal (published in *Formative Writings*) details both her exhaustion and the effects of the petty tyrannies of some of her foremen. Her experiences left her in pieces. Work had been an intellectual concern since her dissertation on Descartes; it now entered her through the scars on her hands and the ache in her muscles. Convalescing with her parents in Portugal, she saw a religious procession, and "the conviction was suddenly borne upon me that Christianity is pre-eminently a religion of slaves, that slaves cannot help belonging to it, and I among others" (1977: 34). It was one of several 'religious' experiences that followed in the train of her physical collapse, leading her away from political writing to subjects related to the experience of affliction, to Christ's suffering and to God. After a brief return to teaching, Weil travelled to Spain at the outbreak of the Civil War to enrol in an anarchist militia on the side of the Republican government. After a brief period at the front during which she rapidly became disillusioned, she stepped into a cooking pot (she had very poor eyesight) and was seriously injured. Convalescing again in 1938, at the Benedictine monastery at Solesmes, Weil had a significant mystical experience related to her severe migraines, and began to pray. In 1940 as the Germans were entering Paris, Weil and her parents took the last train out of Paris to Marseilles. There, she pursued a line of enquiry about whether to be baptized. She became close to an ascetic and intelligent Dominican, Father Perrin, writing a 'spiritual autobiography' for him that is a main source of knowledge about her 'inner' life. She worked for a period at a vineyard owned by Gustave Thibon, and, it seems, undertook some activities on behalf of the French Resistance. She wrote notebooks and published essays, some lauding the Cathar culture of the Languedoc before the Albigensian crusades of the thirteenth century. In 1942 she and her parents received exit visas and Weil made her way to London via Casablanca and New York, where, with help of friends from student days, she took up a post in the Free French forces. She was commissioned to write a briefing document on a possible political philosophy for post-war France, subsequently published as *The Need for Roots*. It had little impact on Charles de Gaulle, and Weil, whose application to become a secret agent in occupied France was rejected, once more became disillusioned, this time with Gaullist French nationalism. Her disordered eating habits, developed over many years, had grown steadily worse, and in a weakened state she contracted tuberculosis and died in August 1943.

PLATO IN WEIL'S THOUGHT

Before sampling elements of Weil's own thought it may be helpful to revisit the role played by Plato's philosophy in her work. This influence, which certainly can be overplayed, may be explored with reference to Weil's understanding of Plato in the history of thought. For Weil, there were two basic points that one must grasp about Plato. The first is that "[h]e was not a man who invented a philosophical doctrine. Unlike all other philosophers (without exception, I believe) he constantly reiterates that he has invented nothing and that he is simply pursuing a tradition, which he sometimes names and sometimes not" (Weil 1968: 91). The second important point about Plato, for Weil, is that the only writings by Plato that have survived are his popular writings, intended for a general – not a specialist – audience. This means it is the responsibility of Plato's readers to fathom from hints in these popular writings what Plato thought. Weil's conclusion was that "Plato is an authentic mystic, and indeed the father of Western mysticism" (*ibid.*: 92). Weil thought that Plato is, in other words (as her teacher Alain had taught), to be read as a poet who carried his readers forwards by means of image and metaphor to truth. Of course, poetry too can convey truth about human life, about beauty, about love and about reality; indeed, there are some truths that are *better* conveyed poetically than though philosophical (or theological) prose. For Weil to describe Plato as a poet is, therefore, to honour him. Thus, for example, Weil understood the well-known allegory of the cave in book seven of the *Republic* as a *parable* of the relationship of this earthly world to the higher reality of the supernatural world. It need not be read as a prosaic account of the relation between two places that exist in the same way: this world and the supernatural world. Rather, Weil suggests, the allegory of the cave may be read as a poem that tells us something about ourselves and our situation. In sum, the cave is the world; the chains are our impoverished imaginations. Plato's parable teaches that our imaginations call us to make a painful journey into the light of day, where truth, beauty, compassion and the good are more real than anything we can imagine. These ideals – truth, beauty, God – are not to be thought of as objects in this world; they are separate, lying outside the cave where all human living occurs. In this sense Weil could say (to her students at Roanne) that, "The wise have to return to the cave, and act there" (1978: 221). It is the poets, not the priests or philosophers or politicians, who are best able to struggle against incredulity and fear until they "reach the stage where power is in the hands of those who refuse it, and not of those whose ambition is to possess it" (*ibid.*).

STEPHEN PLANT

THE NECESSARY NON-EXISTENCE OF GOD

In the remainder of this entry I want to focus on Weil's religious philosophy through the lens of her reflections on love: the love of God and on (what she terms) implicit forms of the love of God. It is not far-fetched to conceive of many of Weil's philosophically religious writings in terms of a love affair with God. In an erotically charged mystical account of days spent in a garret with a Christ-like stranger, written in Marseilles in 1941 or 1942, Weil wrote: "I knew well that he does not love me. How could he love me? And yet deep down within me something, a particle of myself, cannot help thinking, with fear and trembling, that perhaps, in spite of all, he loves me" (1956: vol 2, 638–9). And in a letter written in 1942, Weil compared herself with the fig tree cursed by Jesus on a Jerusalem roadside:

> It is not that I actually do fear [God's anger]. By a strange twist, the thought of God's anger only arouses love in me. It is the thought of the possible favour of God and his mercy that makes me tremble with a sort of fear. On the other hand the sense of being like a barren fig tree for Christ tears my heart. (1977: 64)

In order to fathom the love of God identified in these brief citations we must first wrestle with one of the most stretching aspects of her thought: her understanding of the 'necessary non-existence of God'. God did not feature in Weil's early writings. But from the mid-1930s the problem of whether God may be comprehended by the human mind increasingly came to occupy her. By 1942 she could write to the living Christian she most admired, the Dominican Father Perrin, that she believed she had always been Christian: "I always adopted the Christian attitude as the only possible one. I might say that I was born, I grew up and I always remained within the Christian inspiration" (ibid.: 29). Moreover, her innate 'Christian attitude' was linked to the love of neighbour: "From my earliest childhood I always had also the Christian idea of love for one's neighbour, to which I gave the name of justice" (ibid.: 31). If she judged it impossible to enter the Church by being baptized it was because she was reluctant "to add dogma to this conception of life" (ibid.: 32). Part of her hesitancy as she stood at the door of the Church lay in a dread – learned in part from Plato – of the manner in which belonging within certain social structures inhibited intellectual freedom and integrity. Judaism, Nazism and the Catholic Church were in some degree all judged by Weil to embody Plato's 'Great Beast'.

If Weil did not shape her religious convictions according to the doctrines of the Catholic Church, what were the sources of her beliefs? Weil believed that Jesus Christ embodied deep truths – for example, about the nature of human affliction and about God – but that these truths had also been present in other religious and philosophical traditions throughout human history. The choice facing her

204

(and indeed everyone) was not therefore between being a Christian and being damned, but between truth and falsehood: "[t]here is not a Christian point of view and other points of view; there is truth and error. It is not that anything which isn't Christianity is false, but everything which is true is Christianity" (1970: 80). 'Truth' *included* Christianity, but it was not exclusive to it. On the contrary, she records in a notebook that:

> It is impossible that the whole truth should not be present at every time and every place, available for anyone who desires it. 'Whoever asks for bread'. Truth is bread. It is absurd to suppose that for centuries nobody, or hardly anybody, desired the truth, and then that in the following centuries it was desired by whole peoples.   (*Ibid.*: 302)

In Weil's judgement God's truth did not first enter the world with Jesus. Contrary to Pope Boniface VIII's assertion that outside the Church "there is neither salvation nor the remission of sins", Weil believed that "Every time that a man has, with a pure heart called upon Osiris, Dionysus, Krishna, Buddha, the Tao etc., the Son of God has answered him by sending the Holy Spirit" (1974: 114). What these plural sources of knowledge of God revealed, for Weil, was a singular truth: the love of God is not an illusion. But this, for Weil, is only one half of a pair of contradictory truths, the other half being the inability of the human mind truly to conceive God. This was the problem of 'the necessary non-existence of God', which Weil regarded as an instance of a contradiction or paradox capable of yielding great spiritual truth. Contradictions, Weil thought, functioned something like a koan, on which patient reflection could yield insight. "Impossibility", she wrote, "is the door of the supernatural" (2002: 95). Examples of such contradictions, for Weil, include the doctrine of the Trinity – God is one, and God is three persons – and the mystery of the cross, on which the Christ gave himself and was also punished. But the ultimate contradiction for Weil was God's existence and non-existence:

> A case of contradictories which are true. God exists: God does not exist. Where is the problem? I am quite sure that there is a God in the sense that I am quite sure my love is not illusory. I am quite sure that there is not a God in the sense that I am quite sure nothing real can be anything like what I am able to conceive when I pronounce this word. But that which I cannot conceive is not an illusion.   (*Ibid.*: 114)

Weil understood there to be an interplay of forces in relationships between God and the person, as between persons, analogous to the force of gravity. One person's needs frequently drive others away: need and response are all too often, in Rowan Williams' phrase, "systematically uncoordinated" (Williams 1993: 53). In human relationships it is not uncommon for us, instead of loving someone for who they really are, to fashion them through the distorting lens of our needs into the person we would like them to be. This flaw in the human imagination applies equally, for Weil, when we try to imagine God: we simply cannot know if we are conjuring a false image of God because of the force of our need for a particular kind of deity. The only way in which this may be overcome is to cease attempts to conceive God at all. For this reason, Weil can say that:

> Of two men who have no experience of God, he who denies him is perhaps nearer to him than the other. The false God who is like the true one in everything, except that we cannot touch him, prevents us from ever coming to the true one. The 100 possible thalers in Kant. The same applies to God. We have to believe in a God who is like the true God in everything, except that he does not exist, since we have not yet reached the point where God exists. (2002: 115)

The reference to Kant's comparison between one hundred real and one hundred imaginary thalers, however, reiterates Weil's assertion, cited earlier, that although we may not speak of God as if he is an object in the world of things, there remain some things that we may still say of God, the most important of which is that our love of God is not an illusion: "Nothing which exists is absolutely worthy of love. We must therefore love that which does not exist. This non-existent object of love is not a fiction, however, for our fictions cannot be any more worthy of love than we ourselves, and we are not worthy of it" (*ibid.*: 110). An ideal type of love, for Weil, was the 'courtly love', or colloquially speaking the 'Platonic love', modelled above all in the troubadours of the Languedoc before that culture was suppressed by the Church. Courtly love typically went to great lengths to maintain a distance between lover and beloved in spite of, and even because of, the sense of longing and suffering that distance entailed. In courtly love, therefore, a love song is typically a sad song. In Weil's suggestion that 'love is in proportion to the distance' between God and the individual, one sees such distance given positive value, so long as it is understood that 'distance' is accompanied not by indifference, but rather by a 'courtly' instinct to share in the suffering of the beloved.

The most probing treatment of Weil's 'atheistic theism' to date is that by Rowan Williams. Williams identifies significant tensions in Weil's account of the grammar of the words 'God' and 'love' that may be thought to carry over into her treatment of the forms of the implicit love of God. According to the grammatical rules Weil sets for us, Williams reports:

> we are … able to sort out what we must say about God in order to be talking about God at all; but we cannot affirm that this God exists over against us, an agent within the system of agencies, a subject with whom I can converse, a particular determination of my own existence in the world. (Williams 1993: 55)

There is "never a moment when I can legitimately or intelligibly speak of God as 'existing', as a concrete reality over against me" (*ibid*.: 58). The appropriate response is, therefore, to decreate oneself, to seek to cease to exist, to become transparent in order that one does not get in the way of the flow of love between God and the world. In this process, it is the sheer otherness of God that we are brought to love. But this otherness – as Williams points out– is an "undifferenciated otherness, in the sense that it is indifferent with respect to my specific wants or articulated needs" (*ibid*.: 61). For Weil, only the perfect is deserving of love: if we love something that is imperfect – say, beauty, religion or another person – what we are loving is not really particular: it is the perfection that is glimpsed in the imperfections of the finite. "It is precisely this consideration about the necessary distance between what can be said of God", concludes Williams, "that prompts unease with Weil's analysis of love. She moves very rapidly from the facts of the mobility, fluidity, and discontent of human love to the conclusion that there is an essence of love that is unconditional" (*ibid*.: 63). For Williams, Christianity teaches that love is something learned; it is intrinsically vulnerable, ambiguous, forgetful and sometimes corrupt. It is part of the contingencies of human exchange, and it is within the processes of giving and receiving love, of hurting and of being hurt, of damage and of healing, that we learn of love at all. Weil's discomfort with such contingent forms of love is indicative of a very un-Christian disembodiment.

FORMS OF THE IMPLICIT LOVE OF GOD

Weil argued that direct love of God was impossible, for "God is not present to the soul and never yet has been so" (1977: 76). But although *direct* love of God is impossible, *indirect* love of God is possible by loving certain provisional, natural realities. This indirect love she called the 'implicit love of God'. Weil suggested that there are three ways in which God can be loved implicitly: "The implicit love of God can only have three immediate objects, the only three things here below in which God is really though secretly present. These are religious ceremonies, the beauty of the world and our neighbour" (*ibid*.: 77). In addition, Weil believed friendship was a form of implicit love of God that could be distinguished from that of love for our neighbour. Such forms of the implicit love for God, although veiled, are far from being poor second-bests. For most people, direct love of God is never possible, and the implicit forms of love are the only way for them to love until their death. Even though for most people these forms of love never become direct, nevertheless these implicit loves can be love *for God*, and are not under any circumstances valueless. For a few people – those who learn the lessons of affliction or joy – the implicit forms of love can grow so strong that they are subsumed and perfected, until they become direct forms of love for God. Even in its unperfected forms, implicit love of God can sometimes, Weil continued, reach a high degree of purity and power and even possess the virtue of sacraments. In any case, however, implicit forms of love for God must always precede direct love for God.

The first form taken by the implicit love of God is love of our neighbour. In the parable of the sheep and the goats (Matthew 25:31–46), Jesus suggested that whoever gives to someone who is afflicted is in some sense giving to Christ himself. Within this statement, however, Weil perceived a paradox: "Who but Christ himself can be Christ's benefactor? How can a man give meat to Christ, if he is not raised at least for a moment to the state spoken of by Saint Paul, when he no longer lives in himself but Christ lives in him?" (1977: 77). As well as being present in the person who receives, as Jesus' parable suggests, Christ is also in some sense present in the person who gives. The value of the charitable gift, that is, depends no more on the spiritual qualities of the giver than does the efficacy of the Eucharist on the virtues of the priest. In both cases it is God who gives the gift. In charity Christ can make holy the gift of the greatest sinner: of even a Medici banker, or oil company official. This is because in addition to being an act of fellowship between donor and recipient, an act of charity is a participation in the pure love of God. To be sure, for Weil, it is not possible to conceive of charity in isolation from justice: as well as having qualities associated with love, charity must also entail justice. When confronted by a neighbour in need, Weil argued that in order to be an act of true charity, inequality must somehow be overcome. Otherwise, even when giving to a needy neighbour, the stronger party benefits more than the one who receives their gift: "Almsgiving when it is not supernatural is like a sort of purchase. It buys the sufferer" (ibid.: 84); "The supernatural virtue of justice consists of behaving exactly as though there were equality when one is the stronger in an unequal relationship" (ibid.: 81).

Once neighbour-love is seen in this light, it becomes clear that helping the afflicted person should be instinctive: true charity cannot be motivated, for example, by a desire to save one's soul, or to write off windfall profits against tax, or even to love God implicitly: a person who loves their neighbour "would not", Weil asserts, "think of saying that he takes care of the afflicted for the Lord's sake; it would seem as absurd to him as it would be to say that he eats for the Lord's sake" (1974: 94). In charity a miracle takes place: the giver puts herself in the place of another's affliction. By projecting oneself onto a person who has become a mere object, one gives to them the gift of one's own humanity, even to the point of diminishing one's own humanity for the sake of the enrichment of the other's.

The second form of implicit love is love of the order of the world. This complements love towards our neighbour and, in common with it, requires an act of self-renunciation. The chief instantiation of love of order for Weil lies in the celebration of beauty. However, Weil argued that love for beauty was sadly absent from the Christian tradition, although she acknowledged several exceptions to this rule, including Francis of Assisi. Beauty "is necessity which, while remaining in conformity with its own law and with that alone, is obedient to the good" (2002: 148). A beautiful thing has no objective except to be beautiful, and in this it is unique: beauty is not the means to something else. This quality in beauty is not affected by the passage of time, and thus human appreciation of beauty on earth is one of the few ways to encounter eternity. All individual beauties lead to God, for "The only true beauty, the only beauty which is the real presence of God, is the beauty of the universe. Nothing which is less than the universe is beautiful" (1977: 105).

The third form of implicit love of God is the love of religious practices, by which Weil meant the love that people have for a particular religious tradition. Religion, however, is no more valuable as a form of implicit love of God than the two previous forms: "God is present in religious practices, when they are pure, just as he is present in our neighbour and in the beauty of the world; in the same way and not any more" (*ibid.*: 110). Usually, the form of religion that we love depends on where we were born. A person born into a Hindu family will love God implicitly in Hindu religious practices, while a person born into a Roman Catholic family will love God in the religious practices of Catholicism. Although there are countless ways in which different religions worship God, Weil argued that the basic virtue within each of them remains the same: it lies in the recitation of the name of the Lord. Such worship is nevertheless an implicit and not a direct form of love for God.

The beauty of religions, Weil believed, lies in the intention behind them, and not in their outward forms. Thus, the building in which worship takes place can be ugly, or the priest corrupt, or the singing out of tune: none of this matters. To explain what she meant, Weil suggested that when a mathematician illustrates a mathematical proof on a blackboard or a piece of paper, the straight lines she draws are often not exactly straight, nor the circles she draws exact circles. Nevertheless, the theory the mathematician is illustrating remains perfectly true in spite of her imperfect drawing. Similarly with religious traditions, it is the purity of their content, not of their outward form, that is important. The believer fixes her attention on this purity, and it is in this looking that salvation is to be found.

CONCLUSION

I began this chapter by drawing attention to the fragmentary nature of Weil's thought and the sometimes contradictory qualities of its content. I have concluded with the more positive assessment that there are ways to bring her thinking into focus, for example through the lens of her reflections on God's necessary non-existence and of her understanding of the forms of the implicit love of God. For those who take the trouble to work with and through Weil's writings she can lead her readers in surprisingly fresh and fruitful ways into some of the most important issues in human life and in theology. Wrestling with Weil as Jacob wrestled the angel at Peniel, one can find oneself wrestling God.

FURTHER READING

Bell, R. (ed.) 1993. *Simone Weil's Philosophy of Culture.* Cambridge: Cambridge University Press.

Doering, E. & E. Springsted (eds) 2004. *The Christian Platonism of Simone Weil.* Notre Dame, IN: University of Notre Dame Press.

Levinas, E. 1990. "Simone Weil against the Bible". In *Difficult Freedom: Essays on Judaism*, 133–41. Baltimore, MD: Johns Hopkins University Press.

McLellan, D. 1989. *Simone Weil: Utopian Pessimist.* London: Macmillan.

Moulakis, A. 1998. *Simone Weil and the Politics of Self-Denial.* Columbia, MO: University of Missouri Press.

Ruhr, M. 2006. *Simone Weil: An Apprenticeship in Attention.* London: Continuum.

On BEAUTY see also Vol. 3, Ch. 17. On EXISTENCE OF GOD see also Ch. 11; Vol. 1, Chs 18, 19; Vol. 2, Chs 5, 6, 13, 14; Vol. 3, Chs 6, 12, 13, 14, 15, 21. On LOVE see also Vol. 4, Chs 13, 17. On PLATONISM see also Vol. 1, Chs 11, 14, 15, 17.

17

A. J. AYER

Graham Macdonald

Alfred Jules Ayer was born in London on 29 October 1910. His mother, Reine, was Jewish, and his father, Jules, came from a Swiss Calvinist background. It is clear that from a very early age Ayer was disinclined to believe in any religion. It is reported that, on winning a scholarship to Eton when he was thirteen, he made himself unpopular with his fellow students due to his evangelical atheism (he reports to being "a very militant atheist from the age of about sixteen onwards"; Honderich 1991: 212). The first philosophical book Ayer read was Bertrand Russell's *Sceptical Essays*, and he was much impressed by Russell's advice never to believe a proposition if there was no reason for thinking it true (Rogers 1999: 45). This, he said, remained a motto for him throughout his philosophical career. It appears that he never found a reason for believing any religious doctrine to be true.

Ayer's atheism became, in fact, more radical and a bit more complicated, as he was to form the belief that typical religious statements, such as those about a transcendent deity, were not so much false as meaningless or nonsensical. This view was formed under the influence of an empiricist theory of meaning incorporating a criterion of meaning, the verification principle. The core of the verification principle was that for a statement to be cognitively (or empirically) meaningful, that statement had to be capable of being directly or indirectly 'verified'. That is, the statement had to be capable of being supported by sensory experience. If no such experiences were deemed relevant to the truth (or falsity) of the statement, then the statement was not saying anything that could have any consequences for our experiences in the world, so it was cognitively useless, and hence cognitively meaningless.

Ayer's advocacy of the verification principle entailed that religious statements were not only not significantly affirmable, they were also not significantly deniable, so a typical atheistic statement (for example, 'There are no transcendent deities') was likewise consigned to the category of nonsense. And Ayer was, in this respect, particularly harsh on religious statements. He also thought that moral claims were not capable of being supported by our sensory experience, and so lacked cognitive meaning, but he assigned to them an 'emotive' meaning. Religious statements, on his view, did not have emotive meaning, and so were "absolute verbiage".[1] Much later he was to take a softer line on this:

> I think you can treat, if you're very careful, the affirmation of God's existence as a vacuous hypothesis, in which case it would be, I suppose, false … I would now say – Well, if it offends people to call religion nonsensical, let's call it false. I've become much milder in my old age.
>
> (Honderich 1991: 215)

Ayer's views on these matters were given their initial and most comprehensive formulation in his first and most famous book, *Language, Truth and Logic*, published in 1936 and written when he was only twenty-five. The book was written shortly after Ayer had spent time in Vienna in 1933, attending meetings of the Vienna Circle, a group of mainly Austrian and German philosophers who became known as 'logical positivists', the most famous of whom were Rudolf Carnap and Moritz Schlick. Ludwig Wittgenstein, who occasionally attended these meetings, was an influential figure, particularly for Schlick. Essential to the positivist attitude was a hostility to metaphysics, by which was meant any doctrine or belief whose credibility could not be seen as capable of being supported by the sort of experience that buttresses scientific investigations. The fundamental belief of the positivists was that if one made the kind of theoretical claims typically made by metaphysicians, then those claims ought to be assessable by the means normally used in science, and could not be assessed by any other means. All statements were thus divided into being empirical, or analytic (true in virtue of the meaning of the terms contained therein), or nonsensical. Religious statements were classed as being neither empirical nor analytic, and so, like all other metaphysical statements, nonsensical.

As we have seen, this animosity towards religion and metaphysics was hardened into a criterion of meaningfulness, the criterion supplied by the principle of verification. Although I have given a rough account of what this principle required for meaningfulness, it proved much harder than expected to give it a precise and plausible formulation. Ayer was one of the first to try, and in *Language, Truth and Logic* he formulated the principle in terms of a distinction between strong and weak verification: a statement was strongly verifiable if and only if its truth was conclusively ascertainable on the basis of observation statements, and weakly verifiable if and only if observation statements were deducible from that statement together with 'auxiliary' statements, provided that the observation statements were not deducible only from these auxiliary statements. It was quickly shown that this

---

1. "I've never put religion and morals together. I always said that religion was absolute verbiage. It might possibly have poetical meaning, but that is all" (Honderich 1991: 214).

would not exclude any statement whatever from being meaningful: any statement *P* conjoined with 'if *P* then *O*', where '*O*' is an observation statement, will yield *O*, without this being deducible from 'if *P* then *O*' alone. In the second edition of *Language, Truth and Logic*, published ten years later, Ayer amended the principle to read: a statement is directly verifiable if it is either an observation statement or is such that an observation statement is derivable from it in conjunction with another observation statement (or observation statements), such derivability not being possible from the conjoined observation statement(s) alone. And a statement is indirectly verifiable if, first, in conjunction with certain other premises it entails one or more directly verifiable statements that are not derivable from these other premises alone, and, secondly, that these other premises "do not include any statement that is not either analytic, or directly verifiable, or capable of being independently established as indirectly verifiable" (Ayer 1946: 17). This formulation proved no more successful, with Alonzo Church (1949) showing that it had the same defect in that it allowed *any* statement to be meaningful.[2]

Despite the failure of these attempts to provide a rigorous empiricist criterion of meaning, Ayer continued to hold that there was a close connection between evidence and meaning, maintaining that a satisfactory account of *confirmation* was needed before a foolproof criterion of empirical meaning could be supplied. Given later doubts about whether any theory of confirmation could provide a foundation for a theory of meaning (owing to Quinean doubts relating to the impossibility of ruling out any facts as possibly bearing on the truth of any sentence), it remains unclear how the evidence–meaning connection can be circumscribed.[3]

There is another problem with the principle of verification, one not relevant to its precise formulation. Ayer was an empiricist, and so required all knowledge claims to be adjudicated by our experience. This immediately raises a question about the nature of this experience. In *Language, Truth and Logic* Ayer was committed to phenomenalism: all statements about the world were (in principle) reducible to statements about actual or possible sensory experience, such statements being about our 'sense-data', not about objects in the world. One of the problems this raises is that the 'objectivity' of the external world appears to be sacrificed, since assertions about what are apparently external objects become assertions about one's own experience. One consequence of this view for personal identity is that the self is a set of experiences contained within one body. The extinction of the body meant that the person no longer survived, and hence immortality was impossible. Although Ayer soon relinquished this reductive view

---

2. For discussions of various attempts to overcome deficiencies in empirical criteria of meaning, see Hempel (1950). For a fairly recent discussion and attempt to reformulate the principle of verification, see Wright (1986, 1989).

3. Alvin Plantinga discusses the verificationist, and more broadly empiricist, conception of meaning in relation to claims about God in Plantinga (1967: 164–8). See also Edward Cell (1978: ch. 4). Kai Nielsen responds to Plantinga's criticism in Nielsen (1971: ch. 4).

of assertions about the external world, he retained the empiricism that stood at the heart of both the formulation and application of the verification principle in *Language, Truth and Logic*. A second consequence of the conjunction of verificationism with phenomenalism is that there can be disagreement between two parties as to the meaningfulness of a proposition because they have different experiences relating to that proposition.[4] We will return to this later.

After the publication of *Language, Truth and Logic* Ayer lectured briefly at Christ Church, then became a tutorial fellow at Wadham College, Oxford, before accepting the position of Grote Professor of Philosophy at University College, London. It was at this time that he became more widely known in British intellectual life, chiefly through his participation in many BBC Third Programme broadcasts. One of these broadcasts became particularly celebrated: a debate with Father Copleston on the nature of metaphysics, and in particular on the question whether statements such as 'God exists' are meaningful.[5] The crux of their disagreement concerned the legitimacy of metaphysical claims, Copleston defending the view that metaphysics begins where science leaves off, and Ayer denying that this left metaphysics with a defensible project. For Ayer the relation of philosophy to science was limited to analysing, and showing the connections between, scientific propositions. What philosophy could not do was 'go beyond science' in any more substantial sense, one involving what Ayer called 'transcendental statements', as these did not make the "slightest difference to anything that anyone experiences" (Edwards & Pap 1965: 728). By this one must take Ayer to mean that these transcendental statements, in going beyond what science can explain, also go beyond all the evidence available to scientists, and so in this sense were indifferent to our sensory experience. Copleston, on the other hand, defined metaphysical questioning as concerning "the intelligible structure of reality in so far as it is *not* amenable to the investigation by the methods of empirical science" (*ibid.*: 730). According to Copleston, 'meta-phenomenal reality', although beginning with our sense-experience, is ultimately discerned through intellectual activity, this consisting in intellectual reflection on our sensory experience.

On this topic the debate simply stalled, each questioning the other's central assumptions. Copleston thought what Ayer was saying amounted only to "statements that do not satisfy the principle of verifiability do not satisfy the principle of verifiability" (*ibid.*: 744), whereas Ayer was mystified as to how the non-scientific (metaphysical and religious) statements could be understood.[6] Ayer defended his use of the principle by issuing a challenge to anyone who thought there was a

4. E. L. Mascall (1957) took Ayer to task for interpreting 'experience' in too limited a way. Nielsen discusses this charge in Nielsen (1971: ch. 3).
5. The broadcast took place on 13 June 1949. A transcript is published in Edwards & Pap (1965: 726–56).
6. Much later Ayer admitted to there being a circularity in the way in which the principle could be wielded: "the Principle of Verification commits one to a certain view of the world,

class of expressions that failed the meaningfulness test by the criterion of verifiability but that were still meaningful: "In what sense are they understood? They're not understood in my sense. They aren't parts of a symbolic system. You can't do anything with them, in the sense of deriving any observational consequences from them. What *do* you want to say about them?" (*ibid.*: 745). While both agreed that religious statements are not 'about' reality in the same sense as are scientific statements, Ayer denied while Copleston affirmed that there could be another sense in which they are about reality.

A second feature of the debate, one not immediately relating to the intelligibility of the hypothesis that one can have an intellectual apprehension of metaphysical reality, concerned causation and necessity. Ayer's empiricism embraced a Humean understanding of causation as involving merely contingent generalizations over events. Explanations of events that cited contingent causes could be shown to be false, as the causes could always have been other than those cited by the explanation. Copleston was not content with merely contingent explanations, maintaining that the explanations he was after would not do their explanatory work if they were only contingent: if explanation was to be *fully* satisfactory, necessarily true propositions were required. The non-scientific propositions that Copleston thought were at the heart of both metaphysical and religious thought were non-scientific because their truth was not contingent, hence not liable to verification or falsification by the empirical methods of science. He took the law of non-contradiction to be one such necessary proposition, one required for any reasoning process whatsoever. Ayer, however, had a purely conventional notion of necessity; necessary propositions were only necessary relative to the set of conventions that gave these propositions their (analytic) meaning. He denied that there was one such necessary proposition governing all legitimate moves in the use of different languages, one rule essential to all language games. For Ayer, what Copleston was saying amounted to the claim that in the language game we are presently playing, one of the principles accepted is the law of non-contradiction, and anyone flouting this principle is not reasoning correctly. This conventional reading of necessity could not underwrite any metaphysical or religious truths, so Ayer thought he had deflected any possibility of using such logically necessary truths as a building block for the more ambitious task of justifying the putative necessary truths of metaphysical or religious thought.

As a consequence of his repudiation of intellectual apprehension of *de re* necessary truths, Ayer consistently denied that there was an alternative means (a purely 'rational' way) of supporting beliefs in a necessary being. As we have seen, Copleston did not deny that our reflection began with experience, but he did deny that it was exhausted by that experience; what he wished to affirm was that reason

---

and conversely a certain view of the world is secured by the Principle of Verification" (Ayer 1991: 6).

could engage with experience and go substantially beyond it, and it was this that Ayer denied. Ayer could not see how reason could go beyond experience in a way that was not ultimately responsive to experience, that is, in a way that did not make a difference to what we experienced. And it would be cheating, he thought, if there was said to be a difference, but one that was only discernible after the fact; the difference in experience required by a meaningful claim had to be specifiable in advance of the having of the experience, otherwise the constraint (specifiable loosely as: 'the hypothesis must make a difference to what we can expect to experience') would be too easily satisfied.

Ayer was vulnerable on one point, however, and that was in the manner in which experience was treated. He admitted that not all experience was derived from our senses, there being experience that formed the content of our introspective states. He also admitted that he could not rule out there being mystical experience. A consequence was that he was vulnerable to the believer who insisted that their beliefs had experiential content, one that was available to introspection, and whose content was of a transcendent being. Although he would not deny the coherence of this claim, he could say that this believer could not make the content of their beliefs in the transcendent being intelligible to those who did not share the particular experience. On this view religious statements would form a sort of 'private language'.[7] Ayer did wish to deny that such a possibility could add any cognitive value to our statements; they could not be regarded as increasing our knowledge of the world. Copleston, in a different context, commented, "I simply note in passing that reflection on mystical experience, in so far as its nature can be known from outside, might contribute to the development of a world-view by featuring as one feature or strand in the construction of a general interpretation of reality" (Hahn 1992: 67).

In a later book, *The Central Questions of Philosophy*, Ayer, in considering the classical arguments for the existence of a God, returned to the question of whether the hypothesis that there is a God could be confirmed by experience, concluding this time that unless that hypothesis generated verifiable predictions, then any assumption that God exists is 'theoretically idle' (which is weaker than 'meaningless'; he may have moved to this weaker position owing to the difficulties in arriving at a usable verificationist criterion of meaning). He does not deny that *if* those who maintain that their religious experience justifies their belief in God were sufficient in number, and that they agreed in their accounts of this experience, then it would be possible to credit these experiences as cognitive, and as being experiences of an object. But this would only justify our having a broader conception of what the world contains; no further inferences to the 'unworldy' character of the object of that experience could be sustained.

---

7. Here a Wittgensteinian might argue that such a private language is impossible, but this move is not available to Ayer as he rejected Wittgenstein's argument concerning the impossibility of such a language.

In addressing the classical arguments for the existence of God, Ayer paid particular attention to the ontological argument. He takes this to consist in an argument from three premises to the conclusion that God necessarily exists. The first premise states that God is perfect, meaning at least that no being of greater perfection is imaginable; the second that a real being is more perfect than an imaginary being; the third that were God not to exist then he would be less than perfect; so the conclusion follows that God necessarily exists, or, as Ayer puts it, "his existence follows from his essence, or, in other words, from the way he has been defined" (1973: 214). This way of putting the conclusion is typically linguistic, and leads Ayer to question the Kantian response to the argument, which is to deny that 'exists' is a predicate and so to deny that existence is a property that can be ascribed to any being. Ayer claims that it is open to anybody to include existence in their definition of God, but this would still leave open the question of whether God, thus defined, does exist. That one must conceive of a perfect being as existing does not show, says Ayer, that such a conception does in fact apply to anything.

Ayer then examines a different application of the idea that God is a necessary being: God contains the ground (reason or cause) of his own existence. This is also found wanting, as Ayer claims to find no difference between saying (i) God has no cause, and (ii) God is self-causing. He suggests that the search for an 'ultimate' reason for the existence of the universe, one that would supply purpose and meaning to our lives, is intellectually incoherent. First, we would have trouble finding what this ultimate reason was, but even if that were possible, we would face the question of whether God's purpose was contingent, whether God could have enacted a different plan for the universe. If the answer is affirmative, then we do not have an *ultimate* reason, for we can then ask: why *this* plan? If the answer is negative, then we have to say that it is essential to being God that he has this plan enacted, and we are back to the defects of the ontological argument, as we would still have to show that a being with such an essence existed.

Ayer goes on to tackle the argument from design, which famously claims that the world exemplifies such intricate patterning and adaptive complexity that the only explanation could be that it has come about by design, and moreover by a designer who is God-like. This second claim is addressed first: there is nothing in the argument that tells against multiple designers, says Ayer, nor is there any line of reasoning favouring a designer with the traditional attributes of a God, such as omnipotence and benevolence. The designer must also exist either temporally or atemporally, and Ayer finds difficulty in either supposition. If the designer exists outside time, it is difficult to comprehend how he could act at a time so as to create the universe; if a temporal (albeit eternal) existence is required, then God would have existed before the universe, so the creation of the latter would best be seen as a transformation of events rather than the creation of something out of nothing.

These problems may be viewed as technicalities in the sense that if the argument works, then the character of the designer, and the designer's relation to time, will be secondary (although not unimportant) issues. The major problem with the argument, as Ayer sees it, is that there is no empirical evidence of an overarching plan or purpose. We can see 'local' purposes in our actions, but this cannot license the inference to there being a 'global' purpose, a teleology that governs all that happens. In particular, any thought that the existence of *Homo sapiens* could lend some weight to the assertion that there is a global plan is contradicted by the scientific evidence, which supports the view that we, as a species, are marked for extinction. Here Ayer quotes Russell: "So far as the scientific evidence goes, the universe has crawled by slow stages to a somewhat pitiful result on this earth, and is going to crawl by still more pitiful stages to a condition of universal death" (Ayer 1973: 220, quoting Russell 1957: 25). With what evidence there is telling against the existence of an overarching plan, the argument from design collapses, claims Ayer.

Does the existence of morality provide any evidence for the existence of God? One psychological argument could start with the observation that we (sometimes) behave morally, against our own interests, and that this would be impossible without religious belief providing the necessary moral motivation. Ayer rejects this on empirical grounds, claiming that there is little evidence to show that religious belief is required for moral behaviour, nor that there is any evidence to show that without religious belief we are doomed to amoral selfishness. Even if there were evidence that religious believers behaved more ethically than non-believers, the best this could show, says Ayer, is that religious belief is morally desirable; what it would not show is that those beliefs are true. The more philosophical argument relating morality to religion, that claiming that the authority (or normative force) that morality has can only be derived from a God, Ayer dispenses with on the usual grounds that this authority can only be derived from a being whose goodness has otherwise been certified, thus presupposing the independence of moral goodness from the being who is meant to be its origin.

Towards the end of his life Ayer had a close encounter with death, being 'technically' dead for a few minutes after choking on a piece of smoked salmon. On reviving he reported on what he had experienced during this 'dead' phase in such a way as to provide fodder for those who thought the famous atheist had recanted and 'found God'. In an interview conducted by Professor Ted Honderich (one of Ayer's successors as Grote Professor at University College), Honderich commented that after the experience Ayer seemed to have written more tolerantly of the idea of immortality, or at least that we might survive our deaths. Ayer admitted he had contemplated the idea in one article, but had recanted later:

> No, I still retain my belief we don't survive our deaths. The effect of the experience, though, was to make me more interested in the possibility of survival. Without thinking it *was* a possibility. I was more interested in the question of what circumstances might make it true that one had survived … I think reincarnation might be possible, if

one just legislated. That's to say, supposing it were the case that people did remember, as if it were their own experience, the experience of someone dead. One might choose to say they were the same person.

(Honderich 1991: 226)

Asked if there had been a danger of a deathbed recantation (about the existence of God), Ayer quickly replied, "Oh, no, no. No, none whatsoever. I don't know, I might go ga-ga – but as long as I maintain my present intelligence, no" (*ibid.*). There are, however, different accounts of what Ayer experienced at this time (including whether it was smoked salmon he choked on): see a secondhand report from the doctor at the scene in Cash (2001).

Ayer was philosophically active to the end of his life, spending the last few years responding to articles that were to appear in the volume dedicated to him in the Library of Living Philosophers series, edited by L. E. Hahn. He was admitted to hospital with a collapsed lung early in the summer of 1989, and died on 27 June.

FURTHER READING

Ayer, A. J. (ed.) 1959. *Logical Positivism*. New York: Glencoe Free Press.
Ayer, A. J. 1977. *Part of My Life*. London: Collins.
Ayer, A. J. 1984. *More of My Life*. London: Collins.
Cell, E. 1978. *Language, Existence and God: Interpretations of Moore, Russell, Ayer, Wittgenstein, Wisdom, Oxford Philosophy and Tillich*. Brighton: Harvester.
Copleston, F. 1965. *Contemporary Philosophy*. London: Burns & Oates.
Foster J. 1985. *A. J. Ayer*. London: Routledge.
Martin, M. 1990. *Atheism: A Philosophical Justification*. Philadelphia, PA: Temple University Press.
Nielsen, K. 1971. *Contemporary Critiques of Religion*. London: Macmillan.

On ARGUMENT FROM DESIGN see also Vol. 3, Ch. 23; Vol. 4, Ch. 12. On ATHEISM see also Ch. 6; Vol. 3, Ch. 15; Vol. 4, Chs 2, 10, 20. On CAUSATION see also Vol. 2, Ch. 7. On EMPIRICISM see also Vol. 1, Ch. 7; Vol. 4, Ch. 8. On PHENOMENALISM see also Ch. 15.

18

WILLIAM P. ALSTON

Daniel Howard-Snyder

William P. Alston was born in Shreveport, Louisiana, on 29 November 1921 to Eunice Schoolfield and William Alston. He graduated from high school at age fifteen, and studied music at Centenary College. While serving in the US Army in the Second World War (1942–6), he read philosophy extensively. He earned his PhD in 1951 from the University of Chicago; Alston's dissertation on Alfred North Whitehead was written under the direction of Charles Hartshorne. He held appointments at the University of Michigan (1949–71), Rutgers University (1971–6), the University of Illinois at Urbana-Champaign (1976–80), and Syracuse University (1980–92). Since 1992, he has been Professor Emeritus at Syracuse, where he continued to teach until 2000. During his career, Alston received many honours. He contributed significantly to metaphysics, epistemology and the philosophy of language, psychology and religion.

One will not find a synoptic philosophy of religion in Alston's work, nor much natural theology, although he had an abiding appreciation for both. Rather, one finds historically informed treatments of various problems that arise within theistic religions generally and Christianity specifically, treatments enriched by the tools of analytic philosophy. Alston has been at the forefront of the recent trend for Anglo-American Christian philosophers to take more seriously the Augustinian motto, 'faith seeking understanding'. (He was raised a Methodist and, through various ups and downs and ins and outs, returned to the Church to stay in the mid-1970s. For autobiographical details, see Alston [1995a].) Living out that motto resulted in work on the nature of God and God's action in the world, naturalistic explanations of religious belief, especially Freudianism (Alston 1964a), the Trinity, the Resurrection, the indwelling of the Holy Spirit, prayer, divine command theory, biblical criticism and the evidential value of the fulfilment of divine promises for spiritual and moral development in the here and now. (For a complete bibliography, see Howard-Snyder [2007].) Alston's best work, however, is on the nature of religious discourse, the epistemology of religious experience, the problem of evil and the nature of propositional faith.

RELIGIOUS DISCOURSE

While Alston insists on the indispensable role of non-assertoric speech in religious practice, he is at odds with much contemporary liberal theology over the role of assertion. He disagrees with those who say that no religious assertion is really a statement of fact whose truth-value does not depend on human cognition, and with those who say that human concepts and terms cannot literally apply to God.

Consider these sentences: 'God made a covenant with Abraham', 'God became incarnate in Jesus of Nazareth' and 'There exists an immaterial person who is unlimited in power and knowledge'. Alston holds three theses about such sentences. (1) Absent sufficient reason to the contrary, we should take these sentences to be as they appear: genuine statements of fact, as opposed to mere expressions of feelings and attitudes, directives for behaviour, and the like. As such, they are either true or false. (2) These statements are true if and only if what they are about is as they say it is. Otherwise, they are false. (3) The facts that make these statements true – or false, as the case may be – are what they are independently of our beliefs, theories, conceptual schemes, values, activity and so on. Alston labels the conjunction of (1)–(3) *alethic realism*. Its proponents include theists as well as agnostics and atheists, for example Bertrand Russell. Its detractors deny one or more of (1)–(3).

Those who deny (1) endorse religious non-cognitivism, for example Paul Tillich, Richard Braithwaite, and D. Z. Phillips. The most influential basis for this view, popularized by A. J. Ayer, appealed to the verifiability criterion of meaning (VCM), according to which a non-analytic sentence is a genuine statement (i.e. has a truth-value) only if it is empirically testable, that is, confirmable or disconfirmable by experience. Since religious sentences are not empirically testable, they are not genuine statements (i.e. lack a truth-value).

Even if VCM is true, Alston (2003) argues, it does not follow that no talk about God is empirically testable, for at least two reasons. First, some talk about God occurs in theological contexts that tie that talk to observable historical events thereby rendering it empirically testable. Secondly, if non-sensory religious experience can provide empirical evidence for certain religious beliefs, then it can render statements used to express the content of such beliefs empirically testable.

Most importantly, however, this argument for non-cognitivism is only as plausible as VCM itself. Early in his career, Alston (1954) argued that it was nothing but a bit of metaphysics of the sort its proponents intended to supplant. Later, he stressed four points (1964b, 2003). First, VCM itself is not a genuine statement since it is non-analytic but empirically untestable. If, however, as many insisted, it is merely a proposal for using the predicates 'is a genuine statement', 'is cognitively meaningful' and so on, there is nothing to recommend it. Secondly, given the meaning of some empirically established terms plus a grasp of syntax, a speaker can construct sentences to make statements that are empirically untestable. To illustrate, given the meaning of 'person', 'power', 'knowledge', 'material', 'limit', 'not' and 'exist', one can construct the sentence 'There exists an immaterial person who is unlimited in power and knowledge' and query whether it is true or false despite its empirical untestability. Thirdly, scientific theories contain some statements that are, at best, only indirectly testable, provided the theories of which they are a part include bridge principles: statements that connect them to directly testable statements. But there is no principled way to put restrictions on bridge principles so that statements verificationists want to let in, for example all theoretical sentences, are empirically testable but sentences they want to rule out, for example 'God is perfectly good or it won't rain in Seattle tomorrow', are not. Moreover, since bridge principles are non-analytic, VCM implies they lack truth-value unless they too are testable; but they cannot be tested independently of the broader theories of which they are a part. Fourthly, unless a sentence is already understandable as a factual statement, the question of whether and how it can be empirically tested cannot even arise.

Those who affirm (1) but deny (2) or (3), for example John Hick, affirm a conception of truth other than the minimally realist one expressed in (2), or else claim that the facts that make statements true in the realist sense are not what they are independently of human cognition. As for the denial of (2), Alston (1996a) argues at great length on behalf of (2) and against its rivals. As for the denial of (3), he argues on behalf of (3) on both philosophical (1979, 2001) and religious grounds (1995b). In the latter connection, he argues that it is deeply subversive of the Judaeo-Christian faith. For it is fundamental to that faith that "God is taken to be a real presence in the world, a supreme personal being with whom we can enter into personal relationships, a being Who, to understate it, enjoys a reality in His own right, independently of us and our cognitive doings", a being who is "the source of being for all other than Himself, … an ultimate supreme reality, … that on which everything else depends for its being" (*ibid.*: 45–7). No imaginative construct, no way in which the Real appears, not even Tillich's Being-Itself, can answer to these descriptions. Moreover, arguments for these views endorse an extreme version of the conceptual transcendence of the divine that is based on the false assumption that since human concepts were developed to apply to this-worldly phenomena, they cannot apply to any other reality. Finally, "any form of irrealism is crashingly implausible as an account of the way in which religious beliefs and affirmations are meant (understood) by almost all believers"; as a proposal for reinterpreting them, it is not only intellectually indefensible, but "it would be deeply unsatisfying to practically all religious believers and seekers to be told that the only thing available is a set of make-believes that they can pretend to be real so as to regulate, orient, and guide their lives in certain ways" (*ibid.*: 55–6).

Suppose Alston is correct: religious assertions can be used to make statements of fact. Even so, it might be that no religious statement could possibly be true; that would be the case if it were impossible to refer to God or to truly apply predicates to him.

In response to the question about reference, Alston (1989a) distinguishes two broad positions: descriptivism and direct reference. According to the former, one refers to an individual with a referring expression by having a uniquely exemplified description in mind. According to the latter, one fixes the reference of an expression by virtue of intending to do so when the item is perceptually presented to one on a particular occasion; when others hear the expression, they refer to the item in question by virtue of intending to use it with the same reference as the person they learned it from (Kripke 1972). While mixed modes of reference are typical in general, Alston argues that direct reference to God is primary in religious practice. Most people learn to refer to God by way of learning to refer to God in prayer, sacrament, ritual, and so on, through which they take it they are in experiential contact with God. Moreover, most people intend to refer to what their predecessors refer to, ultimately to what it is the originators of their tradition referred to in experiential encounters with God.

Whether reference to God is primarily direct or descriptive is important for at least two reasons. First, it makes a difference to what is negotiable: if experiential encounter fixes the reference, then what is experienced is the referent of 'God' despite descriptions one had in mind, but if descriptions fix the reference, then, if nothing satisfies them, nothing answers to 'God'. Secondly, it makes a difference to commonality between world religions: if experiential encounter fixes the reference rather than description, it is more likely that religions with radically divergent descriptions of the nature of Ultimate Reality are really in contact with the same being. Taken together, these two points tend to support inclusivism in the debate surrounding religious pluralism.

The problem of theological predication is especially poignant in light of the fact that our talk about God is derived from our talk about creatures, and God is radically different from creatures. In fact, many thinkers suggest that the difference is so radical that our speech cannot apply literally to God; at best, it can apply figuratively, for example metaphorically. Alston's position on these concerns can be summarized under three headings (1989a).

First, some predicates seem to be literally applied to God. Consider some negative predicates, for example 'God is immaterial, atemporal, not restricted to one spatial location, not dependent on anything else for his existence, not identical to Richard Nixon'; or consider some positive relational predicates, for example 'God is thought of by me now', or even 'God comforts us and strengthens us in adversity, forgives the sins of the truly repentant, communicates to us how we should live'. The latter mainly report the effect of God's action on us without saying anything about what God did to bring it about. If, however, God is absolutely simple, as Thomas Aquinas thought (*see* Vol. 2, Ch. 13), no positive non-relational predicate can literally apply to God since that would require God to exemplify a property standardly associated with the predicate, and that implies a distinction between God and God's properties. Alston (1993b) rejects the doctrine of simplicity and the doctrine of analogical predication that goes with it.

Secondly, in contrast to many contemporary theologians, Alston denies that our talk about God is *irreducibly* metaphorical. He argues that in the typical case of using a term metaphorically to express a truth, the speaker presents to the hearer something to which the predicate literally applies (an *exemplar*) and the speaker has in mind some resemblance between the exemplar and the subject, some salient, shared feature the speaker means to draw to the hearer's attention, say *P*. A speaker cannot have *P* in mind without having a concept of *P*, in which case it is possible for others in the speaker's linguistic community to have it too; thus, it is possible, in principle, to semantically correlate a predicate *in the language* with *P*. So the Psalmist truly says 'The Lord is my shepherd' only if it is possible, in principle, to literally express the same truth. Talk about God *cannot* be irreducibly metaphorical.

Thirdly, Alston aims to clarify how personal predicates – both those that ascribe mental states, for example 'knows', 'desires', 'intends', and those that ascribe actions, for example 'makes', 'guides', 'commands', 'forgives' – can apply literally to an immaterial and timeless being. To this end, he makes the general point that features common to the extension of a term need not be features partially constitutive of its meaning; consequently, their application may well have no bodily or temporal requirement. Thus, for example, the predicate in 'God made the heavens and the earth' might literally apply to God since our concept of making something is the concept of bringing something into existence, the concept being silent on how it happens. Furthermore, even if there are bodily and temporal requirements for the literal application of a term, they might be peripheral, in which case they might be simply lopped off or replaced with a functionally equivalent condition; the resulting concept could be literally applied to God.

All of the issues mentioned here are pursued further in Alston (2005).

THE EPISTEMOLOGY OF RELIGIOUS EXPERIENCE

Alston develops a model of the epistemology of religious experience according to which persons' beliefs about the activities, intentions and character of God can owe their justification, in no small part, to their own putative perception of God, in the same general way that ordinary perceptual beliefs about the characteristics of the objects in our immediate environment can owe their justification to perception of those objects and not to arguments. The details have changed over the years, culminating in the model presented in Alston (1991), which is expressed in terms of the notion of a *doxastic practice*: a socially learned, monitored and reinforced constellation of belief-forming dispositions and habits, each of which yields a certain belief from a certain input. But the basic idea is easily understood without this apparatus, despite its importance (Alston 1982; Alston & Fales 2004).

Central to Alston's model is a version of what Richard Swinburne calls the principle of credulity (PC): in general, if one's belief that *x* is so-and-so is based on an experience that *seems* to one to be of *x*'s being so-and-so, then one's belief that *x is* so-and-so is justified, *unless* one has a defeater. One has a defeater just in case one has sufficient reasons to suppose either that (a) one's belief is false (a rebutter) or that (b) one's experience is not, in the circumstances, indicative of the truth (an underminer). To illustrate rebutters, suppose you are having an experience that seems to you to be of a bear behind some bushes ahead of you. Several of your friends who are in a position to tell inform you that there is a burned stump at that spot, but no bear. Their testimony gives you sufficient reason to think that your belief is false, and so your belief is not justified. To illustrate underminers, suppose you are having an experience that seems to you to be of a red wall. Someone who is in a position to know informs you that there is a red light shining on the wall. Their testimony does not give you sufficient reason to think that your belief is false, but it does give you sufficient reason to think that your experience is not, in the circumstances, indicative of the truth, and so your belief is not justified. To illustrate the plausibility of PC, you now believe that there are words before you on the basis of what you take to be a visual experience of words on a page. You do not believe this on the basis of an argument of any sort. Nevertheless, it seems to be a perfectly sensible, rational, justified, warranted belief for you to have, in your circumstances; furthermore, you have no defeaters. PC explains these facts. The main reason to endorse PC, however, is that without it those experientially based beliefs of ours that we tend to think are justified, such as the one of yours just mentioned, would not be justified.

It is crucial to Alston's model that we think of the experiences referred to in PC as *immediate*. One takes it that one is *directly aware* of the object of experience (the bear, the wall, the words), and not indirectly aware of it. To illustrate: when I watch the Mariners from the bleachers of Safeco Stadium and see Ichiro Suzuki smash the ball down the right-field line for a triple, I see him directly, while when I watch the Seahawks on television from a seat at the local sports bar and see Shaun Alexander slice through the defensive line on the television, I see him indirectly, by seeing an electronic image of him. It is also crucial to the model that we think of the justification conferred by experience as *immediate* or *direct*. A belief is *indirectly* or *mediately* justified just when it is justified by *reasons*, other things that one knows or justifiedly believes. A belief is *directly* or *immediately* justified just when it is justified by something other than reasons. One option here is experience, as when I believe the wall is white simply because it appears white to me, or I believe the cat is on the mat simply because it appears so to me. Call the *practice* of forming such mundane perceptual beliefs SP. (Alston's defence of the foundationalist epistemology implicit here can be found in Alston [1989b].)

Now, for many people, it seems to them that they have experiences in which they are directly aware of God's comforting, guiding, forgiving, strengthening and communicating with them, for example. Thus, given PC, if these people believe that God loves them, is guiding them, forgives them, is communicating with them and so on, and those beliefs are based on those experiences, then those beliefs are justified, in the absence of defeaters. Call such beliefs *M-beliefs*, for *manifestation*, and call the *practice* of forming M-beliefs on the basis of those experiences MP.

There are objections to the model, naturally. First, mundane perceptual beliefs are justified on the basis of sense-experience because there is good reason to think that SP is reliable. But there is no good reason to suppose the practice of forming M-beliefs on the basis of putative perception of God is reliable. By way of reply, Alston makes two points.

First, the best arguments we have for thinking that SP is reliable are *epistemically circular*. That is, we assume the reliability of SP in using it to generate or defend at least one of the premises; we rely on the deliverances of SP in order to argue that SP is reliable (Alston 1991, 1993a). If we allow this for SP, we should allow it for MP, in which case those who participate in MP do have good reason to think MP is reliable by way of the deliverances of MP.

Secondly, to suppose that we must have good reason to think that SP is reliable in order to form justified perceptual beliefs on the basis of sense-experience is tantamount to denying PC. PC countenances such beliefs being justified directly on the basis of sense-experience, and not on the basis of arguments for the reliability of SP. To endorse PC yet simply insist that participants in MP must have good reason to think MP is reliable in order for M-beliefs to be justified on the basis of putative perception of God is to evince a *double standard*.

A second objection is that, even though engaging in SP puts us in effective cognitive contact with the world and sensory experience is a basis for directly justified beliefs about objects in the world, there are several differences between SP and sensory experience, on the one hand, and MP and religious experience, on the other hand, that show that MP does not put us in contact with God and, consequently, that religious experience cannot be a basis for directly justified M-beliefs. These differences include the following: (i) SP includes standard ways of checking the accuracy of perceptual beliefs, MP does not; (ii) by engaging in SP we discover regularities that allow us to predict the course of our experience, whereas the same does not hold when we engage in MP; (iii) SP is engaged in by every normal adult, MP is not; (iv) sense-experience is continuous and unavoidable while we are awake, religious experience is not; (v) sense-experience is vivid and richly detailed, religious experience is not. In response, Alston makes two points.

First, although these differences are real, they must not be exaggerated. As for (i), MP does include standard ways of checking the accuracy of M-beliefs, although as in SP they are not conclusive. For example, in diverse religious communities we find these checks: (a) conformity with what would be expected given certain doctrines about the nature and purposes of God; (b) consequences of the experience such as inner peace and spiritual growth; and (c) content of experience that is not likely to have been drummed up by the one who has the experience. With respect to (ii), by engaging in MP its practitioners have discovered that those who are more receptive and spiritually attuned are somewhat more apt to have such experiences. Regarding (iii), many anthropologists argue that not all cultures objectify sense-experience in the same way; if they are right, then, unless we load the dice by defining normality in terms of engagement in SP, SP is not engaged in by every normal adult. Moreover, sociological surveys reveal that many more normal adults take it that they have perceived God on some occasion than the objection lets on. As for (iv), some practitioners of MP report what they take to be the continual presence of God, for example, Brother Lawrence in *The Practice of the Presence of God*. With respect to (v), within sensory modalities we find great diversity in vividness and detail; contrast typical visual experiences with typical aural or gustatory experiences, for example.

Secondly, and much more importantly, there is no good reason to suppose that these differences constitute good reason to distinguish practices and experiences that put us in effective, experiential cognitive contact with reality from those that do not. Regarding (iii) and (iv), neither the degree of dispersal of a practice nor the rarity of its implementation shed any doubt on its capacity to inform us about what the world is like. Think in this connection of connoisseurs, experts and idiot savants, or those blessed with the sort of physical insight that led to the special and general theories of relativity. As for (v), human aural and gustatory experience can put us in contact with the world, and we can form a limited range of justified beliefs on the basis of them, even though those experiences tend to lack the sort of vividness and richness of detail characteristic of normal human visual experience. Likewise, less vivid and rich religious experiences might well put us in contact with God, and we can form a limited range of justified religious beliefs on the basis of them, even if such experiences do not justify other sorts of religious beliefs. Remember: Alston's model is concerned with *M-beliefs*, beliefs to the effect that God loves one, is guiding one, forgiving one, present to one, and communicating with one, not just any belief with a religious content. With respect to (i) and (ii), checks and predictions, to suppose that these constitute indicators of effective cognitive contact with reality is a sort of *imperialism*. It is to suppose that the only sort of reality to which we can have access is one whose character is such as to be conducive to checks and predictions; it is to impose standards that pertain to one practice of forming beliefs about what there is and what it is like to another. In this connection, note that neither introspection nor rational intuition are subject to the sorts of checks and predictions characteristic of SP. So why impose standards that are appropriate only for SP to MP?

A third objection to Alston's model is that whereas we have adequate purely naturalistic explanations of religious experience, we do not have adequate explanations of sense-experience that do not appeal to physical objects and their properties. Alston responds that there is no non-epistemically circular way to rule out various alternative explanations of sensory experience (a point systematically developed at length in Alston [1993a]); it should hardly count against religious experience if it cannot do the same. Moreover, it is not clear whether we have any good purely naturalistic explanation for religious experience, and even if we do, at best it can only account for the proximate causes of religious experience, which leaves it open whether God plays a role in causing such experiences and whether he can be perceived therein.

A fourth objection is that the diversity of religious beliefs that stem from MP counts as reason to think it is unreliable. By way of reply, Alston distinguishes a multitude of things that might be expressed here, arguing that many of them do not pass muster. Still, he concedes that, in light of the most compelling version of the objection, the *degree* of justification that M-beliefs enjoy is less than it otherwise would be. Nevertheless, they can still enjoy a substantial degree of justification despite religious diversity.

THE PROBLEM OF EVIL

Alston's thought about the problem of evil focuses on various versions of the evidential argument from evil, especially those put forward by his former student, William Rowe. Rowe (1979, 1988) asks us to consider some especially horrendous instances of intense suffering, for example a fawn that is trapped in a forest fire caused by lightning being badly burned, suffering for days before dying, or a young girl who is brutally tortured, raped and strangled to death. About these cases, which Rowe labels 'E1' and 'E2', respectively, Rowe contends (roughly) that, so far as we can see, there is no morally sufficient reason for God to permit them; thus, it is reasonable to believe that there is no such reason; thus, it is reasonable to believe that there is no God. In reply, Alston (1996c, 1996d) defends *the agnostic thesis*: grounds for belief in the existence of God aside, we are in no position to infer reasonably that there is no morally sufficient reason on the basis of our inability to conceive of one.

To this end, Alston first canvasses various "theodical suggestions": attempts to explain what reasons might morally justify God in permitting suffering in general. He distinguishes sufferer-centred reasons from non-sufferer-centred reasons. The former include punishment, Hick's (1978) soul-making theodicy, Eleonore Stump's (1985) suggestion that natural evil contributes to God's aim to get us to turn away from things of the world to God by undermining our satisfaction with temporal goods, and Marilyn McCord Adams's (1999) claim that our suffering makes possible a kind of empathetic identification with the suffering of God, which will deepen our intimacy with God, here or in the hereafter. The latter include free will and natural law theodicies. Alston argues that each of these reasons might morally justify God in permitting *some* suffering, perhaps even a good deal of it. However, Alston thinks that, with the possible exception of Adams's theodicy, the sufferer-centred reasons *we know of* do not seem to be live possibilities for God's reason in permitting E1 and E2, especially the former. And non-sufferer-centred reasons could not be the *whole* of God's reason for permitting any suffering, as this would violate demands of divine justice, compassion and love, unless the sufferer was adequately compensated, perhaps in an afterlife. Despite some sympathetic gestures toward some of these reasons, Alston concedes, for the sake of argument, that none of the sufferer-centred reasons could be any part of God's reasons for permitting E1 and E2, and that non-sufferer-centred reasons could not be the whole of God's reason for allowing any case of suffering. Thus, Alston concedes, for the sake of argument, that Rowe's premise is true: so far as we can see, there is no morally sufficient reason for God to permit E1 and E2.

Even given this concession, Alston argues that it is not reasonable to infer that there is no such reason on the basis of this concession. That is because it is reasonable to draw the inference only if it is reasonable to suppose that there is no morally sufficient reason available to God we do not know of, and it is not reasonable to make this supposition. There could be a morally sufficient reason available to God that we do not know of in two ways. First, we might not know all the conditions for the realization of some good that we do know of, for example, perhaps, unbeknown to us, the supreme fulfilment of one's deepest nature or beatific union with God requires horrendous suffering (or its permission). Secondly, there could be some significant good for the sufferer we do not know of, and that good might require horrendous suffering (or its permission). Importantly, these are not wacky, *ad hoc* possibilities; they represent common, sensible themes in lived theistic religions (see the Book of Job among other sacred texts). Alston exhibits why it is unreasonable to suppose that there is no morally sufficient reason outside our ken in three ways, which together underscore the point that it would be unsurprising if there were justifying reasons outside our ken.

First, the pervasiveness of human intellectual progress in evaluative and other matters makes it reasonable to believe that what we now know is only a fraction of what there is to be known. "This creates a presumption that with respect to values, as well as the conditions of their realization, there is much that lies beyond our present grasp" (1996d: 320).

Secondly, Rowe's inference takes "the insights attainable by finite, fallible human beings as an adequate indication of what is available in the way of reasons to an omniscient, omnipotent being" (*ibid*.: 317). But this is like supposing that when I am confronted with the activity or productions of a master in a field in which I have little expertise, it is reasonable for me to draw inferences about the quality of her work just because I 'don't get it'. Suppose I have taken a year of university physics; I am faced with some theory about quantum phenomena and I cannot make heads or tails of it. Certainly it is unreasonable for me to suppose it is likely that I would be able to make sense of it. Similarly for other areas of expertise: painting, architectural design, chess, music and so on.

Thirdly, the inference under discussion "involves trying to determine whether there is a so-and-so in a territory the extent and composition of which is largely unknown to us" (*ibid*.: 318). It is like people who are culturally and geographically isolated supposing that if there were something on earth beyond their forest, they would probably discern it. It is like a physicist supposing that if there were something beyond the temporal bounds of the universe, we would probably know about it (where those bounds are the big bang and the final crunch).

According to Alston, these considerations make it clear that it would not be surprising in the least if there were justifying reasons available to God we do not know of. Thus, it is not reasonable to believe that there are no such reasons on the basis of our inability to think of one. (For critical discussion of the sort of response typified by Alston, see Howard-Snyder [1996] and Trakakis [2007].)

THE NATURE OF PROPOSITIONAL FAITH

It is generally agreed that propositional faith, faith that p, involves two components, one cognitive and the other affective-attitudinal. Traditionally, the cognitive component is thought to be belief and the affective-attitudinal component some complex of tendencies toward certain feelings, desires and behaviour. Alston argues that the cognitive component of propositional faith, both religious and secular, need not be belief; acceptance can play the cognitive role (1996b).

Alston draws a sharp line between belief and acceptance (inspired by Cohen 1992). Belief differs from acceptance in at least three crucial ways. First, belief is a dispositional mental state while acceptance is a mental act. One finds oneself with a belief, whereas accepting p is the adoption or taking on of a positive attitude towards p. Secondly, belief is not under direct voluntary control while acceptance is. Thirdly, while the act of acceptance results in a complex dispositional state much like belief (a state also called 'acceptance'), the complexes differ in an important way. If one believes that p, then, if one considers whether it is the case that p, one will tend to feel that p is the case in the sense that one will be immediately and spontaneously struck with a sense of p being how things are, whereas if one accepts that p, one will definitely not tend to feel that p is the case if one considers whether it is the case that p; the immediacy and spontaneity central to belief is absent.

Alston describes several cases to help clarify the distinction. Consider a field general who must dispose his forces for impending battle with information insufficient to believe any of several competing hypotheses about how he might best deploy them. What does he do? He takes the hypothesis that seems the most likely of the alternatives to be true, he commits himself to its truth, and acts on that basis. In short, he accepts it. A case that does not involve pressure to act can be found in the acceptance of theoretical positions. Alston likens his stance with respect to libertarian freedom in this way. He does not believe it; he does not find himself spontaneously feeling confident of its truth. But he adopts it, regards it as true, and draws various consequences from it in his reasoning.

Alston is concerned to display acceptance as an attractive alternative to belief for the cognitive component of a devout religious faith, especially Christian faith. In this connection, he makes several points. First, both propositional belief and propositional acceptance are found in devout Christians. Some Christians have no doubt that the Christian story is true, while others find it, in T. S. Eliot's words, the least false of the options. Secondly, many biblical and creedal formulations of what is required on the cognitive side are better understood as expressing propositional acceptance rather than propositional belief. Thirdly, worries about a lack of faith are often worries about a lack of belief, worries that might well be mitigated with an understanding of acceptance. Fourthly, faith is thought to be required and meritorious, but if the cognitive component of faith requires belief and belief is involuntary, then faith cannot be required or meritorious. However, if the cognitive component of faith only requires acceptance, then this impediment to faith's being required and meritorious is removed. Fourthly, critics of religious faith often claim that it is unreasonable since religious belief is unreasonable. But if acceptance is sufficient for the cognitive component of faith, the question arises as to whether reasonable acceptance differs from reasonable belief in relevant ways. "Do belief and acceptance have different statuses vis-à-vis the need for evidence, reasons, grounds? Do judgments of rationality and irrationality, justifiability or the reverse, apply differently to them? Or is the same story to be told about the two?" (1996b: 23). If the same story is *not* to be told about the two, then the prospects for reasonable acceptance *absent* reasonable belief may well arise, in which case the unreasonability of religious faith is much less easily established.

In the 1940s, when Alston entered academic philosophy, philosophy of religion in the West was on its deathbed. Today, it is a vibrant, flourishing field within the discipline. It is difficult to measure the influence of a single person on a transformation as dramatic as this, but I venture the conjecture that no single person has done more to contribute to it than William P. Alston.[1]

FURTHER READING

Alston, W., R. M. Gale, G. Pappas & R. Adams 1994. "Symposium on Perceiving God". *Philosophy and Phenomenological Research* **54**: 863–99.

Alston, W., A. Plantinga, N. Kretzmann & R. Audi 1995. "Symposium on *Perceiving God*". *Journal of Philosophical Research* **20**: 1–81.

Lynch, M. & H. Battaly (eds) 2004. *Perspectives on the Philosophy of William P. Alston*. Lanham, MD: Rowman & Littlefield.

Senor, T. (ed.) 1995. *The Rationality of Belief and the Plurality of Faith: Essays in Honor of William P. Alston*. Ithaca, NY: Cornell University Press.

On FAITH see also Ch. 7; Vol. 1, Ch. 13; Vol. 2, Chs 6, 12, 16, 18; Vol. 3, Ch. 8; Vol. 4, Chs 8, 10, 13. On PREDICATION see also Vol. 2, Chs 11, 13, 16. On EVIL/PROBLEM OF EVIL see also Chs 19, 22, 23; Vol. 1, Chs 18, 19; Vol. 2, Ch. 16; Vol. 3, Chs 13, 18, 19; Vol. 4, Chs 12, 18. On RELIGIOUS EXPERIENCE see also Vol. 4, Ch. 15.

---

1. Many thanks to James F. Sennett for helpful comments on an earlier draft.

19

JOHN HICK

Paul Badham

John Harwood Hick was born in Scarborough in Yorkshire on 20 January 1922, the son of a solicitor. He had initially planned to follow the same career, and embarked on the study of law at University College, Hull, but as a result of a conversion experience decided to train for the ministry instead. At this point his career was interrupted by the Second World War. As a committed pacifist, Hick was a conscientious objector to military service, joining instead the Friends' Ambulance Unit in Egypt, Italy and Greece. When the war ended Hick went to Edinburgh University where he took a first in philosophy followed by a DPhil at Oxford on the relationship between faith and knowledge, for which he was supervised by the then Professor of Logic, H. H. Price. Hick's theological training for the Presbyterian ministry was done at Westminster College, Cambridge, and he was ordained to that ministry in 1953. For three years he was a minister in Northumberland where he converted his doctoral thesis into his first major publication. This led to an assistant professorship in philosophy at Cornell. In 1959 he became Stuart Professor of Christian Philosophy at Princeton Theological Seminary. After six years there, Hick returned to Cambridge, initially as a sabbatical Bye-Fellow at Gonville and Caius College, and then as a lecturer in philosophy of religion in the Theological Faculty of Cambridge University. In 1967 he was appointed to the H. G. Wood Chair of Theology at the University of Birmingham, where he stayed for fifteen years. During his last three years at Birmingham, Hick spent half of each year as Danforth Professor of the Philosophy of Religion at Claremont Graduate School (later Claremont Graduate University) in California. This became a full-time appointment in 1982. Hick 'retired' at the age of 70 in 1992 and moved back to Birmingham as a very active member of their Institute for Advanced Research. He also served for ten years as a Visiting Professor of the University of Wales, Lampeter.

HOW HICK'S LIFE SHAPED HIS WORK

It is conventional that discussion of any major thinker's thought should begin with the kind of biographical sketch that I have provided for Hick. But this convention is well founded because the way Hick's thought has developed can be seen to be intimately connected with his experiences of life and with the variety of intellectual milieus in which he worked. That his family background and his initial academic training was in law helps to explain why he has always been concerned to ensure that his thinking had an appropriate evidential basis. The profound conversion experience he underwent at eighteen was, as we shall see, crucial to all his subsequent thinking on religion. His experience of studying philosophy and then philosophy of religion in the early 1950s exposed him to the radical challenge that positivist analytical philosophy was putting to any religious claims, and his first book, *Faith and Knowledge* (1957), was a direct response to that. It was then fortunate for Hick's contribution to philosophy that as a young professor at Princeton he was asked to write a textbook on the philosophy of religion (Hick 1963), as that book became a bestseller and, along with subsequent textbooks and collections of readings, made Hick one of the best-known writers on the philosophy of religion in the English-speaking world. This meant that his subsequent major monographs were immediately read and taken seriously.

It was crucial to Hick's contribution to Christian theology that in the 1960s and early 1970s he taught in theological departments in Cambridge and Birmingham at a time when liberalism was characteristic of much theological thinking and when distinguished colleagues were seeking to reinterpret the doctrine of the Incarnation. It was also important that he left the quintessentially 'English' ethos of Cambridge for the multicultural ethos of Birmingham just at the point when issues of religious pluralism in British society began to surface, and that the importance of this issue was then underlined by his experiences of inter-religious dialogue in California and as a Visiting Professor in India, Sri Lanka and Japan.

RELIGIOUS EXPERIENCE AS FOUNDATIONAL FOR HICK'S UNDERSTANDING OF RELIGION

Hick became a Christian through a powerful evangelical conversion experience while he was a student at University College, Hull. In his autobiography he writes:

> for several days I was in a state of intense mental and emotional turmoil during which I became aware of a higher truth and greater reality ... claiming my recognition ... the reality that was pressing in upon me was not only awesomely demanding but also irresistibly

attractive, and I entered with great joy and excitement into the world
of Christian faith.   (2002: 33)

Hick never doubted that this experience was an encounter with the ultimate divine
reality. But whereas at the time and for several years subsequently he interpreted
this experience within the framework of a fundamentalist faith, and later within
a fairly strict orthodoxy, he subsequently came to see that there was no necessary connection between this experience and the doctrinal framework into which
it was first placed. Like Friedrich Schleiermacher before him (*see* Vol. 4, Ch. 3),
Hick affirmed the reality and authenticity of the experience itself, while insisting
that this did not in any way give binding authority to the system of thought within
which it was first articulated. As we shall see, Hick's experience and his subsequent
interpretation of that experience was to be of crucial importance fifty years later
when he formulated his *Interpretation of Religion*, and still more when he came to
explore *The New Frontier of Religion and Science*.

However, at the time Hick simply took over the complete evangelical package,
including belief in the absolute authority of Scripture and in such doctrines as the
virgin birth, the atoning death and bodily resurrection of Christ, and salvation
as wholly dependent on accepting Christ as one's personal saviour. Part of the
intellectual excitement of Hick's subsequent work is that he was for decades wrestling with the challenge of reconciling the constancy of his 'faith' with the gradual
changes he felt required to make in its intellectual formulation.

FAITH AND KNOWLEDGE

Hick's first book, *Faith and Knowledge* (first published in 1957, and revised and
updated in 1966), developed from his Oxford doctoral thesis. Its importance lies
in the way in which Hick sought to justify religious belief as one possible way of
interpreting reality. Hick believed that none of the various arguments for God's
existence succeeded, and he concluded that we live in an ambiguous universe that
can be 'experienced-as' a wholly naturalistic order, or equally validly 'experienced-
as' the product of a divine creator. The believer is acting rationally if, on the additional basis of religious experience, he or she interprets the world religiously. But,
equally, the sceptic who has not had a religious experience (or has not interpreted
such experiences as they may have had as religious) is rational in espousing a naturalistic atheism. Some religious critics of Hick's position hold that he conceded too
much to atheism in drawing this conclusion. But in the highly sceptical ethos of
mid-twentieth-century philosophy, Hick's work was important. In an intellectual
environment where few philosophers took religion at all seriously it was necessary
to defend the rationality of religious belief as one legitimate way of understanding
reality. Hick successfully did this. He argued that we were living at an 'epistemic
distance' from divine reality. In other words, from the point of view of our theories

of knowledge we cannot know for certain that God exists. There is enough light to enable the believer rationally to embrace the life of faith, but enough ambiguity for the sceptic to be rational in rejecting it. This is important so that faith can be a free response.

During the 1950s a major debate took place between a group of leading British philosophers on the issue of 'theology and falsification'. Antony Flew argued that, in practice, philosophically sophisticated believers accepted the same worldview as their atheist counterparts because, whenever Christian claims were seriously questioned, believers constantly gave ground so that what started out as "brash confident assertions" gradually "died the death of a thousand qualifications" (Flew 1955: 97–8). To meet this objection Hick proposed the theory of 'eschatological verification'. This theory states that there is a real difference between an atheistic and a Christian understanding of reality because one sees our journey through life as leading nowhere, while the other sees life as a journey towards an eternal destiny. These different perspectives affect our whole way of seeing reality, and shape our attitude to life. The Christian claim will either be verified, if eternal life is real, or falsified if it is not. This theory meets the requirement of potential verification even though if there were no life after death no one would be in a position to verify it. It is, however, a meaningful claim and one that makes a fundamental difference to the way life is experienced.

However, in the context of contemporary philosophy the intelligibility of life after death seemed particularly problematical. A dualism of body and mind was widely criticized by leading philosophers. At the same time, Christian theologians insisted that the resurrection of the body rather than the immortality of the soul was the distinctive Christian message. Yet to make sense of bodily resurrection in the light of what we know about nature is a formidable challenge. Although Hick has always been a dualist himself, he believed it was possible to formulate a concept of bodily resurrection that was at least intelligible. He suggested that if God were to create an exact replica of us in another space, possessing complete similarity of all bodily features and full continuity of memory and mental disposition, then the basic criteria of personal identity could be met, and the replicated person could legitimately be said to have survived death. Subsequently, Hick realized that the theory does not depend on 'exact' similarity for that would require life in a physical world identical to our own, which would face innumerable practical problems. However, if one redefined the theory in terms of a replica possessing "sufficient correspondence of characteristics with our present bodies and sufficient continuity of memory with our present consciousness" (Hick 1957: 185), then the thesis could be sustained. Hick's theory has been intensely discussed as a possible way in which the doctrine of the resurrection of the body might be defended today.

HICK'S PHILOSOPHICAL TEXTBOOKS

Hick's initial degree and his doctorate were both taken in departments of philosophy and all his academic appointments have been in philosophy or in philosophy of religion, even when held in an appointment in a department of theology. His research has always focused on philosophical questions, even though the subject matter of such questioning was focused initially on the truth claims of Christianity, and later on the legitimacy of a religious response as such. At this point one should mention the importance of a succession of textbooks Hick produced. Of these, the most important was his *Philosophy of Religion*, first published in 1963 and regularly reprinted and translated over the next forty years, with a fourth edition appearing in 1990. Since this work alone has sold over 600,000 copies and has been distributed worldwide, it is probably through this more than any other work of his that Hick's ideas have become well known. To this might be added his collection of *Classical and Contemporary Readings in the Philosophy of Religion*, which also remains in print after forty years, and his reader on *The Existence of God*, which has likewise been reprinted many times. Hick also wrote a valuable text book on the *Arguments for the Existence of God*, and was the co-editor of an important collection of articles on the ontological argument (*The Many-Faced Argument*). When one is assessing the impact of Hick's work as a philosopher it is important to remember the influence of such works on generations of students across the globe and to recall that Hick's writings have been translated into at least seventeen languages.

However, it is through his own original work that Hick has made his greatest contribution to philosophy, theology and the study of religion. The writing of *Faith and Reason* led Hick to two conclusions. The first was that the credibility of the Christian faith depended on there being at least some response to the problem of suffering. The second followed from this, for if, as Hick thought, any credible theological response to suffering requires belief in life after death, then one must be able to show that such a belief could be rationally spelt out. Hence Hick embarked on two major projects leading to *Evil and the God of Love* in 1966 and to *Death and Eternal Life* ten years later.

EVIL AND THE GOD OF LOVE

Evil and the God of Love (1966, third edition 2007) is arguably Hick's greatest contribution to philosophical discussion. Certainly it is hard to imagine any serious discussion of the problem of evil that does not refer to its arguments. Hick showed that the classic Augustinian explanation of evil as the product of an aboriginal 'fall' was just too much at variance with what evolutionary biology and historical knowledge show about our place in nature. But Hick also demonstrated that from the time of Irenaeus onwards there had always been an alternative

Christian view in which humankind was not created perfect, but was created in a state from which we could gradually progress. Hick showed that if this world had been intended to be a paradise for already perfected beings then the existence of evil would certainly demolish Christian belief in a God of love. However, if this world had been intended to be a place in which we could develop as free responsible agents, then the existence of evil becomes comprehensible as an inevitable part of an environment in which we could exercise both freedom and responsibility. In his theodicy Hick goes on to argue that a real objective material world, governed by regular physical law, offers an environment more suited to the development of responsible agents than an environment in which constant divine intervention always saved humanity from the consequences of its folly or from the heartache and challenge implicit in any finite and physical existence. As a 'vale of soul-making' the hardships and challenges of life can serve a larger purpose, provided of course that there is indeed a soul to make and a larger purpose to serve. Hick's arguments do not 'solve' the problem of evil, the extent and nature of which remains a persistent challenge. But what Hick's work does make clear is that without belief in an afterlife there could be no conceivable answer to the problem of evil. If death means extinction then old age, suffering, disease and death have the last word and thereby bring to nothing any belief that each person matters to an all-sovereign God.

DEATH AND ETERNAL LIFE

Hick's theory of knowledge and his theodicy both illustrate the importance of belief in an afterlife to the philosophical coherence of Christian theism. But belief in a destiny that transcends the limitations of our present existence is also characteristic of almost all the major religious traditions. So in writing *Death and Eternal Life* (1976) Hick resolved to adopt a global perspective, and to draw on insights from any source that might aid our understanding. The result was that his book provides encyclopaedic coverage of human speculation concerning a possible future destiny. One strand of his thought draws together Eastern and Western sources to create a possible hypothesis about what sort of destiny might be imaginable.

Hick speculates that at death our consciousness might temporarily enter a mind-dependent world, somewhat as described in the *Tibetan Book of the Dead* or in the writings of Hick's former supervisor at Oxford, Professor H. H. Price (see Price 1968). This world would be a kind of dream environment built out of our memories and desires, thereby revealing to us their true nature. This would provide an opportunity for life-review, self-revelation and self-assessment. It would also provide opportunity for 'meeting' through telepathic contact with deceased relatives and friends and perhaps an enhanced awareness of the divine. After a period in this *bardo* world the person would be reborn into another embodied existence, not on earth but in another space. Modern physics allows for the possibility of plural spaces and Hick notes that in many Hindu and Buddhist texts reincarnation is spoken of as normally happening in other worlds. Hick believes that a succession of such lives with intervals for reflection in between would provide the most suitable means for the human pilgrimage towards ultimate reality.

WHY HICK CHANGED HIS ATTITUDE TO OTHER FAITHS

In writing *Death and Eternal Life,* Hick consciously drew on a global religious perspective. This reflects a change in his religious understanding since moving to Birmingham in 1967. Before that he had lived in an almost entirely Christian or post-Christian environment. But on coming to Birmingham he was asked to chair a group established to develop a multi-religious syllabus for religious education in Birmingham's schools. His sense of social justice also led him to chair an inter-faith group fighting against racial prejudice, called 'All Faiths for One Race'. In these various capacities he came into close working relationships with leaders of the Hindu, Sikh, Muslim and Jewish communities and he subsequently received invitations to attend worship. Attending worship in mosque, gurdwara, synagogue or temple impressed on Hick a sense that phenomenologically the same kind of activity was taking place as happens in Christian churches. In each place of worship human beings were offering themselves up in dedication and praise to a personal God, addressed and reverenced as creator and Lord. He noticed that themes in hymns and prayers continually overlapped with those of Christian worship, so that if one changed the names one would often not be able to identify from which religion the prayer came. Hick could not square his previous conviction that God can only be known through Christ with the profound commitment to God he saw in the people he was now working among. His move away from Christian exclusivism was not therefore initially derived from new theological arguments but from new life experiences. Naturally, however, such experiences swiftly affected his theological understanding, particularly in relation to the person of Christ.

For many years Hick had believed that commitment to Christ was the only way to salvation, but he had not dwelt on the negative implications of this belief, namely, that those who do not know Christ are not saved, but presumably damned. However, once he did reflect on this a paradox of enormous proportions opened up. For it would make a complete mockery of the claim that God is love if in fact he had so ordered reality that the vast majority of humanity was doomed to perdition. Salvation in this ultimate sense could not therefore depend on Christ alone. Hick felt that the path that scholars such as Karl Rahner had taken to avoid this problem, which involves including everyone within the compass of Christianity, were dishonest to the integrity of both Christianity and of other religions (see Rahner 1966: 122). Against Rahner (*ibid.*), Hick argued that people of other faiths were not "anonymous Christians" who had an "implicit faith" in Christ, nor was the Christ of the Christian story actually at work within other religious traditions. Hick also did not believe that Jesus' death had brought about a change in 'the steadfast love' of God witnessed to by the Hebrew Bible. He therefore could not accept Karl Barth's idea of an "all-inclusive election" brought about by Christ's death (Barth 1956: 117), nor join in Pope John-Paul II's vision that "every human being without any exception whatever has been redeemed by Christ" (John-Paul II 1979: para. 14). Hick thought that to make such claims for Christ and to stress his uniqueness as God incarnate placed Christianity too far apart from other religions, and implied an absoluteness to Christian truth that inevitably diminished the claims of all other religions.

HICK'S INTERPRETATION OF THE INCARNATION AS MYTH OR METAPHOR

Hick therefore came to re-evaluate fundamental Christian doctrines. At first he spoke of *The Myth of God Incarnate* (1977). Later and more helpfully he talked of *The Metaphor of God Incarnate* (1993). He adopted these views not only because of his awareness of the non-Christian religions, but also because he felt that a literal doctrine of the Incarnation was both internally incoherent and also false to the New Testament evidence. He noted that although Christian orthodoxy had affirmed the doctrine of the Incarnation, every attempt to 'explain' in what sense Jesus was simultaneously divine and human had been declared heretical. This is also true today. No modern account of how the Incarnation should be understood has ever won general acceptance. Hick concluded that the reason this had happened was because the doctrine of the Incarnation was not a propositional statement awaiting clarification, but a metaphor inviting a response. Hick noted also that virtually all New Testament scholars reject the authenticity of the "I am" sayings of the Gospels and assume that the historical Jesus had no awareness of being divine. If this is so, Hick argued, then Christianity should cease to make ontological claims about Jesus and instead should accept that Jesus embodied God's love to us in the same true but metaphorical sense as, for example, Churchill embodied the British will to resist the Nazis.

THE PLURALIST HYPOTHESIS

Hick believed that, by seeing the Incarnation of Christ as a myth or metaphor, Christians are better able to see God at work in other lives and in other religious traditions. This became part of his most controversial hypothesis: 'religious pluralism'. At first, on the basis of his Birmingham experience, Hick claimed that 'God has many names', this being the title of a book he published in 1980. But after encountering Advaitic Hinduism in India and Buddhism in Sri Lanka and Japan, he felt that the word 'God' was too closely identified with Christianity and so he spoke of 'The Real' instead. This was developed initially in *Problems of Religious Pluralism* (1985), but was then systematically worked out in his Gifford Lectures, *An Interpretation of Religion* (1989), for which he received the prestigious Grawemeyer Award for significant new religious thinking.

The essence of Hick's philosophy of religious pluralism is that all religions are human responses to a single transcendent Reality. He was convinced that this Reality is objectively real. Hick believed that it would be fatal to religion if a non-realist understanding of religious discourse were to become normative. However, while the religious experience of humanity may enable believers to affirm the existence of transcendent Reality, they cannot with the same certainty endorse what particular traditions say concerning it. This is because what each tradition affirms is always bound up with its overall worldview and understanding. Hence each religion endorses a 'persona' or 'impersona' of the Real. Within each tradition this is the lens through which the Real may be seen. Dialogue may help bring people together and philosophy of religion may clarify understanding. But Hick believed that we are simply not in a position to argue that any one religious tradition should be normative for all. What can be said is that each of the great religious traditions seem capable of leading to human fulfilment and producing a sanctity in which selfishness is overcome and ultimate reality can be encountered and experienced.

THE NEW FRONTIER OF RELIGION AND SCIENCE

In his mid-eighties, Hick produced a new *magnum opus* that wrestled with a topic he had come to see as the central issue of the day. We have already noted that religious experience is foundational to Hick's whole approach. But can we legitimately attach authority to such experiences if they are thought of as simply by-products of chemical and electrical activities within our brains? Within philosophy the relationship between brain and mind has been debated for centuries and from his earliest writings Hick had recognized the importance of such issues. In 1972 he had delivered the Eddington Memorial Lecture on *Biology and the Soul*, much of which reappeared in his *Death and Eternal Life*. However, Hick became aware that the issue was even more important to religious discussion in the twenty-first century because of the ability of neuroscience to show which parts of the brain are associated with religious experience or meditational practice. Forty years ago, although brain–mind identity was already championed by many philosophers, neuroscientists tended to support a dualist understanding. For example, Sir John Eccles, who was awarded the Nobel Prize for his experimental work on the brain, responded to Gilbert Ryle's *Concept of Mind* with the assertion that "[T]he brain is just the kind of machine a ghost could operate" and that "those who hold the

241

materialist philosophy show a complete misunderstanding of the working of the brain" (Eccles 1970: 115, 127). However, Eccles' successors, writing toward the end of the twentieth century, were much more likely to assume that the mind is simply a way of talking about the brain, or at most that the mind is an epiphenomenon of brain processes. Their works have exerted a strong influence on contemporary thinking about the mind. Hick attempted to show, however, that materialist conclusions go beyond the evidence. He demonstrated, through a close reading of the latest research, that the evidence points to correlation rather than identity. It is true that our mental, emotional and religious life is intimately connected with brain processes and other bodily states, but the reverse is equally true. Our thoughts, feelings, religious experiences and beliefs also affect our bodily states. Moreover, neuroscientists do not in practice believe that their own creative theorizing is simply the product of physical happenings within their brains. All wish to be taken seriously as conscious agents making out a rational case for physical determinism. The paradox is that a rational case can only be made if physical determinism is not true, and hence the argument for physical determinism is of necessity self-refuting.

The New Frontier of Religion and Science also provides a fascinating overview of the whole of Hick's religious and philosophical convictions and the way his thinking has broadened and developed through a lifetime of reading and debating. It provides a justification for belief in transcendent reality drawing on the religious experience of humanity as a whole, and shows how much more convincing such an approach is than one that draws solely on the resources of a single religious tradition.

WHY HICK'S PHILOSOPHY IS IMPORTANT

The importance of Hick's work lies in the fact that in the second half of the twentieth century his writings shaped the debates on some of the most vital questions in the philosophy of mind, philosophy of religion, Christian theology and the study of religion. His philosophical and religious writings have generated more than fifty doctoral dissertations and at least thirty-eight books, including works in German, French, Turkish, Chinese and Japanese. Hick's thought has also been much discussed in journal articles and in the writings of other scholars. This does not mean that his writings have gained general assent, for they have generated at least as much opposition as agreement. Nevertheless, Hick repeatedly set the agenda for philosophy of religion in his time. One reason for this is that Hick has focused on genuinely important questions: the challenge to faith posed by the theology and falsification debate of the early 1950s; the problem of how one can continue to justify belief in God in the face of the horrendous evils of the twentieth century; the credibility of believing in life after death; the challenge to Christian theology of taking seriously the religious experiences of people of other faiths; and the challenge to religious experience posed by the findings of contemporary neuroscience. To each of these five issues Hick has responded by producing a major scholarly monograph providing a comprehensive survey of the debate and making an original contribution to it. These have been supported by a range of shorter secondary works that Hick wrote to popularize his conclusions. He has also written student textbooks and encyclopaedia entries, and gladly contributed chapters to edited collections. He is also an enthusiastic conference-goer and has generously accepted invitations to expound his views at universities all over the world. Further, Hick is an extremely clear writer whose arguments can readily be understood. On top of all this, Hick is a person for whom the various debates in the philosophy of religion are existentially real, and although there is considerable consistency in his writings, he does not hesitate to change his position in the light of fresh evidence and fresh experience.

The importance of Hick's early writings has been widely recognized. His concepts of 'epistemic distance' and 'experiencing-as' are generally seen as helpful additions to philosophical thought, while his theodicy is probably the most widely discussed of all attempted 'solutions' to the problem of evil. Hick's more speculative investigations into eternal life have been less influential and the 'replica theory' is more often criticized than affirmed. On the other hand, Hick's conviction that the 'cosmic optimism' of the worlds' religions depends on belief in a final end-state of ultimate value remains highly influential.

Hick's reinterpretation of the doctrine of the Incarnation has been largely rejected by the churches. In part this rejection was based on a misunderstanding of Hick's position and in part on his unfortunate initial choice of the word 'myth' to describe his position. His later and fuller exposition of his position made it clear that he did not 'deny' the incarnation, but instead suggested that it be understood as a metaphorical rather than a propositional claim. Likewise, Hick's theory of religious pluralism has been more often condemned than accepted by faith communities. The theory is persistently caricatured as affirming that all religions are the same. This is certainly something Hick never taught. Instead, his theory of religious pluralism consistently sought to explain the differences between and within religious traditions as deriving from different traditions and worldviews, while at the same time affirming that each of them was derived from different human responses to the one divine Reality. For Hick, the existential truth of his theory was rooted in his conviction that while his own experience of ultimate reality had initially been interpreted within the narrow framework of evangelical fundamentalism, the reality of his experience was not dependent on that interpretation. On the contrary, Hick's belief that he had truly encountered ultimate reality remained crucial to his thinking as his reflection and life-experience broadened out the perspectives of his understanding.

Hick's importance as a philosophical thinker is also illustrated by his lifelong wrestling with issues of personal identity and the mind–body problem. His own contribution demonstrated the possibility of accepting everything that modern science has discovered about the intimate relationship between brain processes and mental events without ruling out the ultimate independence of the mind and the possibility of a future existence beyond our present embodiment.

One theme that consistently runs through Hick's philosophy is his engagement with religious epistemology. How can we legitimately assess religious claims? This issue was as central to *Faith and Knowledge* in 1957 as it was to *The New Frontier of Religion and Science* in 2006. Hick's position is one of critical realism. He has never embraced the kind of postmodernism that thinks that each discipline can engage in its own 'language-game', and he insists that claimed religious truths must be capable of being brought into a relationship with scientific understanding and philosophical awareness. The clearest exposition of this comes in his essay on "Realism versus Non-Realism" in Joseph Runzo's edited work *Is God Real?* (Runzo 1993), in which Hick illustrates the gulf between his position and that of scholars such as Don Cupitt or D. Z. Phillips. It is also significant that, in struggling to find a word for that transcendent reality that Christians experience as 'God' that would be acceptable to people of non-theistic religions, Hick chose the term 'the Real', thus affirming his conviction that the diverse religious experiences and philosophical traditions of humanity represent different human responses to the one ultimate reality.

FURTHER READING

Badham, P. 1990. *A John Hick Reader*. London: Macmillan.

Cheetham, D. 2003. *John Hick: A Critical Introduction and Reflection*. Aldershot: Ashgate.

D'Costa, G. 1987. *John Hick's Theology of Religions: A Critical Evaluation*. Lanham, MD: University Press of America.

Gillis, C. 1989. *A Question of Final Belief: John Hick's Pluralistic Theory of Salvation*. London: Macmillan.

Hewitt, H. 1991. *Problems in the Philosophy of Religion: Critical Studies in the Work of John Hick*. London: Macmillan.

Sharma, A. (ed.) 1993. *God, Truth and Reality: Essays in Honour of John Hick*. New York: St Martin's Press.

Sinkinson, C. 2001. *The Universe of Faiths: A Critical Study of John Hick's Religious Pluralism*. Carlisle: Paternoster Press.

On EVIL/PROBLEM OF EVIL see also Chs 22, 23; Vol. 1, Chs 18, 19; Vol. 2, Ch. 16; Vol. 3, Chs 13, 18, 19; Vol. 4, Chs 12, 18. On SCIENCE see also Ch. 4; Vol. 2, Ch. 12; Vol. 3, Ch. 17; Vol. 4, Chs 7, 11, 12, 15, 17, 19.

20

MARY DALY

Anne-Marie Korte

'If God is male, then the male is god'. With this maxim, launched in the 1970s, American theologian and philosopher Mary Daly (*b.* 1928) opened an unsettling debate in the old disciplines of theology and philosophy of religion. Her book *Beyond God the Father* (1973), written on the back of the second wave of feminism in the Western world, immediately caused a great stir. It marked the start of feminist theology as an influential political and intellectual movement in churches and universities. In her writings Daly sagaciously exposed the patriarchal character and interest of Christian theological reflection and soon her name became a byword for feminist criticism of religion. The intellectual travels into 'metapatriachal' space and time that Daly subsequently undertook, reported in thick books full of sharp observations and hilarious wordplay, confirmed her radical feminist reputation, as did the controversies she evoked by keeping male students out of her classes in university for more than thirty years. Less well known is that her feminist stance also brought her to an original rethinking of the concepts of the subject, language and God in relation to each other, focused on the idea of 'contagious transcendence'.

PURSUING THE HIGHEST AMBITIONS

Mary Daly was born on 16 October 1928 in Schenectady, New York, as the only child of a middle-aged Irish couple.[1] She grew up in an enclosed lower-class Roman Catholic milieu. In the female line of her family, tales of the migration from Ireland due to the famine and of survival in hard circumstances were

---

1. Daly published a very detailed intellectual autobiography: see Daly (1992). She also provided biographical information in the famous new introductions she added to the republications of her first four books.

245

still very present during her youth. Her father was a travelling salesman selling ice cream freezers, which meant that the family could not count on a regular income. Against this background, having a good education – a treasure that both her parents had been denied – became Daly's driving force. Being an excellent student in school, she wanted to become a 'writer', a rather unspecified ideal of living an intellectual life that lured many gifted young women before the second wave of feminism in the 1960s started to offer them more concrete professional prospects.

Building a career as a female scholar was therefore beyond Daly's scope, but being educated in Roman Catholic schools, she was deeply impressed as well as inspired by her female teachers, all nuns who had higher educations. Following their example – but without intending to be a nun herself – she went to study at the College of St Rose in Albany, New York, a private liberal arts college for women founded in 1920 by Roman Catholic Sisters. Although seriously interested in the study of philosophy, for practical reasons Daly could only obtain a BA in English there, which was then followed by an MA in English at the Catholic University of America in Washington, DC. These were the first two of seven 'Catholic' academic degrees that Daly would be awarded in twenty years of academic training, all obtained at the few Roman Catholic theological institutions open to female students in the 1950s and 1960s, before the Second Vatican Council (1962–5) broadened this access.

In Daly's case the fact that she came from a lower-class family and that her father died when she was still in college also influenced her academic prospects and choices. When Daly applied in 1952 to a new PhD course in religion especially for women at St Mary's College in Notre Dame, Indiana, to her enormous relief the college's president, the female poet Sister Madeleva, offered her a scholarship as well as a teaching job. And so at the age of twenty-five, Daly, trained in neo-scholastic philosophy and theology in only a short span of time, obtained her first PhD in the very field she had wanted to study. She immediately set out for a doctorate in philosophy at the University of Notre Dame, but was rejected. Female students were not permitted to follow regular programmes and obtain official Catholic degrees at Notre Dame. Daly accepted a teaching job in theology at a new Roman Catholic college in Brookline, Massachusetts, and took courses in philosophy and theology at Boston College and Harvard Divinity School. Here she attended the lectures of the theologian Paul Tillich and became acquainted with the existentialist philosophy of Simone de Beauvoir and Jean-Paul Sartre. This again strengthened her goal of living a life of the mind.

Convinced that to get the more interesting teaching jobs she needed to have 'sacred' doctorates in theology and philosophy, Daly applied to the Catholic University of America to obtain the highest church-approved degrees in these disciplines. When her application was delayed several times and finally rejected, she applied for entrance to Roman Catholic theological faculties at state universities in Germany and Switzerland that legally could not exclude female students. In

1959 she was admitted to the Faculty of Theology at the University of Fribourg (in Switzerland), a cantonal public university entrusted to the Dominican Order and allowed to grant canonical degrees in theology. Daly acquired a Swiss exchange student scholarship and a teaching job in a Junior Year Abroad programme. Under these conditions, and in the steady company of her mother, she stayed in Fribourg for seven years and gained four more grades, obtaining in the end both her theological (1963) and philosophical doctorate (1965).

THE CHURCH AND THE SECOND SEX

In her later autobiographical writings Daly depicted Fribourg as a medieval storybook town steeped in traditional Roman Catholicism. But in fact her Swiss period was not backwards oriented at all, and Daly here laid the foundation for her whole future oeuvre. Her *de facto* marginalized position in Church and university as a non-European student, a Roman Catholic lay person and above all a young woman, offered particular advantages for her intellectual development. She could engage relatively easily in contemporary philosophy and liberal theology, for she was kept outside the Roman Catholic institutional hierarchy and did not stand under the pressure of its sanctions in case of deviation. Daly's two neo-Thomistic dissertations, on *Speculative Theology* and *Natural Knowledge of God*, reflect this relative leeway. In these studies she gave, alongside firm neo-scholastic reasoning, a remarkably strong and consistent voice to the 'questions of modern people'. Compared to young European monk-theologians such as Edward Schillebeeckx and Johan Baptist Metz, who were engaged in similar studies at that time, Daly did not invest in elaborate reconciliations between neo-Thomism and Enlightenment philosophy, as they did (Metz 1962; Schillebeeckx 1964). She held on to classic Thomistic notions of God, reason and faith, and defended on this basis the premise that all human beings may have 'inductive' and 'intuitive' knowledge of God. At the same time she openly spoke for a new generation in the Western secularizing world: men and women who had a serious interest in religious matters but could not be inspired – or were even appalled – by traditional Christian language and argumentation. In the short version of her theological dissertation she discussed the meaning of theology for "men and women who are not members of the clerus" and she criticized the exclusion of women from higher theological education (Daly 1965).

Daly's incipient interest in feminist issues grew rapidly in the exciting atmosphere of Roman Catholic modernization that accompanied the Second Vatican Council. She visited some sessions of this huge meeting of church leaders, gathering in Rome at that time, and was fascinated as much by the 'spirit of renewal' as by the 'patriarchal pomp' that was shown there. In 1963 she signed a contract with a British publisher to write a book on *Women and the Church*. She was invited to do so after she had published a letter to the editor in a liberal Roman Catholic journal in which she announced that women's emancipation in the church was near at hand.

Daly's *The Church and the Second Sex*, published in 1968, was a moderate and tentative book on gender equality in the Roman Catholic Church. In the first part of this book Daly showed how deeply Christian history is tainted by a patriarchal bias against women. She argued that this "sexual prejudice" contradicts the essence of the Christian message. She conceived her own time as a period of pending renewal, and offered in the second part of her book some "modest proposals" for change, envisioning a post-Vatican II Catholic Church that would transcend its "anachronistic features" and be transformed into "a higher and more adequately human social order". In this order the hierarchical distinctions between clergy and laity and between men and women would be overcome, for they would be of no relevance any longer.

The title of her book made an obvious reference to Beauvoir's famous *The Second Sex* (Beauvoir 1949). Beauvoir's sharp and thorough analysis of the systematic subordination of women in Western society and culture had inspired as well as embarrassed Daly. She partly affirmed Beauvoir's feminist criticism of Roman Catholicism, but against Beauvoir she argued that Christian faith itself bears the 'seeds of transcendence' that make it possible to reform gender relations on a personal and institutional level. According to Daly, Christian faith is capable of furthering the emancipation of women, and we should therefore strive to achieve the full equality and "real partnership" of men and women in all segments and structures of church and society.

In *The Church and the Second Sex* Daly also addressed the internal theological roots of what she labelled 'Christian antifeminism': the concepts of God, revelation, sin, incarnation and church that sustain and perpetuate androcentric views and practices. She remarked that "vague identifications of God with the male sex" abound in Christian theology, despite the paradox that this male God is considered to be above sex. "What can 'masculine' mean if predicated of a Being in which there is no sex?", she wondered (Daly 1968: 181). She called on theologians to rethink notions such as God's masculinity in relation to divine omnipotence, immutability and providence, and to come to a view of God and humanity that would not glorify the status quo any longer, a project that she herself would actually take up in the next five years.

Although in *The Church and the Second Sex* Daly acknowledged that established theological thinking produced a 'built-in resistance' to any social and ecclesial change that would favour women, in this phase of her feminist oeuvre she located the problem only on the level of 'paradoxes' and 'inconsistencies' that could and should be uncovered and overcome. She did not consider the political and psychological consequences of her 'modest proposals', such as the enormous threat to male privilege and power her suggestions actually entailed, and in this sense she was not prepared for the vehement reactions her book evoked, nor for the hostility it met in established academic and ecclesiastical circles.

She finished the book after her return to the United States, where she had accepted a position as Assistant Professor in Theology at the Jesuit-run Boston College. And the book, in Daly's own well-known words, almost finished her (Daly 1975b: 11). In 1969 her two-year contract was not renewed because of the controversial content of *The Church and the Second Sex*. Her termination became a *cause célèbre* and prompted a number of protests at the college and across the country. The nationwide uproar led the College Board to change its view and Daly was granted promotion and tenure. She would stay at Boston College for over thirty years, until she was forcibly retired in 1999 owing to her persistent policy of restricting her women's studies classes to female students.

BEYOND GOD THE FATHER

For Daly the rise of the women's movement in the early 1970s meant a 'spiritual revolution'. The fact that long-established forms of discrimination and misogyny were being openly addressed and countered by women's own initiatives and organizations was revelatory to her. She immediately took part in gatherings and actions of this movement and came out as a lesbian. In 1971 she headed a procession of women out of a service in Harvard Memorial Church in a symbolic exodus from patriarchal religion. The bonds of revolutionary sisterhood became her new ecclesial community, and from a reformist Roman Catholic she turned into a post-Christian radical feminist.

Daly's *Beyond God the Father: Toward a Philosophy of Women's Liberation*, published in 1973, mirrors the first step of this intellectual conversion. The originality of this book lies in the stances Daly took on two fronts simultaneously. By presenting a theological elaboration of the women's movement as a spiritual revolution she challenged established theological thinking as well as emerging radical feminist reflection, neither of which were inclined to see a significant connection between women's emancipation and the concept of God. Daly argued that the feminist movement "is an ontological, spiritual revolution, pointing beyond the idolatries of sexist society and sparking creative action in and toward transcendence. The becoming of women implies universal human becoming. It has everything to do with the search for ultimate meaning and reality, which some would call God" (1973: 6).

As these formulations show, Daly founded her feminist theological project on Tillich's ontological theology, in which Christian theology is elaborated in terms of existentialist philosophy (Tillich 1952, 1953-64, 1954, 1955c). Like Tillich, Daly correlated urgent existential questions and concerns with spiritual reality and theological meaning. She built on Tillich's central concepts of God as the ground of being, human existence as defined by being versus non-being, and faith as existential courage, but she gave these concepts a profoundly different meaning by connecting them to actual situations of feminist struggle and critique. Daly related the 'shock of non-being' to the awareness of women's inferior social position in Western culture and history and to the depth of their 'non-being in patriarchy'. Resisting this non-being, or 'female becoming', is not a matter of confronting existential anxiety in general, but of the courage to be in the face of annihilation caused by the structural evil of patriarchy. According to Daly, "the courage to be is the key to the revelatory power of the feminist revolution" (Daly 1973: 24). This indispensable existential courage Daly defined as the courage to see and the courage to sin, seeing and breaking through the stereotypes and expectations of idealized femininity imposed on women.

Confronting sexism not only leads to radical critique of religiously sanctioned patriarchal power ("If God is male, then the male is god"; Daly 1973: 19), but also to a new redemptive naming of oneself, God, and the world. In patriarchal culture and history, Daly argued, 'the power to name' has been systematically denied to women and current language therefore needs to be 'liberated, castrated and exorcised', wrenched out of its destructive semantic context, to be able to refer to a new reality beyond sexism and institutionalized violence against women. This new naming of the self, God and the world from women's perspective constitutes the becoming of women and reveals at the same time the continuous unfolding of God. Women's 'participation in being' makes God, the ground of being, manifest in new ways. According to Daly, women experience 'transcendence' and 'ultimate meaning' in ways that go beyond the dominant images and oppositions with which God is perceived and defined, in particular beyond the 'male reification of God'. To underline the radical otherness of this hierophany Daly went further than Tillich and posited God not as the ground of being but as the dynamics of all being, ever unfolding and drawing creation toward itself by 'contagious transcendence'. God as 'Be-ing' transcends and transforms creation as well as grounds and encompasses all being. Tillich's ontological theology, in combination with Whiteadian process philosophy and the evolutionary thinking of Teilhard de Chardin, gave Daly the theological and philosophical framework to develop a radical feminist concept of God that did not simply oppose but incorporated and transformed theistic and transcendent aspects of God as elaborated in classic Christian theology.

Daly's most original and famous proposal in *Beyond God the Father* concerns the conceptualization of God as Verb. She wrote:

> Why indeed must 'God' be a noun? Why not a verb – the most active and dynamic of all? Hasn't the naming of 'God' as noun been an act of murdering that dynamic Verb? And isn't the Verb infinitely more personal than a mere static noun? The anthropomorphic symbols for God may be intended to convey personality, but they fail to convey that God is Be-ing. Women now who are experiencing the shock of non-being and the surge of self-affirmation against this are inclined to perceive transcendence as the Verb in which we participate – live, move and have our being. (*Ibid.*: 33–4)

In Daly's concept of God as Verb the most characteristic aspects of her feminist theological project come together. This concept is informed by iconoclasm and kenosis, in a consistent refusal to objectify and to 'gender' God. But remythologization has also shaped this concept, because the idea of God is imaginatively connected to feminist struggle and critique without being linked to gender as such. Daly placed the capacity of naming, which she considered to be constitutive for women's becoming, at the heart of this concept. The founding concepts of Daly's feminist theology of 'naming oneself toward God' and of God as 'the unfolding Verb' also echo the findings of her initial neo-Thomistic studies into 'positive knowledge of God from creatures' and the possibility of 'natural knowledge of God', and are based on the Thomistic threefold epistemology of the *via negativa*, the *via positiva* and the *via eminentiae*.

PATRIARCHY AS RELIGION: THE OBJECTIFICATION OF WOMEN

In *Beyond God the Father* Daly gave a feminist reinterpretation not only of the concept of God, but also of all the other main concepts of Christian systematic theology. This made her book instantaneously successful and created its lasting fame as the classic of feminist theology. Daly defined revelation, creation, sin, Incarnation, Trinity, redemption, church and the eschaton in the light of the process of female becoming and feminist naming, speaking for instance of 'Sisterhood as Anti-Church' and of 'Feminism as Final Cause'. She called this new interpretation 'a feminist liberation of theology'. She explained that epistemologically this approach is double-edged, consisting of a paradoxical recognition of old, stereotypical and of new, liberative ways of perceiving women and everything that is associated with them. This difference between old and new understandings of women addresses the transition from women as object to women as subject of religious reflection, which summarizes the political and philosophical agenda of Daly's whole oeuvre. From Beauvoir, with whom Daly has been in debate during most of her life, she took over the feminist critique of woman as the 'other' of the hegemonic male subject of Western culture and history, and of Western culture and religion as permeated by the stereotyping of women and by their 'objectification'. Daly was particularly fascinated by Beauvoir's thesis that in Western culture both romantic heterosexual love and religion (especially Roman Catholic piety) lure women to accept their status as 'other' in relation to men. The effect of both love and religion, Beauvoir claimed, is that women assent to become objects and betray their autonomy instead of "realizing their potential". Deep veneration for divine men and masculine gods is women's particular – and particularly disastrous – form of "bad faith" (Beauvoir 1949: II, 459–517).

Daly initially assumed that a revised form of Christian faith could counter and overcome this female form of bad faith. In *The Church and the Second Sex* and in *Beyond God the Father* she criticized Christian theology for its stereotyping and objectification of women, and presented a reformulated Christian theology that strongly focuses on women becoming subjects and striving for transcendence. After openly stating her post-Christian position in 1975 (Daly 1975a), Daly began to elaborate Beauvoir's critique of women's 'bad faith' in a far more radical way. Instead of criticizing Christianity and other religions for their patriarchal character, Daly declared that patriarchy functions and legitimizes itself in the same way that religion does:

> Patriarchy is itself the prevailing religion of the entire planet, and its essential message is necrophilia. All of the so-called religions legitimating patriarchy are mere sects subsumed under its vast umbrella/ canopy. They are essentially similar, despite the variations. All – from buddhism and hinduism to islam, judaism, christianity, to secular derivates such as freudianism, jungianism, marxism and maoism – are infrastructures of the edifice of patriarchy. All are erected as parts of the male's shelter against anomie. And the symbolic message of all the sects of the religion that is patriarchy is this: Women are dreaded anomie. Consequently, women are the objects of male terror, the projected personifications of 'The Enemy', the real objects under attack in all the wars of patriarchy. (Daly 1978: 39)

Daly presented a further development of this analytical concept of patriarchy as a religion in her later works. She wrote of a 'phallocratic belief system' and a 'universal religion of phallocracy' that prevent both men and women from believing in women's power and dignity. The results, according to Daly, are the persistent and worldwide objectification of women. All of Daly's later works, written after her 'qualitative leap beyond patriarchal religion' in 1975, are primarily directed against this objectification or 'annihilation' of women and dedicated to their 'becoming' beyond patriarchal religion and the religion of patriarchy.

POST-CHRISTIAN FEMINIST PHILOSOPHY

When, during the 1970s, *The Church and the Second Sex* and *Beyond God the Father* received growing acclamation, their author had already set off for a new and further journey. Daly no longer believed in the transformation of the Catholic Church or in the liberation of theology, and left behind the entire system of myths, symbols, creeds and dogmas of Christianity. This system she now credited for having been her 'springboard' into 'post-Christian time/space', as she stated over and again in the series of new introductions and afterwords that she added to the republications of her theological works. The addition of autobiographical comments to her earlier works became a trademark of Daly's performance as post-Christian feminist author. While this genre allowed Daly to explain and justify her controversial choices, it offered her readers the opportunity to relate her new and often fanciful 'metapatriarchal intellectual travels' to events and developments in Daly's own life.

In 1975 conflicts again revolved around her position at Boston College. She was denied promotion to full professor, on the grounds that her publications to date had been too unscholarly and her academic work less than brilliant. Once more, national protests arose, and Daly was eventually granted promotion (Daly 1991: xiii–xxxv). But ongoing confrontations with the administrative powers and principalities of academic institutions and organizations strengthened Daly to follow her autonomous course beyond 'academentia', as she came to call the academic world. She now openly took a radical feminist position, politically as well as scholarly: she affirmed women's marginality within patriarchal society as a vantage point and urged women to claim their position as critical outsiders. She stated that for women concerned with philosophical and theological questions, building up a feminist tradition requires a radical choice: "[T]here has to be a shift from 'acceptable' female deviance (characterized by triviality, diffuseness, dependence upon others for self-definition, low self-esteem, powerlessness) to deviance which may be unacceptable but which is acceptable to the self and *is* self-acceptance" (1975b: 50). She summoned women to "make the qualitative leap toward self-acceptable deviance as ludic cerebrator, questioner of everything, madwoman and witch" (*ibid.*: 50).

Daly's subsequent series of thick books with playful titles, such as *Gyn/Ecology* (1978), *Pure Lust* (1984), *Webster's First New Intergalactic Wickedary of the English Language* (1987), *Outercourse* (1992), *Quintessence* (1998) and *Amazon Grace* (2006), all obey this call. Although the tone and style of these later works differ greatly from Daly's earlier writings, they continue to reflect the 'passion for transcendence' that had led Daly to pursue the highest degrees of theology and philosophy. The feminist ontology, anthropology and cosmology introduced and outlined in *Beyond God the Father* are taken up in these later works and developed into a "philosophy of what is most intimate and most ultimate", formulated from the perspective of the ones who are excluded, ignored or violated by patriarchal society and androcentric discourse. In particular, the necessity to acknowledge, resist and undo the structural violence that is acted out worldwide against women is addressed in these later works. Daly in these books expanded her critical analyses to include genocide, militarism, nationalism, biotechnology and environmental devastation, seeing them as parallel manifestations of the processes of rape and vivisection that characterize phallic culture. The fact that an incessant fight against the objectification of "women and all sensitive beings" fired her later oeuvre indicates that Daly's post-Christian stance was primarily led by the urge to take pressing moral and political issues into account within philosophical discourse, rather than by a merely scientific or religious rejection of certain theological concepts or suppositions.

As Daly's later works show, the comparison of patriarchy to religion, a radicalization of Beauvoir's existentialist-feminist concept of 'bad faith', not only offered a framework for analysing women's victimization and their compliance to these processes, but such a comparison also opened up strategies for resistance to and escape from patriarchy. It led Daly to design a 'feminist faith' that counters women's objectification and unconditionally affirms women's autonomy, self-actualization and quest for transcendence. In *Beyond God the Father*, Daly had founded this faith in the declaration that feminism is an ontological movement and that the women's revolution brings about participation in being and simultaneously the unfolding of God, "the Verb that has always more to say to us". In her later books, Daly made this position more precise by showing that this participation in and unfolding of 'Metabeing' requires the use of a new language that makes it possible to "realize (one's) transcendence". According to Daly, feminist faith brings this about by way of *meta-pherein*, by the 'spinning' of metaphors that actively carry one from the state of objectification and muteness to self-affirmative and creative being. For Daly this interpretation of feminist faith meant that almost all philosophical and theological concepts she had used earlier to address the 'becoming of women', including her revised concepts of God as Be-ing and Verb, had to be replaced. Taking seriously Beauvoir's finding that women have had neither a history nor a religion of their own, Daly reinvented feminist faith by deconstructing patriarchal religious myths and imagery and reclaiming the fragments of women's lost or suppressed religious heritage. The formulation of this feminist faith both shapes and is shaped by gynocentric language and hermeneutics, which Daly in her later books expressed in creative and steadily evolving newspeak. Her later books could be seen as monumental landmarks, a sort of virtual cathedral of 'elemental faith', as Daly came to designate this feminist faith. 'Elemental' here refers to all spiritual and material realities that have been attacked, suppressed, erased or annihilated by the 'phallocratic belief system'. "[O]ur struggle and quest concern Elemental participation in Be-ing. Our passion is for that which is most intimate and most ultimate, for depth and transcendence" (Daly 1984: vii).

FROM BAD TO BETTER FAITH

In Daly's *Beyond God the Father*, feminist criticism of religion was still inseparable from a dynamic interpretation of religious faith that supports feminism; these were like two sides of the same coin. After her renouncement of Christianity, feminist criticism of religion and feminist religious faith became increasingly separate topics in her work. In the later works we find a sharp distinction between 'bad' and 'good' faith, between religion as an addiction ('opium') and religion as mystical experience ('transcendence'), and between religion's power to tempt women into total subjection versus its capacity to empower them as subjects.

To describe what she meant by such empowerment, Daly borrowed terminology from her study of theology and philosophy (subject–object, self–other, being–non-being, being–Be-ing), as well as from popular psychology (power, energy, centre, life, integrity, authenticity) and from her own, mythical female language (Hag, Crone, Spinster, Voyager, Witch, Goddess). The many equivalents Daly used show that her notion of subjectivity cannot simply be equated with self-determination ('being independent') or with autonomy ('being free of foreign authority'). She speaks interchangeably of the Self, the subject, being, presence, awareness, soul, source, force, integrity, wholeness, strength and centring, while proving that this is not a given or a state of being. It must (still) be actualized, it is a matter of becoming. As becomes manifest in *Gyn/Ecology*, Daly's point of departure is the lack of presence or the 'fragmentation' of the self. Women are obstructed from 'realizing' their self. Among the obstacles are violence against women and 'patriarchal lies', but Daly also mentions the lack of solidarity among women (violence among women, the token woman) and individual women's inner fragmentation ("patriarchy's presence in our own mind"). In *Pure Lust* Daly provided a more profound exploration of women's lack of self-actualization and an enquiry into what constitutes and reinforces inner cohesion. She discussed three aspects of inner cohesion: consciousness, power and 'lust/longing', or, in other words, identifying one's self, asserting the self and extending the self. These aspects were dealt with in three major parts or 'Spheres' of *Pure Lust*, focusing on reason, passion and lust respectively. Daly also established a strong correlation between achieving inner cohesion and naming the self, the world and God.

In some respects, Daly's approach in her later oeuvre resembles that of continental feminist philosophers such as Luce Irigaray, who aligned themselves with the post-structuralist attack on the dominant Western notion of the subject. This resemblance is evident in the importance assigned to the 'revolution of discourse': the use of deconstruction, deviant readings, different semantic connotations and mimetic practices in order to establish and affirm oneself 'as a woman' (Irigaray 1974, 1977, 1987). But unlike Irigaray and other continental feminist philosophers, Daly did not consider the unity and identity of the subject as something that is problematic as such. To her, rather, the main problem is the absence of focus and the lack of re-membering; she considered the moments when one experiences coherence and volume, or 'the constitution of a self', to be 'revelations'.

Daly's later writings contain two different and seemingly contradictory notions of subjectivity. In her criticism of patriarchy as religion, she argued that women need to construct an autonomous self. But what she actually does and achieves and calls for in her writings, while naming, punning and associating, constitute a dismantling of this modern notion of subjectivity. She sings and associates, speaks in different voices, places herself outside any system, shows anger, pleasure and analytical depth, and draws on and cites Western theology, philosophy and mythology as well as contemporary culture; in so doing, she spins and weaves new tapestries of meaning. In so far as Daly identifies and names her way of thinking, she provides images of the self as an intricate knot, consisting of many threads/links: a thinking, feeling, listening and naming entity, which both integrates and reaches out, is self-supporting but also connected to others, and reshaped by them.

In *Quintessence* (1998) Daly adds, in the same playful way, the dimensions of time, duration and exchange to these images of the self. Here, time is assigned a positive meaning in the sense that Daly sees it as the dimension of extension and realization, a dimension women have not yet claimed forcefully enough. Existence in time means more than endurance; it also means realizing volume, substance and continuity. Time not only 'makes a difference' in its historical positioning, but is also the medium through which we can extend in all directions, reach, stand out, connect, be transformed, in short, become more without losing our contours and hence our concreteness as well as our limitations. While many Western theologians and philosophers have regarded time as a limiting factor at the level of the individual – time being directly linked to finiteness and death – Daly seems to regard time as the dimension of transformation and (ex)change.

Daly posited a notion of subjectivity that resides in the tension between 'being' and 'being more'. This tension does not arise from the shocking, distressing or 'impinging' experience of finiteness, individuality and exclusiveness, but from the 'unlocking', affirmative experience of extension, participation and belonging. Daly derived this definition of subjectivity – which is not based on a modern, individualist and androcentric opposition between autonomy and heteronomy – from pre-modern Thomistic religious ontology. This religious ontology assumes that there are various degrees of fullness or intensity of being. An increase in intensity means that persons or things are more involved in an all-transcending or encompassing reality: the fullness and variety of all that is in God. In this view, the way a being actualizes herself (more) is not by resisting or avoiding this all-encompassing reality, but by opening herself up to this 'contagious' reality and knowing herself to be/come part of it. This pre-modern notion allowed Daly to define agency, focus and inner cohesion from a feminist perspective without getting caught in the modern androcentric opposition between autonomy and heteronomy where the subject is represented as 'the self in juxtaposition with the other' and as 'the self inferior or superior to the other'. Neo-scholastic theology therefore offered her an alternative concept of subjectivity that is more suitable for understanding 'female becoming'.

EVALUATION

Daly has been a controversial theologian and philosopher of religion whose writings have received widely divergent reactions: she has shocked as well as thrilled many readers. Her works have been praised for their audacity and creativity, but they have also been sharply criticized for containing ahistoric and undifferentiating analyses of patriarchy and religion, and essentialist, dualistic and 'white' concepts of gender (e.g. Lorde 1984).

Daly has offered a unique and important reconceptualization of God, culminating in her original proposals to speak of God as unfolding Verb and of Metabeing as Metaphor in light of the feminist revolution and of female becoming. Characteristic of Daly is her attempt to reconceive God from a radical feminist perspective without turning to inclusive or female imagery to capture the 'most ultimate and intimate reality'. This distinguishes her project from that of many feminist theologians who search for inclusive or female imagery of God by reinterpreting biblical texts (e.g. Trible 1978; Ruether 1983; Adler 1998), and also distinguishes it from the feminist spirituality movement, which encourages the identification of the divine with the feminine (e.g. Starhawk 1979; Christ 1987, 1997). Daly's radical feminist critique of patriarchal culture and discourse and her passion for transcendence have made her very cautious of any objectification of intimate and ultimate reality. This stance also distinguishes her from continental feminist philosophers such as Irigaray, who has given the concept of God a special place in her project of feminist cultural critique and the positioning of female subjectivity (Irigaray 1984, 1987). Where Irigaray imagines God as 'horizontal' or 'sensible' transcendence that grounds an ethics of sexual difference and mutual recognition of otherness, Daly envisages the divine as continuously evolving and contagious transcendence that evokes connectedness and solidarity between all that is fragile and being threatened. Remarkably, in Daly's project the idea of God is not only unlimited but is also not related to limits, restrictions or any kind of alterity as seen from the perspective of 'female becoming', which shows the fundamental one-sidedness of this approach.

Finally, Daly's project has found most recognition and innovative continuation in the works of several American and British constructive theologians and feminist philosophers of religion (e.g. Keller 1986, 2003; Raphael 1996; Jantzen 1998; Schneider 1998).

FURTHER READING

Cortiel, J. 2001. *Passion für das Unmögliche: Befreiung als Narrativ in der amerikanischen feministischen Theologie*. Essen: Die Blaue Eule.

Durham P. 1997. "Patriarchy and Self-Hate: Mary Daly's Assessment of Patriarchal Religion Appraised and Evaluated in the Context of Karen Horney's Psychoanalytic Theory". *Journal of Feminist Studies in Religion* **13**: 119–30.

Frye, M. & S. Hoagland (eds) 2000. *Feminist Interpretations of Mary Daly*. Pennsylvania, PA: Pennsylvania State University Press.

Großmaß, R. 1989. "Von der Verführungskraft der Bilder: Mary Daly's Elemental-Feministische Philosophie". In *Feministischer Kompaß, patriarchales Gepäck: Kritik konservativer Anteile in neueren feministischen Theorien*, R. Großmaß & C. Schmerl (eds), 56–116. Frankfurt: Campus Verlag.

Hewitt Suchocki, M. 1994. "The Idea of God in Feminist Philosophy". *Hypathia* **9**: 57–68.

Hill, S. 1999. "(Dis)inheriting Augustine: Constructing the Alienated Self in the Autobiographical Works of Paul Monette and Mary Daly". *Literature & Theology* **13**: 149–65.

Korte, A.-M. 1992. *Een passie voor transcendentie: Feminisme, theologie en moderniteit in het denken van Mary Daly*. Kampen: Kok.

Korte, A.-M. 2001. "Horizons of Subjectivity: Religious Faith and Feminist Identity in Mary Daly's Writings". In *Towards a Different Transcendence: Feminist Findings on Subjectivity, Religion and Values*, K. Biezeveld & A.-C. Mulder (eds), 21–48. Oxford: Peter Lang.

Olds, L. 1989. "Metaphors of Hierarchy and Interrelatedness in Hildegard of Bingen and Mary Daly". *Listening* **24**: 54–66.

Raphael, M. 1997. "Thealogy, Redemption, and the Call of the Wild". *Feminist Theology* (May): 55–72.

Ratcliffe, K. 1996. *Anglo-American Feminist Challenges to the Rhetorical Traditions: Virginia Woolf, Mary Daly, Adrienne Rich*. Carbondale, IL: Southern Illinois University Press.

Riswold, C. 2007. *Two Reformers: Martin Luther and Mary Daly as Political Theologians*. Eugene, OR: Wipf & Stock.

Stenger, M. 1982. "A Critical Analysis of the Influence of Paul Tillich on Mary Daly's Feminist Theology". *Encounter* **43**: 219–38.

On LANGUAGE see also Ch. 13; Vol. 2, Chs 4, 11, 12; Vol. 3, Ch. 14; Vol. 4, Chs 3, 8. On THOMISM see also Ch. 9; Vol. 2, Ch. 13.

21

JACQUES DERRIDA

Kevin Hart

Jacques Derrida was born in 1930 in El-Biar near Algiers. He read Henri Bergson and Jean-Paul Sartre in philosophy class at the Lycée Gauthier in Algiers and then encountered Søren Kierkegaard and Martin Heidegger, the reading of whom pushed him to study philosophy rather than literature. In 1949 he moved to France, attending the Lycée Louis-le-Grand in Paris and then studied at the École Normale Supérieure (ENS), where he later taught for the first twenty years of his career. Beginning philosophical life as a phenomenologist, he soon invented a post-phenomenological style of thinking he called 'deconstruction'. Beginning in 1966, with a visit to Johns Hopkins University, Derrida often spent several weeks each year teaching in the United States, most notably at Yale and the University of California, Irvine.

In 1980 Derrida successfully defended his *these d'état* at the Sorbonne, and in 1983 served as the inaugural director of the Collège International de Philosophie while also moving from the ENS to the École des Hautes Études en Sciences Sociales. Throughout the 1970s, 1980s and 1990s he travelled extensively, speaking in Africa, Australia, Europe, Israel, Latin America, Japan and the Soviet Union. A prolific writer, as well as a stylish one, his publications embrace questions of art, literature, politics, psychoanalysis and religion. He died of cancer in 2004.

Most contributions to the philosophy of religion in the twentieth century consist of attempts to develop a new position, or to criticize an old position, with respect to one or more inherited problems: the existence of God, the rationality of belief, the possibility of religious experience, the nature of religious language and so on. Although he has interesting things to say about belief, experience and language, Jacques Derrida does not fit neatly into this model. He is an unusual philosopher of standing in that, over a long and prolific career, he added very little to the standard repertoire of philosophical questions and answers. There is no Derridean solution to the mind–body problem, for example, or a theory of truth to be associated with him, or a comprehensive account of human subjectivity that is peculiar to him. Almost all of his later work comprises responses to diverse invitations, and shows him repeatedly putting into play the ideas that were formulated in his first publications, *Edmund Husserl's "Origin of Geometry": An Introduction* (1962, trans. 1978) and *Speech and Phenomena* (1967, trans. 1973). This is not a matter of simply applying old ideas to new topics, since in his view those ideas do not exist independently of their contexts, their languages and the signatures of the authors whose texts provoke his engagement with them. Inevitably, then, one does not find a systematic approach to any traditional problem in the volumes of Derrida's writings. Yet one finds many essays, some of which are highly inventive, in which the notions we have come to associate with him – *la différance, le supplément, la trace* – are constantly redeployed in slightly different ways in order to rethink the ideas that form the Western philosophical tradition.

At times Derrida says that deconstruction, the philosophical position for which he is known, is strictly neither a position nor philosophical. If 'position' means affirming a thesis about being, knowing, judging or acting that has been reached by a tried and tested method, then deconstruction is not a position. Rather, it is an ensemble of practices of close reading that reveal how philosophical motifs can be found, folded in unique ways, in Western writing from Plato to Paul Celan. Deconstruction "cannot be separated from performatives, from signatures, from a given language" (Derrida 1996: 217). And if 'philosophical' refers to motifs that are specific to philosophy understood as an inherited set of discourses – metaphysics, epistemology, logic and the rest – that turn on a relation with presence, then Derrida says that deconstruction is not philosophical. On the contrary, the task of deconstruction, as he saw it, is to question philosophy as a formal discourse, and to do so from a place, or non-place, that is neither inside nor outside philosophy as he conceives it. He calls this place or non-place *la différance*, by which he means a quasi-transcendental structure of differing and deferring that can be found to be at work in any form of inscription.

Of course, if one looks beyond Derrida's general pronouncements on deconstruction he can be seen to commend and defend various philosophical positions. Some are first-order views (e.g. one should hold to reflective rather than dogmatic faith). Others involve a subtle arrangement of first- and second-order views: for example, he is a soft antinomian with respect to law (maintaining that justice does not coincide with the law) and a non-cognitivist with respect to judgement (holding that there is no theoretical assurance that one has acted justly). So it can be seen that Derrida proposes various positions in the philosophy of religion, especially in the last twenty years of his writing life. Specifically of interest are the following views: that God, as understood within Christianity, is a metaphysical entity, one whose existence he cannot affirm; that the relation between religion and ethics is formally undecidable; that religion is not natural but that a certain religiosity is universal; that one can and should affirm a messianicity without reliance on any positive messianism; and that prayer presumes the possibility of God's absence. If Derrida would deny that, in holding these views and supporting them with reasons, he was doing philosophy of religion, he would at least concede that he was participating in philosophy, taken as a set of conventions, without fully belonging to it. In fact, one might say that Derrida not only contributed to the philosophy of religion but also extended its borders. In several essays on biblical texts, he introduces for our times a new subdiscipline we might call 'philosophy and Scripture' (see "Towers of Babel" in Derrida [2002], and "Of an Apocalyptic Tone Newly Adopted in Philosophy" in Derrida [1992]). More generally, he finds questions of religion and theology folded in areas where they are not usually expected. For instance, his account of translation involves consideration of what he calls a 'theology of translation', he traces the complex relation of writing and priestly authority, and his analysis of political authority points to a 'mystic foundation' (see Derrida 1979b, 2002, 2004). One might also point out that his study of the gift, most notably in *Given Time I* (1991, trans. 1992), has prompted theologians (John Milbank, in particular) and philosophers with a theological bent (Jean-Luc Marion, especially) to clarify the theological implications of gift giving.

DERRIDA'S GENERAL APPROACH TO PHILOSOPHY

Before considering the views about religion that Derrida came to hold, it will be worthwhile to dwell on his general approach to philosophy. For his take on the discipline strongly influences how he regards religion and theology. There are philosophical motifs, he contends, that can be found throughout Western discourse, even in subjects that appear unrelated to philosophy as it has been practised from Parmenides to Levinas. Literature and politics, history and art criticism, economics and theology, are all regulated by references to *logos, morphe, nous, ousia* and *telos*, among others. More generally, all Western discourse, including that of religion, is structured by what Derrida calls "the metaphysics of presence". Accorded a far wider scope than is usual, "presence" has several dimensions: ontic (the temporal presence of beings), ontological (the determination of being as presence) and epistemological (a subject's self-presence or presence to another subject). Derrida claims that all metaphysics is that of presence but that it does not form a homogeneous unity. His early work can be understood as showing how some moderns and contemporaries – Husserl, Foucault, Levinas, Lévi-Strauss and Saussure – seek to reform philosophy or leave its jurisdiction only to find themselves still in the grip of some of its deepest assumptions, while other philosophers, stalwart metaphysicians such as Plato and Hegel, offer glimpses of what exceeds the metaphysics of presence.

GOD AND PRESENCE

Read quickly, the works of his first maturity such as *Of Grammatology* (1967, trans. 1997) and *Writing and Difference* (1967, trans. 1979) seem to identify God and presence, and were this indeed the case he would be committed to the judgements that God is a metaphysical entity and that all discourse on God is metaphysical in his sense of the word. It is easy to point to textual evidence to support this view. For example, we read, "God is the name and the element of that which makes possible an absolutely pure and absolutely self-present self-knowledge" (Derrida 1997a: 98). When examined closely, however, these early works say something quite different. "Only infinite being can reduce the difference in presence", we are told. And then we hear a qualification: "In that sense, the name of God, *at least as it is pronounced within classical rationalism*, is the name of indifference itself" (*ibid.*: 71, emphasis added). That is, the name of God is metaphysical when and only when it is spoken within the terms of classical rationalism. The possibility is therefore opened that appeals to God need not be metaphysical, or at least not simply metaphysical.

This possibility of a non-metaphysical theology can be clarified by looking at the word 'onto-theology', first used by Immanuel Kant in the *Critique of Pure Reason* (A 631, B 659) but given a new sense by Heidegger in his "The Onto-Theo-Logical Constitution of Metaphysics". For Heidegger, metaphysics has an onto-theo-logical structure, by which he means that it turns on an ambiguity that goes back to Aristotle's definition of metaphysics as *on hē on* (*Metaphysics* 1005a). On the one hand, metaphysics is the study of beings in general, ontology; while, on the other hand, it is the study of the most elevated or deepest ground of beings, the *theion*, in which case it is theiology. Notice that 'theiology' is not 'theology': the latter word denotes a metaphysical enterprise when and only when it figures God as the highest or the lowest ground. Can God be construed as non-metaphysical in this sense? Derrida was doubtful that Christianity was able to do so, although he sometimes implied that the situation is different in Judaism. There is no doubt that he was fascinated by the possibility that apophatic or negative theologies – that is, theologies that deny, neutralize or suspend all the predications of God given by positive theologies – speak of a deity that is not metaphysical. Yet on his reading of Pseudo-Dionysius the Areopagite (*see* Vol. 1, Ch. 20) and Meister Eckhart, the denial of the predicate of being to the deity always presumes a hyper-essential being. God would therefore be a metaphysical entity, and talk of God would remain metaphysical, even if a partial deconstruction has taken place. Meister Eckhart, for example, might be seen in his German homilies to have unravelled scholastic claims about God as the ground of being, and to affirm a faith of "wandering joy", as Reiner Schürmann has it (see Eckhart 2001), while nonetheless remaining committed to certain assumptions of Neoplatonism.

Deconstruction should not be regarded as offering an external or even an entirely hostile critique of religion in general and of Christianity in particular. It has a heritage that comes from Christianity and has roots in Jewish prophecy. Derrida freely admitted that 'deconstruction' refers not only to Heidegger's 'Destruktion' but also "to Luther's *destruuntur*" (Derrida 2005: 33), the word that the Reformer used in the *Heidelberg Disputation* (1518) to translate Paul's citation of the Lord's words, "I will destroy the wisdom of the wise" (1 Corinthians 1:19), a warning that is of course a citation from Isaiah 29:14. So deconstruction reaches an internal limit when dealing with Scripture. Also, it makes no claim to be able to reject claims of immediate religious experience. With Kierkegaard (*see* Vol. 4, Ch. 13), Derrida holds that faith exceeds philosophical categories. If grace is given to someone

> in a way that is absolutely improbable, that is, exceeding any proof, in a unique experience, then deconstruction has no lever on this. And it should not have any lever. But once this grace, this given grace, is embodied in a discourse, in a community, in a church, in a religion, in a theology … then deconstruction, a deconstruction, may have something to say, something to do, but without questioning or suspecting the moment of grace. (Derrida 2005: 39)

One cannot deconstruct God, but only discourses about God; and this is one reason why Derrida is unable to say directly that he is an atheist.

NEGATIVE THEOLOGY AND PRAYER

As early as 1968, when discussing his essay "Différance" at a meeting of the Societé Française de Philosophie, Derrida was faced with the objection that deconstruction is itself a mode of negative theology. Brice Parain observed that *la différance* "is the source of everything and one cannot know it: it is the God of negative theology" (Derrida 1985: 130). To which Derrida responded, "Difference [i.e. *la différance*] is not, it is not a being and it is not God" (*ibid.*: 132). Neither God nor *la différance* can be known since neither can be placed in a category. Yet whereas God transcends the categories, existing *a se* and enjoying the status of absolute singularity, *la différance* is anterior to all categories and fails to coincide with itself. In Kantian terms we can say that God, for Derrida, is transcendent and transcendental, while *la différance* is transcendental but does not form a ground (that is, it is quasi-transcendental). The same view is elaborated in detail in "How to Avoid Speaking" (1987, trans. 1989a), where Derrida offers close readings of the accounts of the Good in Plato (*see* Vol. 1, Ch. 4) and God in Pseudo-Dionysius, Meister Eckhart and Heidegger. The essay proposes a matrix of ideas that enlivened Derrida's later writing. Some of these, most importantly the nature of avoidance and denegation, are drawn from writings of the same period: *Of Spirit: Heidegger and the Question* (1987, trans. 1989b) and "Desistance" (1986, trans. 1989c). Others – the uniqueness of the other, whether human or divine; the primacy of revealedness over revelation; and the impossibility of prayer being directed exclusively to God – are taken up in later pieces such as "Faith and Knowledge: The Two Sources of

'Religion' at the Limits of Reason Alone" (1996, trans. 1998) and the three essays collected in English translation in *On the Name* (1995a).

Of particular interest in "How to Avoid Speaking", both in itself and for his later thought, is Derrida's reading of the prayer that opens Pseudo-Dionysius' *Mystical Theology*. Derrida works with the assumption that prayer must be a pure invention each time and must take place in a moment of full presence, in the silent communion of soul and God, and not be contaminated by codes and repetition. He distinguishes two traits in the opening prayer: (i) an address to the other as other, and (ii) an encomium to the Trinity. The encomium is needed for the prayer to be directed to the Christian God, and yet this very determination compromises the purity of the prayer: the other is no longer wholly other but has been fashioned by concepts and metaphors, by codes and scripts. Derrida then notes that, after praying, Pseudo-Dionysius quotes his prayer in addressing the person to whom his treatise is dedicated, Timothy. The prayer, the quotation of the prayer, and the apostrophe to Timothy all presume the possibility of repetition. Indeed, as soon as the prayer is verbalized, even silently, it is diverted from its unique and singular addressee, and the moment of pure communion with God has been divided. So prayer cannot be insulated in a singular moment of full presence; it is always and already subject to mechanical repetition.

A common-sense objection to this argument is that there is no need to make the assumptions that Derrida does: that prayer must be singular and unrepeatable, and that, for a prayer to be authentic, only God should be able to receive it. The very model of prayer for Christians is the "Our Father," which the faithful believe to have been given by Jesus himself. Each time one prays the "Our Father" one is repeating it, and in church and at prayer meetings many others will certainly overhear it. Of course, the prayer is to be said with attention, both to the words and to the addressee, and in that sense it is said freshly each time it is said properly. This stress on attention when reciting a formula generates a weaker version of Derrida's original conclusion. And in a later conversation on prayer he endorses this weaker version: "each time I pray, I must imply 'I am different.' It's a different prayer, it's new, I don't simply repeat like a recording, I am not just repeating the prayer I've learned or rituals" (Derrida *et al.* 2001: 67). So authentic prayer involves both an inevitable reference to codes and an attempt at complete freshness in addressing the deity. The weaker account is more convincing than the stronger. Even so, one might demur over Derrida's highly Romantic suggestion that a prayer is "a poem. A prayer is a language that you have to invent" (*ibid.*). Few prayers are linguistically inventive, and there is a powerful tradition, best represented by Samuel Johnson, that argues that such invention is both impossible and undesirable. "Man admitted to implore the mercy of his Creator and plead the merits of his Redeemer is already in a higher state than poetry can confer" (Johnson 1905: vol. 1, 291). One's recitation of a prayer might be inventive, in the sense that an attempt is made to read the words as though they are spoken for the first time, thereby responding to the awe of addressing one's maker, or meditating on the words in a singular manner over the course of a long period. Even so, one might object that Derrida takes insufficient account of the passivity of the subject in the higher reaches of prayer. One does not always strive to prove one's sincerity to God; sometimes one simply places oneself at God's disposal.

Needless to say, Derrida would reply that this theology of contemplative prayer ascribes full presence to God. Now a believer might respond in either or both of two ways without thereby disagreeing with Derrida's central contention about the metaphysics of presence. Either one can affirm this divine presence, and say that although writing divides all representations it can no more determine the deity's reality than it can any person's. No quasi-transcendental structure of repetition gives us the right to restrict the ontic or ontological population of reality, as Derrida himself admits. Or one can say that this presence does not function as a ground in any ontic, ontological or epistemological way. One loves God in a mode without mode (*modus, sine modo*), it will be said, referring to a patristic commonplace that Bernard of Clairvaux (*see* Vol. 2, Ch. 9) popularized in *De deligendo Deo* (On loving God) 1.1, and this love precedes philosophical constructions. Both responses would tend to assimilate deconstruction to a religious attitude, iconoclasm, rather than set it against religious belief as such. Of course, this sort of general agreement with Derrida's case against the metaphysics of presence does not oblige anyone also to agree with his specific claims about God, faith, revelation or prayer.

Let us stay with prayer. "The possibility that God remains eternally absent, that there might be no addressee at the other end of my prayer is the condition of the prayer", he insists (Derrida *et al.* 2001: 63). The view is rephrased a little later: "the possibility for Him not to listen to, not to respond to His name, is included in the essence of the prayer" (*ibid.*). One might accept Derrida's claim that each prayer is a call but not accept either conclusion that he draws from it: that the call might have no addressee, and that the call might not be answered. A believer will be reconciled in faith to the possibility that God might not answer his or her prayer in the terms of the petition. But no believer will pray in the belief that the prayer might not be heard at all. The soldier who supposedly prayed before the battle of Blenheim, "O God, if there be a God, save my soul, if I have a soul!" is a not a model that any believer can take seriously. It is true that one can write a poem that mentions the name of God without ever intending to use it. Jules Supervielle begins his "Prière à l'inconnu" as follows: "Voilà que je me suprends à t'adresser la parole, / Mon Dieu, moi qui ne sais encore si tu existes" (And so it is that I find myself addressing a word to you, / My God, I who does not yet know if you exist) (Supervielle 1996: 363, my trans.). Yet no one can pray in adoration or with a burning petition without intending to use the word 'God' rather than mention it. Derrida says, "there should be a moment of atheism in the prayer" (Derrida *et al.* 2001: 63), and it must seem that way to a non-believer who, after all, sees a prayer in terms of a risk that one might be fooled into asserting the existence of an addressee. For a believer, however, who enjoys a settled belief in God, a more appropriate claim would be that 'there should be a moment of iconoclasm in the prayer'. Belief in God does not come with deductive knowledge of what God is, and one's inherited images of the deity are certainly open to doubt.

DERRIDA'S PHILOSOPHY OF RELIGION

Most of Derrida's work in the philosophy of religion in the latter part of his writing life is done with reference to Kant, Kierkegaard, Heidegger and Levinas. A Kierkegaardian accent can be heard in the way in which he assimilates prayer to risk, and in general it must be said that Protestant emphases can be felt more powerfully than Catholic ones in his views of prayer and belief. If Augustine (*see* Vol. 1, Ch. 18) impinges on his thought, as he does before and after "Circumfession" (1991, trans. 1993), it is chiefly the *Confessions*, not the studies of grace and the Trinity, and there is no evidence of a serious or prolonged engagement with Anselm or Aquinas. In general, as Derrida says in "Faith and Knowledge", his position derives from an attempt to revamp Kant's *Religion within the Boundaries of Mere Reason* (1793). The rational religion that Derrida advocates is linked to republican ideals: not a state that can be inspected now or at any given time in the future but a "democracy to come," that is, all the sum of all possibilities that the idea of democracy contains within itself and that can be drawn upon by an endless desire for justice (which Derrida sharply distinguishes from right). No ecclesial structures or priestly rituals will characterize this rational religion. Nor will it be a natural religion. Instead, it will turn on a "universalizable culture of singularities" (Derrida 1998: 18). Each person is regarded as being absolutely singular and therefore holy, and my relation with the other person is predicated on the other's faith in me.

This natural faith, as we might call it in order to distinguish it from supernatural faith, is what Derrida calls '*croyance*' in "Faith and Knowledge" (§§10–11, 32, 43). That society presumes a faith other than that infused by God for ordinary commerce to take place is not a new idea. In Christian theology it goes back at least to Aquinas (*see* Vol. 2, Ch. 13), who discusses it in his *Commentary on Boethius' De Trinitate* (q. III, art. 1.3). Yet Derrida will resist the claim that *croyance* is natural, insisting that it is social. Nor is it restricted to the sphere of the human, for animals also exhibit faith in one another. A culture of singularities would not be universal in that it bespeaks a communitarian fusion. Not at all: a difference between myself and the other person is always retained by dint of the quasi-transcendental priority of *la différance* (or, as he calls it from time in time in his later works, *khora*). Nonetheless, this structure impinges on anyone and everyone, and in that sense it is universal. The universality of *la différance* distinguishes it from belief in any messianism such as one finds in the Abrahamic religions. On the contrary, Derrida argues that *la différance* is itself a structure of messianicity that, being prior to any historical revelation, is free from all positive messianism and does not depend on any; and it is this structure that marks the affirmation of a new religion elaborated at the limits of reason alone. Although Derrida holds to the word 'religion', it might be more accurate to call what he affirms to be 'religiosity', although even this might be more than is strictly warranted by his minimal philosophical faith. For as we shall see, Derrida's new version of Kant's *Religion within the Limits of Reason Alone* does not admit a sharp distinction between religion and ethics.

Before turning to that important issue, however, something should be said about 'religion'. As Derrida notes, the word comes from the Latin *religio*, and he observes that Latinity has been globalized, and that the word 'religion' has developed a power to incorporate all manner of things in it that once had little or nothing to do with it. In "Faith and Knowledge" he calls this process *mondialatinisation* (globalatinization). Its power derives from an alliance of Christianity (especially in its North American formations), capitalism and tele-technology. Today 'religion', an English word "that has been to Rome and taken a detour to the United States" (Derrida 1998: 29), imposes itself in world politics in an imperial manner. Derrida detects a double bind in this globalatinization. On the one hand, it "produces, weds, exploits the capital and knowledge of tele-mediatization", while, on the other hand, "it reacts immediately, *simultaneously*, declaring war against that which gives it this new power" (*ibid.*: 46). Religion today immunizes itself against tele-technology while destroying its own immune system. Such is the strange logic of all messianisms – Christian, Jewish and Islamic – he thinks, and hence the need to listen again to Kant and refigure his thought for our own times. In doing so we would once again protect ourselves, as rational agents, from fanaticism in all its forms. There is no doubt in his mind that positive messianisms can lead to fanaticism, and wanting to protect justice for all he commends what he calls 'messianicity without messianism'.

This messianicity is, Derrida says, "the opening to the future or to the coming of the other as the advent of justice, but without horizon of expectation and without prophetic prefiguration" (*ibid.*: 17). No positive revelation is assumed here. Following Kant, Derrida affirms reflective over dogmatic faith; and, borrowing Heidegger's distinction between *Offenbarung* and *Offenbarkeit*, revelation and revealedness, he asserts the priority of the latter. Two things are odd about this assertion. In the first place, Derrida translates *Offenbarkeit* as 'révélabilité' or 'revealability', thereby giving the word a transcendental twist that it does not have in the original German. And in the second place, although Derrida recognizes that *Offenbarung* and *Offenbarkeit* arrange themselves in the form of an aporia, and insists that an aporia must always be negotiated, there is no negotiation, no attempt to find, as he said earlier in *Politics of Friendship*, "a structure of experience in which the two poles of the alternative cease to oppose one another to form another node, another 'logic', another 'chronology', another history, another relation to the order of orders" (1997b: 25 n.26). Instead of pondering what would happen if *Offenbarung* were prized over *Offenbarkeit* – if revelation were to reveal the possibility of revealedness or the capacity to receive revelation – Derrida affirms the priority of *Offenbarkeit* and thereby prizes the methodological priority of human categories over the act of divine self-communication. His new rational religion can therefore be seen by Christian eyes to continue the liberal Protestant tradition that looks back to Kant and Schleiermacher (*see* Vol. 4, Ch. 3), and to oppose the post-liberal tradition that draws inspiration from Karl Barth and Hans Urs von Balthasar. Unlike liberal Protestantism, however, messianicity without messianism has no Christology and no doctrine of God. While it is possible to conceive some philosophers finding the position attractive, it is impossible to imagine anyone actually being religiously converted to it.

In *The Gift of Death* (1992, trans. 1995) Derrida assimilates his position on religion to several major currents of modern philosophy. The general view is an attempt to think religion without "*the event of a revelation or the revelation of an event*" (Derrida 1995b: 49). Philosophers who support this view in different ways include Kant and Hegel, Kierkegaard and Heidegger; and, in our own times, we can add to their number Levinas and Patočka, Ricoeur and Marion. They all belong, Derrida says, to a tradition "that consists of proposing a non-dogmatic doublet of dogma, a philosophical and metaphysical doublet, in any case a *thinking* that 'repeats' the possibility of religion without religion" (*ibid.*). Perhaps the first thing to say about this "non-dogmatic doublet" is that it is not restricted to modern philosophy. Attempts to cash out the truths of religion in terms of philosophy can be found in antiquity and the medieval ages: generations of Platonists maintained that the One could be reached by dialectic, while Ibn-Rushd (Averroes; *see* Vol. 2, Ch. 10) argued that the one truth can be approached from various directions, including the philosophical. By the same token, a quest for a non-dogmatic interpretation of religion has been a concern of modern theology. Karl Rahner, for one, argues that "transcendental experience" yields "experience of transcendence" which is a vague, unthematic (and therefore non-dogmatic) experience of God (see Rahner 1982: 20). More surprising is that Derrida secures non-dogmatic religion at the cost of its being metaphysical, and makes no remark, as one would expect, that this metaphysics needs to be brought under critique. It might be noted that many philosophers, from Aristotle to Kant to contemporary modal logicians, take possibility to be a metaphysical notion, although, to be sure, there are alternatives. Husserl does not regard eidetic possibility as metaphysical, and Derrida claims that possibility, as he uses the word, is internally divided and therefore not metaphysical (see Derrida 1998: 49). And finally, it should be kept in mind that not all the philosophers that Derrida names construe religion without religion by way of the primacy of ethics, as he does and as Kant and Levinas do. Marion, for instance, could be seen to secure the content of the Christian faith as eidetic possibility.

The ethics at issue in Derrida's own understanding of religion without religion is not that developed by Kant but is a modified version of the ethics elaborated by Levinas. There is no recourse to a universal moral law but an appeal to my responsibility for the other person: Derrida takes this from his sustained engagement with Levinas. Yet there is no responsibility without the risk of irresponsibility: Derrida draws this from his reading of Kierkegaard. In fact, Derrida's most intriguing comments on ethics and religion turn on his attempt to make Kierkegaard and Levinas converse with one another, and once again we are reminded that Derrida tends to do philosophy by way of the history of philosophy. What Kierkegaard and Levinas have in common is that "Neither one nor the other can assure himself of a concept of the ethical and of the religious that is of consequence; and consequently they are especially unable to determine the limit between these two orders" (Derrida 1995b: 84). If so, this would be a difficulty for each of them. Let us see why.

Kierkegaard's thought turns on a distinction between the orders of the ethical and the religious, but can this distinction be rigorously sustained? It cannot, Derrida says. "Kierkegaard would have to admit, as Levinas reminds him, that ethics is also the order and respect for absolute singularity, and not only that of the generality or of the repetition of the same. He cannot therefore distinguish so conveniently between the ethical and the religious" (*ibid.*: 84). There is similarly a difficulty for Levinas, for he maintains that the otherness of the other human being is distinct from the otherness of God. Yet "for his part, in taking into account absolute singularity, that is, the absolute alterity obtaining in relations between one human being and another, Levinas is no longer able to distinguish the infinite alterity of God and that of every human. His ethics is already a religious one" (*ibid.*). In each case, it seems, the border between ethics and religion cannot be drawn without interruption.

Reflection on Kierkegaard and Levinas leads Derrida to affirm one of his most controversial statements, "Tout autre est tout autre" (Derrida 1995b: ch. 4), which can be translated, 'Each and every other is wholly other'. The import of this apparent tautology (in French) is that every person, perhaps including every animal, is absolutely singular and therefore cannot be assimilated to the generality of any universal. Critics of Derrida will object that the statement is implausible because it denies all analogy between persons. I may be different from you, but I am not different in each and every way. Another objection is that with this statement Derrida erases the difference between the other person and God. Only God is absolutely singular, and human beings are only relatively singular. Our uniqueness is real, it will be freely admitted, but it does not turn on existing *a se* like God or being the absolutely singular God-man, Jesus Christ. Derrida's defenders on this point will reply that this objection assumes there is a clear and rigorous distinction between ethics and religion but that, as shown, no such distinction can be drawn. And Derrida's critics on this point will object that questions of borders, as Derrida discusses them, are informed wholly by *Offenbarkeit* and that a distinction between ethics and religion can and should be reinstated by granting primacy to *Offenbarung*. If one begins one's philosophy of religion with the idea of a free creator who reveals himself, then it will indeed be possible to distinguish ethics and religion. And if one does not, the philosophy of religion that we inherit from Kant and that is refined by Derrida will always exert pressure on any attempt to separate ethics and religion.

FURTHER READING

Caputo, J. 1997. *The Prayers and Tears of Jacques Derrida: Religion without Religion*. Bloomington, IN: Indiana University Press.
Coward, H. & T. Foshay (eds) 1992. *Derrida and Negative Theology*. Albany, NY: SUNY Press.
Hart, K. 2000. *The Trespass of the Sign: Deconstruction, Theology and Philosophy*, 2nd edn. New York: Fordham University Press.
Hart, K. & Y. Sherwood (eds) 2005. *Derrida and Religion: Other Testaments*. New York: Routledge.
O'Leary, J. 1985. *Questioning Back: The Overcoming of Metaphysics in Christian Tradition*. Minneapolis, MN: Winston Press.
Taylor, M. 1984. *Erring: A Postmodern A/theology*. Chicago, IL: University of Chicago Press.

On ETHICS see also Chs 12, 15; Vol. 1, Ch. 11; Vol. 2, Chs 4, 8; Vol. 3, Ch. 9; Vol. 4, Chs 13, 19. On NEGATIVE THEOLOGY see also Vol. 2, Ch. 11. On PRAYER see also Vol. 1, Chs 13, 18; Vol. 3, Ch. 5.

22

ALVIN PLANTINGA

James F. Sennett

In the halcyon days of post-positivisitic analytic philosophy, philosophy of religion and philosophical theology were considered by many to have been relegated to the forgotten realms of outmoded superstition they so richly deserved. Antony Flew's (1961, 1984) sophisticated recasting of David Hume's concerns over miracles and natural theology, John Mackie's (1955) stunning attack on the free will defence, R. M. Hare's (1955) sensible non-cognitive analysis of religious language, and many other enticing rebuttals of classical theism dominated the landscape and bode ill for any future progress in the philosophical defence of traditional belief.

Anyone aware of the state of analytic philosophy of religion at the start of the twenty-first century knows that the current picture could not be more radically different from that just described. Research programmes abound, and many of the philosophers conducting them profess and defend a profound belief in Western theism in general and Christianity in particular. There are many reasons for this amazing turnaround and many philosophers who share the credit, among them William Alston, Richard Swinburne and Nicholas Wolterstorff. But there can be no doubt that one of the premier champions of this team is the American philosopher Alvin Plantinga.

Alvin Carl Plantinga was born on 15 November 1932, in Ann Arbor, Michigan. He received philosophy degrees from Calvin College (AB in 1954), the University of Michigan (MA in 1955), and Yale University (PhD in 1958). He held permanent teaching positions at Wayne State University and Calvin College before assuming the John A. O'Brien Chair in Philosophy at the University of Notre Dame in 1982, which he holds at the time of writing. He also served as director of the Center for Philosophy of Religion at Notre Dame from 1984 to 2002. Plantinga has received numerous academic fellowships and has given dozens of named lectureships, including two appointments to deliver the Gifford Lectures at Aberdeen University. He has published more than a dozen books and well over one hundred articles and chapters in journals, magazines and books.

Plantinga's influence on contemporary philosophy of religion has been profound, but it has not stood alone. He has, along the way, made significant contributions to analytic metaphysics and epistemology as well. He developed a vocabulary for possible worlds discourse and modal logic in *The Nature of Necessity* (1974b) that is still in common usage throughout the discipline. Furthermore, the externalist theory of knowledge articulated in *Warrant and Proper Function* (1993b) has provided some of the liveliest discussion in post-Gettier epistemological research. More will be said about these and other influences as they pertain to Plantinga's philosophy of religion. It must suffice here to say that very few contemporary philosophers have had both the breadth and depth of impact on the discipline that Plantinga has.

PLANTINGA'S PHILOSOPHY OF RELIGION: AN OVERVIEW

Plantinga's influence on contemporary philosophy of religion can be charted along two axes: content and methodology. The former has, naturally, received the most attention from proponents and critics alike. But the latter may be the more wide-ranging, since many philosophers of religion concerned with subjects far afield from any Plantinga has ever broached nonetheless adopt procedural approaches traceable to his pioneering technique. A proper analysis of Plantinga's philosophy of religion must take both dimensions into account. The approach taken here will be content-oriented and largely chronological. Nonetheless, this approach will be explicitly peppered with references to at least four methodological tools frequently employed by Plantinga and now in common usage in analytical philosophy of religion.

Plantinga's philosophy of religion career has moved through several stages:

- *The rational theism stage*: an initial foray into the requirements for rational theism, represented most notably in *God and Other Minds* (1967). As will be shown, this stage prepared the way for much of what was to come over the next three decades.
- *The modal stage*: an exploration of the implications of modal metaphysics for classical philosophy of religion issues. This study resulted in his famous modal version of the ontological argument and his highly influential version of the free will defence. Both were presented in *The Nature of Necessity* (1974b) and *God, Freedom and Evil* (1974a).
- *The reformed epistemology stage*: a detailed defence of theistic belief from a reformed theological perspective. This stage divides into two substages. The first is most fully represented in his landmark article "Reason and Belief in God" (1983), and the second in the massive tome *Warranted Christian Belief* (2000).[1]

---

1. At the time of writing, Plantinga is engaged in a fourth major stage of research, which could be called the *Science and Religion Stage*: a so far somewhat sporadic examination of various issues at the crossroads of science and religion. This stage began with two controversial

Along the way Plantinga has also offered new and creative critiques of arguments for and against the existence of God (1967), a powerful attack on *a priori* probability and other notions crucial to any inductive form of the argument from evil (1979, 1988), and occasional ventures into the deepest waters of philosophical theology, with typically well-argued and surprising results (1980, 1982, 1986).

The methodological approaches to philosophy of religion Plantinga has pioneered and shaped include:

- An *indirect approach* to the defence of theism that challenges the sceptic to make the charges against belief explicit and philosophically rigorous enough to establish their point without proving too much. Absent such philosophical sophistication (Plantinga believes), theism enjoys a sort of rationality by default, as do many commonly held beliefs that lack either strict philosophical defence or indisputable philosophical refutation.
- A *descriptive approach* to philosophy of religion issues that begins with the facts of religious belief and takes them at face value, then attempts normative analysis that retains as much of the legitimacy of these facts as is philosophically feasible.
- A *modest approach* that understands rationality and other epistemic virtues to be person-relative in the sense that it is possible for a given body of epistemic grounding to render a given theist rational or justified[2] even though the same grounding may not award the same epistemic status to everyone who considers it.
- A *mature approach* that utilizes the best tools analytic philosophy has to offer, including sophisticated logical instruments such as modal logic and probability theory and advanced dialectical enquiries that interact with and utilize the most current theories and approaches in epistemology, philosophy of science and other related disciplines.

---

articles in 1991: a critique of Darwinian evolutionary theory (1991b) and an argument that philosophical naturalism is irrational given Darwinian evolutionary theory. (This argument was first presented in Plantinga [1991a], and was later revised and expanded to become chapter twelve of *Warrant and Proper Function* [1993b]. The latter was reprinted as chapter four in Plantinga [1998].) This phase is ongoing, and was the subject of Plantinga's 2005 Gifford Lectures. I do not treat this stage in the present chapter because of its ongoing nature; both its conclusions and its impact on the state of contemporary philosophy of religion are unclear at this point.

2. While the terms 'rational', 'justified' and their cognates are sometimes differentiated in their connotations, the epistemological intricacies usually at stake need not concern us here. For the balance of this chapter I shall consider the concepts of epistemic rationality and justification synonymous and shall use them and their cognates interchangeably. Furthermore, I do not understand either of them to entail knowledge of a true belief that bears them. Thus care will be taken in discussion of the reformed epistemology stage to distinguish between them both (with their internalist implications) and Plantinga's externalist notion of warrant.

UNIVERSITY OF WINCHESTER
LIBRARY

All of these approaches reflect the best of late-twentieth-century analytical philo-sophical attitudes. Furthermore, they are carried out in the context of clear, precise argumentation. Although the waters of Plantinga's philosophy often run deep, they are seldom murky. Plantinga's influence has served to spark a very important maturation in the philosophy of religion. Today's practitioner must be well trained in the best contemporary philosophy has to offer in order to keep up.

THE RATIONAL THEISM STAGE: OTHER MINDS AND MODEST THEISM

In *God and Other Minds* (1967) Plantinga takes on what may be the oldest and most venerated objection to theistic belief: that it cannot be rational because the fundamental theistic claim – that there exists an omniscient, omnipotent and morally perfect creator and sustainer of the universe – lacks demonstrative argu-ment. Plantinga does not challenge this premise. In fact, the entire first section of his book appears to be a rigorous and detailed defence of it. He systematically dismantles several forms of the cosmological argument, the teleological argument and the ontological argument, concluding that none of the classical theistic proofs delivers the demonstrative confirmation of theism that the medieval scholastics and modern natural theologians claimed for them.

However, in the remainder of the book Plantinga challenges the hidden premise behind this traditional objection: the assumption that there can be no rational theistic belief without good argument. Plantinga begins his rebuttal by showing that the fundamental atheistic claim – that there is no such creator as that described above – is in the same philosophical boat as its contradiction, lacking demonstrative argument. The second part of *God and Other Minds* is devoted to rebutting the most common arguments against theism, most notably the argu-ment from evil in both deductive and inductive forms. The result is a disturbing dialectical parity that forebodes a pessimistic agnosticism, given the assumption that rational belief requires good argument.

In the third section of the book Plantinga turns to the philosophical chestnut known as "the problem of other minds": the question of how we can know or rationally believe that others have conscious lives similar to our own. Plantinga examines the most common and, he argues, most promising argument for the rationality of belief in other minds, the argument from analogy. This argument, like all the theistic and atheistic arguments examined previously, is flawed and therefore fails to compel rational assent to its conclusion. In fact, Plantinga shows that the logical failing of the argument from analogy is identical to the logical failing he found in the teleological argument.

This intriguing discovery leads Plantinga to a careful examination of the nature of rational belief and its relationship to philosophical argument, resulting in the conclusion that demonstrative proof is seldom, if ever, a requirement for ration-ality. We certainly do not consider ourselves irrational in believing that there are other minds, even when shown that there is no compelling philosophical argument for the conclusion. But then why should we think such a failing renders our theistic belief irrational? The closing words of *God and Other Minds*, although provisional, nonetheless portend a revolution in the philosophical defence of theism:

> Of course there may be other reasons for supposing that although rational belief in other minds does not require an answer to the epistemological question [i.e. why do you believe; what good reasons do you have for your belief?], rational belief in the existence of God does. But it is certainly hard to see what these reasons might be. Hence my tentative conclusion: if my belief in other minds is rational, so is my belief in God. But obviously the former is rational; so, therefore, is the latter. (1967: 271)

It is important to note that there are two different ways of interpreting Plantinga's conclusion, depending on one's interpretation of the argumentative failure he has exposed. One the one hand, we might opt for what could be called the 'weak rationality thesis' (WRT):

WRT: It is possible for one to be rational in holding theistic belief even though one is aware of no rationally compelling or demonstrative argument for such belief.

Here 'rationally compelling or demonstrative' connotes that anyone fully appreciative of the argument must respond with theistic belief on pain of irrationality. This is a weak interpretation because it is consistent with rational theistic belief under two different scenarios: (i) one having theistic argument that is convincing to her, but that she understands would not necessarily be convincing to everyone; and (ii) one having no awareness of any theistic argument that is convincing to her or to anyone else. The *strong* rationality thesis (SRT), however, excludes the first of these scenarios and allows only the latter.

SRT: It is possible for one to be rational in holding theistic belief even though one is aware of no convincing theistic argument at all.

These two interpretations both play into the development of Plantinga's thought. In the modal stage Plantinga presents a version of the ontological argument that he understands to fill the bill of WRT: an argument that may well serve to support rational belief in some although it cannot be considered compelling or demonstrative, and will be unconvincing to many. In the reformed epistemology stage, Plantinga explores the implications of SRT, offering a full-blown theory of rational theistic belief *sans* argument at all, compelling or otherwise.

Although early and preliminary, the rational theism stage of Plantinga's career is already teeming with the methodological nuances that would help to transform and revitalize philosophy of religion in the coming years. His defence of rational theism in *God and Other Minds* is indirect in that he concentrates on showing the lack of formidable charge against theism; there is no decisive argument against it nor any defensible reason to reject if for lack of positive argument. It is descriptive in that it turns on the undeniable claim that belief in other minds is considered patently rational, and that any attempt to deny such would be unacceptably revisionary, leading to a pervasive scepticism that belies the analytical project. It is modest in that Plantinga nowhere charges the atheist with irrationality or claims that theism must be accepted by all on pain of irrationality. And it is mature in that the criticisms of classic arguments in all three parts of the book utilize state-of-the-art concepts and tools in logic, metaphysics and epistemology.

THE MODAL STAGE: MODERN LOGIC AND TRADITIONAL THEISM

The Nature of Necessity (1974b) is considered by many to be Plantinga's finest work. It is not a study in philosophy of religion but rather the construction of a full-scale theory of modality – of the concepts of necessity, possibility and contingency. The book is considered foundational to the discipline of modal metaphysics, along with the works of David Lewis, Saul Kripke, and Ruth Marcus. Plantinga is a modal realist, arguing for the existence of possible worlds as maximally consistent states of affairs, an analysis that proves less problematic than the more tempting inclination to think of them as sets or propositions and more intuitively pleasing than Lewis' controversial reification thesis. He is also an actualist, holding that entities bear properties only in worlds in which they exist. These and other features of his work lead to a semantics and logical structure that many consider the most workable in the field. In the last two chapters of his book Plantinga applies his modal framework to two subjects in the philosophy of religion that had already occupied a great deal of his attention in previous work: the ontological argument and the free will defence against the argument from evil.[3]

The modal ontological argument

In chapter ten of *The Nature of Necessity*, Plantinga presents a version of the ontological argument examined in the previous decade by Norman Malcolm

---

3. These two subjects are also treated, along with other issues in philosophy of religion, in Plantinga (1974a): treatments reprinted as chapters two and three in Plantinga (1998). While these discussions lack the sophisticated logical framework of the versions in *The Nature of Necessity*, they are nonetheless technical and detailed enough to gainsay the label 'popular' often affixed to them.

(1960) and Charles Hartshorne (1962): a modal version, in chapter 3 of Anselm's *Proslogion*, one chapter over from the saint's more popular offering. Here Anselm (*see* Vol. 2, Ch. 6) concentrates on the *necessity* of God's unsurpassable greatness, rather than on its purported facticity. Plantinga had examined and dismissed Malcolm's version of this argument (albeit reluctantly) in *God and Other Minds*. In *The Nature of Necessity* he revisits his criticism and presents a way to repair it, resulting in what he claims to be a sound version of the argument.

Defining *maximal excellence* as the property of bearing maximal degrees of all great making properties and *unsurpassable greatness* as the property of bearing maximal excellence in all possible worlds, Plantinga offers:

(P1) "There is a possible world in which unsurpassable greatness is exemplified."

(P2) "The proposition *a thing has unsurpassable greatness if and only if it has maximal excellence in every possible world* is necessarily true."

(P3) "The proposition *whatever has maximal excellence is omnipotent, omniscient, and morally perfect* is necessarily true."

Therefore,

(C1) "*Possesses unsurpassable greatness* is instantiated in every world."

Therefore,

(C2) "There actually exists a being who is omnipotent, omniscient, and morally perfect, and has these properties in every world." (Plantinga 1974b: 216)[4]

Given the actualist thesis, that entities bear properties only in worlds in which they exist, this argument is valid in S5 modal logic. (P2) and (P3) are true by stipulated definition.

So all of the dialectical attention is focused on the truth-value of (P1). And here Plantinga exercises his modest approach to philosophy of religion, stating simply, "The only question of interest, it seems to me, is whether its main premise ... is *true*. I think this premise is indeed true. Accordingly, I think this version of the Ontological Argument is sound" (*ibid.*: 216–17). In response to the charge that the argument is question-begging, he asserts:

> It is by no means obvious that anyone who accepts its main premise does so only because he infers it from the conclusion. If anyone *did* do

---

4. Plantinga numbers (P1), (P2), (P3) and (C1) as (42)–(45), respectively. He does not number (C2), but it is a quotation taken from his text.

that, then for him the argument is dialectically deficient …; but surely [it] need not be thus dialectically deficient for one who accepts it.

(Ibid.: 218)

In other words, Plantinga is not claiming to have *proved* the existence of God in any strong or compelling way. But he does claim to have constructed an argument that passes WRT muster: it is possible that one be rational in believing that the theistic God exists based on one's epistemically virtuous acceptance of this argument. There may be many who remain rationally unconvinced of (P1) or who see its only possible defence to be a question-begging one, and for them the argument could never rationally ground theism. But this does nothing to confute Plantinga's claim.[5]

The modal free will defence

In chapter nine of *The Nature of Necessity,* Plantinga offers a modal version of the free will defence (FWD) against the logical argument from evil. The logical argument is so-called because it alleges that the concepts of God and evil are logically exclusive – in modal terms: necessarily, if one exists the other does not; they cannot both exist in the same possible world. Since we know that there is evil, we can be certain that God does not exist. The FWD argues that the concepts are compatible, and could both be actualized in a world with free moral beings. The responsibility for evil in such a world would rest with the free beings who cause it; furthermore, God is justified in creating them because the good of human freedom outweighs any evil such beings may cause.

John Mackie (1955) offers a formidable rebuttal to the FWD. He points out that the logic of freedom entails that there is some possible world in which all free beings always behave properly.[6] Mackie then argues that God is responsible for the evil that free beings cause because he could have created such a world. God was not limited to the creation of worlds in which free beings caused evil.

Plantinga's FWD is a modal refutation of Mackie's argument, grounded in a concept he calls 'transworld depravity' (TD). TD lends modal credence to the driving intuition behind the FWD: that whether or not a free being chooses to do evil is finally and solely up to that free being, not to God. More precisely, for God to create a world with free beings and no evil, he requires the cooperation of all

5. In Sennett (1989; 1992: 24–8), I argue that Plantinga's argument is question-begging in an unavoidable way; namely, that one can *understand* the proposition asserted by (P1) only if one already understands it to entail (C2). However, I have been forced to rethink my position owing to recent work by Ruloff (2004).

6. Throughout this discussion a libertarian view of freedom is assumed: that free actions are not determined. While Mackie confesses commitment to a compatibilist view of freedom, his argument does not require it.

free beings in that world. Divine omnipotence does not entail such cooperation. The logic of freedom dictates that it is possible that a given free being would not offer such cooperation regardless of what God does. Such a free being suffers from TD. Whether or not a being suffers from TD is a contingent matter: true in some worlds and false in others. Therefore, it is a contingent matter whether or not *every possible free being* suffers from TD.[7] Hence, there is at least one possible world in which they all do. In such a world there will be evil no matter what God does. Hence, God and evil coexist in a world in which every possible free being suffers from TD. Hence, it is possible that God and evil coexist. So the FWD is successful and the logical argument fails.

When endorsing his FWD, Plantinga displays none of the philosophical modesty heretofore noted. Instead he states categorically, "I therefore conclude that the Free Will Defense successfully rebuts the charge of inconsistency brought against the theist. If evil is a problem for the believer, it is not that the existence of evil … is inconsistent with the existence of God" (1974b: 193). Plantinga considers his argument decisive, and it is not coincidental that, since the 1970s, the attention in philosophy of religion has shifted dramatically away from the logical argument from evil to the *inductive* argument from evil.[8]

Although it does not display his characteristic modesty, Plantinga's FWD does exemplify the mature approach to philosophy of religion, perhaps more vividly than any other aspect of his corpus. Indeed, the logical intricacies of TD and the other concepts involved are so complex that virtually every critic who has argued that the defence fails has been shown actually to have misunderstood it in some crucial way. And, when the misunderstanding is corrected, the criticism dissolves.[9]

THE REFORMED EPISTEMOLOGY STAGE:
NATURALIZED EPISTEMOLOGY AND SUPERNATURAL BELIEF

Above, I noted that Plantinga's rejection of the objection that theistic belief requires good argument to be rational could be interpreted in either a weak or

---

7. Given Plantinga's actualism, this statement is inaccurate. Possible but unactual beings bear no properties at all. Plantinga couches his discussion in terms of *essences*, the sets of essential properties of any free being. As abstract objects, essences exist necessarily, even in worlds where they are not exemplified in beings. I sacrifice technical accuracy for simplicity.
8. Also called the *probabilistic, empirical*, and *evidential* argument (from evil) in the literature. This argument presupposes that God and evil are compatible, and instead charges that the extent and intensity of evil in the world count as strong inductive evidence against the existence of God. See Plantinga (1979, 1988) for his criticisms of this version of the argument.
9. See Sennett (1992: 60–61) for a clarification of several vital points that have been misunderstood by critics, and an exposition of how Mackie in particular got it wrong (Mackie 1982: 174).

a strong sense (WRT and SRT). The modal ontological argument serves as a fine example of a WRT defence of theism. In the early 1980s Plantinga began a long and extensive programme of SRT defence, which he labelled 'reformed epistemology' (RE) since it advocates a view reflective of Calvinist theology.[10]

RE challenges evidentialism: the view that rational theistic belief must be based on propositional evidence.[11] Foundationalist epistemology distinguishes between beliefs that are based on other beliefs and those that are based on some non-doxastic phenomenon, such as rational intuition or perceptual experience. Such beliefs are *properly basic*. Evidentialism amounts to the claim that theistic belief cannot be properly basic.[12] RE argues contrariwise and offers an account of what rational theistic belief *sans* argument might look like.

The early defence of reformed epistemology

In "Reason and Belief in God" (Plantinga 1983), the foundational document of the RE programme, Plantinga argues that evidentialism is historically grounded in an epistemological theory he calls 'classical foundationalism' (CF):

CF: "A proposition p is properly basic for a person S if and only if p is either self-evident to S or incorrigible for S or evident to the senses for S" (1983: 59).

Self-evident beliefs include any beliefs whose truth is clear beyond doubt without reflection, such as simple truths of logic and arithmetic. Incorrigible beliefs are those that, if believed, must be true. Paradigm cases include beliefs about one's own psychological states, such as *I feel hungry*. Beliefs evident to the senses are those presented so vividly by the senses as to make questioning them ludicrous. Obviously theistic belief does not fall under any of these categories; thus, if CF is true, so is evidentialism.

Plantinga offers two arguments that CF is false. First, it is too strong. Many ordinary beliefs (e.g. those about the past, the future, other minds, personal identity, etc.) are not of the kinds endorsed by CF, nor derivable from such. Hence, if CF is true, then such beliefs are categorically irrational. However, since I am

---

10. Plantinga developed the early stages of the RE programme with his good friend and (then) colleague at Calvin College, Nicholas Wolterstorff.

11. That is, a person S is rational in believing theistic proposition p just in case there is some other (possibly conjunctive) proposition q such that (i) S rationally believes that q; (ii) q provides S with good evidence for p; and (iii) S believes that p on the basis of q.

12. Thus evidentialism is merely a view on the epistemology of theistic belief, not an attack on its rationality. Many theists are evidentialists. In fact, Plantinga traces the doctrine to John Locke (among others), and some of the most ardent critics of RE have been other theistic philosophers.

clearly rational in my belief about, say, where I was thirty seconds ago, CF must be false. This argument is an expansion and deepening of the *God and Other Minds* argument, and reflects both the modest and indirect approaches seen there. But it is the second argument that Plantinga sees to be decisive. CF itself is neither self-evident, or incorrigible, nor evident to the senses, nor is there any good argument for it from such beliefs. Hence, either CF is false or it cannot be rationally believed. It is *self-referentially incoherent*: irrational by the very criterion it establishes.

In "Reason and Belief in God", Plantinga offers little more than this refutation of CF by way of argument for RE. Since CF is false, there is no reason to assume evidentialism true, hence no reason to deny RE. So the argument is indirect in the sense that has become familiar to us: RE is vindicated by lack of reason to reject it.

Plantinga responds to two obvious objections to RE: the Great Pumpkin objection and the grounding objection. The first of these is a *reductio ad absurdum*, claiming that if theistic belief can be properly basic, any belief at all could be, including Linus' belief in the Great Pumpkin in Charles Shultz's classic comic strip *Peanuts*. Plantinga responds that RE is simply and solely about theistic belief, and has no implications whatsoever about any other kinds of beliefs. Each candidate for proper basicality must be judged on its own merits. The grounding objection charges that theistic belief without argument has no such merits: that it is groundless, based on nothing. Plantinga responds that the obvious cases of proper basicality (those named in CF, other minds' belief, etc.) are grounded in some sort of experience; hence, if theistic belief is properly basic, it too is grounded in experience. As such it is no more groundless than perceptual belief or beliefs about our current psychological states.

This early stage of RE defence is clearly driven by Plantinga's indirect approach. The arguments of "Reason and Belief in God" and its surrounding corpus are exercises in dodging objections with precious little in the way of positive argument. Nor is Plantinga simply being coy or evasive. A major purpose of his throughout this period is to clear out traditional but flawed prejudices against the idea of rational theism. Plantinga's driving question is: why *shouldn't* we consider theistic belief properly basic? And his verdict is that there is no defensible answer to that question. Of course, this project is also a modest one. Plantinga is not claiming that theistic belief is properly basic for all who hold it, much less that everyone should hold properly basic theistic belief. Rather, the clearest message of the early RE project is that there is philosophical room for the idea that some theists hold some of their theistic beliefs in a properly basic way: a triply modest thesis.

Reformed epistemology and proper function

In the latter stage of the RE project Plantinga moves away from concern over theistic belief to concern over specifically Christian belief, and away from concerns about rationality to concerns about knowledge. The switch began when

Plantinga raised the question: what would it take for basic theistic belief, if it is indeed true, to count as knowledge? This led naturally to the more general question of what epistemologists sometimes call 'the conversion property': that property, whatever its nature, that converts true belief into knowledge. In his early RE forays, Plantinga became convinced that rationality or justification (understood in the internalist, Cartesian sense recently championed by Roderick Chisholm and others) has little or nothing to do with knowledge. He turned his attention instead to externalist concerns, represented most notably by Alvin Goldman.[13]

Plantinga coins the term 'warrant' to refer to the conversion property, then argues that the most promising attempts to account for warrant fail (1993a). He then presents his own theory, dubbed 'proper function', which states (roughly) that a belief has warrant if and only if it is produced by properly functioning epistemic faculties operating in an environment conducive to their proper function. While some faculties function properly by processing beliefs to generate new beliefs (e.g. faculties of reason or induction), many other faculties function immediately to produce beliefs directly from experience. When such faculties are functioning properly in a proper environment, the beliefs they produce are warranted and, if true, constitute knowledge. So my belief about what I had for breakfast, produced immediately on my memorial reflection by my cognitively unimpaired memorial faculty, is warranted and basically so.

It is this concept of properly functioning epistemic faculties that becomes the locus of Plantinga's latter defence of RE. In *Warranted Christian Belief* (2000) he develops the 'Aquinas/Calvin model', arguing that properly functioning human beings in receipt of divine grace have a cognitive faculty or mechanism – Calvin's *sensus divinitatis* – that produces immediate and fully warranted Christian beliefs under appropriate conditions. In other words, this faculty produces warranted beliefs in the same way that perceptual and memorial faculties do. They are properly basic – warranted without propositional support. Plantinga's conclusion is that if the fundamental doctrines of Christianity are true, then Christian belief is typically warranted in a basic way and constitutes knowledge. Whether or not they are true is, of course, the concern of the metaphysics of religion, not its epistemology.

In the introduction to *Warranted Christian Belief*, Plantinga distinguishes between two different objections to Christianity (and theism in general): the *de facto* objection that its central claims are simply false, and the *de jure* objection that the question of their truth is irrelevant since they have no warrant – even if they are true, no one can ever know that they are. We might think of these as metaphysical and epistemological objections, respectively, and it is natural to assume that they are philosophically independent issues. It is, after all, quite possible for

---

13. While Plantinga acknowledges a conceptual debt to Goldman, he believes Goldman's reliabilist programme ultimately fails. See Plantinga (1993b).

something to be true even though no one can ever know that it is true. However, the Aquinas/Calvin model entails that the question of Christian belief's warrant cannot be divorced from the question of its truth. If Christianity is true (as the Christian believes it is), then the Christian's beliefs constitute (or can constitute) knowledge.

CONCLUSION

The philosophical approaches explicated throughout this chapter must be kept in focus as one works to master Plantinga's thinking. To lose sight of them is to invite misunderstanding and confusion. This is especially true of the modest approach and the mature approach. It is a common mistake for critics and proponents alike to read Plantinga's claims as broader or deeper than he intends. He is primarily concerned with carving out epistemically acceptable room for theistic belief, not forcing its undeniability down the throats of unbelievers. His aims are not by any means timid, but they are, for the most part, limited and carefully articulated.

On the other hand, the philosophical sophistication of Plantinga's work must not be underestimated. Plantinga is one of the most meticulous and careful philosophers of his generation. He leaves no dialectical stone unturned. Consequently, any perceived weakness in his work more often indicates failure of scrutiny on the part of the exegete; a more careful reading often reveals Plantinga's anticipation of, and response to, the perceived difficulty. Plantinga's methodology is quintessentially analytical, and any approach to it that is anything less will invite misinterpretation and rob one of challenging contemplation and rewarding insight.

FURTHER READING

Baker, D. (ed.) 2007. *Alvin Plantinga*. Cambridge: Cambridge University Press.
Beilby, J. (ed.) 2005. *Epistemology as Theology: An Evaluation of Alvin Plantinga's Religious Epistemology*. Aldershot: Ashgate.
Crisp, T., M. Davidson & D. Vander Laan (eds) 2006. *Knowledge and Reality: Essays in Honor of Alvin Plantinga on his 70th Birthday*. Dordrecht: Springer.
Hoitenga Jr., D. 1992. *Faith and Reason from Plato to Plantinga: An Introduction to Reformed Epistemology*. Albany, NY: SUNY Press.
Kvanvig, J. (ed.) 1996. *Warrant in Contemporary Epistemology: Essays in Honor of Plantinga's Theory of Knowledge*. Lanham, MD: Rowman & Littlefield.
McLeod, M. 1993. *Rationality and Theistic Belief: An Essay on Reformed Epistemology*. Ithaca, NY: Cornell University Press.
Sennett, J. 1992. *Modality, Probability, and Rationality: A Critical Examination of Alvin Plantinga's Philosophy*. New York: Peter Lang.
Sennett, J. 1998. "The Analytic Theist: An Appreciation". In *The Analytic Theist: An Alvin Plantinga Reader*, J. Sennett (ed.), xi–xviii. Grand Rapids, MI: Eerdmans.

Sennett, J. 2003. "Reformed Epistemology and the Rationality of Theistic Belief". In *God Matters*, R. Martin & C. Barnard (eds), 219–31. New York: Longman.

Tomberlin, J. & P. van Inwagen (eds) 1985. *Alvin Plantinga*. Dordrecht: Reidel.

On EPISTEMOLOGY see also Vol. 3, Ch. 18. On FREE WILL see also Vol. 1, Ch. 18; Vol. 2, Chs 2, 7, 9, 19; Vol. 3, Chs 9, 15. On ONTOLOGICAL ARGUMENT see also Ch. 5; Vol. 2, Ch. 6. On EVIL/ PROBLEM OF EVIL see also Chs 19, 23; Vol. 1, Chs 18, 19; Vol. 2, Ch. 16; Vol. 3, Chs 13, 18, 19; Vol. 4, Chs 12, 18. On RATIONALISM see also Vol. 3, Chs 18, 20, 22.

23

RICHARD SWINBURNE

Bruce Langtry

Richard Swinburne (*b.* 1934) retired from his position as Nolloth Professor of the Philosophy of the Christian Religion at the University of Oxford in 2002. He is perhaps the foremost philosopher of religion of the past hundred years. In addition, he has contributed to the philosophy of space and time, confirmation theory, general metaphysics and epistemology, and the philosophy of mind. His work in these areas has frequently been generated and applied in the course of his reasoning about God and religious faith. For example, the first half of *The Christian God* consists of general essays on substance, thisness, causation, time and necessity. Swinburne himself is a Christian.

BARE NATURAL THEOLOGY: THE CONTENT OF THEISM

Swinburne assumes that statements about God have substantial, controversial metaphysical implications: as found in the writings of such authors as Augustine, Aquinas, Descartes, Locke and Leibniz (*see* Vol. 1, Ch. 18; Vol. 2, Ch. 13; Vol. 3, Chs 8, 12, 13), as well as the speech of most non-philosophical believers, they are not to be interpreted as attempts at fiction or myth, or as consisting entirely in disguised expressions of one's values. This assumption is, obviously, consistent with recognizing that many statements about God are best interpreted as involving analogical predication or metaphor.

Natural theology consists in the discussion of God's existence and nature, conducted without appeal to the authority of revelation; it includes contributions by agnostics and atheists as well as by theists. Swinburne distinguishes between *bare natural theology* and *ramified natural theology*. The former argues for or against *bare theism*, the doctrine that God exists. Swinburne identifies God as the omnipotent, omniscient, perfectly good and perfectly free creator of the universe. He does not deal with conceptions of God held by Neoplatonists and process theologians. He carefully explains God's attributes in ways intended to show the coherence of bare theism, and he argues that there are significant necessary connections between the attributes. Ramified natural theology investigates more specific religious doctrines (Swinburne 2005: 117).

Here I shall highlight two attributes of God that Swinburne understands differently from many theists: perfect freedom and necessity. In various different places (Swinburne 1993: 148, 152; 1994: 68, 128; 2004: 7, 98, 104), Swinburne explains God's perfect freedom by saying:

- nothing, not even God's own past states, in any way causally influences God to do what he does;
- what counts is God's being subject to no *non-rational* influences;
- God's perfect freedom consists in his being subject to no causal influences *that he does not himself control*;
- God's freedom of choice operates only for cases in which he does not have overriding reasons to performing one action rather than any of the alternatives.

Swinburne holds that the existence of God is not logically necessary. Is God nevertheless in some other way a necessary being? His most recent answer (2004: 96) is that God's existence is 'factually necessary', by which he means that God's nature guarantees that if he exists at any time then he exists at all times, and the state of affairs *God's existing at some time or other* does not depend on any other state of affairs.[1]

BARE NATURAL THEOLOGY: DOES GOD EXIST?

Probability and explanation

In this chapter 'probability' means the *inductive probability* of one proposition relative to another: the extent to which the former, if it were true, would give reason for believing the latter.[2] Now, we often say that the extent to which p gives a good reason for believing q is a contingent matter, dependent on the truth of some other proposition r. What Swinburne has in mind by inductive probability, however, is a relationship solely between the two propositions; if r seems relevant to our enquiries into q, then we should consider the probability of q relative to the compound proposition, p & r. In many cases, the inductive probability of q relative to p can be given a numerical value in the range from 0 to 1, but in many cases all that can be said is (say) that the probability is high, or higher than that of some

---

1. For earlier accounts, see Swinburne (1993: 274ff., 277; 1994: 144–9, 179).
2. Swinburne distinguishes between inductive probability, physical probability and statistical probability.

other proposition *s* relative to *p*. The inductive probability of *q* relative to *p* in cases where *p* is a tautology is called the *intrinsic probability* of *q*. Swinburne maintains that all propositions have intrinsic probabilities.

Since the inductive probability of *q* relative to *p* does not depend on the truth of any other proposition, how high or low it is is a logically necessary, *a priori* matter (whether or not we human beings have access to its value using *a priori* reasoning). Accordingly, Swinburne identifies inductive probability with *logical probability*, understood as the measure of inductive support that would be accorded by a 'logically omniscient' person: one who is omniscient about logical necessities and logical possibilities, and has correct criteria of when *p* gives a good reason for believing *q*.

What inductive criteria should we use? Swinburne in effect appeals to what is actually considered best practice in contemporary science and history, and in informal reasoning about everyday matters. His account centres on forming explanatory hypotheses. Other things being equal, a hypothesis that provides a good explanation of some body of evidence is probable relative to that evidence.[3]

Swinburne distinguishes two different basic patterns of explanation: inanimate and personal. Inanimate explanation proceeds in terms of initial conditions (one of which is frequently designated 'the cause' and the other the conditions under which the cause operated) and the laws of nature. In personal explanation, it is persons who are the causes, and they cause in virtue of their powers, beliefs and purposes. Swinburne argues that personal explanation is unanalysable in terms of inanimate explanation (2004: ch. 2, esp. 38–44).

In practice it is impossible to assess the probability of a hypothesis relative to the conjunction of all the things we know and (and can use without circularity). What typically happens instead is that we identify various arguments for and against the hypothesis, and we then try to weigh these different arguments to reach an overall verdict. In assessing the bearing of some body of truths on the hypothesis, it is often useful to distinguish two components of the body of truths: the specific considerations described as 'the data' (such as the results of some recent experiment), and the 'background evidence' (such as the results of previous experiments). Swinburne discusses five criteria that determine the extent to which an explanatory hypothesis is probable relative to some body of truths:

- Does the hypothesis yield the data? That is, is the data highly probable relative to the conjunction of the hypothesis and the background evidence? (This question concerns what is called the 'explanatory power' of the hypothesis.)
- How probable is the hypothesis relative to background evidence alone?
- How probable is the data relative to background evidence alone?

---

3. The converse is not true. *The fuel gauge says 'Empty'* may be highly probable relative to *The fuel tank is empty*, but the former does not explain the latter.

- How great is the scope of the hypothesis? That is, in conjunction with background evidence, how much does it say and imply about how things are? The greater the scope, the less the probability relative to any data (given this background evidence).
- How simple is the hypothesis? Other things being equal, the simpler it is, the more probable it is.

Simplicity in turn has several criteria. For scientific hypotheses, the criteria Swinburne lists include the number of entities the hypothesis postulates, the number of kinds of entity it postulates, the unity of the hypothesis and its mathematical simplicity. Swinburne acknowledges that some philosophers have quite different views about inductive criteria to his own, and that some philosophers deny that simplicity plays a fundamental role.[4]

The structure of Swinburne's cumulative approach

In *The Existence of God*, Swinburne's case for (bare) theism moves through many stages. He begins by considering bare theism's intrinsic probability, which is determined by merely the content of *God exists*. In each subsequent stage, he identifies additional considerations that raise the probability of theism higher than it was in the preceding stages. He finally reaches a point where he is able to claim that the probability of theism, relative to the conjunction of all the considerations so far identified, is greater than 0.5 (Swinburne 2004: 341–2).

Plainly 'more than 0.5' is not enough to justify believing that theism is true: agnosticism leaning slightly towards theism might be the most reasonable stance. In *The Resurrection of God Incarnate*, however, Swinburne argues that theism is highly probable relative to the conjunction of the foregoing considerations with the detailed historical evidence concerning Jesus.

In the first stage of his cumulative case, Swinburne argues that the intrinsic probability of theism is a lot higher than the intrinsic probabilities of rival hypotheses about what, if anything, caused there to be physical things or physical events.[5] *Physical things or physical events were caused by an omnipotent intelligent agent* is simpler than *They were caused by a single intelligent agent possessing such-and-such finite powers* because a finite limitation calls for explanation of why there is just

---

4. The foregoing paragraphs have been based on the exposition in Swinburne (2001: chs 3 and 4).
5. Swinburne himself holds a ramified version of theism, according to which God is a Trinity. He argues, however, that *God exists* entails *There are at least three divine beings*. If so, then the intrinsic probability of the latter is not less than the intrinsic probability of the former. See Swinburne (1994: ch. 8; 2004: 342–5).

that particular limit, in a way that limitlessness does not (*ibid.*: 97).[6] Furthermore, God's attributes are tightly linked; for example, Swinburne argues that it is necessary that an omnipotent, omniscient and perfectly free being also be perfectly good. The comparative internal simplicity of theism makes it a better stopping-point for explanation than rival proposed stopping-points: a better point at which to say, 'That is just the way things are'. The foregoing remarks are important at later stages of Swinburne's case.

Consider now the probability of various hypotheses purporting to explain *why there exists a complex physical universe*. Theism has the initial advantage over its rivals of higher intrinsic probability. It also possesses superior explanatory power. God's perfect goodness gives God a reason to create a complex physical universe, and his omnipotence guarantees that he can do so, whereas rivals, such as *The complex physical universe was created by a committee of finite spiritual beings*, need to postulate additional special propensities of these beings to create such a universe.

How about *scientific* explanations of the existence of a complex physical universe? The states appealed to in a scientific explanation will themselves be complex. Consider, for example, a causal account in terms of a big bang: at this stage, the occurrence of a big bang is not a part of our background evidence, but maybe it is a good explanatory hypothesis. For a big bang to do its explanatory job, however, it must be complex: for example, it must be supposed to be of a kind such that there would not be an immediate re-collapse but rather the emergence of an enduring, complex universe.

It is often protested that explanations in terms of God should be ruled out because a good hypothesis should make falsifiable predictions, but this criticism rests on some very doubtful assumptions (which there is no space to discuss here).

Swinburne concludes that, relative to *There exists a complex physical universe*, theism is more probable than it is relative to merely *There are physical things or events*, and is more probable than any rival explanatory hypothesis. Similarly, Swinburne argues that relative to the slightly more specific proposition *There exists a complex physical universe that conforms to simple, formulable scientific laws*, theism is more probable than it is relative to merely *There exists a complex physical universe*, and is more probable than any rival explanatory hypothesis. For here, too, theism has genuine explanatory value and is very simple.

The foregoing pattern is repeated many times. Swinburne pleads the theoretical virtues of bare theism with respect to the following truths:

---

6. Swinburne thinks that scientists would agree with him that *The universe is infinitely large* is simpler than *The universe is 1023 km in diameter* and *The universe is more than 105 km in diameter*, even though there are good reasons for holding that the universe is in fact not infinitely large.

- there exists a complex physical universe governed by simple scientific laws;
- the universe is 'fine tuned' for the existence (at some time and place or other) of bodies suited for the acquisition of true beliefs about the environment, and for the formation of aims and intentions in the light of desires;[7]
- such bodies give rise to the conscious life typical of human beings;
- human beings have moral awareness;
- there are opportunities for free agents to make choices that make important differences to themselves, each other and the physical world; and
- there occur experiences that seem (epistemically) to the subjects to be experiences of God or of some other supernatural thing.

By the time we have reached the second of these truths, we are counting as part of background evidence many statements accepted by contemporary physicists as uncontroversial. Going beyond these statements to postulate the activity of God is attractive because doing so has genuine explanatory value and involves an onto-logically economical, very simple hypothesis.

Objections to the existence of God, based on evil

Swinburne claims not only that moral and natural evil does not disconfirm theism but also that, speaking broadly, moral and natural evil *confirm* theism. He argues as follows:

- It is good that there exist finite agents who have free (and therefore undeter-mined) choices in morally important matters, and that they have a great degree of responsibility for each other's well-being. Therefore God, if he exists, has good (although not decisive) reasons for bringing free agents into existence and permitting them to make and implement many morally wrong choices, including choices to harm other people, or to abstain from preventing their being harmed, through negligence or malice.
- Hence it is not surprising, given that God exists, that there are large-scale moral evils such as war: for they are typically the result of a great many morally wrong actions and omissions by a great many individuals, for example wrong actions and omissions that facilitated the rise and ongoing dominance of a tyrant. Death limits the extent of any individual's suffering, and opens up the possibility of especially weighty courage and self-sacrifice as well as especially serious wrongdoing.
- It is not surprising, given that God exists, that there are natural evils such as floods and earthquakes. It is very good that free creatures learn by rational

---

7. The words 'fine tuned' as used in this context do not have built in to their very meaning the implication that there is a person who is engaged in fine tuning.

enquiry, and by responding rationally to evidence they encounter. Natural evils greatly extend the scope for causally and morally important free decisions, by providing people with the responsibility and opportunity to acquire knowledge needed to make such decisions – for example, decisions on where to build towns, and what disaster-relief organizations to set up. There is a second reason why God might permit not only human beings but also the 'higher' animals such as bears and deer to inhabit hazardous environments. Doing so makes possible various goods for them, such as courage, sympathetic concern for other animals, intentional action to avoid danger or rescue offspring from danger and so on.

- It is not surprising, given that God exists, that both human beings, and also animals lacking free will and moral awareness, experience pain, which is biologically useful given that they inhabit hazardous environments. A mere absence of the good would not serve. Any alternative to pain that might be biologically useful as a warning and deterrent would be an evil, because it would have to be strongly disliked.
- It is good, given that a person's loved ones have come to harm, that he or she be distressed rather than respond to such events calmly.

It is often objected that (i) there are particular occurrences of evil such that neither they nor any other particular state of affairs at least as bad are logically necessary for some outweighing good, and (ii) even if this is not so, God might have produced a lot less evil than we actually find while still securing or making possible the good states of affairs described above. In both ways, there is too much evil, and (iii) God has no right to cause or allow some people (notably, children) to undergo great suffering and deprivation so that others may benefit.

Swinburne responds to these objections, first, by maintaining that theism is not committed to the falsity of (i). Instead, the relevant requirement is that for each particular occurrence of evil, God's allowing it (or some state at least as bad) is the only morally permissible way in which God can bring about a logically necessary condition of some outweighing good. He adds that the correct requirement is in fact fulfilled. Of course, it is impracticable to show this by working through every difficult particular occurrence one by one; instead, one must make the claim plausible by generalizations about typical kinds of evil.[8] Secondly, he recommends that we try some thought experiments to test how highly we value various goods that play vital roles in his theodicy. Thirdly, he repeats the point that if God ensured that there was much less evil (relative to population size) than there actually is then the result would be a 'toy world', one in which human choices mattered much less than they actually do.

---

8. Swinburne points out that the correct requirement is compatible with there being no goods that individually require God's allowing some particular bad state, while all the good states together require God's allowing all the bad states together.

Does God have the *right* to allow some people to undergo serious suffering and harm, for the sake of making possible various goods accruing largely to other people? Swinburne appeals to analogies with human parents and their dependent children. In virtue of having brought us into existence, and having given us many good things, and continuing to sustain our lives from moment to moment, God has extensive rights (and also extensive duties) with respect to us. A parent has the right to cause or allow his or her child to suffer somewhat to benefit others. But there are limits on such rights. God must give people a life that is, on balance, good. Since plainly there are many people whose lives between birth and death are not on balance good, it follows that these people must be given a life after death that is sufficiently good that their total period of existence meets the requirement.

Swinburne concedes that this last affirmation makes his resulting theory more complicated than bare theism, and therefore less epistemically probable. In the light of this, he concedes that known truths about evil decrease the probability of his theistic position. But, he argues, it does not do so very much, since, quite apart from considerations with respect to evil, God would have reasons for providing a good life after death for many human beings, and so might well actually do so, because his doing so would be a good act.[9]

Swinburne sums up his overall case for the existence of God in chapter fourteen of *The Existence of God* (second edition). Consider the body of evidence that omits detailed historical information about Jesus but includes all other relevant information, *including all known truths about evil.* Relative to this body of evidence, Swinburne claims, bare theism is more probable than not.

RAMIFIED NATURAL THEOLOGY: EXPLICATING SOME CHRISTIAN DOCTRINES, AND THEIR PROBABILITY RELATIVE TO BARE THEISM

Swinburne aims to interpret some specifically Christian doctrines in such a way as to exhibit their internal coherence, and to argue that, relative to bare theism, there is a non-negligible probability that each of them is true. Obviously his own personal views would probably have been different if his life had not been heavily influenced by Christianity. Nevertheless what matters in this context is not the causal origins of his beliefs, but rather whether there are good arguments for his conclusions.

For reasons of space, it will be necessary to pass over Swinburne's treatments of many topics in Christian theology, including original sin, sanctification, heaven, hell, the authority and interpretation of the Bible, and the Church.

---

9. Swinburne's most recent discussion of evil is in Swinburne (2004: chs 10, 11); for his remarks about an afterlife see *ibid.*, 262, 264–6.

Atonement

Swinburne holds that whether or not they realize it, almost all human beings have wronged God, directly or indirectly, for example by being ungrateful to him, or by violating obligations that he has legitimately imposed on them as conditions attached to his gifts (including life itself). Grave wrongdoing against people in God's care constitutes grave wrongdoing against God. Human beings can wrong God even if they do not believe that he exists, just as sailors might believe that an island is uninhabited and nevertheless wrong the inhabitants by killing a goat they find there or by polluting a stream.

Swinburne supports his account of atonement in the divine–human case by appealing to widespread moral intuitions about human–human cases. In general, he says, when a person wrongs someone they must not, morally speaking, simply walk away from the resulting damaged moral status (guilt): they must deal with it by making atonement, and thereby either repair the current interpersonal relationship or remove a barrier to a possible future one. What this involves can vary, but in serious cases making atonement involves four components: repentance, apology, reparation and penance.

God could have deemed some minimal degree of repentance and apology to constitute adequate atonement for human wrongdoing against him, and he could have forgiven us on this basis. Nevertheless, it is good that God take our wrongdoing so seriously as to require something very substantial by way of atonement. Swinburne holds that God has reason to help us by providing some very valuable reparation to which we can join our repentance and apology and that we can offer to him to make an acceptable atonement. One appropriate way of doing this – Swinburne does not argue that it is God's only option[10] – would be to become incarnate, live a perfect life among us and allow himself to be killed, so that we have the opportunity to offer his perfect life to him as part of atonement.

Revelation

Suppose that God exists, and we have substantial duties towards him that we often violate, and God has provided opportunities for us to make atonement for our wrongdoing and to become members of the Church: a fellowship whose members are dedicated to helping each other and outsiders to lead lives that are truly worth living and to attain a very good afterlife. In that case, we urgently need to know that all these things are so. Without divine revelation hardly anyone would possess such information. Accordingly, Swinburne argues, God has good reasons to reveal it to us.

---

10. Swinburne sometimes seems to say that the only proper offering to God would be something not owed to God anyway, and that a perfect offering must consist in a perfect life of some rational agent, but he does not argue these things, and eventually veers away from committing himself to them (2003: 41–4).

A revelation might be expressed in statements that were philosophically rigorous and involved no presuppositions that were peculiar to any specific culture or range of cultures. But doing so would not remove all opportunities for misunderstanding by hearers influenced by the concerns and interests of their own culture. Even a revelation of this kind would need to be complemented by divine guidance as to how it can be properly interpreted. It is at least as likely that God would choose to give a revelation while expressing it (or allowing it to be expressed) in terms of one specific culture, possibly through many prophets and authors speaking and writing from many different standpoints over many generations and employing many different literary genres. If God proceeded in this way, then one would expect him also to provide some kind of help with interpretation.

How might we recognize a genuine revelation from among the many candidates? Its content – although not the presuppositions in terms of which it is cast – must be relevant, not evidently false, and accompanied by positive evidence in favour of its being genuine. The candidate divine revelation needs to be accompanied by some 'seal' or 'signature' that could have originated only from God and which (given the conventions of most cultures) either apparently occurred in answer to a prayer for or prediction of an authenticating sign or else manifestly made a major contribution to the promulgation of the candidate revelation. Very strong evidence would be provided by a prophet's predicting a miracle that subsequently occurred.[11]

The Trinity

There seem to be three main ways of understanding the orthodox doctrine of the Trinity:

1. The Father, the Son and the Holy Spirit are everlasting modes of God, who is a substance. Each of the three is a distinct person, a rational, conscious agent, but God is not. When people declare that God believes, intends and so on, what they say is a manner of speaking, made true by the believing, intending and so on of one or more of the three divine persons. God is the metaphysically basic entity that unifies the three, and whose nature generates the omnipotence, omniscience and perfect goodness possessed by the three rational, conscious agents, along with their beliefs, intentions and so on.
2. The Father, the Son and the Holy Spirit are not beings but modes of God who is the one and only divine rational, conscious agent.
3. The Father, the Son and the Holy Spirit are rational, conscious agents, and God is the collective entity they constitute. The Father, the Son and the Holy

---

11. Swinburne's account of the nature of miracles is explained in Swinburne (1971: ch. 1; 2004: 277–82).

Spirit are not modes but substances. The statement *Each of the three is God* should be understood as saying that each of them is omnipotent, omniscient and perfectly good. *There is only one God* should be understood as saying that the source of all other things is indivisible, in that its three members are, necessarily, completely dependent on each other for their existence, and are jointly behind each other's acts. God, the collective entity, can properly be described as having beliefs and intentions and as being omnipotent, omniscient and perfectly good, but only in a derivative sense.

Swinburne holds the third of these views, which he regards as a legitimate interpretation of the traditional doctrine, rather than a substitute for it. This third view is called *Social Trinitarianism*.

Swinburne argues not only that the Social Trinitarianism is coherent but also that the probability that the doctrine is true, given the truth of bare theism and of a certain metaphysical assumption about thisness – but independently of any considerations derived from revelation – is greater than (even if only slightly greater than) the probability of any rival account of the divine nature.[12]

The Incarnation

The classical account of the Incarnation contains four central affirmations:

- Jesus is one individual, who possessed a divine nature, before he was conceived by Mary.
- He acquired a human nature in the course of Mary's pregnancy, while still retaining his divine nature.
- In virtue of his divine nature, Jesus was, throughout his earthly career, essentially omnipotent, omniscient and perfectly good.
- He is identical with God the Son, the second person of the Trinity.

How can Jesus' supposed omnipotence and omniscience be reconciled with various New Testament passages that seem to imply that Jesus, during his earthly career, was weak, ignorant of various important things and subject to temptation? Swinburne provides an interpretation of the Incarnation doctrine in a way that affirms these implied truths rather than explaining them away as merely apparent.

He does so by claiming that the incarnate Jesus has a human body and a divided mind. In becoming incarnate, Jesus acquired a human 'belief system' in addition to his divine one. It is in the light of his human belief system that he entertained the

---

12. Swinburne (1994: 191). Swinburne has explained that a substance has thisness if and only if it is not individuated solely by its properties (*ibid*.: 34), where the word 'property' is being used in a very broad sense (*ibid*.: 10).

thoughts connected with his brain, interpreted the data obtained though his eyes and performed actions through his body. This body, if it were to be human, could not have had capacities radically different from those of other human bodies. So there are limits to the powers he acquired in virtue of acquiring a human body; for example, he could not run 100km in an hour. In becoming incarnate, Jesus retained his divine way of acting and forming beliefs, while acquiring in addition a human way of operating that involved limited, fallible cognitive, volitional and executive powers.

Thus the question 'Could Jesus, during his earthly career, turn water into wine?' requires a complicated answer. Plainly, his divine nature enabled him to decide to turn water into wine and to carry out that decision. But how did things stand from the viewpoint of his human nature? First, he could ask God the Father to turn water into wine for him, just as Moses could have. (People sometimes say that they are renovating their house when they have employed a builder to do the work for them.) Secondly, if Jesus, with his human cognitive system, was aware of his divine nature and knew how to engage his divine executive and cognitive powers, then he could do so and thereby be said, even from the standpoint of his human nature, to turn water into wine. If each of the foregoing two possibilities were unavailable, then Jesus could not, during his earthly career and from the standpoint of his human nature, turn water into wine.

Swinburne is aware of a major alternative theory of the Incarnation – the kenotic theory – according to which a divine individual can temporarily abandon omnipotence and omniscience, while remaining divine. He rejects this alternative.

He argues that God could become incarnate in a way that involved subjecting himself to temptation, but only to do a lesser good, not to do wrong.

What good reasons does God have for becoming incarnate as a human being? The first reason is to make available to human beings a means by which their broken relationship with God can be repaired. Secondly, God would judge it a good thing to identify with human beings and to share the suffering to which he subjects them for the sake of greater goods. The third reason is to provide information and encouragement to us with respect to how we should live, by showing us an actual example of a human life lived perfectly in very difficult circumstances; such a person is not likely to arise naturally.

Swinburne claims that the foregoing considerations together make it at least as probable as not that if God exists (and he brings human beings into existence, etc.) then he will become incarnate, and live a perfect human life among human beings. He claims also that these reasons together do not provide much by way of grounds for expecting more than one incarnation.

RAMIFIED NATURAL THEOLOGY: A CASE FOR
THE TRUTH OF CHRISTIANITY

Overview of the issues

In investigating whether Christianity is true, Swinburne argues, we need to answer the following questions:

1. What is the probability of *God exists* relative to the evidence considered in bare natural theology?
2. Can the central Christian doctrines be interpreted in such a way that each is internally coherent and morally non-defective?
3. Does God have good reasons to reveal key truths about himself to human beings and to provide human beings with some way of making atonement for their wrongdoing against him?
4. Does he have good reasons to become incarnate as a human being?
5. Does the alleged Christian revelation in general bear authenticating marks that God might be expected to provide, and do so to a greater extent than any rival religion?
6. What observable features would we expect a person's life to have, if it was to recognizably be the earthly life of God incarnate?
7. Is the detailed historical evidence we actually possess such that we would find this kind of evidence if Jesus in fact led the specified sort of life, and also rose from the dead?
8. Do epistemological considerations concerning miracles rule out the possibility of our concluding, on the basis of historical testimony, that a bodily resurrection had occurred?

Questions 1–4 have already been dealt with.

The alleged Christian revelation and other alleged revelations

Swinburne argues that there is only one serious candidate for being a religion whose doctrines are to be believed on the grounds that they have been revealed. Buddhism does not even purport to be such a religion. As I indicated earlier, Swinburne holds that to be recognizable as genuine revelation, a candidate must be accompanied by some sign that manifestly could have originated only from God. He argues that neither Hinduism nor Islam fulfils this requirement, and that Judaism does so to a far lesser extent than Christianity (Swinburne 1991: 95–7). So how credible is Christianity?

Was Jesus God incarnate? Did Jesus rise from the dead?

After partially dealing with question 5 via his detailed discussion of the content of Christian doctrine and related matters such as the status of the Bible, Swinburne turns to questions 6 and 7. For a human life to recognizably be the earthly life of God incarnate the following must be true:

- The person's public behaviour must be characteristic of a perfect human life, which includes helping others, and providing people with encouragement in their efforts to improve the human condition.
- The person must teach people verbally how to live in order that we may see how to apply his pattern of life to the circumstances of people whose age, sex, social class and culture differ from his own. This teaching should include information about how we are to interact with God, as well as information about the afterlife. It should be plausibly true and deep. The person must claim God's authority for that part of his teaching that human beings cannot discover for themselves.
- The person must show us that he believes himself to be God Incarnate, although he need not explicitly declare this.
- He must teach that his life and death provide a means of atonement, making God's forgiveness available for those who repent of their sins.
- He must found a 'Church' in which his teaching is to be handed on to people in new generations and cultures. Moreover, his Church must actually continue to grow and make his teaching available to new generations and cultures.
- The success of the person's life must be made possible only by an evident violation (or 'quasi-violation') of natural laws, which contemporaries can recognize as God's authenticating approval of the person's life.

Swinburne observes that, as a matter of historical fact, there is no serious known candidate other than Jesus for satisfying all, or even most, of these requirements.

In chapters four to nine of *The Resurrection of God Incarnate*, Swinburne surveys the historical evidence we have about Jesus, assesses its general historical reliability and offers detailed empirical arguments, based on this evidence, for the view that Jesus in fact fulfilled all of the conditions stated above.

Many historians specializing in New Testament studies reach conclusions incompatible with Swinburne's. But, he thinks, the arguments of many of these historians are wholly or partly vitiated by two mistaken assumptions that pervade their work: first, that we should proceed by ignoring the probability, relative to background evidence, that God exists, is able to act miraculously and would have good reason to do so in certain circumstances; and secondly, that philosophical considerations rule out the possibility of our concluding, on the basis of historical testimony, that a bodily resurrection had occurred.[13]

Swinburne's overall conclusion with respect to the resurrection of Jesus is that his answers to questions 1–8 make it very probable that Jesus was God Incarnate who rose from the dead.

There is an important corollary. For reasons already explained, if Jesus rose from the dead then his doing so constituted God's public endorsement of his teaching. Chapter seven of *The Resurrection of God Incarnate* has argued that Jesus' teaching included the atonement doctrine. Swinburne has also argued that the view that God would become incarnate in order to provide an atonement for human wrongdoing has a significant prior probability. It follows that the atonement doctrine is probably true (although not as probable as the occurrence of the resurrection).

FAITH AND REASON

Swinburne acknowledges that there may well be some people who hold a justified basic belief that God exists, or that some more specific religious doctrine is true, but he doubts that there are many such people. Most theists need arguments, at least to back up the deliverances of whatever religious experiences they may have. Swinburne explains various conceptions of rational outcomes of religious enquiry, generated by more and less demanding criteria of rationality. Rejecting the view that religious enquiry is pointless, he argues that individuals have a moral obligation to try to discover the truth about central religious matters.

For how long should we investigate, and in what depth? The answer will depend partly on the time and other resources that are available, given our moral obligations and the goodness of doing other things. Even if one currently thinks it unlikely that any religion is correct, there is much at stake, so it is very important that one's conclusions should be correct; and few people can truly say that they have *no* time to spend on an investigation. Of course, some people have said that rational religious enquiry is pointless because knowledge of transcendent realities is impossible, but Swinburne rejects this claim.

When should we pursue some religious goal or other, and in connection with which religion, if any, should we pursue it? The answer will depend on the value of the goal if it is attained and on the probability of our obtaining the goal by following this or that way. Swinburne argues that some major religions score better in terms of one or both of these criteria than other major religions do, and so he denies that they are all equally worth following. In doing so, he indicates the

---

13. For Swinburne's discussion of epistemological issues concerning miracles, see Swinburne (1971: chs 2–6; 2004: 284–8).

criteria by which the probabilities of different religious creeds can be compared, and also sketches considerations that provide *prima facie* reasons for favouring the Christian creed over alternative ones.

FURTHER READING

Bradley, M. 2002. "The Fine-Tuning Argument: The Bayesian Version". *Religious Studies* **38**: 375–404.

Draper, P. 2001. "Critical Notice of *Providence and the Problem of Evil*". *Noûs* **35**: 456–74.

Hasker, W. 2002. "Is Christianity Probable? Swinburne's Apologetic Program". *Religious Studies* **38**: 253–64.

Swinburne, R. 1989. *Responsibility and Atonement*. Oxford: Clarendon Press.

Swinburne, R. [1986] 1997. *The Evolution of the Soul*, rev. edn. Oxford: Clarendon Press.

Swinburne, R. 1998. *Providence and the Problem of Evil*. Oxford: Clarendon Press.

On NATURAL RELIGION/THEOLOGY see also Vol. 3, Chs 4, 6, 7, 11, 12, 13, 19, 23; Vol. 4, Chs 8, 12. On EVIL/PROBLEM OF EVIL see also Chs 19, 22; Vol. 1, Chs 18, 19; Vol. 2, Ch. 16; Vol. 3, Chs 13, 18, 19; Vol. 4, Chs 12, 18. On REVEALED RELIGION see also Vol. 3, Ch. 22; Vol. 4, Ch. 12. On REVELATION see also Ch. 8; Vol. 1, Ch. 14; Vol. 2, Chs 11; Vol. 3, Chs 7, 11, 16; Vol. 4, Chs 5, 11. On THE TRINITY see also Ch. 12; Vol. 1, Chs 14, 17, 20; Vol. 2, Chs 2, 8, 15; Vol. 3, Chs 3, 9, 17; Vol. 4, Ch. 4.

24

LATE-TWENTIETH-CENTURY ATHEISM

Graham Oppy and N. N. Trakakis

In 1948, the BBC broadcast a debate between Bertrand Russell and Father Frederick Copleston on the existence of God (Russell & Copleston 1957). In that debate, Copleston claims: (i) that the existence of God can be proved by a metaphysical argument from contingency; and (ii) that only the postulation of the existence of God can make sense of our religious and moral experience. Russell replies by giving diverse reasons for thinking that these two claims are incorrect: there are various ways in which Copleston's argument from contingency fails to be persuasive, and there are more plausible alternative explanations of our religious and moral experience. While there are many significant changes of detail, it is fair to say that the debate between Russell and Copleston typifies exchanges between theists and atheists in the second half of the twentieth century, and it is also fair to say that Russell's contribution to this debate typifies the approaches of late twentieth-century atheists.[1]

Speaking very roughly, we might divide the activities of atheists in the following way. First, some atheists have been concerned to argue that religious talk fails to be meaningful: there is no serious discussion to be had about, for example, the existence of God because one cannot even meaningfully deny the existence of God. Secondly, many atheists have been concerned to develop alternative worldviews to the kinds of worldviews that are presented in the world's religions; and, in particular, many atheists have been concerned to develop naturalistic worldviews that leave no room for any kinds of supernatural entities. Thirdly, some atheists have been interested in discussions of the ground rules for the arbitration of debates between theists and non-theists; and, in particular, some atheists have wanted to insist that there is an initial presumption in favour of atheism that leaves theistic opponents carrying the argumentative burden of proof. Fourthly, many

---

1. A more recent (and more developed) version of a very similar debate can be found in Smart & Haldane (1996).

atheists have been concerned to raise objections against the plethora of theistic arguments that have been advanced, in particular on behalf of the claim that God exists. Fifthly, some atheists have also been concerned to advance argument on behalf of atheism and, in particular, on behalf of the claim that God does not exist. Sixthly, in the early part of the twenty-first century, some 'new' atheists have attempted to advance overarching critiques of religion – not merely theistic religion – in which even moderate religious belief is characterized as barbaric superstition. In what follows, we shall survey all of these different spheres of activity of atheists in the second half of the twentieth century.[2]

Some philosophers have taken great pains to distinguish different varieties of non-belief, that is, different ways in which philosophers who do not accept the claim that God exists view that claim. While we can distinguish between 'weak agnosticism', 'strong agnosticism', 'weak atheism', 'strong atheism' and the like, for the purposes of the present chapter we shall just use the term 'atheism' to refer to all of those who are non-believers, that is, all of those who fail to accept the claim that God exists. Given this terminological stipulation, it follows that there are many atheists who are also religious believers: for what unites 'atheists' is merely their failure to accept the theistic hypothesis that God exists, and there are many religious traditions that fail to endorse the claim that God exists.

ALLEGED PROBLEMS WITH RELIGIOUS LANGUAGE

One of the perennial temptations in philosophy is the thought that we can describe boundaries to intelligible thought and intelligible utterance that place much philosophical and religious thought and talk on the wrong side of that boundary. At the mid-point of the twentieth century, there were two powerful philosophical traditions – logical positivism and ordinary-language philosophy – that endorsed different ways of filling out this perennially tempting thought. The impact of those two traditions can be seen very clearly in the articles collected together in the influential anthology of Antony Flew and Alasdair McIntyre (1955).

On the logical positivist line of thought, the reason why religious claims are meaningless is that, while clearly not being mere truths of reason, those claims are insusceptible of empirical verification. The crude articulation of this line of thought by A. J. Ayer (1936) went on to receive further development in the work of such writers as John Wisdom (1944–5) and Flew (1961, 1984), and significant

---

2. Although the focus in this chapter is on developments in the English-speaking analytic tradition, atheism has also had a strong presence in the so-called continental tradition, particularly in the atheistic stream of existentialism (the most significant figure here being Jean-Paul Sartre, although Simone de Beauvoir, Albert Camus and Martin Heidegger are also often placed in this group). On the fortunes of atheism in more recent continental philosophy, in postmodern thought especially, see Caputo (2007).

elaboration of this type of approach can also be seen in the work of Kai Nielsen (1982) and Michael Martin (1990). While there has been strenuous criticisms of this line of thought from theistic philosophers – see, for example, Alvin Plantinga (1967, 2000) – it is also worth noting that many atheistic philosophers have been prepared to reject the view that religious claims are literally meaningless (e.g. Mackie 1982; Sobel 2004).

On the ordinary-language philosophy line of thought, the leading idea is that religious claims should be given some kind of non-cognitivist construal, that is, they should not be supposed to be in the business of stating facts. There are many different ways in which this fundamental idea might be further developed. On one way of thinking, religious assertions are *expressive*; for example, according to R. B. Braithwaite (1955), religious assertions are expressions of intentions to act in certain specified ways. On another way of thinking, the only standards to which religious claims are answerable are standards that are internal to religious language games: there is no single conception of 'the business of stating facts' to which common sense, science and religion are all answerable. Some philosophers – for example D. Z. Phillips (1976) – have supposed that this latter way of thinking need not be uncongenial to religion; however, others – for example Stephen T. Davis (2001) – have supposed that the 'Wittgensteinian' way with religion amounts to the embrace of atheism.

At the end of the twentieth century, there were still some atheistic philosophers inclined to the view that, for example, the claim that God exists is literally meaningless. However, it seems safe to say that many more atheistic philosophers were inclined to follow the line taken by John Mackie and Jordan Howard Sobel, a line that leads to the search for evidence or reasons that bear on the assessment of the truth status of the claim that God exists.

THE RISE OF NATURALISTIC PHILOSOPHY

One of the major post-Second World War developments in philosophy has been the rise to prominence of naturalism and naturalistic philosophy. While naturalistically inclined philosophers disagree about many matters, they characteristically agree that the natural world forms a causally closed system, and that there are no causal exchanges that do not form part of that causally closed system. Thus, naturalistically inclined philosophers typically agree that there are no supernatural agents – no spooks, no gods, no ghosts, no unembodied minds or souls – because supernatural agency, by definition, requires causal interactions that form no part of that causally closed system that is the natural world. Among the matters on which naturalistically inclined philosophers disagree are such questions as whether all that exists belongs to the natural world; whether all that exists 'comes down' to elementary particles and microphysical events; and whether there is anything that resists explanation by the methods that are characteristic of the natural sciences.

In many senses, W. V. Quine is the father of modern naturalistic philosophy. Quine held the view that everything that belongs to the natural world 'comes down' to elementary particles and microphysical events, but he allowed that there are things – numbers, functions, classes – that do not belong to the natural world. (Alas, Quine gave no very clear account of what it is for the natural world to 'come down' to elementary particles and microphysical events, a question that has received much closer attention in more recent times.) Furthermore, Quine gave special prominence to the methods that are characteristic of the natural sciences in the project of describing and understanding the natural world. While it is perhaps not quite right to say that he denied that there is anything that resists explanation by the methods that are characteristic of the natural sciences, he was certainly inclined to insist on the use of the methods that are characteristic of the natural sciences in a diverse range of enquiries. In particular, Quine is very well known for his insistence that epistemology should be 'naturalized', that is, for his insistence that epistemology should be reconceived as a scientific study of the relationship, in human beings, between the inputs of sensory experience and the neural states that are prompted by those inputs. Moreover, Quine is also very well known for his insistence that, because the idioms that we typically use in making ascriptions of beliefs and desires resist smooth incorporation into a properly scientific world-view, those idioms should be accorded only a second-class status, and should not be thought fit for the purposes of *serious* description and understanding of the world. (For a very brief outline of Quine's beliefs, see Quine [1966].)

After Quine, naturalistic philosophy has developed in various directions. Some naturalists hold the thesis that everything in the natural world 'supervenes' on elementary particles and microphysical events, whereas other naturalists hold merely that everything in the natural world is 'constituted by' elementary particles and microphysical events. Some naturalists suppose that there are no such things as numbers, functions and classes; other naturalists suppose that numbers, functions and classes are denizens of the natural world; and yet other naturalists continue to agree with Quine that numbers, functions and classes exist, but not as parts of the natural world, and not in such a way as to be engaged in causal interaction with the natural world. Some naturalists suppose that it is indeed true that there is nothing that resists explanation by the methods that are characteristic of the natural sciences; but many naturalists suppose that, at the very least, there are many legitimate domains of enquiry that we can pursue only via the methods of enquiry of the social sciences, the humanities and so forth.

Alongside the rise of naturalistic philosophy, there has been a parallel rise in naturalistic investigations of religious practices, customs and beliefs. While the project of arriving at a naturalistic explanation of religion was at least understood by David Hume (*see* Vol. 3, Ch. 19), and while various early attempts at naturalistic explanations of religion were enunciated during the nineteenth century, it is fair to say that the move to develop naturalistic explanations of religion really began to gather momentum towards the end of the twentieth century. In particular, the close of the twentieth century saw the beginnings of some bold, interdisciplinary projects – drawing on anthropology, linguistics, cognitive science, neuroscience, evolutionary theory and a range of other disciplines – that seek to provide satis-factory naturalistic accounts of religion. Important examples of these types of projects include: Thomas Lawson and Robert McCauley (1990), Pascal Boyer (2001), Scott Atran (2002) and Daniel Dennett (2006).

DEBATING THE BURDEN OF PROOF

Some atheistic philosophers – including Flew (1976) and Michael Scriven (1966) – have argued that there is a 'burden of proof' on believers in the existence of God. In particular, these atheistic philosophers argue that the default position, adopted by all *reasonable* people in the absence of compelling arguments to the contrary, is either atheism or agnosticism. If theists cannot provide arguments that ought to persuade reasonable atheists to renounce their atheism and become theists then, on this line of thought, those theists are convicted of irrationality in their theistic beliefs. (Among subsequent writers, Martin [1990: 29] "remains neutral" on the question whether there is a presumption of atheism, but in a way that suggests some sympathy for the view that the 'burden of proof' rests with theists. Similarly, Keith Parsons [1989] suggests at least some sympathy for the view that the 'burden of proof' rests with theists.)

Against these atheistic philosophers, other atheistic philosophers have thought that there is something improper in the legalistic invocation of the concept of 'burden of proof' in the context of philosophical debate about the existence of God. Thus, for example, David Lewis (1993) ends with the observation that "some will want to play on by debating the burden of proof. Myself, I think that this pastime is as useless as it is undignified" (*ibid.*: 172). Furthermore, other atheistic philosophers have worried that there is a conflation of requirements on debate (argumentation) and requirements on belief at work in the suggestion that theists suffer under a 'burden of proof'. While it seems right to think that doxastic respon-sibility requires that believers have sufficiently good grounds for their beliefs, it is not at all clear how this requirement connects to the demand that believers have evidence that supports their beliefs, or to the demand that believers adduce accept-able chains of reasoning that terminate in statements of the beliefs in question, or to the demand that believers find arguments that ought to persuade reasonable atheists to take on those theistic beliefs.

RESPONDING TO THEISTIC ARGUMENTS

During the heyday of logical positivism and ordinary-language philosophy, phil-osophers typically took a very dismissive view of arguments for the existence

305

of God. Consider, for example, W. T. Stace: "I simply cannot bear to discuss the dreary logomachy of the ontological argument. Probably Broad has completely demolished the argument. But I cannot bring myself to think that it needs demolishing" (1959: 180). However, the last four decades of the twentieth century witnessed much interesting criticism of arguments for the existence of God on the part of atheistic philosophers of religion. Of course, this period also witnessed much interesting criticism of arguments for the existence of God on the part of theistic philosophers of religion. Thus, for example, Plantinga (1967) provides exemplary critiques of some of the best-known arguments for the existence of God. Nonetheless, much of the most interesting criticism of arguments for the existence of God in this period has come from the pens of atheistic philosophers.

Some of this critical work is local, and consists in the detailed criticism of a particular argument or family of arguments, often within the compass of a single journal article or book chapter. Examples of this kind of critical work include: Lewis' (1970) discussion of Anselm's ontological argument; William L. Rowe's (1975) discussion of cosmological arguments, including arguments from contingency; Michael Tooley's (1981) discussion of Plantinga's ontological argument; Paul Draper's (1997) discussion of William Lane Craig's *kalām* cosmological argument; Alan Hájek's (2003) discussion of Pascal's wager; and Elliott Sober's (2003) discussion of the argument for design.

Some of the interesting critical work has had a wider scope, and criticizes a wide range of arguments for the existence of God within the bounds of a single work. While there are earlier attempts to provide a synoptic discussion of arguments about the existence of God – as, for example, in Wallace Matson's (1965) very readable, but somewhat flawed book – the first really significant book of this kind is Mackie (1982). In that work (*The Miracle of Theism*), Mackie provides careful and incisive critiques of ontological arguments, cosmological arguments, arguments for design, arguments from consciousness, moral arguments and Pascalian wagers (in the service of constructing an overall case for the conclusion that there is no God). Other works constructed according to a similar plan, and covering much of the same range of arguments, include Martin (1990), Nicholas Everitt (2004) and Sobel (2004). Of works in this genre, Sobel's *Logic and Theism* established a new benchmark: although it has a more limited range than Mackie (1982), Sobel (2004) provides much more painstaking and detailed analyses of the arguments that it covers.

Apart from books that attempt to provide overarching critiques of arguments for the existence of God, there are also some shorter works that aim to show that cases for the existence of God can be mimicked by equally good (or bad) cases for the existence of alternative deities, for example a perfectly evil God or a morally indifferent God. A nice example of this genre is provided by Christophe New (1993), who provides inversions of a large family of arguments for the existence of God, each of which purports to establish the existence of an omnipotent, omniscient and maximally evil being.

ARGUING FOR ATHEISM

Much of the most interesting recent work done by atheistic philosophers has focused on attempts to argue directly against the truth of theism (and directly for the truth of atheism). As in the case of responses to theistic arguments, some of this work has been local, focusing on particular kinds of considerations, while other instances of this kind of work have attempted to construct an overarching case for atheism (e.g. Matson 1965; Mackie 1982; Martin 1990; Le Poidevin 1996; Everitt 2004).

J. N. Findlay (1948) attempts an ontological disproof of the existence of God. While this proof is not strong – among other things, it is vitiated by reliance on a conventionalist conception of necessity – it does point the way towards an interesting global criticism of ontological arguments for the existence of God: in a large range of cases, ontological arguments for the existence of God can be 'paralleled' by arguments for the conclusion that God does not exist. Findlay himself quickly gave up on his ontological disproof; and perhaps there has been no subsequent atheist philosopher who has supposed that there are successful ontological disproofs of the existence of God. Nonetheless, many atheistic philosophers have supposed that most (if not all) ontological arguments for the existence of God are disabled by these 'parallel' arguments for the conclusion that God does not exist.

Quentin Smith (1991) attempts a cosmological disproof of the existence of God, drawing on contemporary cosmological theorizing. In particular, Smith argues that there is some kind of inconsistency between big bang cosmology and theism. Given the fluid state of contemporary cosmological theorizing, it is unclear how much importance could be attributed to Smith's argument even if it were otherwise unexceptionable. And, in any case, there is much else in Smith's argument that has proven to be controversial. Other atheist authors have hinted at different cosmological disproofs of the existence of God: there are arguments in William L. Rowe (1975) that suggest that considerations about contingency point strongly to the conclusion that God does not exist. Here, the idea is roughly this: if there is contingency, then there is brute, unexplained *initial* contingency. Theism is committed both to the claim that there is contingency – this is required by the assumption that we have libertarian freedom – and to the claim that there is no brute, unexplained *initial* contingency – this is required by the assumption that God provides a complete explanation for the existence and nature of the world even though there is no contingency in God.

Wesley C. Salmon (1979) attempts a teleological disproof of the existence of God. Salmon's proof is elaborated into a whole battery of teleological disproofs in Martin (1990). The idea behind this style of disproof is that we have inductive evidence – based on universal human experience – that certain kinds of created entities are typically created by creators with certain kinds of properties. Given that the universe is an entity of the kind in question, we can infer that if it has a creator, then that creator has the properties in question: embodiment, fallibility,

finitude, being a worker with pre-existing materials, being one member of a creative team, and so forth. But a creator with these properties would not be the God
of monotheistic religions. Everitt (2004) gives an argument from scale that runs
along somewhat similar lines. Here, the motivating question is whether one would
expect the God of traditional theism to create the kind of universe in which we
actually live; and the line that Everitt takes is that more or less everything that
modern science tells us about the size and scale and nature of the universe reveals
that universe to be strikingly inapt as an expression of a set of divine intentions of
the kind that is postulated by traditional theism.

Perhaps predictably, many of the direct arguments that recent atheistic philosophers have launched against theism have involved considerations about evil.
Mackie (1955) launched an intensive investigation of logical arguments from evil:
of arguments that purport to show that there is a logical inconsistency between
the claim that God exists and some well-established claim about evil (e.g. that
there is evil in the world, or that there is moral evil in the world, or that there is
horrendous evil in the world, or the like). While many theists suppose that these
kinds of arguments are defeated by the free will defence elaborated by Plantinga
(1965), there are some atheist philosophers who continue to pursue and defend
logical arguments from evil (see e.g. Gale 1991).

Rowe (1979) provoked a similarly intensive investigation of evidential arguments from evil: of arguments that purport to show that the claim that God exists is
implausible, or improbable, or not worthy of belief, in the light of certain evidence
about the nature and extent of kinds of evil in our universe. On Rowe's account,
it is highly improbable that particular instances of the suffering of animals and
young children would be permitted by an all-powerful, all-knowing and perfectly
good God. While some theists have maintained that Rowe's evidential argument
from evil is in no better shape than Mackie's logical argument from evil – see, for
example, the theistic contributions to Daniel Howard-Snyder (1996) – there are
many atheist philosophers who continue to think that Rowe's evidential argument
from evil does embody powerful grounds for atheism.

Draper (1989) presents another kind of evidential argument from evil. On
Draper's account, there is good *prima facie* reason to reject theism deriving from
the negative evidential impact on theism of the observations that we make, and
the testimony that we encounter, concerning human and animal experiences of
pain and pleasure. (The observations that we make, and the testimony that we
encounter, concerning human and animal experiences of pain and pleasure, are
much more likely on the hypothesis that neither the nature nor the condition of
sentient beings on earth is the result of benevolent or malevolent actions performed
by non-human persons, than they are on the hypothesis that the nature and condition of sentient beings on earth is the result of the actions of an omnipotent, omniscient and perfectly good God.) Draper's argument has occasioned a considerable
amount of critical discussion from theistic philosophers such as Plantinga and
Howard-Snyder; it seems doubtful that this discussion has yet been exhausted.

There are other arguments that atheists have mounted against theism that are not strictly speaking arguments from evil, but which are arguments in the same ballpark. So, for example, John Schellenberg (1993) mounts a sustained argument against the existence of God on the grounds of divine hiddenness: if there were an omnipotent, omniscient and perfectly good God, surely there would be much better evidence available to all of the existence of such a being. Similarly, Theodore Drange (1998) mounts an argument against the existence of God on the grounds of non-belief: if there were an omnipotent, omniscient and perfectly good God, surely there would not be so many reasonable, intelligent and well-informed people who fail to believe that God exists. The arguments of Schellenberg and Drange have both been widely discussed; see, for example, Howard-Snyder and Paul Moser (2002), for a selection of critical responses to Schellenberg's argument.

Apart from logical arguments from evil, there are other arguments that purport to raise logical difficulties for theism. Mackie (1955) also initiated contemporary debate about the paradoxes of omnipotence: what should a theist say in response to the question whether God can make a stone so heavy that God is unable to lift that stone? (On the one hand, if God cannot make such a stone, then there is something God cannot do, and so God is not omnipotent. On the other hand, if God can make such a stone, then there is something that God cannot do, namely, lift the stone that God is able to make.) While this simple version of the paradox of omnipotence seems easily met – not even God can be expected to do that which is logically impossible, and at least one half of the dilemma prompted by our question implicitly requires God to do something that is logically impossible – discussion of more complex versions of this argument has continued into the twenty-first century.

Patrick Grim (1983) is the first of a series of papers that develops arguments for the conclusion that it is impossible for there to be an omniscient being. According to Grim, the very notion of omniscience is beset by logical paradox: there is no collection of truths that could form the object of knowledge of an omniscient being; and, besides, there are perspective-dependent truths that can be grasped only from perspectives other than the one that would be occupied by God (if there were such a being). While Grim has pursued his arguments in debate with numerous theistic opponents – including, notably, Plantinga (see Plantinga & Grim 1993) – it is probably fair to say that his arguments have not found as much support as the corresponding arguments that have been developed in connection with the notion of divine omnipotence.

Of course, there are many other arguments that are taken to raise logical problems for theism. There are questions about divine foreknowledge and human freedom; see John Martin Fischer (1994) for contributions by some contemporary atheists to this debate. There are questions about divine freedom; Rowe (2004) marks one recent attempt to argue that an omnipotent, omniscient and perfectly good being could not have the kind of freedom that is required for moral responsibility, praise and gratitude. There are also many questions about less commonly discussed divine attributes, and particular theological doctrines. So, to take a small number of examples among many: Richard M. Gale (1991) argues for the claim that the doctrine of divine simplicity is incoherent; Martin (1997) argues that there are many logical difficulties in the traditional theistic conception of heaven; and Lewis (1997) argues that the doctrine of the atonement is not worthy of belief. One of the interesting developments in analytic philosophy of religion in the latter part of the twentieth century has been the wider range of topics that have been investigated using the tools of analytical philosophy: this broadening of range has been true of atheistically motivated philosophers no less than it has been true of theistically motivated philosophers.

THE 'NEW' ATHEISM

The beginning of the new millennium has witnessed a perhaps unexpected surge in public enthusiasm for books that take a highly critical view of theism, and of religion in general. Works by the 'new atheists' – Richard Dawkins, Sam Harris, Christopher Hitchens, Michel Onfrey, Anthony Grayling, Daniel Dennett, and others – have found a large global audience, often occupying prominent positions in bestseller lists.

The works of these 'new atheists' have been written against the background of broader changes in attitudes towards religion and religious belief over the course of the second half of the twentieth century. Census figures across the Western world indicate that, for much of the latter half of the twentieth century, organized religion was in something approaching decline. While there was some increase in the number of those claiming to have no religion, there was much greater increase in the number of those who claimed to belong to no organized religion. Church numbers maintained a steady downwards slide; and the percentage of people who attended church only very infrequently continued to increase.

Of course, these general trends were not uniform. Moreover, and more importantly, even while the *overall* trends indicated that organized religion was in decline, these trends were not necessarily replicated in the fortunes of the *evangelical* branches of at least some of the major religions. In particular, in the United States, the last part of the twentieth century witnessed strong gains for evangelical Christianity, especially in the so-called 'red' states. As evangelical Christians came to have more influence on the Republican party and its policies, the influence of evangelical Christian beliefs could be discerned in a diverse range of social trends: a greater push for evangelical Christian home schooling (and schooling outside the public education system); more intense evangelical Christian opposition to legal recognition of gay relationships and other legal entitlements for gay couples; greatly increased evangelical Christian support for equal recognition of the theory of intelligent design in public school biology classes; massive diversion of public funds from secular social service organizations to evangelical Christian organizations under the label of 'faith-based initiatives'; increased evangelical Christian promotion of 'abstinence only' sex education programmes in public schools; and so on across the full range of evangelical Christian activity.

In other parts of the world, the latter part of the twentieth century witnessed gains for evangelical branches of other major world religions. In particular, evangelical Islam made considerable gains in many corners of the globe – in the Middle East, Africa and Asia – and there were also some gains for evangelical Hinduism, most notably in India. And, along with the rise of support for evangelical forms of several of the major world religions, there has also been a rise in political and social tensions – and, in many cases, political and social *violence* – in which matters of evangelical religious disagreement have played some kind of role. While the causal aetiology is unclear, it is uncontroversial that evangelical religion is one of the causal factors involved in, for example, the rise of Al Qaeda, the 9/11 attacks, suicide bombings in the Middle East and skirmishes on the India/Pakistan border.

Writers such as Harris (2005, 2006), Hitchens (2007) and Dawkins (2006) argue, not only that the recent rise of evangelical religion marks a serious slide back towards a dark and barbarous past, but that even religious moderation marks a set of irresponsible cultural and intellectual accommodations with a best-rejected ancient heritage. In their view, teaching the beliefs of evangelical religionists to children is tantamount to child abuse; and, in general, "religious faith represents so uncompromising a misuse of the power of our minds that it forms a kind of perverse cultural singularity – a vanishing point beyond which rational discourse proves impossible" (Harris 2005: 25). Critics of the 'new atheists' have not been slow to wonder at the sheer magnitude of the assertions that the 'new atheists' make: in claiming that even religious moderates are irrational in their religious beliefs, the 'new atheists' commit themselves to the view that more than 90 per cent of all the adults on the planet have simply irrational religious beliefs.

While it certainly should not be supposed that all atheists are enthusiastic supporters of the 'new atheists', it seems plausible to suppose that the 'new atheism' will occupy a prominent position in academic debates about religion and religious belief in the immediate future. Indeed, because – at least in the area of philosophy – evangelical Christians have made considerable inroads into the academy (particularly, but not only, in the United States), one expects that arguments involving the 'new atheists' will grow even noisier in the coming years.

FURTHER READING

Antony, L. (ed.) 2007. *Philosophers Without Gods: Meditations on Atheism and the Secular Life.* Oxford: Oxford University Press.

Hitchens, C. (ed.) 2007. *The Portable Atheist: Essential Readings for the Nonbeliever.* Cambridge, MA: Da Capo Press.

Martin, M. (ed.) 2007. *The Cambridge Companion to Atheism*. Cambridge: Cambridge University Press.

Martin, M. & R. Monnier (eds) 2003. *The Impossibility of God*. Amherst, NY: Prometheus.

Martin, M. & R. Monnier (eds) 2006. *The Improbability of God*. Amherst, NY: Prometheus.

On ATHEISM see also Chs 6, 17.

CHRONOLOGY

1900   Death of **Friedrich Nietzsche** (*see* Vol. 4, Ch. 18), who spent his last eleven years as an invalid.
        Max Planck discovers the law of blackbody radiation that ushers in quantum theory, earning Plank the Nobel Prize for Physics in 1918.

1901   Rudolf Steiner founds anthroposophy.
        Australia passes Immigration Restriction Act to underpin its White Australia Policy.

1902   Women in Australia gain voting rights.
        William James publishes his Gifford Lectures as *The Varieties of Religious Experience*.

1903   A wave of anti-Jewish pogroms start in Russia.
        Emmeline Pankhurst, British woman suffragist, founds the Women's Social and Political Union.

1905   Albert Einstein's 'annus mirabilis', the year in which he publishes four papers that revolutionized physics, one of which includes his formulation of the equivalence of mass and energy ($E = mc^2$).

1906   Birth of **Emmanuel Levinas**, French philosopher who developed an ethical form of phenomenology.
        Albert Schweitzer publishes *The Quest of the Historical Jesus*.
        Gandhi launches a programme of passive resistance in South Africa in response to discrimination against the Indian minority.

1908   Earthquake kills 200,000 in Sicily and southern Italy.
        Gideon's International begins to distribute free Bibles.
        Death of **Edward Caird** (*see* Vol. 4, Ch. 16).

1909   Birth of **Simone Weil**, French social philosopher and mystic.
        Louis Bleriot makes the first aeroplane flight across the English Channel.
        Einstein introduces the concept of wave–particle duality in physics.

1910   Birth of **A. J. Ayer**, leading representative of logical positivism.
        Deaths of **William James**, best known in philosophy for his pragmatism and 'radical empiricism', and Leo Tolstoy, author of *War and Peace* and *Anna Karenina*.
        China abolishes slavery.
        Establishment of the first kibbutz in Palestine.

1911   Death of **Dilthey** (*see* Vol. 4, Ch. 15).

American archaeologist Hiram Bingham discovers Machu Picchu, the site of ancient Inca ruins in the Peruvian Andes.

1912   Carl Jung publishes *The Psychology of the Unconscious*, resulting in a formal break with Sigmund Freud.
        Formation of the precursor to the African National Congress, dedicated to the abolition of apartheid in South Africa.

1913   British geologist Arthur Holmes publishes *The Age of the Earth*, estimating the Earth to be 1.6 billion years old, far older than had been believed (the Earth is now believed to be 4.55 billion years old).

1914   Death of **Peirce** (*see* Vol. 4, Ch. 17).
        The assassination of Archduke Franz Ferdinand of Austria precipitates the First World War.

1915   German meteorologist and geophysicist Alfred Wegener publishes his theory of continental drift.

1916   Death of **Royce** (*see* Vol. 4, Ch. 19).
        Assassination of Russian peasant and mystic Grigory Rasputin.
        Easter Rising in Ireland in which republicans aimed to end British rule.
        Launch of Cabaret Voltaire nightclub in Zurich, which played an important part in the formation of the Dada art movement.

1917   Death of **Durkheim** (*see* Vol. 4, Ch. 21).
        October revolution in Russia, led by Vladimir Lenin.
        Execution of Dutch dancer Mata Hari by the French on charges of spying for Germany during the First World War.
        US Congress legislates for Prohibition.

1918   Spanish flu pandemic, resulting in approximately 50 million deaths worldwide.
        The armistice treaty is signed between the Allies and Germany, bringing the First World War to an end.

1919   Establishment of the League of Nations, precursor of the United Nations.

1920   The Nineteenth Amendment to the US Constitution guarantees votes for women.

1921   Birth of **William P. Alston**, American philosopher who has made influential contributions to philosophy of language, epistemology and Christian philosophy.
        Publication (in German) of Wittgenstein's *Tractatus Logico-Philosophicus*.

1922   Birth of **John Hick**, English philosopher of religion best known for his work on the problem of evil and defence of religious pluralism.
        Moscow proclaims the creation of the Union of Soviet Socialist Republics (USSR).

1923   Martin Buber publishes *I and Thou*.
        Conclusion of the Irish Civil War.
        Hyper-inflation in Germany, leading to economic collapse.

1925   Prosecution of John Scopes in Dayton, Tennessee, for teaching evolutionary theory to schoolchildren.
        Publication of the first volume of Adolf Hitler's *Mein Kampf*.
        Publication of Franz Kafka's *The Trial*.

1927   Werner Heisenberg announces the uncertainty principle.
        Martin Heidegger publishes *Being and Time*.

1928   Birth of **Mary Daly**, radical feminist philsopher and theologian who taught at Boston College for thirty-three years.

Publication of the final volume of Havelock Ellis' seven-volume groundbreaking *Studies in the Psychology of Sex*.

Egyptian religious and political leader Hassan al-Banna founds the Muslim Brotherhood.

1929   Lateran Treaty establishes papal sovereignty over Vatican City.

Heinrich Himmler assumes command of the German SS.

Edwin Hubble demonstrates the expansion of the universe.

The Wall Street stock market crashes, initiating the Great Depression.

1930   Birth of **Jacques Derrida**, French philosopher of deconstruction.

Gandhi leads the Dandi Salt March, drawing worldwide attention to the Indian independence movement.

1931   Death of American inventor Thomas Edison.

Japanese occupation of Manchuria in north-east China.

1932   Birth of **Alvin Plantinga**, Professor of Philosophy at the University of Notre Dame and widely considered as one of the leading Christian philosophers today.

1933   Hitler becomes chancellor of Germany, and five weeks later the first Nazi concentration camp in Germany is established at Dachau.

1934   Birth of **Richard Swinburne**, Nolloth Professor of the Philosophy of the Christian Religion at the University of Oxford (1985–2002) and regarded as one of the world's foremost defenders of natural theology.

Chinese Communists under Mao Zedong begin the massive military retreat from Jiangxi to Shaanxi, known as the Long March.

1935   Nuremberg laws strip Jews of their German citizenship.

Italy, under fascist leader Benito Mussolini, invades Ethiopia.

Joseph Stalin initiates 'Great Terror' campaign, including 'show trials' of leading Communists and the arrest and execution of millions of people from all sections of Soviet society.

1936   **Ayer** publishes *Language, Truth, and Logic*.

Start of the Spanish Civil War.

Germany and Japan establish a pact against the Soviet Union.

1937   The Basque town Guernica is heavily bombed by German planes in support of Franco's forces during the Spanish Civil War, an incident that inspired Pablo Picasso's famous painting, *Guernica*.

Japanese troops occupy Nanjing and massacre up to 300,000 civilians.

1938   Saudi Arabia begins to export oil;.

The Dust Bowl crisis in the Great Plains of the United States reaches a peak.

The Nazi Kristallnacht pogrom results in the destruction of Jewish property and the arrest and deportation of thousands of Jews to concentration camps.

1939   Death of **Sigmund Freud** (*see* Vol. 4, Ch. 20), founder of psychoanalysis.

Hitler orders the invasion of Poland, and in response Great Britain and France declare war on Germany, thus initiating the Second World War.

1940   End of the Winter War between the Soviet Union and Finland.

Allied troops are evacuated from Dunkirk to England in a flotilla of hastily assembled boats, and the German air force carpet bombs Coventry and assails London in the Battle of Britain and the Blitz.

Assassination of Leon Trotsky, presumably on Stalin's orders.

Discovery of prehistoric cave paintings at Lascaux, southwestern France.

1941   Death of **Henri Bergson**, French philosopher and winner of 1927 Nobel Prize for Literature.

The Soviet Union is invaded by the Axis powers in Operation Barbarossa, and Japanese aeroplanes attack Pearl Harbour, thus bringing the US into the war.

Hermann Göring commissions Reinhard Heydrich to carry out a "final solution to the Jewish question".

1942   C. S. Lewis publishes *The Screwtape Letters*.

Gandhi launches the Quit India Movement to campaign for Indian independence.

Initiation of the Manhattan Project to develop the first atomic bomb.

Fall of Singapore to the Japanese army.

1943   Death of **Weil**.

Jean-Paul Sartre publishes *Being and Nothingness*.

The Battle of Stalingrad ends with the surrender of German forces and the Allies invade Italy, leading to the fall of Mussolini, with Italy then becoming a battleground between Allied and German forces.

1944   Invasion of Normandy by Allied forces, the Blitz continues with V1 and V2 flying bombs used in raids on London and the first wave of Japanese kamikaze missions takes place against the Allies in the Pacific campaign.

From May 1942 to September 1944, more than 4,200,000 Jews are killed in such death camps as Auschwitz, Treblinka, Belzec, Chelmno, Majdanek and Sobibor.

Establishment of the World Bank and the International Monetary Fund.

1945   Death of US president, Franklin D. Roosevelt.

Allied firebombing of Dresden. After atomic bombs are dropped on Hiroshima and, three days later, on Nagasaki, Japan surrenders signalling the end of the Second World War, the bloodiest conflict in history.

Karl Popper publishes *The Open Society and Its Enemies*.

1946   The world's first peacetime atomic weapons test is conducted at Bikini Atoll in the central Pacific Ocean.

The Nuremberg Trials against former Nazi leaders are concluded.

1947   Death of **Alfred North Whitehead**, professor of mathematics and philosophy.

Primo Levi, Italian chemist of Jewish descent and survivor of Auschwitz, publishes his first memoir, *If This Is a Man*.

Discovery of the Dead Sea Scrolls.

1948   The cold war intensifies with the Soviet Union's blockade of Berlin.

The state of Israel is proclaimed, leading to the immediate invasion of Israel by the armies of five Arab states.

The Universal Declaration of Human Rights is ratified by the UN.

Establishment of the World Council of Churches.

Gandhi is assassinated by a Hindu extremist.

1949   The United States and its European allies form the North Atlantic Treaty Organization (NATO).

Establishment of the People's Republic of China under Chairman Mao.

The Soviets explode their first atomic warhead, thus ending the American monopoly on the atomic bomb.

Simone de Beauvoir publishes feminist classic, *The Second Sex*.

1950   The Soviet-supported communist government of North Korea invades US-supported South Korea in 1950, setting off the Korean War.

1951   Death of **Ludwig Wittgenstein** in Cambridge, his last words being, "Tell them I've had a wonderful life!"

1952   Death of **John Dewey**, American philosopher and educator.
Mother Teresa opens a hospice in Calcutta for the terminally ill.

1953   Death of Soviet dictator Stalin.
End of the Korean War.
Watson and Crick report double-helical structure of DNA.

1954   Sun Myung Moon launches the Unification Church.

1955   Death of Einstein, the most influential physicist of the twentieth century, best known for his special and general theories of relativity.

1956   Mao's Hundred Flowers Campaign begins, granting Chinese greater freedom of speech.
Anti-Communist revolution in Hungary is brutally suppressed by Soviet troops.
In the Suez Crisis in Egypt, British and French forces are dispatched to occupy the canal zone, but are later forced to withdraw.

1957   Establishment of the European Economic Community.
Launch of the Sputnik satellite by Soviet Union, inaugurating the space age.

1959   Fidel Castro comes to power in Cuba.

1961   East Germany erects the Berlin Wall.

1962   Death of Niels Bohr, the Danish physicist who played a leading role in the development of quantum theory.
The Second Vatican Council is convened by Pope John XXIII.
Adolf Eichmann is hanged by the state of Israel for his part in the Holocaust.

1963   US president John F. Kennedy is assassinated during a motorcade in Dallas.

1964   The Palestine Liberation Organization (PLO) is formed.
Nelson Mandela is sentenced to life imprisonment and is incarcerated at Robben Island Prison in South Africa.

1965   Deaths of religious existentialists **Martin Buber** and **Paul Tillich**, and of Winston Churchill, British prime minister during the Second World War.
Assassination of the African-American Muslim leader, Malcolm X.
Escalation of the US military engagement in Vietnam.

1966   Start of the Cultural Revolution in China.

1967   Communist guerrilla leader Che Guevara is captured and executed in Bolivia.

1968   Death of **Karl Barth**, Swiss Protestant theologian and author of the monumental *Church Dogmatics*.
Assassination of US civil rights leader Martin Luther King, Jr.
Massacre of Vietnamese civilians by US soldiers at My Lai.
Warsaw Pact troops invade Czechoslovakia.

1969   Death of **Karl Jaspers**, German philosopher and one of the founders of existentialism.
Design of the first programmable computer microchip.
Woodstock Music Festival is attended by some 400,000 people.

1970   Death of **Bertrand Russell**, leading British philosopher, mathematician and social reformer.
Germaine Greer publishes *The Female Eunuch*.

1971   Founding of Greenpeace.
Idi Amin seizes control in Uganda and establishes a brutal dictatorship.
Civil war escalates in East Pakistan, leading to the independence of Bangladesh.

1972   British troops kill thirteen civilians in Londonderry, Northern Ireland on 'Bloody Sunday'.

1973   Death of **Jacques Maritain**, French Thomist philosopher.
Death of Pablo Picasso, one of the greatest and most influential artists of the twentieth century and the founder (with Georges Braque) of cubism.
Yom Kippur War between the Arab states and Israel.
Roe v. *Wade* establishes abortion rights for women in the US.

1974   Augusto Pinochet comes to power in Chile.
The Watergate scandal leads to the resignation of US president Richard Nixon.

1975   The Khmer Rouge, under the leadership of Pol Pot, takes power in Cambodia, launching reign of terror during which as many as 1.5 million Cambodians died.
Bill Gates and Paul Allen found Microsoft.

1976   Death of **Martin Heidegger**, widely influential German philosopher often considered a founder of existentialism, and death of the chairman of the Chinese Communist Party, Mao Zedong.

1977   Death in police custody of Steve Biko, South African political leader who founded a national "black consciousness" movement to combat racism and apartheid.

1978   Louise Brown becomes the world's first baby to be conceived by *in vitro* fertilization (IVF).

1979   The Khmer Rouge government is overthrown by invading Vietnamese troops.
Sandinistas take power in Nicaragua, ending forty-six years of dictatorship by the Somoza family.
Soviet troops invade Afghanistan.

1980   Death of Jean-Paul Sartre, popular French existentialist whose funeral was attended by 25,000 people.
Iraq, under the leadership of Saddam Hussein, invades Iran.

1981   Investigators in New York and California report the first official case of AIDS (since then some 25 million people have died of the disease).

1982   The Falklands War between the United Kingdom and Argentina.

1983   US-led invasion of Grenada in the West Indies overthrows military coup.
French and American researchers identify the HIV virus.
Gerry Adams becomes president of Sinn Fein, the political wing of the Irish Republican Army (IRA).

1984   Assassination of Indian prime minister Indira Gandhi by Sikh extremists.
Devastating famine in Ethiopia.

1985   In the Iran-Contra affair the US National Security Council sells weapons to Iran and the funds are given to the Contras, the US-backed rebels fighting to overthrow the Marxist-oriented Sandinista government of Nicaragua.
Mikhail Gorbachev is appointed general secretary of the Soviet Communist party.

1986   The core module of the Soviet Mir space station is launched into Earth orbit.
A nuclear power station explodes at Chernobyl.

1987   Foundation of Hamas, militant Palestinian Islamic movement.
Significant US stock market collapse.

1988   End of the protracted Iran–Iraq War.
Iraqi forces quell Kurdish resistance using chemical weapons.

Auung San Suu Kyi forms opposition party, the National League for Democracy, in Myanmar (Burma).

Pan Am flight 103 is brought down by terrorists near Lockerbie, Scotland, killing all 259 passengers and crew members.

1989   Death of **Ayer**.

Ayatollah Khomeini issues a fatwa against Salman Rushdie for allegedly having blasphemed Islam in his novel *The Satanic Verses*.

The Soviet Union completes the withdrawal of troops from Afghanistan.

Demonstrations in Tiananmen Square are forcibly repressed by the Chinese government, with the loss of hundreds of lives.

The communist regime of Romanian leader Nicolae Ceausescu is overthrown.

1990   Nelson Mandela is released from prison.

The Hubble Space Telescope is placed into orbit abound the Earth.

More than 100,000 people participate in a pro-democracy rally in Moscow.

Iraq invades Kuwait, leading to the First Gulf War.

The Human Genome Project starts.

1991   Slovenia and Croatia declare their secession from the Yugoslav federation, inaugurating civil war.

The US-led coalition defeats Iraq and liberates Kuwait.

Gorbachev resigns as president of the Soviet Union, and the Commonwealth of Independent States (comprising Russia and eleven other former Soviet republics) replaces the crumbling Soviet Union.

1992   Civil war and devastating famine in Somalia, leading to interventions by United Nations and United States.

The Church of England votes to ordain women as priests.

The European Union (EU) is created.

1993   Eighty members of the Branch Davidian religious sect are killed after a fifty-one-day standoff near Waco, Texas.

In the Israel–PLO accords, Israel recognizes the PLO and agrees to implement limited self-rule for Palestinians in the West Bank and Gaza Strip.

1994   Rwanda genocide, with more than 800,000 civilians, primarily Tutsi, killed.

Russian troops enter Chechnya.

In South Africa's first multiracial elections, marking the end of apartheid, the African National Congress (led by Nelson Mandela) lands an overwhelming victory.

1995   Death of **Levinas**.

Bosnian Serbs massacre thousands of Muslims in Srebrenica.

A terrorist attack in Oklahoma city kills 168 people.

Israeli prime minister Yitzhak Rabin is assassinated.

1996   Birth of Dolly the sheep, the first clone of an adult mammal.

The Taliban captures Kabul and gains effective control of Afghanistan.

1997   The Kyoto Protocol is adopted, with the aim of reducing the emission of gases that contribute to global warming.

1998   Suharto is forced from office in Indonesia.

Terrorist bombing of US embassies in Kenya and Tanzania.

Fighting between Serbs and Albanians escalates in Kosovo.

1999   Eleven EU nations adopt the Euro as their shared currency.

2000   Death of **Charles Hartshorne**, American process philosopher and theologian, and W. V. Quine, influential Harvard philosopher and logician.

George W. Bush wins presidency after one of the closest and most controversial elections in American history.

2001 Netherlands becomes the first country to legalize euthanasia.
Ancient statues of the Buddha are destroyed by the Taliban in Afghanistan.
The former president of Serbia and Yugoslavia Slobodan Milosevic is arrested and later turned over to the UN war crimes tribunal in The Hague.
Terrorist attacks against the World Trade Center and the Pentagon, on 11 September.
The American energy company Enron, one of the most successful companies in the world, files for bankruptcy as revelations of systematic corruption and mismanagement followed.

2002 The US invasion of Afghanistan removes the Taliban from power.
Alleged al-Qaeda terrorists are detained at the US military prison at Guantánamo Bay.
The civil war in Sierra Leone ends.

2003 Genocidal civil war in the Darfur region of Sudan.
In the Second Gulf War, the US-led invasion of Iraq deposes dictator Saddam Hussein.

2004 Death of **Derrida**.
Multiple bomb blasts in Madrid kill at least two hundred rail commuters.
Photographs of US soldiers abusing Iraqi prisoners in Abu Ghraib prison near Baghdad are published.
More than 300 people, nearly half of them children, die as Chechen rebels seize a school in the town of Beslan.
An earthquake measuring 9.0 on the Richter scale strikes the floor of the Indian Ocean, unleashing a tsunami on the shores of Indonesia, Sri Lanka, South India, Thailand and other countries, killing over 200,000 people and leaving many more homeless.

2005 Death of Pope John Paul II
Suicide bomb attacks in London kill fifty-two people.
Hurricane Katrina causes widespread damage and loss of life in Gulf Coast region of the United States, especially in New Orleans.
Eighty thousand people die in an earthquake in Kashmir.

2006 Saddam Hussein is executed in Baghdad after being convicted of crimes against humanity.
North Korea conducts missile and nuclear tests.
War breaks out in Somalia.

2007 Assassination of former prime minister of Pakistan, Benazir Bhutto, the first woman leader of a Muslim nation in modern history.

2008 Global financial crisis is triggered, with the US government creating a $700 billion Treasury fund to purchase failing bank assets.
Barack Obama wins the US presidential election, becoming the first African-American president.
Fidel Castro resigns as president of Cuba.

2009 Victoria undergoes the deadliest bushfires in Australia's history.
Outbreak of swine flu pandemic.
Civil unrest in Iran following the presidential election.
Death of **William Alston**

2010 230,000 die in Haiti earthquake.
Sovereign debt crises in Greece, Ireland, Portugal, Spain, and other European countries.
780,000 cubic metre oil spill in the Gulf of Mexico.
Death of **Mary Daly**.

2011   Tsunami kills 16,000 and triggers Fukushima nuclear power plant meltdown in Japan. World population reaches 7 billion.

Deaths of Osama bin Laden (founder of al-Qaeda), Kim Jong Il (ruler of North Korea), and Muammar al-Qaddafi (leader of Libya).

2012   Death of **John Hick**.

Aung San Suu Kyi of Myanmar (Burma), after spending much of the past two decades under house arrest, is finally permitted to receive the Nobel Peace Prize she was awarded in 1991 "for her non-violent struggle for democracy and human rights."

CERN announces discovery of the long-sought Higgs boson, the so-called 'God particle'.

BIBLIOGRAPHY

Adams, M. M. 1999. *Horrendous Evils and the Goodness of God*. Ithaca, NY: Cornell University Press.

Adler, S. 1998. *Engendering Judaism: An Inclusive Theology and Ethics*. Boston, MA: Beacon Press.

Alston, W. 1954. "Are Positivists Metaphysicians?". *Philosophical Review* **63**: 42–57.

Alston, W. 1964a. "Psychoanalytic Theory and Theistic Belief". In *Faith and the Philosophers*, J. Hick (ed.), 63–102. New York: St Martin's Press.

Alston, W. 1964b. *Philosophy of Language*. Englewood Cliffs, NJ: Prentice-Hall.

Alston, W. 1979. "Yes, Virginia, There is a Real World". *Proceedings and Addresses of the American Philosophical Association* **52**: 779–808.

Alston, W. 1982. "Religious Experience and Religious Belief". *Noûs* **16**: 3–12.

Alston, W. 1989a. *Divine Nature and Human Language: Essays in Philosophical Theology*. Ithaca, NY: Cornell University Press.

Alston, W. 1989b. *Epistemic Justification: Essays in the Theory of Knowledge*. Ithaca, NY: Cornell University Press.

Alston, W. 1991. *Perceiving God: The Epistemology of Religious Experience*. Ithaca, NY: Cornell University Press.

Alston, W. 1993a. *The Reliability of Sense Perception*. Ithaca, NY: Cornell University Press.

Alston, W. 1993b. "Aquinas on Theological Predication: A Look Backward and a Look Forward". In *Reasoned Faith: Essays in Philosophical Theology in Honor of Norman Kretzmann*, E. Stump (ed.), 145–78. Ithaca, NY: Cornell University Press.

Alston, W. 1995a. "A Philosopher's Way Back to the Faith". In *God and the Philosophers*, T. Morris (ed.), 19–30. New York: Oxford University Press.

Alston, W. 1995b. "Realism and the Christian Faith". *International Journal for Philosophy of Religion* **38**: 37–60.

Alston, W. 1996a. *A Realist Conception of Truth*. Ithaca, NY: Cornell University Press.

Alston, W. 1996b. "Belief, Acceptance, and Religious Faith". In *Faith, Freedom, and Rationality*, D. Howard-Snyder & J. Jordan (eds), 10–27. Lanham, MD: Rowman & Littlefield.

Alston, W. 1996c. "The Inductive Argument from Evil and the Human Cognitive Condition". In *The Evidential Argument from Evil*, D. Howard-Snyder (ed.), 97–125. Bloomington, IN: Indiana University Press.

Alston, W. 1996d. "Some (Temporarily) Final Thoughts on Evidential Arguments from Evil". In *The Evidential Argument from Evil*, D. Howard-Snyder (ed.), 311–32. Bloomington, IN: Indiana University Press.

Alston, W. 2001. *A Sensible Metaphysical Realism*. Milwaukee, WI: Wisconsin University Press.

Alston, W. 2003. "Religious Language and Verificationism". In *The Rationality of Theism*, P. Copan & P. Moser (eds), 17–34. New York: Routledge.

Alston, W. 2005. *Divine Mystery and Our Knowledge of God: The Taylor Lectures*, delivered *in absentia* at Yale Divinity School.

Alston, W. & E. Fales 2004. "Does Religious Experience Justify Religious Belief?". In *Contemporary Debates in Philosophy of Religion*, M. Peterson & R. Vanarrogon (eds), 135–63. New York: Blackwell.

Aquinas, T. 1941. *Summa Theologiae*. Ottawa: Collège Dominicain d'Ottawa.

Aquinas, T. 1961. *Commentary on the Metaphysics of Aristotle*, John P. Rowan (trans.). Chicago, IL: Henry Regnery Company.

Aquinas, T. 1963. *Commentary on the* De Trinitate *of Boethius*. In *St Thomas Aquinas, The Division and Methods of the Sciences: Questions V and VI of his Commentary on the* De Trinitate *of Boethius Translated with Introduction and Notes*, A. Maurer (ed.), 3–84. Toronto: Pontifical Institute of Mediaeval Studies.

Atran, S. 2002. *In Gods We Trust: The Evolutionary Landscape of Religion*. New York: Oxford University Press.

Aubrey, E. 1941. "The Religious Symbol". *Journal of Liberal Religion* **2**: 201–2.

Ayer, A. J. 1936. *Language, Truth and Logic*. London: Victor Gollancz.

Ayer, A. J. 1946. *Language, Truth, and Logic*, 2nd edn (1st edn, 1936). London: Gollancz.

Ayer, A. J. 1973. *The Central Questions of Philosophy*. Harmondsworth: Penguin.

Ayer, A. J. 1991. "A Defence of Empiricism". In *A. J. Ayer: Memorial Essays*, A. Phillips Griffiths (ed.), 1–16. Cambridge: Cambridge University Press.

Balthasar, H. von 1992. *The Theology of Karl Barth*. San Francisco, CA: Ignatius.

Barth, K. 1933. *Theological Existence Today: A Plea for Theological Freedom*, R. Hoyle (trans.). London: Hodder & Stoughton.

Barth, K. 1956–77. *Church Dogmatics*, 13 vols, G. Bromiley & T. Torrance (eds). Edinburgh: T&T Clark.

Barth, K. 1956. *Church Dogmatics II*. Edinburgh: T&T Clark.

Barth, K. 1964. *Revolutionary Theology in the Making: Barth-Thurneysen Correspondence, 1914–1925*, J. Smart (trans.). Richmond, VA: John Knox.

Barth, K. 1968. *The Epistle to the Romans*, E. Hoskyns (trans.). Oxford: Oxford University Press.

Barth, K. 1973. *Karl Barth – Eduard Thurneysen: Briefwechsel*, vol. 1. Zurich: Theologischer Verlag.

Barth, K. 1978. *The Word of God and the Word of Man*, D. Horton (trans.). Gloucester: Peter Smith.

Barth, K. 1982. *Die christliche Dogmatik im Entwurf*, G. Sauter (ed.). Zürich: TVZ.

Beauvoir, S. de 1949. *Le deuxième sexe* I, *Les faits et les mythes*; II, *L'expérience vécue*. Paris: Gallimard.

Bergson, H. [1889] 1910. *Time and Free Will: An Essay on the Immediate Data of Consciousness*, F. L. Pogson (trans.). London: George Allen and Sons.

Bergson, H. 1911. *Creative Evolution*, A. Mitchell (trans.). London: Macmillan. Originally published as *L'Évolution créatrice* (Paris: Presses Universitaires de France, 1907).

Bergson, H. 1946. *The Creative Mind: An Introduction to Metaphysics*, M. Andison (trans.). New York: Philosophical Library.

Bergson, H. [1935] 1977. *The Two Sources of Morality and Religion*, R. Audra & C. Brereton, with the assistance of W. Carter (trans.). Notre Dame, IN: University of Notre Dame Press. Originally published in French as *Les deux sources de la morale et de la religion* (Paris: Presses Universitaires de France, 1932).

Bergson, H. [1896] 1988. *Matter and Memory*, N. Paul & W. Palmer (trans.). New York: Zone Books.

Bergson, H. 2007. *An Introduction to Metaphysics.* Basingstoke: Palgrave-Macmillan.

Bishop, J. 2007. *Believing by Faith: An Essay in the Epistemology and Ethics of Religious Belief.* Oxford: Clarendon.

Blackwell K. 1985. *The Spinozistic Ethics of Bertrand Russell.* London: Allen & Unwin.

Blood, B. P. 1874. *The Anesthetic Revelation and the Gist of Philosophy.* Amsterdam, NY: n.p.

Bochenski, I. 1961. *Contemporary European Philosophy*, 2nd edn, D. Nicholl & K. Aschenbrenner (trans.). Berkeley, CA: University of California Press.

Boyer, P. 2001. *Religion Explained.* London: Heinemann.

Braiterman, Z. 1998. *(God) After Auschwitz.* Princeton, NJ: Princeton University Press.

Braithwaite, R. B. 1955. *An Empiricist's View of the Nature of Religious Belief* (The Ninth Arthur Stanley Eddington Lecture). Cambridge: Cambridge University Press.

Breslauer, S. 1980. *The Chrysalis of Religion.* Nashville, TN: Abingdon.

Buber, M. 1949a. *Paths in Utopia*, R. Hull (trans.). London: Routledge & Kegan Paul.

Buber, M. 1949b. *The Prophetic Faith.* New York: Harper & Row.

Buber, M. 1952. *Eclipse of God*, M. Friedman *et al.* (trans.). New York: Harper & Row.

Buber, M. 1956. *The Tales of Rabbi Nachman*, M. Friedman (trans.). New York: Horizon.

Buber, M. 1958. *Hasidism and Modern Man*, M. Friedman (ed. and trans.). New York: Horizon Press.

Buber, M. 1965a. *The Knowledge of Man*, M. Friedman (trans.). New York: Holt, Rinehart and Winston.

Buber, M. 1965b. *Daniel: Dialogues on Realization*, M. Friedman (trans.). New York: Holt, Rinehart and Winston.

Buber, M. 1967a. "Autobiographical Fragments". In *The Philosophy of Martin Buber*, P. Schilpp & M. Friedman (eds), 3–37. La Salle, IL: Open Court.

Buber, M. 1967b. "The Philosopher Replies". In *The Philosophy of Martin Buber*, P. Schilpp & M. Friedman (eds), 689–741. La Salle, IL: Open Court.

Buber, M. 1967c. *On Judaism.* New York: Schocken Books.

Buber, M. 1969. *The Legend of the Baal-Shem*, M. Friedman (trans.). New York: Schocken Books.

Buber, M. [1923] 1970. *I and Thou*, W. Kaufmann (trans.). New York: Scribner's.

Buber, M. 1982. *On the Bible.* New York: Schocken Books.

Busch, E. 1976. *Karl Barth*, J. Bowden (trans.). Philadelphia, PA: Fortress.

Busch, E. 2004. *The Great Passion: An Introduction to Barth's Theology*, G. Bromiley (trans.). Grand Rapids, MI: Eerdmans.

Calvin, J. 2006. *Institutes of the Christian Religion*, 2 vols, J. McNeill (ed.), F. Battles (trans.). Lousiville, KY: Westminster John Knox Press.

Caputo, J. 2007. "Atheism, A/theology, and the Postmodern Condition". In *The Cambridge Companion to Atheism*, M. Martin (ed.), 267–82. Cambridge: Cambridge University Press.

Cash, W. 2001. "Did Atheist Philosopher See God When He Died?". *National Post* (3 March), http://gonsalves.org/favorite/atheist.htm (accessed July 2009).

Cell, E. 1978. *Language, Existence and God: Interpretations of Moore, Russell, Ayer, Wittgenstein, Wisdom, Oxford Philosophy and Tillich.* Brighton: Harvester.

Chalier, C. 1993. *Lévinas: L'utopie de l'humain.* Paris: Albin Michel.

Christ, C. 1987. *Laughter of Aphrodite: Reflections on a Journey to the Goddess.* San Francisco, CA: Harper & Row.

Christ, C. 1997. *Rebirth of the Goddess: Finding Meaning in Feminist Spirituality.* New York: Routledge.

Church, A. 1949. "Review of *Language, Truth, and Logic*". *Journal of Symbolic Logic* **14**: 52–3.

Clayton, P. 1997. *God and Contemporary Science.* Grand Rapids, MI: Eerdmans.

Cochrane, A. 1976. *The Church's Confession under Hitler*. Pittsburgh, PA: Pickwick Press.

Cohen, L. 1992. *Belief and Acceptance*. New York: Oxford University Press.

Cohen, R. 1994. *Elevations: The Height of the Good in Rosenzweig and Lévinas*. Chicago, IL: University of Chicago Press.

Cone, J. 1990. *A Black Theology of Liberation*. Maryknoll, NY: Orbis.

Daly, M. 1965. *The Problem of Speculative Theology*. Boston, MA: Thomist Press.

Daly, M. 1966. *Natural Knowledge of God in the Philosophy of Jacques Maritain*. Rome: Officium Libri Catholici.

Daly, M. 1968. *The Church and the Second Sex*. London: Geoffrey Chapman.

Daly, M. 1973. *Beyond God the Father: Toward a Philosophy of Women's Liberation*. Boston, MA: Beacon Press.

Daly, M. 1975a. "The Qualitative Leap Beyond Patriarchal Religion". *Quest* **1**: 20–40.

Daly, M. 1975b. *The Church and the Second Sex: With a New Feminist Postchristian Introduction by the Author*. New York: Harper & Row.

Daly, M. 1978. *Gyn/Ecology: The Metaethics of Radical Feminism*. Boston, MA: Beacon Press.

Daly, M. 1984. *Pure Lust: Elemental Feminist Philosophy*. Boston, MA: Beacon Press.

Daly, M. 1985a. *The Church and the Second Sex: With the Feminist Postchristian Introduction and New Archaic Afterwords by the Author*. Boston, MA: Beacon Press.

Daly, M. 1985b. *Beyond God the Father: Toward a Philosophy of Women's Liberation. With an Original Reintroduction by the Author*. Boston, MA: Beacon Press.

Daly, M. 1987. *Websters' First New Intergalactic Wickedary of the English Language* (conjured in cahoots with Jane Caputi). Boston, MA: Beacon Press.

Daly, M. 1991. *Gyn/Ecology: The Metaethics of Radical Feminism: With a New Introduction by the Author*. Boston, MA: Beacon Press.

Daly, M. 1992. *Outercourse: The Bedazzling Voyage Containing Recollections from My Logbook of a Radical Feminist Philosopher*. San Francisco, CA: Harper.

Daly, M. 1998. *Quintessence … Realizing the Archaic Future: A Radical Elemental Feminist Manifesto*. Boston, MA: Beacon Press.

Daly, M. 2006. *Amazon Grace: Re-Calling the Courage to Sin Big*. New York: Palgrave-Macmillan.

Davidson, D. 2001. "On the Very Idea of a Conceptual Scheme". In his *Inquiries into Truth and Interpretation*, 183–98. Oxford: Oxford University Press.

Davis, S. T. 2001. "Critique [of Phillips' 'Theism without Theodicy']". In *Encountering Evil: Live Options in Theodicy*, 2nd edn, S. T. Davis (ed.), 161–73. Louisville, KY: Westminster John Knox Press.

Dawkins, R. 2006. *The God Delusion*. London: Bantam Press.

Dennett, D. 2006. *Breaking the Spell: Religion as a Natural Phenomenon*. London: Allen Lane.

Derrida, J. 1973. *Speech and Phenomena*, D. Allison (trans.). Evanston, IL: Northwestern University Press.

Derrida, J. 1978. *Edmund Husserl's "Origin of Geometry": An Introduction*, J. Leavey, Jr (trans.). Stony Brook, NY: N. Hays.

Derrida, J. 1979a. *Writing and Difference*, A. Bass (trans.). London: Routledge & Kegan Paul.

Derrida, J. 1979b. "Scribble (writing-power)", C. Plotkin (trans.). *Yale French Studies* **58**: 117–47.

Derrida, J. 1985 "The Original Discussion of Différance (1968)", D. Wood *et al.* (trans.). In *Derrida and Difference*, D. Wood & R. Bernasconi (eds), 129–50. Warwick, CT: Parousia Press.

Derrida, J. 1989a. "How to Avoid Speaking: Denials". In *Languages of the Unsayable: The Play of Negativity in Literature and Literary Theory*, S. Budick & W. Iser (eds), 3–70. New York: Columbia University Press.

Derrida, J. 1989b. *Of Spirit: Heidegger and the Question*, G. Bennington & R. Bowlby (trans.). Chicago, IL: University of Chicago Press.

Derrida, J. 1989c. "Desistance", C. Fynsk (trans.). In P. Lacoue-Labarthe, *Typography: Mimesis, Philosophy, Politics*, C. Fynsk (ed.), 1–42. Cambridge, MA: Harvard University Press.

Derrida, J. 1992. *Given Time: I. Counterfeit Money*, P. Kamuf (trans.). Chicago, IL: University of Chicago Press.

Derrida, J. 1993. "Circumfession", G. Bennington (trans.). In J. Derrida & G. Bennington, *Jacques Derrida*, 3–315. Chicago, IL: University of Chicago Press.

Derrida, J. 1995a. *On the Name*, T. Dutoit (ed.), D. Wood *et al.* (trans.). Stanford, CA: Stanford University Press.

Derrida, J. 1995b. *The Gift of Death*, D. Wills (trans.). Chicago, IL: University of Chicago Press.

Derrida, J. 1996. "*As if* I were Dead". In *Applying: To Derrida*, J. Brannigan, R. Robbins & J. Wolfreys (eds), 212–26. London: Macmillan.

Derrida, J. 1997a. *Of Grammatology*, G. Spivak (rev. and corrected ed., trans.). Baltimore, MD: Johns Hopkins University Press.

Derrida, J. 1997b. *Politics of Friendship*, G. Collins (trans). London: Verso.

Derrida, J. 1998. "Faith and Knowledge: The Two Sources of 'Religion' at the Limits of Reason Alone", S. Weber (trans.). In *Religion*, J. Derrida & G. Vattimo (eds), 1–78. Cambridge: Polity Press.

Derrida, J. 2002. *Acts of Religion*, G. Anidjar (ed.). New York: Routledge.

Derrida, J. 2004. "Theology of Translation". In his *Eyes of the University: Right to Philosophy 2*, J. Plug *et al.* (trans.), 64–80. Stanford, CA: Stanford University Press.

Derrida, J. 2005. "Epoché and Faith: An Interview with Jacques Derrida". In *Derrida and Religion: Other Testaments*, Y. Sherwood & K. Hart (eds), 27–50. New York: Routledge.

Derrida, J. & G. Vattimo (eds) 1998. *Religion*. Cambridge: Polity Press.

Derrida, J., M. Govrin & D. Shapiro 2001. *Body of Prayer*, K. Shkapich (ed.). New York: Irwin S. Chain School of Architecture.

Dewey, J. 1969–91. *The Collected Works of John Dewey, 1882–1953: The Early Works of John Dewey, 1882–1898; The Middle Works of John Dewey, 1899–1924; The Later Works of John Dewey, 1925–1953*, J. A. Boydston (ed.). Carbondale, IL: Southern Illinois University Press.

Diamond, D. 2005. "Wittgenstein on Religious Belief: The Gulfs between Us". In *Religion and Wittgenstein's Legacy*, D. Phillips & M. von der Ruhr (eds), 99–137. Aldershot: Ashgate.

Drange, T. 1998. *Non-Belief and Evil: Two Arguments for the Non-Existence of God*. Buffalo, NY: Prometheus Books.

Draper, P. 1989. "Pain and Pleasure: An Evidential Problem for Theists". *Noûs* **23**: 331–50.

Draper, P. 1997. "A Critique of the *Kalām* Cosmological Argument". In *Philosophy of Religion*, 3rd edn, L. Pojman (ed.), 42–7. Belmont, CA: Wadsworth.

Eccles, J. 1970. *Facing Reality*. London: Longmans.

Eckhart, M. 2001. *Wandering Joy: Meister Eckhart's Mystical Philosophy*, R. Schürmann (ed. & trans.). Great Barrington, MA: Lindisfarne Books.

Edwards, P. & A. Pap (eds) 1965. *Introduction to Modern Philosophy*, rev. edn. New York: Free Press of Glencoe.

Everitt, N. 2004. *The Non-Existence of God*. London: Routledge.

Fackenheim, E. 1967. "Martin Buber's Concept of Revelation". In *The Philosophy of Martin Buber*, P. Schilpp & M. Friedman (eds), 273–96. La Salle, IL: Open Court.

Fackenheim, E. 1970. *God's Presence in History*. New York: New York University Press.

Findlay, J. N. 1948. "Can God's Existence be Disproved?". *Mind* **57**: 176–83.

Fischer, J. M. (ed.) 1994. *God, Foreknowledge and Freedom*. Stanford, CA: Stanford University Press.

Flew, A. 1955. "Theology and Falsification". In *New Essays in Philosophical Theology*, A. Flew & A. MacIntyre (eds), 96–9. London: SCM Press.

Flew, A. 1961. *God and Philosophy*. New York: Harcourt, Brace, & World.

Flew, A. 1976. *The Presumption of Atheism and Other Essays*. New York: Barnes & Noble.

Flew, A. 1984. *God: A Critical Inquiry*. La Salle, IL: Open Court.

Flew, A. & A. MacIntyre (eds) 1955. *New Essays in Philosophical Theology*. London: SCM Press.

Ford, L. 2000. *Transforming Process Theism*. Albany, NY: SUNY Press.

Ford, L. 2003. "On the Origin of Process Theism". *Process Studies* 32: 270–97.

Ford, L. 2006a. "Whitehead's Creative Transformations: A Summation". *Process Studies* 35: 134–64.

Ford, L. 2006b. "Enduring Subjectivity". *Process Studies* 35: 291–318.

Friedman, M. 1986. *Martin Buber and the Eternal*. New York: Human Sciences Press.

Friedman, M. 1991. *Encounter on the Narrow Ridge: A Life of Martin Buber*. New York: Paragon House.

Gale, R. M. 1991. *Arguments For and Against the Existence of God*. Cambridge: Cambridge University Press.

Gibbs, R. 1992. *Correlations in Rosenzweig and Lévinas*. Princeton, NJ: Princeton University Press.

Griffin, D. 2001. *Reenchantment without Supernaturalism: A Process Philosophy of Religion*. Ithaca, NY: Cornell University Press.

Griffin, D. (ed.) 2005. *Deep Religious Pluralism*. Louisville, KY: Westminster John Knox Press.

Grim, P. 1983. "Some Neglected Problems of Omniscience". *American Philosophical Quarterly* 20: 265–76.

Hahn, L. E. (ed.) 1992. *The Philosophy of A. J. Ayer*. La Salle, IL: Open Court.

Hájek, A. 2003. "Waging War on Pascal's Wager". *Philosophical Review* 112: 27–56.

Hallward, P. 2006. *Out of This World: Gilles Deleuze and the Philosophy of Creation*. London: Verso.

Hare, R. M. 1955. "Theology and Falsification". In *New Essays in Philosophical Theology*, A. Flew & A. MacIntyre (eds), 99–103. London: SCM Press.

Harnack, A. 1978. *What Is Christianity?*, T. Saunders (trans.). Gloucester, MA: Peter Smith.

Harris, S. 2005. *The End of Faith: Religion, Terror and the Future of Reason*. New York: W. W. Norton.

Harris, S. 2006. *Letter To A Christian Nation*. New York: Knopf.

Hartshorne, C. 1941. "Whitehead's Idea of God". In *The Philosophy of Alfred North Whitehead*, P. Schilpp (ed.), 513–60. New York: Tudor Publishing Company.

Hartshorne, C. 1948. *The Divine Relativity: A Social Conception of God*. New Haven, CT: Yale University Press.

Hartshorne, C. 1961. "Tillich's Doctrine of God". In *The Theology of Paul Tillich*, C. Kegley & R. Bretall (eds), 164–95. New York: Macmillan.

Hartshorne, C. 1962. *The Logic of Perfection*. La Salle, IL: Open Court.

Hartshorne, C. 1972. *Whitehead's Philosophy: Selected Essays, 1935–1970*. Lincoln, NE: University of Nebraska Press.

Hartshorne, C. 1987. "Bergson's Aesthetic Creationism Compared to Whitehead's". In *Bergson and Modern Thought: Towards a Unified Science*, A. Papanicolaou & P. Gunter (eds), 369–82. Chur, Switzerland: Harwood Academical Press.

Hartshorne, C. & W. Reese 1953. *Philosophers Speak of God*. Chicago, IL: University of Chicago Press.

Heidegger, M. [1946] 1976. *Brief über den Humanismus*. In *Gesamtausgabe*, vol. 9, *Wegmarken*, F.-W. von Herrmann (ed.). Frankfurt: Klostermann. Published in English as *Letter on Humanism*, F. Capuzzi (trans.), in *Pathmark*, W. McNeill (ed.) (Cambridge: Cambridge University Press, 1998).

Heidegger, M. [1927] 1977. *Sein und Zeit* , F.-W. von Herrmann (ed.). In *Gesamtausgabe*, vol. 2. Frankfurt: Klostermann. Published in English as *Being and Time*, J. Macquarrie & E. Robinson (trans.) (Oxford: Blackwell, [1962] 2006).

Heidegger, M. [1953] 1983. *Einführung in die Metaphysik*, P. Jaeger (ed.). In *Gesamtausgabe*, vol. 40. Frankfurt: Klostermann. Published in English as *Introduction to Metaphysics*, G. Fried & R. Polt (trans.) (New Haven, CT: Yale University Press, 2000).

Heidegger, M. [1979] 1988. *Prolegomena zur Geschichte des Zeitbegriffs*, P. Jaeger (ed.). In *Gesamtausgabe*, vol. 20. Frankfurt: Klostermann. Published in English as *History of the Concept of Time, Prolegomena*, T. Kisiel (trans.) (Bloomington, IN: Indiana University Press, 1985).

Heidegger, M. 1989. *Beiträge zur Philosophie [Vom Ereignis]* F.-W. von Herrmann (ed.). In *Gesamtausgabe*, vol. 65. Frankfurt: Klostermann. Published in English as *Contributions to Philosophy: From Enowning*, P. Emad & K. Maly (trans.) (Bloomington, IN: Indiana University Press, 1999).

Heidegger, M. [1984] 1993. *Hölderlins Hymne "Der Ister"*, W. Biemel (ed.). In *Gesamtausgabe*, vol. 53. Frankfurt: Klostermann. Published in English as *Hölderlin's Hymn "The Ister"*, W. McNeill & J. Davis (trans.) (Bloomington, IN: Indiana University Press, 1996).

Heidegger, M. [1987] 1994. *Zollikoner Seminare*, M. Boss (ed.). Frankfurt: Klostermann. Published in English as *Zollikon Seminars: Protocols, Conversations, Letters*, M. Boss (ed.), F. Mayr & R. Askay (trans) (Evanston, IL: Northwestern University Press, 2001).

Heidegger, M. [1980] 1996. *Erläuterungen zu Hölderlins Dichtung*, F.-W. von Herrmann (ed.). In *Gesamtausgabe*, vol. 4, Frankfurt: Klostermann. Published in English as *Elucidations of Hölderlin's Poetry*, K. Hoeller (trans.) (New York: Humanity Books, 2000).

Heidegger, M. 1997. *Besinnung*, F.-W. von Herrmann (ed.).In *Gesamtausgabe*, vol. 66, Frankfurt: Klostermann. Published in English as *Mindfulness*, P. Emad & T. Kalary (trans.) (London: Continuum, 2006).

Heidegger, M. 2000. "Only a God Can Save us Now". *Spiegel* interview with Rudolf Augstein and Georg Wolff, 23 September 1966, fuller, corrected version. In *Reden und andere Zeugnisse eines Lebensweges*, H. Heidegger (ed.), *Gesamtausgabe*, vol. 16. Frankfurt: Klostermann. Originally published in *Der Spiegel* (31 May 1976), 193–219. (The fuller version is translated with the cooperation of Dr Herrmann Heidegger at www.eco.utexas.edu/~hmcleave/350kPEEHeideggerSpiegel.pdf [accessed July 2009].)

Heidegger, M. 2002. "The Onto-Theo-Logical Constitution of Metaphysics". In his *Identity and Difference*, J. Stambaugh (trans.), 42–106. Chicago, IL: University of Chicago Press.

Heidegger, M. [1943] 2003a. *Nietzsches Wort "Gott ist Tot"*. In *Gesamtausgabe*, vol. 5, *Holzwege*, F.-W. von Herrmann (ed.). Frankfurt: Klostermann. Published in English as "Nietzsche's Word: 'God Is Dead'", in M. Heidegger, *Off The Beaten Track*, J. Young & K. Haynes (eds & trans.), 157–99 (Cambridge: Cambridge University Press, 2002).

Heidegger, M. [1935–6] 2003b. *Der Ursprung des Kunstwerkes*. In *Gesamtausgabe*, vol. 5, *Holzwege*, F.-W. von Herrmann (ed.). Frankfurt: Klostermann. Published in English as "The Origin of the Work of Art", in M. Heidegger, *Off The Beaten Track*, J. Young & K. Haynes (eds & trans.), 1–56 (Cambridge: Cambridge University Press, 2002).

Heidegger, M. [1986] 2005. *Seminare*, C. Ochwadt (ed.). In *Gesamtausgabe*, vol. 15. Frankfurt: Klostermann.

Heidegger, M. 2006a. *Geschichte der Philosophie von Thomas von Aquin bis Kant*, H. Vetter (ed.). In *Gesamtausgabe*, vol. 23. Frankfurt: Klostermann.

Heidegger, M. [1957] 2006b. *Identität und Differenz*, F.-W. von Herrmann (ed.). In *Gesamtausgabe*, vol. 11. Frankfurt: Klostermann. Published in English as *Identity and Difference*, J. Stambaugh (trans.) (New York: Harper & Row, [1969] 2002).

Hempel, C. 1950. "Problems and Changes in the Empiricist Criterion of Meaning". *Revue Internationale de Philosophie* **11**: 41–63.

Hempel, C. 1959. "The Empiricist Criterion of Meaning". In *Logical Positivism*, A. J. Ayer (ed.), 108–29. Glencoe, IL: Free Press.

Hick, J. 1957. *Faith and Knowledge*. London: Macmillan.

Hick, J. 1963. *Philosophy of Religion*. Englewood Cliffs, NJ: Prentice-Hall.
Hick, J. (ed.) 1964a. *Classical and Contemporary Readings in the Philosophy of Religion*. Englewood Cliffs, NJ: Prentice-Hall.
Hick, J. (ed.) 1964b. *The Existence of God*. New York: Macmillan.
Hick, J. 1966. *Faith and Knowledge*, 2nd edn. London: Macmillan.
Hick, J. 1968. *Christianity at the Centre*. London: SCM Press.
Hick, J. 1970. *Arguments for the Existence of God*. London: Macmillan.
Hick, J. 1972. *Biology and the Soul*. Cambridge: Cambridge University Press.
Hick, J. 1976. *Death and Eternal Life*. London: Collins.
Hick, J. (ed.) 1977. *The Myth of God Incarnate*. London: SCM Press.
Hick, J. 1978. *Evil and the God of Love*, rev. edn. New York: Harper & Row.
Hick, J. 1979. *The Center of Christianity*. New York: Harper & Row. [2nd edn of *Christianity at the Centre* (1968)]
Hick, J. 1980. *God Has Many Names*. London: Macmillan.
Hick, J. 1983. *The Second Christianity*. London: SCM Press. [3rd edn of *Christianity at the Centre* (1968)]
Hick, J. 1985. *Problems of Religious Pluralism*. London: Macmillan.
Hick, J. 1989. *An Interpretation of Religion*. London: Macmillan.
Hick, J. 1990. *Philosophy of Religion*, 4th edn. Englewood Cliffs, NJ: Prentice-Hall.
Hick, J. 1993. *The Metaphor of God Incarnate*. London: SCM Press & Westminster John Knox Press.
Hick, J. 1995. *The Rainbow of Faiths*. London: SCM Press & Westminster John Knox Press. [Published in America as *A Christian Theology of Religions*.]
Hick, J. 2001. *Dialogues in the Philosophy of Religion*. Basingstoke: Palgrave.
Hick, J. 2002. *John Hick: An Autobiography*. Oxford: Oneworld.
Hick, J. [1999] 2004a. *The Fifth Dimension*, 2nd edn. London: SCM Press.
Hick, J. 2004b. *An Interpretation of Religion*, 2nd edn. London: Macmillan.
Hick, J. 2005. *The Metaphor of God Incarnate*, 2nd edn. London: SCM Press & Westminster John Knox Press.
Hick, J. 2006. *The New Frontier of Religion and Science*. Basingstoke: Palgrave.
Hick, J. [1966] 2007. *Evil and the God of Love*, 3rd edn. London: Macmillan.
Hick, J. & A. McGill (eds) 1968. *The Many-Faced Argument: Recent Studies on the Ontological Argument for the Existence of God*. London: Macmillan.
Hitchens, C. 2007. *God Is Not Great: How Religion Poisons Everything*. New York: Twelve/ Warner Books.
Honderich, T. 1991. "An Interview with A. J. Ayer". In *A. J. Ayer: Memorial Essays*, A. Phillips Griffiths (ed.), 209–26. Cambridge: Cambridge University Press.
Horowitz, R. 1988. *Buber's Way to "I and Thou"*. New York: Jewish Publication Society.
Howard-Snyder, D. (ed.) 1996. *The Evidential Argument from Evil*. Bloomington, IN: Indiana University Press.
Howard-Snyder, D. 2007. "William P. Alston: A Bibliography", www.ac.wwu.edu/~howardd/ alston/bibliographies/writingsbyalston/writingsbyalston.htm (accessed July 2009).
Howard-Snyder, D. & P. Moser (eds) 2002. *Divine Hiddenness: New Essay*. Cambridge: Cambridge University Press.
Husserl, E. [1900–1901] 1970. *Logical Investigations*, J. Findlay (trans.). London: Routledge & Kegan Paul.
Irigaray, L. 1974. *Speculum: De l'autre femme*. Paris: Minuit.
Irigaray, L. 1977. *Ce Sexe qui n'en est pas un*. Paris: Minuit.
Irigaray, L. 1984. *Éthique de la différence sexuelle*. Paris: Minuit.
Irigaray, L. 1987. *Sexes et parentés*. Paris: Minuit.
James, W. 1975– . *The Works of William James*, 17 vols. Cambridge, MA: Harvard University Press.

Janicaud, D. 2000. *Phenomenology and the "Theological Turn": The French Debate*. New York: Fordham University Press.

Jantzen, G. 1998. *Becoming Divine: Towards a Feminist Philosophy of Religion*. Manchester: Manchester University Press.

Jaspers, K. 1960. *The Perennial Scope of Philosophy*, R. Manheim (trans.). London: Routledge & Kegan Paul.

Jaspers, K. 1962. *The Great Philosophers*, H. Arendt (ed.), R. Manheim (trans.). New York: Harcourt, Brace & World.

Jaspers, K. [1958] 1963. *The Atom Bomb and the Future of Man*, E. Ashton (trans.). Chicago, IL: University of Chicago Press.

Jaspers, K. 1967. *Philosophical Faith and Revelation*, E. Ashton (trans.). New York: Harper & Row.

Jaspers, K. 1970. *Philosophy, vol. 2: Existential Elucidation*, E. Ashton (trans.). Chicago, IL: University of Chicago Press.

Jaspers, K. 1971. *Philosophy, vol. 3: Metaphysics*, E. Ashton (trans.). Chicago, IL: University of Chicago Press.

Jaspers, K. 1973. *Way to Wisdom: An Introduction to Philosophy*, R. Manheim (trans.). New Haven, CT: Yale University Press.

Jaspers, K. 1986. *Karl Jaspers: Basic Philosophical Writings: Selections*, E. Ehrlich, L. Ehrlich & G. Pepper (eds and trans.). Athens, OH: Ohio University Press.

Jaspers, K. & R. Bultmann 1958. *Myth and Christianity: An Inquiry into the Possibility of Religion without Myth*, N. Guterman (trans.). New York: Noonday Press.

John-Paul II 1979. *Redemptor Hominis*. Rome: Encyclical.

Johnson, S. 1905. "Waller". In *Lives of the English Poets*, vol. 1, G. Hill (ed.), 249–300. Oxford: Clarendon Press.

Kant, I. [1793] 1996. *Religion within the Boundaries of Mere Reason*. In his *Religion and Rational Theology*, A. Wood & G. Di Giovanni (eds & trans.), 39–215. Cambridge: Cambridge University Press.

Keller, C. 1986. *From a Broken Web: Separation, Sexism, and Self*. Boston, MA: Beacon Press.

Keller, C. 2003. *Face of the Deep: A Theology of Becoming*. London: Routledge.

Kepnes, S. 1992. *The Text as Thou: Martin Buber's Dialogical Hermeneutics and Narrative Theology*. Bloomington, IN: Indiana University Press.

Kierkegaard, S. 1985. *Philosophical Fragments*, H. Hong & E. Hong (eds & trans.). Princeton, NJ: Princeton University Press.

Kierkegaard, S. 1991. *Practice in Christianity*, H. Hong & E. Hong (eds & trans.). Princeton, NJ: Princeton University Press.

Kierkegaard, S. 1992. *Concluding Unscientific Postscript to "Philosophical Fragments"*, H. Hong & E. Hong (eds & trans.). Princeton, NJ: Princeton University Press.

Kohanski, A. 1982. *Martin Buber's Philosophy of Interhuman Relation*. London: Associated University Presses.

Kripke, S. 1972. *Naming and Necessity*. Cambridge, MA: Harvard University Press.

Lawson, T. & R. McCauley 1990. *Rethinking Religion: Connecting Cognition and Culture*. Cambridge: Cambridge University Press.

Lemke, A. 1984. "Der Unveröffentlichte Nachlass von Rudolf Bultmann". In *Rudolf Bultmanns Werk und Wirkung*, B. Jaspert (ed.), 194–207. Darmstadt: Wissenschaftliche Buchgesellschaft.

Le Poidevin, R. 1996. *Arguing For Atheism: An Introduction to the Philosophy of Religion*. London: Routledge.

Levinas, E. 1988. *Autrement que savoir: Emmanuel Lévinas*. Paris: Éditions Osiris.

Levinas, E. 1991. *Otherwise than Being, or, Beyond Essence*, A. Lingis (trans.). Dordrecht: Kluwer.

Levinas, E. 1994. *Outside the Subject*, M. Smith (trans.). Stanford, CA: Stanford University Press.

Levinas, E. 1998a. "God and Philosophy". In his *Of God Who Comes to Mind*, B. Bergo (trans.), 55–78. Stanford, CA: Stanford University Press.

Levinas, E. 1998b. "Hermeneutics and the Beyond". In his *Of God Who Comes to Mind*, B. Bergo (trans.), 100–110. Stanford, CA: Stanford University Press.

Levinas, E. 1998c. "The Idea of the Infinite in Us". In his *Entre Nous: Thinking of the Other*, M. Smith & B. Harshav (trans.), 219–22. New York: Columbia University Press.

Lewis, D. 1970. "Anselm and Actuality". *Noûs* **4**: 175–88.

Lewis, D. 1993. "Evil for Freedom's Sake?". *Philosophical Papers* **22**: 149–72.

Lewis, D. 1997. "Do We Believe in Penal Substitution?". *Philosophical Papers* **26**: 203–9.

Lorde, A. 1984. "An Open Letter to Mary Daly". In her *Sister Outsider: Essays and Speeches*, 66–71. Trumansburg, NY: Crossing Press.

Macdonald, G. & C. Wright (eds) 1986. *Fact, Science, and Morality*. Oxford: Blackwell.

Mackie, J. 1955. "Evil and Omnipotence". *Mind* **64**: 200–212.

Mackie, J. 1982. *The Miracle of Theism: Arguments For and Against the Existence of God*. Oxford: Clarendon Press.

Malcolm, N. 1960. "Anselm's Ontological Arguments". *Philosophical Review* **69**: 41–62.

Malcolm, N. 2001. *Ludwig Wittgenstein: A Memoir*. Oxford: Oxford University Press.

Maritain, J. 1938. *Science and Wisdom*, B. Wall (trans.). London: Sheed & Ward.

Maritain, J. 1939a. *Antisemitism*. London: Geoffrey Bles, Centenary Press.

Maritain, J. 1939b. *A Preface to Metaphysics: Seven Lectures on Being*. London: Sheed & Ward.

Maritain, J. 1944. *The Twilight of Civilization*. New York: Sheed & Ward.

Maritain, J. 1955a. *An Essay on Christian Philosophy*, E. Flannery (trans.). New York: Philosophical Library.

Maritain, J. 1955b. *Bergsonian Philosophy and Thomism*, M. Andison & J. Andison (trans.). New York: Philosophical Library.

Maritain, J. 1958a. *The Range of Reason*. New York: Scribner's.

Maritain, J. 1958b. *Reflections on America*. New York: Scribner's.

Maritain, J. 1959. *An Introduction to Philosophy*, E. Watkin (trans.). London: Sheed & Ward.

Maritain, J. 1966. *The Person and the Common Good*, J. Fitzgerald (trans.). Notre Dame, IN: University of Notre Dame Press.

Maritain, J. 1967. *Approaches to God*, P. O'Reilly (trans.). New York: Macmillan.

Maritain, J. 1968. *The Peasant of the Garonne: An Old Layman Questions Himself about the Present Time*, M. Cuddihy & E. Hughs (trans.). New York: Holt, Rinehart & Winston.

Maritain, J. 1973. *A Christian Looks at the Jewish Question*. New York: Arno Press.

Maritain, J. 1977a. *Creative Intuition in Art and Poetry*. Princeton, NJ: Princeton University Press.

Maritain, J. 1977b. *Existence and the Existent*, L. Gallantiere & G. Phelan (trans.). Garden City, NY: Doubleday, Image Books.

Maritain, J. & R. Maritain 1959. *Liturgie et contemplation*. Paris: Desclée de Brouwer.

Maritain, J. & R. Maritain 1960. *Liturgy and Contemplation*. New York: P. J. Kennedy & Sons.

Maritain, R. 1945. *We Have Been Friends Together: The Memoirs of Raïssa Maritain*. New York: Longmans, Green.

Martin, M. 1990. *Atheism: A Philosophical Justification*. Philadelphia, PA: Temple University Press.

Martin, M. 1997. "Problems with Heaven", www.infidels.org/library/modern/michael_martin/heaven.html (accessed July 2009).

Mascall, E. L. 1957. *Words and Images: A Study in Theological Discourse*. London: Longmans.

Matson, W. 1965. *The Existence of God*. Ithaca, NY: Cornell University Press.

Maurer, A. (ed.) 1963. *St Thomas Aquinas, The Division and Methods of the Sciences: Questions V and VI of his Commentary on the* De Trinitate *of Boethius translated with Introduction and Notes*. Toronto: Pontifical Institute of Mediaeval Studies.

Maurer, A. 1974. "The Unity of a Science: St. Thomas and the Nominalists". In *St Thomas Aquinas, 1274–1974, Commemorative Studies*, A. Maurer (editor-in-chief), 269–91. Toronto: Pontifical Institute of Mediaeval Studies.

McCormack, B. 1995. *Karl Barth's Critically Realistic Dialectical Theology: Its Genesis and Development 1909–1936*. New York: Oxford University Press.

McInerny, R. 2003. *The Very Rich Hours of Jacques Maritain: A Spiritual Life*. Notre Dame, IN: University of Notre Dame Press.

Mendes-Flohr, P. 1989. *From Mysticism to Dialogue: Martin Buber's Transformation of German Social Thought*. Detroit, MI: Wayne State University Press.

Metz, J. 1962. *Christliche Anthropozentrik: Über die Denkform des Thomas von Aquin*. Munich: Kösel Verlag.

Monk, R. 1991. *The Duty of Genius*. London: Vintage.

Moore, G. 1903. "The Refutation of Idealism". *Mind* **12**: 433–53.

Morris, T. 1987. *Anselmian Explorations: Essays in Philosophical Theology*. Notre Dame, IN: University of Notre Dame Press.

Mougel, R. (editor-in-chief) 1982– . *Oeuvres complètes de Jacques et Raïssa Maritain*, 16 volumes. Fribourg: Éditions universitaires/Paris: Editions St Paul.

New, C. 1993. "Antitheism". *Ratio* **6**: 36–43.

Nielsen, K. 1971. *Contemporary Critiques of Religion*. London: Macmillan.

Nielsen, K. 1982. *An Introduction to the Philosophy of Religion*. London: Macmillan.

Nielsen, K. & D. Phillips 2005. *Wittgensteinian Fideism?* London: SCM Press.

Nietzsche, F. 1999. *Nachlaß 1885–1887*. In *Friedrich Nietzsche: Kritische Studienausgabe*, vols 1–15, G. Colli & M. Montinari (eds). Berlin: de Gruyter.

Oppy, G. 1996. *Ontological Arguments and Belief in God*. Cambridge: Cambridge University Press.

Oppy, G. 2006. *Arguing about Gods*. Cambridge: Cambridge University Press.

Ott, H. 1993. *Martin Heidegger: A Political Life*. London: HarperCollins.

Ott, H. 1995. "Heidegger's Catholic Origins". *American Catholic Philosophical Quarterly* **69**: 137–56.

Owens, J. 1981. "The Grounds of Ethical Universality in Aristotle". In *Aristotle: The Collected Papers of Joseph Owens*, J. Catan (ed.), 148–63. Albany, NY: SUNY Press.

Parsons, K. 1989. *God and the Burden of Proof*. Buffalo, NY: Prometheus.

Pétrement, S. 1976. *Simone Weil: A Life*, R. Rosenthal (trans.). London: Mowbrays.

Phillips, D. Z. 1976. *Religion without Explanation*. Oxford: Blackwell.

Plantinga, A. 1965. "The Free Will Defense". In *Philosophy in America*, M. Black (ed.), 204–20. Ithaca, NY: Cornell University Press.

Plantinga, A. 1967. *God and Other Minds: A Study of the Rational Justification of Belief in God*. Ithaca, NY: Cornell University Press.

Plantinga, A. 1974a. *God, Freedom and Evil*. Grand Rapids, MI: Eerdmans.

Plantinga, A. 1974b. *The Nature of Necessity*. Oxford: Oxford University Press.

Plantinga, A. 1979. "The Probabilistic Argument from Evil". *Philosophical Studies* **35**: 1–53.

Plantinga, A. 1980. *Does God Have a Nature?* Milwaukee, WI: Marquette University Press.

Plantinga, A. 1982. "How To Be An Anti-Realist". *Proceedings of the American Philosophical Association* **56**: 47–70.

Plantinga, A. 1983. "Reason and Belief in God". In *Faith and Philosophy*, A. Plantinga & N. Wolterstorff (eds), 16–93. Notre Dame, IN: University of Notre Dame Press.

Plantinga, A. 1984. "Advice to Christian Philosophers". *Faith and Philosophy* **1**: 253–71.

Plantinga, A. 1986. "On Ockham's Way Out". *Faith and Philosophy* **3**: 235–69.

Plantinga, A. 1988. "Epistemic Probability and Evil". *Archivio di Filosofia* **56**: 557–84.

Plantinga, A. 1991a. "An Evolutionary Argument against Naturalism". *Logos* **12**: 27–49.

Plantinga, A. 1991b. "When Faith and Reason Clash: Evolution and the Bible". *Christian Scholar's Review* **21**: 8–32.

Plantinga, A. 1993a. *Warrant: The Current Debate*. New York: Oxford University Press.

Plantinga, A. 1993b. *Warrant and Proper Function*. New York: Oxford University Press.

Plantinga, A. 1998. *The Analytic Theist: An Alvin Plantinga Reader*, J. Sennett (ed.). Grand Rapids, MI: Eerdmans.

Plantinga, A. 2000. *Warranted Christian Belief*. New York: Oxford University Press.

Plantinga, A. & P. Grim 1993. "Truth, Omniscience, and Cantorian Arguments: An Exchange". *Philosophical Studies* **71**: 267–306.

Plato 1961. *Republic*, P. Shorey (trans.). In *The Collected Dialogues of Plato: Including the Letters*, E. Hamilton & H. Cairns (eds), Bollingen Series 71. New York: Random House, Pantheon Books.

Price, H. 1968. "Survival and the Idea of Another World". In *Brain and Mind: Modern Concepts of the Nature of Mind*, J. Smythies (ed.), 1–33. London: Routledge.

Quine, W. 1966. "What I Believe". In *What I Believe*, G. Unwin (ed.), 70–75. London: Allen & Unwin.

Rahner, K. 1966. *Theological Investigations*, vol. 5. London: Darton, Longman & Todd.

Rahner, K. 1982. *Foundations of Christian Faith: An Introduction to the Idea of Christianity*, W. Dych (trans.). New York: Crossroad.

Raphael, M. 1996. *Thealogy and Embodiment: The Post-Patriarchal Reconstruction of Female Sacrality*. Sheffield: Academic Press.

Redpath, P. A. 1987. "Romance of Wisdom: The Friendship between Jacques Maritain and St Thomas Aquinas". In *Understanding Maritain: Philosopher and Friend*, D. Hudson & M. Mancini (eds), 91–113. Macon, GA: Mercer University Press.

Rhees, R. 1984. *Ludwig Wittgenstein, Personal Recollections*. Oxford: Oxford University Press.

Rhees, R. 2001. "On Religion: Notes on Four Conversations with Wittgenstein", D. Phillips (ed.). *Faith and Philosophy* **18**: 409–15.

Rhees, R. 2005. *Wittgenstein on Certainty: There – Like our Life*. Oxford: Blackwell.

Rogers, B. 1999. *A. J. Ayer: A Life*. London: Grove Press.

Rowe, W. L. 1968. *Religious Symbols and God: A Philosophical Study of Tillich's Theology*. Chicago, IL: University of Chicago Press.

Rowe, W. L. 1975. *The Cosmological Argument*. Princeton, NJ: Princeton University Press.

Rowe, W. L. 1979. "The Problem of Evil and Some Varieties of Atheism". *American Philosophical Quarterly* **16**: 335–41.

Rowe, W. L. 1988. "Evil and Theodicy". *Philosophical Topics* **16**: 119–32.

Rowe, W. L. 2004. *Can God Be Free?* Oxford: Oxford University Press.

Ruether, R. 1983. *Sexism and God-talk: Toward a Feminist Theology*. Boston, MA: Beacon Press.

Ruloff, C. 2004. "Plantinga's S5 Modal Argument, Obvious Entailment, and Circularity: A Response to Sennett". *Philo* **7**: 71–8.

Runzo, J. (ed.) 1993. *Is God Real?* London: Macmillan.

Russell, B. 1916. "Religion and the Churches". In his *Principles of Social Reconstruction*, 137–54. London: Allen & Unwin.

Russell, B. 1917. "The Place of Science in a Liberal Education". In his *Mysticism and Logic*, 31–9. London: Allen & Unwin.

Russell, B. 1930. *The Conquest of Happiness*. London: Allen & Unwin.

Russell, B. 1935. *Religion and Science*. Oxford: Oxford University Press.

Russell, B. 1945. *History of Western Philosophy*. New York: Simon & Schuster.

Russell, B. 1946. *History of Western Philosophy*. London: Allen & Unwin.

Russell, B. 1952. *The Impact of Science on Society*. London: Allen & Unwin.

Russell, B. 1954. *Human Society in Ethics and Politics*. London: Allen & Unwin.

Russell, B. 1957. "Has Religion Made Useful Contributions to Civilization?". In his *Why I Am Not a Christian and Other Essays on Religion and Related Subjects*, 27–42. London: Allen & Unwin.

Russell, B. 1959. *My Philosophical Development*. New York: Simon & Schuster.

Russell, B. 1961. *History of Western Philosophy*. London: Allen & Unwin.

Russell, B. 1968. *Unpopular Essays*. London: Allen & Unwin.

Russell, B. 1975. *Autobiography*. London: Unwin Paperbacks.

Russell, B. 1997a. "Reply to Criticisms". In *The Collected Papers of Bertrand Russell, Volume 11: Last Philosophical Testament, 1943–68*, J. Slater & P. Köllner (eds), 18–64. London: Routledge.

Russell, B. 1997b. "Is There A God?". In *The Collected Papers of Bertrand Russell, Volume 11: Last Philosophical Testament, 1943–68*, J. Slater & P. Köllner (eds), 543–48. London: Routledge.

Russell, B. 1999. *Russell On Religion: Selections from the Writings of Bertrand Russell*, L. Greenspan & S. Andersson (eds). London: Routledge.

Russell, B. & F. Copleston 1957. "The Existence of God: A Debate Between Bertrand Russell and Father F. C. Copleston". In B. Russell, *Why I Am Not A Christian and Other Essays on Religion and Related Subjects*, 133–53. London: Allen & Unwin.

Ryle, G. 1949. *The Concept of Mind*. London: Hutchinson.

Sagan, C. 1996. *The Demon Haunted World: Science as a Candle in the Dark*. London: Headline.

Salmon, W. C. 1979 "Experimental Atheism". *Philosophical Studies* **35**: 101–4.

Sartre, J.-P. [1943] 1956. *Being and Nothingness*, H. Barnes (trans.). New York: Philosophical Library.

Scheler, M. [1929] 1958. *Philosophical Perspectives*, O. Haac (trans.). Boston, MA: Beacon Press.

Scheler, M. [1920] 1960. *On the Eternal in Man*, B. Noble (trans.). London: SCM Press.

Scheler, M. [1927] 1961a. *On Man's Place in Nature*, H. Meyerhoff (trans.). New York: Noonday.

Scheler, M. [1912] 1961b. *Ressentiment*, W. Holdheim (trans.). Glencoe, NY: Free Press.

Scheler, M. [1913] 1970. *The Nature of Sympathy*, P. Heath (trans.). Hamden, CT: Archon Books.

Scheler, M. [1913, 1916] 1973a. *Formalism in Ethics and Non-Formal Ethics of Values*, M. Frings & R. Funk (trans.). Evanston, IL: Northwestern University Press.

Scheler, M. [1933] 1973b. *Selected Philosophical Essays*, D. Lachterman (trans.). Evanston, IL: Northwestern University Press.

Scheler, M. 1992. *On Feeling, Knowing, and Valuing: Selected Writings*, H. Bershady (ed.). Chicago, IL: University of Chicago Press.

Schellenberg, J. L. 1993. *Divine Hiddenness and Human Reason*. Ithaca, NY: Cornell University Press.

Schillebeeckx, E. 1964. *Openbaring en theologie*. Baarn: Nelissen.

Schilpp, P. & M. Friedman (eds) 1967. *The Philosophy of Martin Buber*. La Salle, IL: Open Court.

Schleiermacher, F. 1999. *The Christian Faith*, H. Mackintosh & J. Stewart (eds). Edinburgh: T&T Clark.

Schneider, L. 1998. *Re-Imagening the Divine: Confronting the Backlash against Feminist Theology*. Cleveland, OH: Pilgrim Press.

Schönbaumsfeld, G. 2007. *A Confusion of the Spheres. Kierkegaard and Wittgenstein on Philosophy and Religion*. Oxford: Oxford University Press.

Scriven, M. 1966. *Primary Philosophy*. New York: McGraw-Hill.

Sennett, J. 1989. "God and Possible Worlds: On What There Must Be". *Southern Journal of Philosophy* **27**: 285–97.

Sennett, J. 1992. *Modality, Probability, and Rationality: A Critical Examination of Alvin Plantinga's Philosophy*. New York: Peter Lang.

Smart, J. & J. Haldane 1996. *Atheism and Theism*. Oxford: Blackwell.

Smith, Q. 1978a. "Max Scheler and the Classification of Feelings". *Journal of Phenomenological Psychology* **9**: 114–38.

Smith, Q. 1978b. "Scheler's Critique of Husserl's Theory of the World of the Natural Standpoint". *Modern Schoolman* **55**: 387–96.

Smith, Q. 1979. *Phenomenology of Feeling: A Critical Development of the Theories of Feeling in Husserl, Scheler and Sartre*. London: University MicroFilms International.

Smith, Q. 1991. "Atheism, Theism and Big Bang Cosmology". *Australasian Journal of Philosophy* **69**: 48–65.

Smith, Q. 1997. *Ethical and Religious Thought in Analytic Philosophy of Language*. New Haven, CT: Yale University Press.

Sobel, J. H. 2004. *Logic and Theism*. Cambridge: Cambridge University Press.

Sober, E. 2003. "The Design Argument". In *God and Design*, N. Manson (ed.), 27–54. London: Routledge.

Spiegelberg, H. 1971. *The Phenomenological Movement*, vol. 1. The Hague: Martinus Nijhoff

Stace, W. T. 1959. "Broad's Views on Religion". In *The Philosophy of C. D. Broad*, P. Schilpp (ed.), 171–95. New York: Tudor.

Starhawk 1979. *The Spiral Dance: A Rebirth of the Ancient Religion of the Great Goddess*. San Francisco, CA: Harper & Row.

Stump, E. 1985. "The Problem of Evil". *Faith and Philosophy* **2**: 392–420.

Supervielle, J. 1996. *Œuvres poétiques complètes*. Paris Gallimard.

Swinburne, R. 1971. *The Concept of Miracle*. London: Macmillan.

Swinburne, R. 1991. *Revelation*. Oxford: Clarendon Press.

Swinburne, R. [1977] 1993. *The Coherence of Theism*, rev. edn. Oxford: Clarendon Press.

Swinburne, R. 1994. *The Christian God*. Oxford: Clarendon Press.

Swinburne, R. 2001. *Epistemic Justification*. Oxford: Clarendon Press.

Swinburne, R. 2003. *The Resurrection of God Incarnate*. Oxford: Clarendon Press.

Swinburne, R. [1979; rev. 1991] 2004. *The Existence of God*, 2nd edn. Oxford: Clarendon Press.

Swinburne, R. [1981] 2005. *Faith and Reason*, 2nd edn. Oxford: Oxford University Press.

Thurneysen, E. (ed.) 1973. *Karl Barth – Eduard Thurneysen Briefweschsel*, vol. 1. Zurich: TVZ.

Tillich, P. 1940. "The Religious Symbol". *Journal of Liberal Religion* **2**: 13–33.

Tillich, P. 1951. *Systematic Theology*, vol. 1. Chicago, IL: University of Chicago Press.

Tillich, P. 1952. *The Courage to Be*. London: Collins.

Tillich, P. 1953–64. *Systematic Theology*, 3 vols. London: Nisbet & Company.

Tillich, P. 1954. *Love, Power and Justice: Ontological Analyses and Ethical Applications*. Oxford: Oxford University Press.

Tillich, P. 1955a. *Biblical Religion and the Search for Ultimate Reality*. Chicago, IL: University of Chicago Press.

Tillich, P. 1955b. "Theology and Symbolism". In *Religious Symbolism*, F. Johnson (ed.), 107–16. New York: Harper & Brothers.

Tillich, P. 1955c. *The New Being*. New York: Scribner's.

Tillich, P. 1957a. *Dynamics of Faith*. New York: Harper & Bros.

Tillich, P. 1957b. *Systematic Theology*, vol. 2. Chicago, IL: University of Chicago Press/

Tillich, P. 1961. "The Religious Symbol". In *Religious Experience and Truth: A Symposium*, S. Hook (ed.), 301–21. New York: New York University Press.

Tillich, P. 1963. *Systematic Theology*, vol. 3. Chicago, IL: University of Chicago Press.

Tooley, M. 1981. "Plantinga's Defence of the Ontological Argument". *Mind* **90**: 422–7.

Trakakis, N. 2007. *The God Beyond Belief: In Defence of William Rowe's Evidential Argument from Evil*. Dordrecht: Springer.

Trible, P. 1978. *God and the Rhetoric of Sexuality*. Philadelphia, PA: Fortress Press.

Vycinas, V. 1961. *Earth and Gods: An Introduction to the Philosophy of Martin Heidegger*. The Hague: Martinus Nijhoff.

Webster, J. 1995. *Barth's Ethics of Reconciliation*. Cambridge: Cambridge University Press.

Weil, S. 1956. *The Notebooks of Simone Weil*, A. Willis (trans.). London: Routledge.

Weil, S. 1968. *On Science, Necessity, and the Love of God*, R. Rees (ed. & trans.). Oxford: Oxford University Press.

Weil, S. 1970. *First and Last Notebooks*, R. Rees (ed. and trans.). Oxford: Oxford University Press.

Weil, S. 1974. *Gateway to God*, D. Raper, M. Muggeridge & V. Sproxton (eds). Glasgow: Collins/Fontana.

Weil, S. 1977. *Waiting on God*, E. Craufurd (trans.). London: Fountain Books.

Weil, S. 1978. *Lectures in Philosophy*, H. Price (trans.). Cambridge: Cambridge University Press.

Weil, S. 1988. *Oppression and Liberty*, A. Wills & J. Petrie (trans.). London: Ark Paperbacks.

Weil, S. 2002. *Gravity and Grace*, G. Thibon (ed.), E. Crawford & M. von der Ruhr (trans.). London: Routledge.

White, A. 1896. *A History of the Warfare of Science with Theology in Christendom*. New York: D. Appleton and Company.

Whitehead, A. N. 1925. *Science and the Modern World*. New York: Macmillan.

Whitehead, A. N. 1926. *Religion in the Making*. New York: Macmillan.

Whitehead, A. N. [1929] 1978. *Process and Reality: An Essay in Cosmology*, corrected edn, D. Griffin & D. Sherburne (eds). New York: Free Press. First published (New York: Macmillan, 1929).

Williams, R. 1993. "The Necessary Non-existence of God". In *Simone Weil's Philosophy of Culture*, R. Bell (ed.), 52–76. Cambridge: Cambridge University Press.

Winch, P. 1987. *Trying to Make Sense*. Oxford: Blackwell.

Wisdom, J. 1944–5. "Gods". *Proceedings of the Aristotelian Society* **45**: 185–206.

Wittgenstein, L. 1953. *Philosophical Investigations*, G. Anscombe, R. Rhees & G. von Wright (eds), G. Anscombe (trans.). Oxford: Blackwell.

Wittgenstein, L. 1966. *Lectures and Conversations on Aesthetics, Psychology and Religious Belief*, C. Barrett (ed.). Oxford: Blackwell.

Wittgenstein, L. 1977. *Culture and Value*, G. von Wright (ed.), P. Winch (trans.). Oxford: Blackwell.

Wittgenstein, L. 1993. *Philosophical Occasions: 1912–1951*, J. Klagge & A. Nordmann (eds). Indianapolis, IN: Hackett.

Wittgenstein, L. 2002. *Tractatus Logico-Philosophicus*, B. McGuinness & D. Pears (trans.). London: Routledge.

Wright, C. 1986. "Scientific Realism, Observation, and the Verification Principle". In *Fact, Science, and Morality*, G. Macdonald & C. Wright (eds), 247–74. Oxford: Blackwell.

Wright, C. 1989. "The Verification Principle: Another Puncture – Another Patch". *Mind* **98**: 611–22.

INDEX

Tillich, Paul
  assertions concerning being-itself 136,
    140–42
  biographical details and major writings
    113
  concept of non-being 133–4
  The Courage to Be 133–4
  distinction between symbols and signs
    139–40
  existentialism 133
  God as the ground of being 57, 138
  on the human quest for being-itself 134
  identification of God with being-itself
    137–8, 140–41
  linguistic versus non-linguistic signs and
    symbols 139
  on necessary truth of the reality of being-
    itself 142–3
  on notion of 'existence' as incompatible
    with the nature of God 137–8
  philosophical identification of God with
    being-itself versus 'God' in religious
    discourse 135–6
  Systematic Theology 135
  theory of religious experience 141–2
  theory of religious symbols 138–41
transcendence
  as absolute being 120–21
  in boundary situations 124–5
  ciphers of 122–3
  in interpersonal communication 125–6
  Jasper's concept 120
  and the realization of one's own Existenz
    123–4
Trinitarian doctrine
  of Karl Barth 151–2
  Swinburne's account 294–5

verifiability criterion of meaning (VCM)
  222–3
verificationism, and phenomenalism 213–
  14, 216
Vienna Circle 212

Weber, Max 5
Weil, Simone
  'atheistic theism' 206–7
  biographical details and major writings
    199–203
  on forms of the implicit love of God
    207–9

influence of Plato in her thought 203
Lectures in Philosophy 201
on love of the order of the world 208–9
on love of religious practices 209
on the necessary nonexistence of God
  204–6
on neighbour-love 208
Oppression and Liberty 201
sources of her beliefs 204–5
Whewell, William, on religion and science
  5
White, Andrew Dickson, *A History of the
  Warfare of Science with Theology in
  Christendom* 5
Whitehead, Alfred North
  biographical details 53, 56
  on 'concrescence' 59–60
  influence of Hume 56
  non-temporality of formative elements
    57–88
  Principia Mathematica 53
  principle of concretion/limitation 56–7,
    60
  process philosophy and the nature of
    divine perfection 54–6
  Process and Reality 54, 58–9
  process theism 56–64
  Religion in the Making 58
  Science and the Modern World 56
  significance and influence 53
  on subjective aims 59–63
  theory of creation 63–4
Wilson, E. O. 5
Wisdom, John 302
Wittgenstein, Ludwig
  biographical details and major writings
    161–2
  conception of religious belief 163–4
  contribution to philosophy of religion
    162
  Culture and Value 162
  emphasis on existential dimension of faith
    164
  fideism 169
  on God's existence 170–73
  his philosophy 162
  implications of his conception of religious
    belief 164
  influence of Kierkegaard 163
  influences on his conception of religious
    belief 163

UNIVERSITY OF WINCHESTER LIBRARY